O F 1

OXFORD MONOGRAPHS IN
INTERNATIONAL LAW

General Editor: PROFESSOR VAUGHAN LOWE
*Chichele Professor of Public International Law in the
University of Oxford and Fellow of
All Souls College, Oxford*

The Decolonization of International Law

OXFORD MONOGRAPHS IN INTERNATIONAL LAW

The aim of this series is to publish important and original pieces of research on all aspects of international law. Topics that are given particular prominence are those which, while of interest to the academic lawyer, also have an important bearing on issues that touch upon the actual conduct of international relations. Nonetheless, the series is wide in scope and includes monographs on the history and philosophical foundations of international law.

The Decolonization of International Law: State Succession and the Law of Treaties

MATTHEW CRAVEN

Professor of International Law, School of
Oriental and African Studies, University of London

OXFORD

UNIVERSITY PRESS

OXFORD
UNIVERSITY PRESS

Great Clarendon Street, Oxford OX2 6DP

Oxford University Press is a department of the University of Oxford.
It furthers the University's objective of excellence in research, scholarship,
and education by publishing worldwide in

Oxford New York

Auckland Cape Town Dar es Salaam Hong Kong Karachi
Kuala Lumpur Madrid Melbourne Mexico City Nairobi
New Delhi Shanghai Taipei Toronto

With offices in

Argentina Austria Brazil Chile Czech Republic France Greece
Guatemala Hungary Italy Japan Poland Portugal Singapore
South Korea Switzerland Thailand Turkey Ukraine Vietnam

Oxford is a registered trade mark of Oxford University Press
in the UK and in certain other countries

Published in the United States
by Oxford University Press Inc., New York

British Library Cataloguing in Publication Data

Data available

Library of Congress Cataloging in Publication Data

Data available

Typeset by Newgen Imaging Systems (P) Ltd., Chennai, India
Printed in Great Britain
on acid-free paper by
Biddles Ltd., King's Lynn.

ISBN 978–0–19–921762–5

1 3 5 7 9 10 8 6 4 2

Preface

It is one of the paradoxes of international law that the location of its theoretical foundations in the consent of States was articulated with greatest clarity during the period when the coexistence of extensive colonial empires made the idea of consent no more than a remote fiction as far as most inhabitants of the world were concerned. In this reflective and original study, Professor Craven explores the manner in which the implications of the consensual basis of international law and its fundamental principle of sovereign equality were handled during the period of radical transformation in the international legal order associated with decolonization. In doing so he offers an incisive critique of the Law of State Succession, of importance not only to those concerned now with the fragmentation (and, perhaps soon, the combination) of existing States and the aftershocks of that process, but to all those interested in pinning down the bases upon which the international legal order is built.

AVL

All Souls College, Oxford
June 2007

Contents

Table of Cases

Table of Cases

Table of Treaties

Introduction

By the early 1990s international lawyers were, once again, engaging with an issue which, for the most part, had been left to one side since the era of decolonization. With the dismemberment of the United Socialist Soviet Republic (USSR), the Socialist Federal Republic of Yugoslavia (SFRY) and Czechoslovakia, and with the unification of Germany and Yemen, they were confronted with a range of international legal questions that appeared to require some sort of answer. What would happen to the treaties of the former German Democratic Republic (GDR)?[1] Who would be responsible for the arms reduction commitments of the former Soviet Union?[2] Who had claims to the monetary reserves in the International Monetary Fund of the former Yugoslavia?[3] What would happen to the seats of North and South Yemen in the United Nations?[4]

The answers to these and many other such questions seemed to fall squarely within the framework of the law of state succession,[5] the subject of which had been partially codified in two Vienna Conventions, the 1978 Vienna Convention on State Succession in Respect of Treaties,[6] and the 1983 Vienna Convention on State Succession in Respect of Property, Archives and Debt.[7] There were plenty of issues that fell outside the compass of these two Conventions (such as matters

[1] D Papenfuss, 'The Fate of the International Treaties of the GDR within the Framework of German Unification', 92 AJIL (1998).

[2] G Bunn and J Rhinelander, 'The Arms Control Obligations of the Former Soviet Union', 33 VaJIL (1993) 323.

[3] P Williams, 'State Succession and the International Financial Institutions: Political Criteria v Protection of Outstanding Financial Obligations', 43 ICLQ (1994) 776.

[4] Agreement on the Establishment of the Republic of Yemen, (1990) 30 ILM (1991) 820. R Goy, 'La Réunification du Yémen', AFDI (1990) 249; K Bühler, *State Succession and Membership in International Organizations: Legal Theories Versus Political Pragmatism* (2001).

[5] Some of the most prominent works are D O'Connell, *State Succession in Municipal and International Law* (1967) vols I and II; D O'Connell, *The Law of State Succession* (1956); E Feilchenfeld, *Public Debts and State Succession* (1931); A Keith, *The Theory of State Succession with Special Reference to English and Colonial Law* (1907); O Udokang, *Succession of New States to International Treaties* (1972); A Cavaglieri, *La dottrina della successione di stato a stato e il suo valore giuridico* (1910); A Hershey, 'The Succession of States', 5 AJIL (1911) 285; W Jenks, 'State Succession in Respect of Law Making Treaties', 29 BYIL (1952) 105; B Stern, *La Succession d'États* (2000); Y Makonnen, *International Law and the New States of Africa* (1983); L Chen, *State Succession Relating to Unequal Treaties* (1974); R de Muralt, *The Problem of State Succession with Regard to Treaties* (1954) 18.

[6] Vienna Convention on State Succession in Respect of Treaties, 17 ILM (1978) 1488.

[7] Vienna Convention on State Succession in Respect of Property, Archives and Debts, 1983, 22 ILM (1983) 306.

relating to the survival of local law,[8] questions of nationality,[9] responsibility for international delicts,[10] and membership in international organisations),[11] but even as regards the issues addressed within the Conventions themselves, there were doubts as to whether they were to be of any assistance. Neither of the Conventions, at that stage, had entered into force, and their applicability in the context of the events arising in the 1990s was almost universally doubted. Not only was it evident that the applicability of such agreements to the new states as they were to emerge was a point of some contention, but a recurring point of criticism was that, having been drafted with the particular facts of decolonization in mind, the Conventions were in only very small part declaratory of customary international law[12] and were largely inapplicable in the very different contexts arising in the 1990s.[13] This led, naturally enough, various organizations including the International Law Commission, the International Law Association and others to re-examine the question of State succession in light of emerging contemporaneous practice. It also led to the production of a considerable body of literature on the question of succession, much of which was directed towards an evaluation as to whether the rules of succession that had been so painfully pieced together in the 1960s and 1970s remained of significance.

Nearly two decades have passed since the inaugural events of 1989 and the time for writing a book on their political, economic, social or cultural significance might have passed. The time also, for writing another book evaluating the two Vienna Conventions on State Succession by reference to those events may also be gone. As always, the transitory and almost ephemeral problems of succession quickly pass out of mainstream discourse. Yet there is something that remains in the subject which is curiously enduring. One can provide an answer as to whether international law requires that new states honour the contractual obligations of the predecessor, suggest also how it might respond to the problem of membership in regional economic organisations, but still the sense that any answer will be both highly contingent if not speculative will remain. The questions of State

---

[8]   eg S Rosenne, 'The Effect of Change of Sovereignty upon Municipal Law', 27 BYIL (1950) 267.

[9]   eg Y Onuma, 'Nationality and Territorial Change: In Search of the State of the Law', *8 Yale J W Pub Order* (1981); R Donner, *The Regulation of Nationality in International Law* (2nd ed. 1994); V Mikulka, 'First Report on State Succession and its Impact on the Nationality of Natural and Legal Persons', A/CN4/467 (1995), Yrbk ILC 1995, II; 'Second Report', A/CN4/474, 1996; Yrbk ILC, 1996, II; 'Third Report', A/CN4/480, (1997), Yrbk ILC, 1997, II; 'Fourth Report on Nationality in Relation to the Succession of States', A/CN4/489 (1998), Yrbk ILC, 1998, II; ILC *Draft Articles on Nationality of Natural Persons in Relation to the Succession of States*, GA Resn 55/153, (2000) Annex.

[10]   eg C Hurst, 'State Succession in Matters of Tort', 5 BYIL (1924) 163; M Volkovitsch, 'Righting Wrongs: Towards a New Theory of State Succession to Responsibility for International Delicts', 92 Colum LR (1992) 2162.

[11]   See Bühler, n 4 above.

[12]   D Vagts, 'State Succession: The Codifiers' View', 33 VaJIL (1992–3) 275, p 276.

[13]   cf Criticism by O'Connell, 'Reflections on th State Succession Convention' 39 ZaöRV (1979) 725, p 726 (1978); I Sinclair, 'Some Reflections on the Vienna Convention on Succession of States in Respect of Treaties', in K Hakapää (ed), *Essays in Honour of Erik Castrén* (1979) 149.

succession, precisely because they do involve a disruption to the conditions of normality (often in a much more profound way than, for example, situations of military occupation) seem to ask by way of response something more than may be provided by an elaboration of State practice, or a recitation of evidence demonstrating a necessary *opinio iuris*. Also implicated are questions concerning received ideas of statehood, of the basis of obligation in international law, of the relationship between law and politics, of international law's simultaneous commitment to continuity and change. It is, in other words, a subject which, through its presentation of itself as a moment of crisis, brings all else into contemplation.

At the outset, it should be made clear that the object of this book is not to provide an exhaustive account of State practice, nor indeed to present a prospectus on the 'current state of the law'. It is perfectly arguable that far too much time has been spent collating and distilling instances of State practice – as might be exemplified in the reports of the UN Secretariat put together in the 1960s and 1970s, and in the work of the Council of Europe's Committee of Legal Advisors (CAHDI) in the 1990s – conversely, rather too little time has been spent reflecting upon what is at stake, and why it is that the subject has been framed in the way it has. Projects of documentation undoubtedly serve a useful purpose in the doctrinal construction of rules of customary international law, but all too frequently end up as something of a surrogate for a more open or transparent discussion as to the character of underlying discourses that appear to structure those kinds of legal intervention. That one might begin to examine the practice of international organizations as regards their policies concerning the admission of 'new States' to membership, for example, not only poses questions as regards the kind of rule one is seeking to uncover (a 'right of membership' perhaps or a 'deferral' to the rules of the organization), but also leaves in the air the broader questions concerning the significance of institutional membership, the relationship between membership and organizational capacity, and the broader role that such decisions might have in disposing of a range of other more concrete, or specific, concerns regarding, for example, access to resources invested within those institutions.

Indeed, it is all the preliminary or supplementary questions – the questions that seem to precede or flow from the articulation of particular substantive rules of succession – that appear most puzzling. On the one hand, there are the preliminary questions concerning the application of rules of succession – questions that concern the identification of a State as 'new' or 'old', questions that concern the application of rules of succession to cases which do not appear to involve a 'change in sovereignty' (such as territories under international administration or emerging from belligerent occupation), questions that surround the differentiation between State and governmental change. All of these appear to require some kind of initial response before engaging in the process of deciding whether this or that obligation has been inherited. On the other hand, there are also the supplementary questions concerning how far a particular substantive rule might be taken.

What are the implications, in other words, of the articulation of a rule of non-inheritance of treaty obligations in the case of States emerging from a condition of dependence? Would this apply with equal ease to the case of Kazakhstan as it would to that of Tanzania? To what agreements, furthermore, might this extend? Of course, in many respects these supplementary questions are not supplementary at all, but condition the kinds of examples one might go in search of for purposes of elaborating of a particular rule of customary international law, and to the way in which one may go about 'cutting' that practice so as to delineate the margins of any particular rule. But it is evidently the way in which the subject of succession appears to wrap around itself in this manner that makes it particularly intriguing.

With such thoughts in mind, the purpose of this book may be said to be effectively twofold. The first, preliminary, object is to try to develop a sense of what seems to be at stake when international lawyers turn to the question of succession. What is it that is to be achieved in the development of this particular field of law? And why is it that the subject appears to be either so abstract or so intractable? In the years since 1990, the International Court of Justice has had reason to examine the question of succession on at least four different occasions and yet, on only one of them, did it make any definitive pronouncement upon the issue. Its evasiveness was not, it seems clear, a product of the lack of relevant practice or argumentation on the point. Nor indeed were those arguments entirely superfluous. In fact, there is reason to suppose that had it taken a definitive stand on the issue, it would not have been forced into a position of near contradiction in its approach to Serbia's membership in the United Nations in two of its most recent decisions: the *Legality of the Use of Force*[14] and the *Bosnia Genocide* cases[15]. Something other than the standard problems associated with the identification or construction of customary international law appear to have been in play, and part of the purpose of this book is to uncover what they might be.

The second object of this book, as the title suggests, is to examine how it was that international lawyers understood decolonization and what significance that process had for the understanding of their own discipline. At first sight, this may appear to have only a somewhat tangential relationship to my first concern, but it seems important for two reasons. First of all, as suggested above, decolonization was a particularly significant experience in the context of the codification of the law of State succession during the 1960s and 1970s, and it is precisely because of the closeness of this relationship that many have regarded the two Vienna Conventions to be largely irrelevant in the context of the events surrounding the collapse of States in Eastern Europe in the 1990s. Codification, in other words, seemed to occur at an inopportune moment – codifying the law in relation to

[14] *Legality of the Use of Force (Serbia and Montenegro v Belgium) Preliminary Objections,* Judgment ICJ Rep 2004, 279.
[15] *Case Concerning the Application of the Convention on the Prevention and Punishment of the Crime of Genocide,* ICJ, Judgment of 26 Feb 2007.

events whose time would quickly pass. But this, of course, is to prompt certain questions: what was it about decolonization that people regarded as so unique as a form of social or political change? If, as many seemed to assume to be the case, it was a question of putting into practice the principle of self-determination, did this not also have similar relevance in the context of post-Soviet transition? And if not, why not?

Secondly, if an understanding of the significance of decolonization appears important for evaluating the terms of the two Vienna Conventions on State succession, it is also apparent that same relationship works in the other direction. Whilst, for the most part, decolonisation has been understood in terms of a series of quite formal questions of status or territorial title (such as the criteria of statehood and recognition, self-determination and *uti possidetis*), it is apparent that the determinants of what independence really seemed to signify for international law were cast in terms of succession – these were the rules that seemed to determine whether, and to what extent, 'newly independent States' could really assert themselves to be 'new', and for resistance to colonial rule to be articulated in ways other than merely in terms of a right to self-government. The rules on succession, in other words, would provide a language for generating knowledge about either the profundity or superficiality of decolonization.

Yet, as I hope the title of the book indicates, my concern is to do more than simply examine the existence of a passing relationship between the doctrine of State succession and decolonization. I am also suggesting that part of the problem with the formulation and codification of the law of State succession may be related to the idea that decolonization was a radical or constitutive moment: a moment at which international lawyers were faced not only with the task of managing political change on the 'outside', but of managing the decolonization of the legal imagination itself. To explain my position, in this respect, it is perhaps worthwhile explaining briefly why I have *not* chosen to entitle this work 'the international law of decolonization'. It strikes me that to talk about an international law of decolonization is problematic for several reasons. To begin with, it seems to suggest that there existed a body of rules or principles governing decolonization whose articulation or identification preceded the events themselves. This was evidently not the case, and even if the two Vienna Conventions might be read as encapsulating what a law of decolonization might have looked like, they effectively did so after the event. Furthermore, such a posture also supposes that decolonization could be accomplished merely through the articulation of a set of particular rules about recognition or inheritance and quite apart from any engagement with the conditions for participation in the 'international legal community' (for want of a better phrase). The difficulty, of course, was not merely the formal one as to the basis upon which 'new' States may be deemed to have consented to the terms of a legal order in advance of the moment of their admission, but the sense that the legal order itself was one burdened by a disciplinary history of active involvement in the encouragement, fostering or promotion of colonization in the first place (through ideas such as the 'standard of civilisation'.)[16] Decolonization, in other words, was not something that could simply be managed without simultaneously putting in question the very basis upon which the law itself had been constructed.

What I am thus suggesting, is that it was within the framework of the doctrine of State succession that international lawyers – both of a radical and mainstream disposition – sought to work through the substantive implications of the perceived need to 'universalize' international law by the emancipation of colonial territories, at the same time as renegotiating what membership in the international legal community might entail. Decolonization was a moment of disciplinary anxiety and introspection; a moment at which the emancipation of the colonized world had to be accompanied by the simultaneous emancipation of the idea of international law. The discourse of succession was thus not merely a language through which the transition from one status to another might be managed, but the language in which the full implications of colonialism and its unravelling could be explored and discussed. Not surprisingly, however, there were several different accounts as to what colonialism seemed to mean, several different accounts as to what its undoing might entail, several different accounts, furthermore, as to what its significance might be today. And it is with a view to exploring such stories that this book is primarily concerned.

One final remark should be made here about the particular focus of the book – and particularly the emphasis placed upon the question of succession to treaties in the second and third parts. To have focused upon the general question of succession would have resulted in a book twice as long but somewhat less detailed in its analysis. I wanted to capture the idiosyncrasies of various debates and points of argument arising in the context of decolonization and so a somewhat narrower focus was obviously desirable. From here, the choice seemed to be to focus either on property and debt (the 1983 Vienna Convention) or treaties (the 1978 Vienna Convention), and my choice of the latter resulted from a sense that the arguments were, in many respects, more variegated and of broader relevance given the wide range of matters that fell within the compass of treaty law. By the same token, it was also clear that since part of my argument was about the relationship between the ideas of 'status' and 'autonomy' this could be best explored in the context of treaty relations, as I hope will become clear.

---

[16] G Gong, *The Standard of Civilisation* (1984); C Alexandrowicz, *An Introduction to the History of the Law of Nations in the East Indies* (1967); M Koskenniemi, *The Gentle Civiliser of Nations: The Rise and Fall of International Law 1870–1960* (2002).

I

Critical Diagnostics

1. Introduction

In an application to the International Court of Justice on the 20 March 1993, Bosnia-Herzegovina instituted proceedings against the Federal Republic of Yugoslavia (Serbia-Montenegro), (FRY), alleging that it had violated obligations under the Genocide Convention (1948) by encouraging and promoting acts of genocide in Bosnia during the conflict in the former Yugoslavia in 1992–93.[1] It was to be nearly 14 years before the ICJ delivered judgment in the case, and by all accounts it was something of a victory for each side. Serbia, as it was to become, was held to have breached its obligations under the Genocide Convention by actively failing to prevent genocide during the siege of Srebrenica in 1995; it was not held, however, to have been directly responsible for, or complicit in, those acts itself.[2] There were several obvious reasons for the length of proceedings in this case (one might mention here, the evidential complexities associated with gathering of the necessary information, the need to deal with the purported discontinuance of proceedings in 1999, and the difficulties of timetabling associated with proceedings in contiguous cases such as that brought by Croatia in 1999[3] and the 'NATO' cases of 1999).[4] But one significant source of delay was found in the fact that having issued a judgment in 1996 dealing with preliminary objections in which it concluded that it had *prima facie* jurisdiction, the Court was then faced with a request to revise that judgment in light of the emergence of a 'new fact' – namely Serbia's admission to the United Nations in 2000 – which retrospectively put in question its status as a party to the Statute of the ICJ at the time at which the application was submitted to the Court.[5] This request was denied by

---

[1] *Case Concerning the Application of the Convention on the Prevention and Punishment of the Crime of Genocide*, ICJ, Judgment of 26 Feb 2007.

[2] ibid, paras 385–450.

[3] *Application of the Convention on the Prevention and Punishment of the Crime of Genocide* (Croatia v Serbia and Montenegro), 2 July 1999.

[4] *Legality of the Use of Force (Serbia and Montenegro v Belgium) Preliminary Objections*, Judgment ICJ Rep 2004, 279.

[5] *Application for Revision of the Judgment of 11 July 1996 in the Case concerning Application of the Convention on the Prevention and Punishment of the Crime of Genocide (Bosnia and Herzegovina v Yugoslavia) Preliminary Objections (Yugoslavia v Bosnia and Herzegovina)*, Judgment, ICJ Reps 2003, 7.

the Court in 2003, which eventually left the way open to a final judgment, which was delivered in February 2007.

At every stage of the proceedings, there were a series of perplexing issues which dogged the Court. At the outset, the Federal Republic of Yugoslavia (Serbia-Montenegro) had disputed the Court's exercise of jurisdiction (which was based, in part, upon article IX of the Genocide Convention) on the grounds that Bosnia-Herzegovina was not to be regarded as a party to the Genocide Convention (or at least, not at the relevant moments in time).[6] Although Bosnia and Herzegovina had been recognized by the EC member States in April 1992,[7] and had later submitted a 'notification of succession' to the Genocide Convention on 29 December in the same year,[8] this was not, as far as the FRY was concerned, an effective legal act and was not such as to allow Bosnia and Herzegovina to bring proceedings under the Genocide Convention against it. In the main, the FRY's contention here concerned the illegality of Bosnia and Herzegovina's claim to independent statehood (as being constituted in violation of the 'principle of equal rights and self-determination of peoples'), but it had also claimed in earlier proceedings that there was 'no rule' of general international law which 'gives Bosnia-Herzegovina the right to proclaim unilaterally that it is now a party to the Genocide Convention merely because the former Socialist Federal Republic of Yugoslavia was a party to the Convention.'[9] There was not, in other words, any possibility of Bosnia and Herzegovina having automatically become party to the Genocide Convention by way of succession.

At a later stage, Serbia and Montenegro went on to dispute their own participation in the Genocide Convention – a claim which was partially premised upon the idea that, as successor states, neither of them had automatically inherited the obligations of the former Socialist Federal Republic of Yugoslavia.[10] The story behind such claims was obviously complicated by the fact that the FRY initially claimed to be the 'continuation' of the SFRY (in which its continued participation in multilateral agreements was taken as axiomatic), but then later abandoned that position in 2000 when it applied for membership in the United Nations, proclaiming itself to be a successor State.[11] Its 'accession' to the Genocide Convention in 2001, with an appended reservation limiting the jurisdiction of the Court, was obviously designed to put in question that it had been party to that agreement at the time at which the alleged acts of genocide occurred.

---

[6] *Application of the Convention on the Prevention and Punishment of the Crime of Genocide,* Preliminary Objections, Judgment, ICJ Rep 1996, 595, pp 604–9.

[7] Bosnia was recognized by the EC member States on 6 April 1992, Keesing's, vol 38, pp 38704, 38833 (1992). According to the Badinter Commission, Bosnia-Herzegovina obtained its independence on 6 Mar 1992, Opinion no 11, 32 I L M, p 1589.

[8] ICJ Rep 1996, 595, p 610.

[9] ICJ Rep 1993, 3, para 24.

[10] *Application for Revision of the Judgment of 11th July 1996,* ICJ Rep 2003, 7, p 12, para 18.

[11] It was further complicated by the separation of Montenegro from Serbia in 2006. above, n 1, paras 67–79.

For the Court to have denied the applicability of the Genocide Convention to the events at that time would almost have been unthinkable: it was surely at precisely such moments of state collapse or secessionary conflict that the Convention's guarantees needed to be maintained in place. Of course, it was possible to argue that the obligation to prevent and punish genocide was both a general (ie customary) as well as conventional obligation, and that participation or non-participation in the Convention was largely irrelevant for those purposes. But as far as proceedings before the ICJ were concerned, it was clear that being a party to the Genocide Convention (and more specifically, acceptance of Article IX) was of critical importance for purpose of establishing the Court's jurisdiction.[12] So, if the Court was to have anything to say about the allegations of genocide in Bosnia, it would have to deal with the questions of succession that had been raised.

In the first phase, the Court appeared to be faced with two fairly straightforward questions: first, was it possible for Bosnia to be regarded as party to the Genocide Convention in virtue of it being a 'successor State' to the former Socialist Federal Republic of Yugoslavia (SFRY)? Secondly, and if the answer was in the affirmative, did that mean that Bosnia could be regarded as party to the Convention at the time at which the alleged atrocities took place? As regards the first questions, although the Court indicated that Bosnia 'could become a party to the Convention through the mechanism of State succession'[13] it refused to be drawn on the issue as to whether this was, in fact, the case, or whether it had rather simply acceded to the Convention. The reason for this was not immediately obvious. The Court might have relied upon Article 34[14] of the Vienna Convention on Succession of States in Respect of Treaties (1978)[15] by way of establishing a principle of general succession to multilateral agreements.[16] It might also have relied upon Bosnia's notification of succession as an exercise of a 'right of option' consistent with Article 17 of the same Convention.[17] It might even have pursued the argument promoted by Bosnia, and supported by Judge Weeramantry in his Separate Opinion, to the effect that there exists a principle of automatic succession to 'humanitarian' treaties.[18] The obvious benefit of insisting upon some form

---

[12] Art IX provides: 'Disputes between Contracting Parties relating to the interpretation, application or fulfilment of the present Convention, including those relating to the responsibility of a State for genocide or for any of the other acts enumerated in Article III, shall be submitted to the International Court of Justice at the request of any of the parties to the dispute'.

[13] ICJ Rep 1996, 595, paras 20, 24.

[14] Art 34(1) provides that 'When a part or parts of the territory of a State separate to form one or more States, whether or not the predecessor State continues to exist: . . . (a) any treaty in force at the date of the succession of States in respect of the entire territory of the predecessor State continues in force in respect of each successor State so formed'.

[15] Vienna Convention on the Succession of States in Respect of Treaties (1978), 1946 UNTS 3.

[16] cf Separate Opinion of Judge Tomka, ICJ Rep (2007) paras 31–36.

[17] Art 17 reads: 'a newly independent State may, by a notification of succession, establish its status as a party to any multilateral treaty which at the date of the succession of States was in force in respect of the territory to which the succession of States relates'.

[18] Judge Weeramantry, Separate Opinion, ICJ Rep 1996, 640, pp 645–52.

of succession would have been, as Judge Shahabuddeen pointed out, to avoid the existence of a time-gap in the protection afforded by the Convention between the date at which Bosnia became independent, and the date at which its accession to the Convention became effective.[19] The Court's failure to do so, however, left it in the difficult position of having to establish a basis for the applicability of the Convention (and hence its jurisdiction) in relation to acts which potentially took place before Bosnia became party to the Convention. That it did, by the curious, and perhaps extravagant, expedient of construing the Convention as one whose obligations are not 'temporally limited'[20] (shorthand for suggesting that the conventional prohibition on genocide, and hence the Court's jurisdiction in relation to such acts, may be retroactive in operation)[21] was perhaps only symptomatic of its underlying desire to avoid the issue of succession at all costs.

As suggested, by the time at which the Court dealt with the issue at the Merits phase, it was faced with the additional complication of Serbia's claim not to have been party to the Genocide Convention at the time of the institution of proceedings – a claim which had been addressed on a fairly summary basis in 1996. There the Court had noted that Serbia-Montenegro had made the following proclamation on the 27 April 1992: 'The Federal Republic of Yugoslavia, continuing the State, international and political personality of the Socialist Federal Republic of Yugoslavia, shall strictly abide by all commitments that the Socialist Federal Republic of Yugoslavia assumed internationally in the past'.[22]

Relying upon Serbia-Montenegro's stated intention to remain bound by the commitments 'to which the former Yugoslavia was party', and noting that 'it has not been contested that Yugoslavia was party to the Genocide Convention', the Court concluded that 'Yugoslavia was bound by the provisions of the Convention on the date of the filing of the Application in the present case, namely on 20 March 1993.'[23] When it said this issue was not 'contested' the Court was, of course, being a little disingenuous: certainly neither party disputed Serbia-Montenegro's participation in the Genocide Convention – both however

[19] Judge Shahabuddeen, Separate Opinion, ICJ Rep 1996, 634, p 635.

[20] ICJ Rep 1996, 595, p 617 para 34 ('the Genocide Convention...does not contain any clause the object or effect of which is to limit in such manner the scope of its [the Court's] jurisdiction *ratione temporis*, and nor did the Parties themselves make any reservation to that end....The Court thus finds that it has jurisdiction in this case to give effect to the Genocide Convention with regard to the relevant facts which have occurred since the beginning of the conflict which took place in Bosnia-Herzegovina'.)

[21] This argument was clearly finessed by the Court's observation that the prohibition of Genocide was a customary rule and one operating *erga omnes*. It is important to recall, however, that the point in issue was not one as to whether Serbia was entitled to commit acts of Genocide, but whether the Court had jurisdiction in relation to claims concerning the application of the Genocide convention. On this point see S Rosenne, 'Automatic Treaty Succession', in J Klabbers and R Lefeber (eds) *Essays on the Law of Treaties* (1998) 97, pp 103–5.

[22] ibid, p 610, para 17. The intention to remain bound by international treaties was confirmed in an Official Note of 27 Apr 1992 from the Yugoslav Mission in New York to the Secretary General. UN SCOR, 47th session, Annex, UN Doc S/23877 (1992).

[23] Ibid.

had very different reasons for coming to that conclusion. For its part, Serbia-Montenegro simply worked on the supposition that as the 'continuing state', its participation in multilateral agreements would continue unless prejudiced by the changing circumstances. For Bosnia's part, the argument would no doubt have been something along the lines that Serbia-Montenegro had either acceded or succeeded to the Convention. Given this difference of opinion, and given furthermore the Court's subsequent conclusion in the *Use of Force* cases that Serbia-Montenegro's earlier claim to be the continuation of the SFRY was of negligible legal significance,[24] there might have been reason to reconsider this assumption. That it chose rather to treat its 1996 judgment on the issue as res judicata can thus be seen, once again, to be indicative of a desire to avoid, if at all possible, the question of succession.[25]

So what prompted the International Court to evade the issue of succession which was so obviously the one which it was called upon to decide? Why was it reluctant to rely upon the terms of the 1978 Vienna Convention when they were so obviously available to it? The first, and most obvious explanation was that, as nearly every commentator at the time made clear, the law of State succession was largely confused and resistant to simple exposition.[26] Not only did there seem to be a lack of clarity[27] and imprecision[28] in the substantive rules, but there also appeared to be no obviously agreed theoretical structure.[29] State practice, in that regard, appeared too diffuse, or heterogeneous,[30] to be pulled within the frame

[24] It is notable that the Court did not decide whether Serbia-Montenegro was, or was not, a party to the Genocide Convention in 1999, ICJ Rep 2004, 279.

[25] Above, n 1, para 140. See further, Separate Opinion of Judge ad hoc Kreća, ICJ Rep (2007), paras 61–74.

[26] Stern remarks that 'La succession d'Etats apparaît comme l'un des problèmes le plus complexes du droit international.', B Stern, *La Succession d'États* (2000) p. 27; S Oeter, 'German Unification and State Succession', ZaöRV (1991) 349 (the law of succession is 'chaotic'); M Koskenniemi and M Lehto, 'La succession d'Etats dans l'ex-URSS, en ce qui concerne particulièrement les relations avec la Finlande', AFDI (1992) 182 (the idiosyncratic nature of each situation makes generalisation difficult); G Hafner and E Kornfeind 'The Recent Austrian Practice of State Succession: Does the Clean Slate Still Exist?', ARIEL 1996/1, 1, p 2.

[27] E Castrén, 'Obligations of States Arising from the Dismemberment of Another State, 13 ZaöRV (1951) 753; I Brownlie, *Principles of Public International Law* (5th edn 1998) p 650 ('State succession is an area of great uncertainty and controversy.').

[28] Verzijl notes, for example, that: '[t]he face of pre-existing treaties is extremely difficult to determine in a global manner, not only because of the wide variety of the conditions under which new independent States come into existence and of the subject matters regulated by such treaties, but also owing to the fact that international practice and doctrine in this field show an unusual degree of divergence. This is true to such an extent that one feels inclined to ask if this is not a domain on which positive international law still exhibits a genuine and grave lacuna'. J Verzijl, *International Law in Historical Perspective* (1974) p 170.

[29] The ILC commented, for example, that '[a] close examination of State practice afforded no convincing evidence of any general doctrine by reference to which the various problems of succession in respect of treaties could find their appropriate solution'. YBILC (1974) vol. II, Pt i, at 168, para 51. Oeter similarly speaks about the lack of a 'common theoretical basis', above, n 26, p 355. Hafner and Kornfeind, above, n 26, p 355.

[30] R Jennings, 'General Course on Public International Law', 121 Hague Recueil (1967) 112, p 437 (State succession 'is a subject which presents such a rich diversity of practice as to give some

of any clear-cut set of rules or principles,[31] and theories of succession too abstract, or too universal to be of much assistance. There seemed, in other words, to be either a problem with the subject matter (too 'political' for anything sensible to be said on the matter)[32] or a problem with the way in which legal scholars had tried to address it.[33] When faced with such deficiencies, the perception that the problem of succession was one of considerable importance, yet was incapable of being effectively addressed, verged on the parodic.[34] And with such thoughts in mind, the Court would undoubtedly have had to proceed with caution.

Apart from such general concerns with the subject matter, there were also some quite obvious formal difficulties associated with relying upon the terms of the Vienna Convention of 1978. Although the SFRY had ratified the Vienna Convention in 1980, the Convention had only come into force in 1996 following its subsequent ratification by several of the successor States emerging from the former Yugoslavia.[35] Its applicability to the events in 1991–2 would have been problematic both for the reason that its terms were explicitly held to be 'prospective' rather than retrospective in orientation,[36] and because of the obvious point,

plausibility to a surprisingly varied range of theoretical analysis and doctrine'); Castrén, above, n 27, p 753 ('The elucidation of this question is rendered difficult by the absence of general international treaties and in view of the great instability in the practice observed by different States in different periods. It is, therefore, not surprising to find that differences of opinion, even with regard to certain fundamental aspects of the problem, prevail in the doctrine of the law of nations.') D O'Connell, 'Recent Problems of State Succession in Relation to New States', 130 Hague Recueil (1970) 95, p 116 ('A record of what newly independent States have done, or of the attitudes which they have struck, often leads, not to concordance, but to incoherence, and the systematic treatment of the facts of so-called "State practice" rarely rises above the anecdotal.').

[31] M Koskenniemi, 'Report of the Director of Studies of the English-speaking Section of the Centre', in M Koskenniemi and P Eisemann, *State Succession: Codification Tested Against the Facts* (1997), 65; V Degan, 'La Succession d'États en Matière de Traités et les États Nouveaux (Issue de L'Ex-Yougoslavie)', 42 AFDI (1996) 206, p 207. Brownlie, above, n 27, p 650 ('it is perfectly possible to take the view that not many settled legal rules have emerged as yet').

[32] A common theme in many writings was the emphasis given to 'political considerations'. See eg, E Castrén, 'Aspects Récents de la Succession d'Etats', 78 Hague Recueil (1951) 385.

[33] Hall famously criticized international lawyers for all too often merely copying one another, W Hall, *A Treatise on International Law* (4th edn, 1895) p 98. O'Connell was rather more scathing in his assessment of his contemporaries: 'never before has international legal scholarship been so barren of philosophical reflection, or so preoccupied with the ephemeral, as it is today; and this deficiency of intellectual resources may be said to have inhibited the juristic exposition of the problem of State succession more than of other international legal problems'. O'Connell, 'Recent Problems', above, n 30, p 102.

[34] Hoelflich complains that '[h]aving examined the history of the law of State succession to public debts, one begins to feel rather depressed and confused and even despairing of ever discovering a "settled" principle of international law'. M Hoeflich, 'Through a Glass Darkly: Reflections Upon the History of the International Law of Public Debt in Connection with State Succession', Uni Ill L Rev (1982) 39, p 65.

[35] The Convention currently has 19 signatories and 21 parties. Those that have ratified are: Bosnia and Herzegovina, Croatia, Cyprus, Czech Republic, Dominica, Ecuador, Egypt, Estonia, Ethiopia, Iraq, Liberia, Montenegro, Morocco, St Vincent and the Grenadines, Serbia, Seychelles, Slovakia, Slovenia, the Former Yugoslav Republic of Macedonia, Tunisia, and Ukraine.

[36] eg art 7(1) ('... the Convention applies only in respect of a succession of States which has occurred after the entry into force of the Convention except as may otherwise be agreed.').

alluded to during the drafting of the Convention, that its applicability would depend upon the prior question as to whether the 'successor States' in question could be regarded as party to the Vienna Convention itself.[37] The relevance of the Vienna Convention, in other words, would depend upon the operation of the same rules that it was designed to bring into effect. If the Court was to rely upon the Convention, then, it could only plausibly do so by way of arguing either that the party concerned was in a position to decide on a unilateral basis to apply the terms of the Convention to its own succession (which, although partly envisaged within the Convention,[38] really just returned to the original problem of possible objection by third parties), or that the terms of the Convention were reflective of general international law.

In respect of the latter possibility, there were two obvious difficulties. The first concerned the general assumption that if a rule of inheritance was identified as having the status of customary international law, all 'new' States would be automatically bound by it by reason of an inescapable obligation to honour pre-existent customary international law, whatever its content and irrespective of consent. Whilst such an article of faith has never been seriously questioned, neither has it easily been explained. It was always evident, for example, that 'Austinian' accounts that sought to locate the authority of (international) law in the will of the sovereign, were most vulnerable to arguments about succession, since it was precisely the location of sovereignty which was put in question in such cases. If consent provided the basis for obligation, how might 'new' States be incorporated into the legal order without any effective evidence for having consented to the applicable rules? If consent was relevant, it could thus only be sustained by way of being diffused – as, for example, by way of resort to the idea of tacit consent, acquiescence or perhaps estoppel. But even here it was evident that such arguments were still at risk of falling into self-justification. In the latest version of *Oppenheim's International Law*, for example, Jennings and Watts begin by suggesting that '[i]t is not possible to say why international law as a whole is binding upon the international community without entering the realm of non-legal considerations'.[39] They go on to argue, nevertheless, that 'practical

---

[37] As the ILC was to note in the midst of its work on state succession in the 1970s (Yrbk ILC, 1974, II, pt. i, p 170, para 62.): 'Since a succession of States in most cases brings into being a new State, a convention on the law of succession in respect of treaties would *ex hypothesi* not be binding on the successor State unless and until it took steps to become a party to that convention; and even then the convention would not be binding upon it in respect of any act or fact which took place before the date on which it became a party. Nor would other States be bound by the convention in relation to the new State until the latter had become a party'.

[38] Art 7(3) of the Convention provides that a successor State may, at the time of ratifying the Convention 'make a declaration that it will apply the provisions of the Convention provisionally in respect of its own succession of States which has occurred before the entry into force of the Convention in relation to any other signatory or contracting State which makes a declaration accepting the declaration of the successor State'. Both the Czech Republic and Slovakia purported to rely upon art 7(3) in applying the Convention to their own succession.

[39] R Jennings and A Watts, *Oppenheim's International Law* (9th edn. 1992) I, p 14, s 5.

realities' suggest that the basis lies in the 'common consent' of members of the international community. This is immediately qualified however:

This "common consent" cannot mean, of course, that all States must at all times expressly consent to every part of the body of rules constituting international law, for such common consent could never in practice be established. . . . The common consent that is meant is thus not consent to particular rules but to the express or tacit consent of states to the body of rules comprising international law as a whole at any particular time. Membership of the international community carries with it the duty to submit to the existing body of such rules, and the right to contribute to their modification or development in accord-ance with the prevailing rules for such processes. *Thus new States which come into existence and are admitted into the international community thereupon become subject to the body of rules for international conduct in force at the time of their admittance. No single State can say on its admittance into the community of nations that it desires to be subjected to such and such rules of international law and not to others.* [emphasis added][40]

For all its overt simplicity, the kinds of subtle equivalences this explanation puts in play are altogether problematic. On the one hand, the idea of common consent brings to mind a kind of informal 'voting' system in which both affirm-ation and abstention are taken as positive signals. On the other hand, however, it also seems to operate as a condition for membership in which the possibility of dissent (a necessary implication of being balloted) is excluded from the outset. 'Tacit consent', in other words, seems to have two decisively different meanings depending upon whether the subject of that consent is, or is not, *already* under-stood to be a participant in the legal order. This, of course, is also to bring to mind the idea of a territorially incomplete international order. In order for there to be 'new' States, or for participation in the legal order to be constructed along the lines of membership, there presumably has to be some space *outside* that order – either from which those new States emerged, or in which non-members may reside. But it is in the construction of this fictional space as a way of under-pinning the argument about common consent ('fictional' in the sense that none of the advocates of this kind of reasoning would actually accept its existence)[41] that the reasoning clearly becomes most tendentious. As will be seen, however, it is precisely through the advancement, and subsequent subversion, of this idea of 'newness' that much scholarship relating to succession has proceeded.[42]

---

[40] ibid. See also, T Franck, *The Power of Legitimacy Among Nations* (1990) pp 190–1 ('new States are deemed to be obliged to comply with the duties of statehood not because they agree to do so, but because they have satisfied requirements for the recognition of their right to membership in the community. The obligations, so to speak, come with the rights.').

[41] Jennings and Watts (above, n 39, pp 4–5) for example, speak frequently about the existence of 'universal' as opposed to 'particular' or 'general' international law. ('That part of international law that is binding on all States, as is far the greater part of customary law, may be called *univer-sal* international law', (ibid, 4); 'One can also distinguish between those rules of international law which, even though they may be of universal application, do not in any particular situation give rise to rights and obligations *erga omnes*, an those which do', (ibid, 4–5)).

[42] Below, pp 135–47.

The second, and more prosaic, difficulty was associated with the way in which the Vienna Convention itself had been drafted. As most commentators felt at liberty to declare, the Convention was never representative of customary international law, nor was it ever intended to be – and that was particularly true of Articles 16 and 34 which might have been relied upon by the ICJ in the Bosnia case.[43] The real concern, as far as most commentators on the Convention seemed to suggest, was that the Vienna Convention had been drafted at a time at which decolonization was in full flood. The International Law Commission – whose draft articles formed the basis for the Convention – had been explicitly instructed to draft articles taking into account 'the views of States which have achieved independence since the Second World War',[44] and the Convention, as a result, was largely oriented to the elaboration of principles of succession in relation to 'newly independent States'. The definition of 'newly independent States' furthermore, had obviously been influenced by the application of the principle of self-determination which, according to the contemporary orthodoxy, meant that it was to be largely confined to former colonial dependencies (occasionally referred to as 'salt-water colonies').[45] This, in fact, formed the basis for the different rules elaborated in Articles 16 and 34 respectively and which suggested that, whilst consent was important for purposes of determining the fate of treaty obligations in case of decolonization, in other contexts it was far less important, and in some circumstances succession could be regarded as occurring automatically irrespective of any act on the part of the successor State.

The point was, however, not simply that it was hard to choose as to which of these provisions should be applicable in case of Bosnia and Herzegovina (as far as the latter was concerned, either provision would suffice), but that the framework of decolonization had so distorted the project of codification that it was impossible to take anything at face value. Article 34, for example, was criticized, in particular, for appearing to conflate two very different categories of case (those relating to the dissolution of States, and those concerning the separation of part of a State)[46] and was thought as a result to be a largely speculative provision.[47] But this, in some senses, was just symptomatic of a more general perception that, for all the work that had been put in by the ILC in detailing and archiving State practice – deliberating as to which analogies should apply, trying to discern

---

[43] See generally the discussion as to the status of art 34 in the *Gabčíkovo-Nagymaros Project* case (Hungary v Slovakia), ICJ Rep 1997, 7. See below, pp 239–44.

[44] GA Resn 1902 (XVIII), 18 Nov 1963.

[45] A newly independent State was a successor State 'the territory of which immediately before the date of the succession of States was a dependent territory for the international relations of which the predecessor State was responsible'. Art 2(1)(f), 1978 Vienna Convention. The ILC draft articles make clear that the kinds of 'dependent territories' the ILC had in mind were colonies, trusteeships, mandates, and protectorates. Commentary to draft art 2, Yrbk ILC, 1974, II, paras 6–7.

[46] eg, Z Zimmermann, *Staatennachfolge in völkerrechtliche Vertäge* (2000) p 860. Quoted in Separate Opinion of Judge Tomka, ICJ Rep 2007, p 15, para 33, n 12.

[47] cf dissenting opinion of Judge Kreca, ICJ Rep 1996, 658, pp 775–90; Hafner and Kornfeind, above, n 26, p 3.

evidence of *opinio iuris* from selected texts – it had spent far too much time looking backwards rather than forwards. The drafters had become obsessed with a transient form of political change and had disregarded the obvious possibility that 'future' cases of succession would assume a very different character.[48] As it turned out, post-socialist transition in the 1990s was almost uniformly regarded as quite different from decolonization,[49] and as a consequence, the frame and orientation of the Convention appeared to be largely useless. When thus seen in terms of its specific aim – to codify and develop progressively the law of State succession – the Vienna Convention could only be regarded as something of a failure[50] (even if, as it turns out, *some* of its provisions gained subsequent endorsement).[51]

As these forms of explanation may suggest, my main concern in this book is twofold. First of all, my intention is to explore this general attitude to the 1978 Convention: why was it that codification of the law of State succession seemed to be so difficult, and so fraught? What was it about the subject of succession that seemed to defy the possibility of effective law-making? Secondly, and further to that, I am concerned with examining the way in which the story of decolonization has been and continues to be, told within this field of law, and within international law more generally. Why is it that decolonization seems to represent such a specific instance of practice for purposes of policy making in this field? What does this seem to say about international lawyers' understanding of their own disciplinary history, and their engagement with parallel instances of political change? As both of these sets of questions suggest, I am not concerned with trying to indicate where things went wrong, to vindicate any or all of the provisions of the 1978 Convention, or indeed to suggest alternative formulations that better reflect past or present State practice. Nor am I going to attempt to detail how far contemporary practice has either converged with, or moved away from, the positions adopted within the Convention. Those kinds of studies have already been undertaken elsewhere,[52] and in many respects the continued fascination with the recording and archiving of the infinite variety of instances of practice has, in a very perverse way, tended to draw attention away from an examination of the way in which the issue has been approached and what seems to be at stake.

Broadly speaking, the orientation of this work is both diagnostic and exploratory. It is exploratory in the sense that I want to investigate and understand the

[48] This was the substance of contemporaneous criticism. eg, I Sinclair, 'Some Reflections on the Vienna Convention on Succession of States in Respect of Treaties', in *Essays in Honour of Erik Castren* (1978) 149, p 181; D O'Connell, 'Reflections on the State Succession Convention', 39 ZaöRV (1979) 725.

[49] cf R Mullerson, *International Law, Rights and Politics* (1994) pp 64–7.

[50] eg, Reply of Republic of Hungary in the *Gabcikovo-Nagymaros Project* case, p 173, para 3.157. (asserting that the 1978 Convention 'is widely regarded as an unsuccessful exercise in international law-making and which does not correspond to subsequent practice'.)

[51] *Gabčikovo-Nagymaros Project* case, above, n 43, p 72, para 123 (concerning art 12); *Continental Shelf* case (Tunisia/Libya) Judgment 24 Feb 1982, ICJ Rep 1982, para 84.

[52] eg Stern, above, n 26; Koskenniemi *et al* above, n 31; Hafner and Kornfeind, above, n 26.

ideas and assumptions that went to inform the process of codification (eg the role played by the notion of self-determination and the differing interpretations thereof, the basis upon which a rule of succession was thought capable of elaboration, and the way in which notions of sovereignty or personality informed the project) and through that, to also generate a sense of the place that the history of decolonization might have within contemporary accounts of international law. It is also diagnostic in the sense that I want to try to pinpoint why it is that international lawyers have struggled with the topic of State succession – to look beyond, in that sense, standard complaints about the inconsistency of practice or the theoretical uncertainty, and try to generate an understanding of why it is that this inconsistency or uncertainty has emerged. To put this second point in a slightly different way, I want to treat the concerns that usually animate criticism of the law of State succession as symptomatic rather than causal, even if it may not be the case that my diagnosis will necessarily be productive of the kind of clarity that may be conducive to present or future policy-making. The reason for this is simple enough – without some further understanding of why it is that practice seems so chaotic or why theory so redundant, there is neither the opportunity to intervene effectively as a policy-maker nor to situate oneself in respect of such activities. Without, in brief, knowing what the question is, we are at a loss for understanding how to evaluate, or react to, what appears to be happening around us.

Certain things also need to be added about the way in which this book is written and the particular focus adopted. To begin with, as will soon become evident, this book is largely written in narrative form rather than in the form of some analytical/doctrinal statement of the law of State succession. Parts II and III of the book, in particular, are dedicated to telling a story about the way in which a variety of international lawyers and agencies approached the question of succession in respective periods of time (1960s-70s, and the 1990s onwards), with a view to examining the different kinds of themes to emerge, the different understandings given to the idea of succession, the different impulses that were to shape their response to the problems arising. In the course of doing so, I will be examining, in particular, the stories being told by the various protagonists as to *their* understanding of the present and past of the law and practice of State succession.

There are two broad reasons for taking this approach to the subject. In the first place, I am concerned with highlighting the use of historical narratives in the context of doctrinal engagement with issues of international law. In a formal sense, of course, this is a necessary, and indeed inevitable, activity. Whether, for example, as a matter of determining the content of customary international law through an analysis of past and contemporary State practice, interrogating the precedential value of judicial decisions, construing international agreements by reference to the *travaux preparatoires*, or identifying the applicable law or the 'critical date' in the context of dispute resolution, some engagement with the past and its relationship to the present is inescapable. This activity is obviously a very particular one – it is employed, above all else, for the purpose of identifying those rules, principles, or institutional techniques that have cemented themselves within the code. Treaties, judicial pronouncements, diplomatic exchanges, and scholarly writings are thus all plundered instrumentally for the purpose of elucidating a normative pedigree or, as Kennedy puts it, to generate 'a list of factors and a holding'.[53]

What I find most interesting about this, however, is not so much the persistence of the narrative in legal argumentation or (re)statement, but the critical character of the stories being told in the process. I implicitly draw, in this sense, upon the kind of post-Foucauldian historiography that highlights the way in which the past is continually re-read and re-written for ideological or other effect. The past, in other words, is viewed not as something merely 'there' to be interpreted, or available to us in unmediated form, but something that is constructed backwards through the identification of relevant texts and materials, through interpretation, and through the mode of emplotment, in which choices are continually made as to how, and in what way, its salience may be presented.[54] If this is the case, then we might be prompted to look, not so much at the accuracy of the historical narratives – how far, for example, one might sustain an argument about the general approach to treaty succession in the 1960s – but rather to the kinds of meaning that the narrators sought to generate through the telling of those stories. What lies behind, in other words, either a story about the progressive evolution of the law of succession from the 19th century onwards, or about a story that is one of its continued 'restatement' or 're-formulation'?[55]

A second reason for utilizing a narrational methodology in this work (ie to write it, in a sense, as a story about stories) is in the way that it allows me to explore, in a much more reflective way, the manner in which particular arguments or ideas have been, and continue to be, utilized. As I will suggest later, for example, the principle of self-determination was read in very different ways, and to very different effect, by different participants in the process of codification. In one direction it was taken as an idea which might sustain the continuity of

---

[53] D Kennedy, 'The Disciplines of International Law', 12 Leiden JIL (1999) 1, p 82. ('The rhetorical gestures and motives of scholars and statesmen are extremely hard to compare across time as applications of similar ideas or contributions to a single institutional project. Moreover, it is unlikely that historical actors were primarily concerned, or even noticed, the relationship between their actions and a transcendent historical development of something which would later come to be summarized as 'international law'. The complexity of the historical record – different ideas about what 'law' was, different attitudes about 'sovereignty' and 'war' and 'right' – tend to disappear when one looks at historical events for evidence of what 'the law' about some transhistorical phenomenon like 'conquest' or 'sovereign immunity' has been.').

[54] I draw here very loosely on the work of those such as M Foucault, 'Neitzsche, Genealogy, and History' in P Rabinov (ed), *The Foucault Reader* (1986) 76; H Kellner, *Language and Historical Representation* (1989); R Young, *White Mythologies* (2nd edn 2004); H White, *The Content of the Form: Narrative Discourse and Historical Representation* (1987).

[55] For a useful account of the themes of 'restatement' and 'renewal' and a contrasting 'genealogical' approach to international legal history see N Berman, 'In the Wake of Empire', 14 Am ULR (1998–99) 1523.

existing legal relations by telling a story about decolonization as one of evolution rather than as radical change. In another direction, it was taken as an idea that was radically to transform and disrupt international legal relations, severing the past from the present.[56] The point is, however, that my 'meta-narrative' (for want of a better expression) allows an exploration of the variability of such arguments without forcing a conclusion one way or another as to which was a more credible or 'acceptable' interpretation of the principle. Certainly conclusions were drawn as to the significance or relevance of the principle of self-determination, but the narrative itself reminds us of the open texture of ideas, the presence of dissonant voices, and of our constructive role as narrators in bringing to light, and silencing, the stories that others might tell. The narrative *can* be one of closure and normative insight (and typically a modernist story of progress and fruition) but it can also be one of repetition, indeterminacy and inconclusiveness.[57]

I have talked thus far about the way in which I approach the subject, but there is also the question of the particular focus of this work. Why, at a time in which the most pressing questions relating to succession appear to be those that have ensued from the territorial reconfiguration of Europe post 1989, would I spending most of my time discussing decolonization? The full answer to this question, I hope, will emerge as the work progresses, but several initial reasons may be given at the outset. One initial point to make, however, is that this is not intended to be a book *solely* or even *primarily* about the law of State succession. It is also a book about the way in which international lawyers have tended to approach decolonization, and the significance of decolonization for the understanding of their own discipline.

From the middle of the 20th century, at least, international lawyers had to confront quite directly the somewhat uncomfortable fact that international law (or the purveyors thereof) had done as much to assist colonization in the late 19th century as to resist it. Its toleration of conquest and its denial of 'native' sovereignty in Africa and Asia were only part of the picture. Alongside this were doctrines – of *terra nullius*, of subjugation, of annexation, of treaties as equal bargains, of sovereignty full and partial – all of which were to suggest that international lawyers were complicit actors in a broader imperial project. This was, of course, to change in the 20th century. According to many standard accounts, the Charter era, and the accompanying process of decolonization, brought colonialism as a practice to an end. The hierarchical ordering of international society that engendered the expansion of colonial empires was replaced by a commitment to formal equality; the continuance of colonial rule replaced by a commitment to the fostering of self-determination; and the tolerance of forcible annexation replaced by a general prohibition on the use of force.

[56] Below, pp 82–90.
[57] On the significance of the choice between 'romantic' and 'tragic' modes of narrative emplotment to tell the story of the colonial and post-colonial experience, see D Scott, *Conscripts of Modernity: The Tragedy of Colonial Enlightenment* (2004).

Such an account of the 'problem of colonialism', however, scarcely engaged with the relationship between colonial practice and the imperial designations that supported it. Even if colonialism, as an idea, was associated with the establishment of colonial settlements or the assumption of formal rule over territories in Africa and Asia, it could by no means easily be separated from a broader discourse of Empire. From the early 20th century many had begun to associate imperial policy with the expansion of capitalism, and the exploitation of colonial territory for economic gain.[58] Whilst the kind of balance-sheet approach to economic history that this seemed to prompt was problematic enough, what it did signal was two things. On the one hand, it was to suggest that a discourse of imperialism could extend beyond the parameters of the colonial territory itself, and into the semi-colonial periphery (in the form, perhaps, of an 'imperialism of free trade').[59] On the other hand, it was also to suggest the possible continuity of those imperial relations beyond the moment of decolonization itself. If economic expansion (such as the opening of new markets and investment opportunities)[60] was the key, formal rule was merely a contingent variable. These two themes have remained in subsequent post-colonial discourse even if the focus of the latter has extended considerably beyond the realm of political economy. As Said explains it, 'imperialism' should be understood as representing 'the practice, the theory, and the attitudes of a dominating metropolitan centre ruling a distant territory' for which 'colonialism', strictly concerned with the implanting of settlements on distant territories, is merely one of its (accidental)[61] consequences.[62] He concludes that whilst 'colonialism has largely ended...imperialism...lingers where it has always been, in a kind of general cultural sphere as well as in specific political, ideological, economic, and social practices'.[63] Said's specific endeavour was to

---

[58] This general theme is often referred to as the Hobson-Lenin thesis. See J Hobson, *Imperialism: A Study* (1905); V Lenin 'Imperialism: The Highest Stage of Capitalism', in 1 *Collected Works of VI Lenin* (1917) 495.

[59] See J Gallagher and R Robinson, 'The Imperialism of Free Trade', 6 *Economic History Review* (1953) 1. This thesis prompted a lively academic debate as regards the accuracy of their characterization of mid-Victorian policy concering free trade. eg O MacDonagh, 'The Anti-Imperialism of Free Trade', 14 *Economic History Review* (1962) 489; R Moore, 'Imperialism and "Free Trade" Policy in India, 1853–4', 17 *Economic History Review* (1964) 135; D Platt, 'The Imperialism of Free Trade: Some Reservations', 21 *Economic History Review* (1968) 296; B Semmel, *The Rise of Free Trade Imperialism* (1970); P Cain and A Hopkins, *British Imperialism: Innovation and Expansion, 1688–1914* (London: Longmans, 1993) pp 8–10.

[60] For the view that imperialism may be understood as a 'largely economic rather than largely territorial enterprise', see G Spivak, *A Critique of Postcolonial Reason: Toward a History of the Vanishing Present*, (Cambridge, Mass, Harvard University Press, 1999) 3.

[61] cf J Seeley, *The Expansion of England* [1883] (London: Macmillan, 1931) p 143 (The British acquisition of India 'was made blindly. Nothing great that has ever been done by Englishmen was done so unintentionally, so accidentally, as the conquest of India . . . in India we meant one thing, and did another.') On this theme more generally, B Porter, *Absent-Minded Imperialists: Empire, Society and Culture in Britain* (2004).

[62] E Said, *Culture and Imperialism* (1993) p 8.

[63] ibid.

locate the continuance of an imperial ideology in the cultural frames of reference of Western art and literature – initially at the level of a textual 'discourse' that combined knowledge and power in the creation and domination of the 'Orient'.[64] But it had obvious resonance also for the generic discourse of international law many of whose doctrines – of personality, recognition, sovereignty, and territory – seemed to have internalized an imperial ideology of dominance and subordination in which the 'colonized other' is constructed as a constant object of intervention.[65]

In a strange way, this was always clear to those international lawyers conscripted to manage decolonization in the middle of the 20th century. However one was to view the process, decolonization raised a good many more questions than those related to the obvious issues of sovereignty, self-determination, recognition or territorial title. It was a moment at which quite virulent and hostile debates opened out relating to the rules of succession – rules that purported to govern everything from the location of boundaries, to decisions as to whether the 'newly independent' States could automatically regard themselves as members of international organizations, whether they were entitled to overseas assets or liable for public debt, whether they had an obligation to respect contracts or concessionary agreements relating to that territory, or whether there were any constraints governing the granting or withholding of nationality. It was here, rather than in decisions concerning, for example, the process by which new States would gain admission to the 'family of nations', that the real sense of what decolonization actually seemed to mean for international lawyers starts to become clear.

If the doctrine of State succession thus appeared to put at centre stage the problem of imperialism, it was also critical in understanding the significance or otherwise of decolonization as a process by which international lawyers could distance themselves from the history of their own discipline. The problem of a lingering 'imperialism' could only be supplanted if it came to be resisted in the doctrine and practice of State succession. But there were many things to be negotiated here. One was the character of the new law of State succession: how was it to resist the imperial urge other than by the appropriation of the forms and designation of the nation-State (and the prerogatives of 'sovereignty') which were already substantially under attack in mainstream discourse? Would this not merely signal the return of a discredited tradition that reified sovereignty and paid insufficient attention to the developing law of human rights amongst other things? Another question was that of timing: if the law of State succession was to play

---

[64] There is an acknowledged ambivalence in his work both as regards the orientation of such knowledge formations (to intentionally dominate?) and their representative function (does the Orient pre-exist the discourse?). See, R Young, *Postcolonialism: An Historical Introduction* (Oxford: Blackwell, 2001) pp 390–1.
[65] A Anghie, *Imperialism, Sovereignty and the Making of International Law* (2004).

a part in resisting imperialism, then how might it be reconstructed along anti-colonial lines prior to the fact of decolonization itself? Insofar as it was always clear that the identification of a customary international law of State succession was dependent upon the weight of established practice (in classical terms, a 'constant and uniform usage'), wouldn't the putative law of decolonization always be too late? As will be seen, these two issues have been recurrent points of discussion: on the one part, in arguments about the need to transcend the old categories of sovereignty when dealing with questions of succession; on the other in arguments about the temporal finitude of decolonization itself.

Thus far, I have suggested that in order to understand the relationship between international law and imperialism, one must pay attention to the apparent role played by the law of State succession in the course of decolonization. But there is another angle on this which I would also like to bring out, and which relates back to my earlier comments about trying to assume a diagnostic posture on contemporary discussions of the law of State succession. Here, I would like to suggest that there seems to be some connection between two apparently distinct themes in the current discourse of succession: one theme being that mentioned above, namely the marginalization of the experience of decolonization from contemporary legal analysis; the other being the emergence of a (albeit under-theorized) species of pragmatism which is overtly unselfconscious about the kind of agenda that is being set. I will ultimately be suggesting that, far from being marginal, decolonization provided the only coherent framework by which it was possible to perceive or understand the real meaning or significance of the law of State succession, and the insistent separation of the contemporary scene from its immediate historical precursors has only been such as to make it entirely unclear as to what the stakes might be.

In the following sections of the first part of this book, I will be trying to set the scene for the narratives that follow. I will shortly begin with a brief history of the idea of succession in which I will try to lay out the changing shape of legal discourse in the period prior to the project of codification in the 1960s, and will continue by examining in a little more detail, several features of the discourse as it was to develop during that time. What I am mainly concerned with, here, is to identify the main theoretical, conceptual, and analytical 'moves' that have assisted in the formation of this particular field of international law, with a view to bringing to the forefront some of the quandaries that have tended to be ill-articulated in mainstream accounts. I will also, in passing, be trying to associate those ideas and 'developments' with what appear to be background accounts of the relationship between international legal discourse and the colonial confrontation. In the spirit of the very subject matter, I want to bring to the fore what seems to be 'exceptional' or 'aberrational' about the idea of State succession, and how such crises may bring to the surface the theoretical fragility of the discipline of international law. Before I do so, however, I begin with one or two general remarks about some of the general 'themes' that appear to underpin approaches to the question of succession.

2. The Themes of Succession

At the beginning of his influential book on State succession, written in 1956, O'Connell begins with the following description of the subject:

The transfer of territory from one national community to another gives rise to legal problems of a difficult and complex character. Such transfers have been frequent in modern history, and often drastic in their extent and consequences. They have been effected in a variety of ways: by violent annexation, by peaceful cession, by revolution or emancipation of subject regions, and by extensive territorial resettlements. Despite their formal differences these changes possess one common feature; one State ceases to rule in a territory, while another takes its place. This is a fact which has legal consequences. A sudden and often serious influence is exerted upon the international relations of the territory concerned, and upon its economic, social, and legal structure. The body of law which has been built up for the solution of the problems arising from transfer of territory has for its object the minimizing of the effects of this change.[66]

In terms of what is commonly taken to be the function of the law of State succession this is an admirable description. It is about solving the legal problems arising from the many varied forms of territorial change (usually going under the terminology of cession, secession, annexation, unification, dismemberment, absorption, or independence), with a view to minimizing the effects of such change upon the stable relations between States. As O'Connell explains the role of the law of State succession, one can sense it to be both reactive and transitional. It is *reactive* in the sense that, as he puts it, it is concerned with the management of the many consequences of factual changes in the geography of rule. This may include decisions not merely as to the fate of treaties, as to entitlement to assets or responsibility for debt, but also as to questions of nationality, responsibility, or the continuity of contracts and concessions. It is also *transitional* in the sense that it mediates between the 'before' and 'after' of political change, operating not so much as a set of ongoing prescriptions for daily life, but as a contingent discourse of intervention, the concern of which is to return the world as far as possible back to a condition of 'normality'. The *reactive* character of the law of succession thus points towards the non-legal (political, economic, or cultural) nature of the problem, and its *transitional* character to the mediating role it seeks to play between the 'politics' of change and the 'law' of continuity.

Although not departing in any obvious way from the way in which the subject is normally conceived, O'Connell's description seems to invite us to think about two questions: one concerns the significance of this normative-empirical distinction between the 'factual event' (which seems to take place outside law) and its consequences (the management of the effects of political change through law); the other concerns the contingent or expedient nature of the law of State

---

[66] D O'Connell, *State Succession* (1956), p 3.

succession as a form of transitional intervention. On the first of these issues, O'Connell seems to present the issue as one concerned with a move from politics to law – a story about the tragedy of political change (which, as he suggests, can be 'drastic' in its consequences, dividing communities and depriving individuals of their homes and possessions) the effects of which are to be regulated and 'minimized' through the intervention of international law. The international law of State succession may be seen, in other words, as providing a means by which innocent parties (third States and their nationals) may be protected from forms of revolutionary change that might otherwise put them, their possessions and other entitlements, at risk. This 'heroic' stance, of course, is not merely one assumed in the name of those actors whose legal entitlements or expectations are immediately affected by the changes in question. It is also about protecting international law itself. Here, as Lauterpacht put it, the role of the law of State succession is to fill a gap 'caused by events which threaten otherwise to destroy the *continuity of the international legal order*'. [emphasis added][67]

The immediate difficulty presented by this idea of the law of State succession as a technical response to certain factual/political events in the outside world is that the events themselves are already partially foreseen within various pre-constructed doctrinal categories. O'Connell cites in the quotation above, various examples including the cases of 'annexation', 'peaceful cession', 'revolution', and the 'emancipation of subject regions', with which one might also include other possible categories: dismemberment, unification, and perhaps secession. These, ultimately, are not merely neutral descriptions of events, as O'Connell himself was perfectly aware, but are seen to carry with them particular implications. In the Vienna Convention of 1978, for example, very different consequences seem to apply depending upon whether a case in question is seen to be one of decolonization, unification, or dismemberment. Those category descriptions, of course, relate to events whose origin will undoubtedly be socially over-determined (in the sense that no one 'causal explanation' will suffice), but it is also evident that, as far as lawyers engaged with the question of succession are concerned, the doctrinal categories of succession will construct their understanding of what has actually occurred, just as much as the categories themselves may seem to be matters of observation. At the centre of their debates stand questions such as: what kinds of changes constitute a succession of States? Does a revolutionary change in the social or political order constitute a crisis for which rules of succession are required? How might one differentiate, if at all, between the collapse of a federal State and the disintegration of a unitary State? Whatever view taken, it is evident that in seeking to answer such questions, the 'facts' are no longer to be taken as speaking for themselves, but are made relevant for the purpose of attributing certain consequences to them.

---

[67] H Lauterpacht, *Private Sources and Analogies of International Law* (1927) p 129.

In this sense, far from merely being reactive, the doctrine of State succession appears to be both causal and symptomatic – it is something that inserts itself at the *centre* of the political crisis[68] with which it seeks to engage, at the same time as seeking to address its consequences. This is to give it a fundamentally conflicted character: its very invocation ('this is a case of state succession') signalling on one side the radical and destabilizing character of the crisis and providing a language for the expression of those ideas, whilst on the other, overtly normalizing those events by presenting them as already foreseen and regulated by an overarching international legal order ('these are the rules applicable in case of the cession of territory'). This has certain obvious consequences as regards the characterization of the law of State succession. Whilst its objective might be said to be the 'minimization' of the effects of political change, it is also obviously about the simultaneous recognition of that change: about order *and* disorder, about securing the continuity of certain legal relationships, *and* about legitimizing the discontinuity of others. The 'ends' of succession are thus much harder to articulate than might at first seem obvious.

One or two further remarks may be made, in this context, about the putative distinction that O'Connell and others appear to make between the 'law' and 'politics' of State succession. When speaking about succession, there are evidently many different kinds of politics in play. On the one hand, there appears to be a politics of personal and communal identity associated with questions such as whether those affected by a change in sovereignty will owe allegiance to the 'new' sovereign, whether they will be entitled to rights of citizenship or have security in their possessions, whether they will remain with, or be divided from, their community. On the other hand there is an international politics associated with the role that 'great powers' or the 'international community' may assume in territorial settlements, or with the question of institutional membership or the maintenance of stability, peace, and good order. There is also, and more obviously, a politics of nationalism informed by principles such as 'sovereignty', 'self-determination' or 'permanent sovereignty over natural resources', the effect of which may be to encourage or deny the continuation of 'inherited obligations'. To observe that such considerations are always in play is, ultimately, rather banal. But of course, when people speak about such politics in this context, they have in mind the idea that the law of State succession is effectively opposed to such forms of politics: that it must be able to order, resist, or control the exercise of power which might otherwise be seen to dominate the stage. The purpose of a law of State succession, on

---

[68] For the view that this is the place in which the idea of self-determination resides see N Berman, 'Sovereignty in Abeyance: Self-Determination and International Law', 7 Wisc ILJ (1988–89) 51. Berman takes the view, however, that the 'traditional' law of State succession, insofar as it is concerned with 'identifying the sovereign to whom legal responsibility is to be attached', is only concerned with 'a *post hoc* evaluation of whether, and with what result, the crisis has come to a decisive conclusion' (pp 79–82). Such an argument, however, supposes both a determinacy as to the content of the law of State succession, and that one's reading of the nature and character of the 'crisis' would be unaffected by considerations as to what consequences might flow therefrom.

such a view, is found in its capacity to resist the ordering potential of an uncon-
strained politics:[69] the 'politics' of State succession is always to be identified in
the 'absence of law' and vice versa (the failure to identify 'settled' rules relating
to the inheritance of treaty obligations or the partition of debt becomes, thereby,
an *indica* of the extent to which the topic remains effectively political). The more
political it is seen to be, furthermore, the greater the apparent need for some kind
of regulation, but the more difficult such regulation might become.

This kind of opposition between the 'law' and 'politics' of succession remains
problematic for several reasons. First of all, even if this argument were to be taken
at face value – politics happening in the space left by law (or, perhaps, in the
interstices of existing rules) – it is entirely unclear as to precisely where the move
from law to politics or vice versa takes place. To say, for example, that there are
'no rules governing succession to treaty obligations in case of new States', is not
to say that there are no legal principles available to argue one's side in a case.
Arguments about sovereignty, consent or the honouring of commitments will
always still be to hand, albeit that there will be no obvious way in which such
claims might be prioritized, or outcomes 'determined'. The absence of a rule of
automatic succession, for example, will still offer the opportunity for one side
to argue the discontinuity of existing relationships by reason of the priority of
sovereignty (consent to obligations), and for the other to argue their continuance
by reason either of their intangible nature (such obligations being 'unaffected' by
the change), or the limited character of the change (that it did not constitute a
'succession' in the first place).

That there is always law to hand, of course, doesn't lead to the conclusion that it
is determinative. The supposition may be, of course, that a new State, in deciding
whether to honour overseas debts or otherwise oppose the fact of indebtedness,
will be guided primarily by a range of economic, political or other considerations,
the lawyers being brought in at the last moment (if at all) to articulate some kind
of plausible justification. But then again, to call the outcome of such decisions
'politics', is only to emphasize (along with scholars as diverse as Lauterpacht[70]
and Morgenthau[71]) the interwoven fabric of legal and political discourse. That
this led both Lauterpacht and Morgenthau to radically different conclusions (in
one direction to the need for impartial third party adjudication, in the other to
an examination of the social-psychological motors of power-relations) was not to
displace their common insight that calling something 'essentially political' was
largely a rhetorical move, shorthand for something else entirely.[72] To the extent

---

[69] See below Lauterpacht's arguments in favour of codification, pp 94–5.

[70] H Lauterpacht, *The Function of Law* (1933) p 159 ('the non-justiciability of a dispute…is
nothing else than the expression of the wish of a State to substitute its own will for its legal
obligations.').

[71] H Morgenthau, *Die internationale Rechtspflege, ihr Wesen und ihre Grenzen* (1929) pp 62–72.

[72] For an admirable discussion see M Koskenniemi, *The Gentle Civiliser of Nations: The Rise and
Fall of International Law 1870–1960* (2002) pp 366–9, 440–5.

that international law provides a vocabulary by which one may make arguments about, for example, relative entitlements to social and material resources following political change is always to make clear that the argument, if there is an argument at all, is about surrogacy: how far does law legitimize a particular politics, or how far, by contrast, does calling something 'political' really involve some form of normative/ legal assertion? Neither of these questions demands that one situate law and politics in two different places, or assumes that the prioritization of one is to be associated with the marginalization of the other. Both are ways of describing and appraising the same social activities – one through the medium of the political actor, the other through that of the legal subject – and the critical point is not, therefore, *whether* law *or* politics, but *what kind* of law and politics is ushered in or invoked in a particular context.

Thus far, I have spoken about the character of the law of State succession as being a putatively *reactive* endeavour, and have suggested in the process that it is far more than that: it is also partially constitutive of the crisis that it seeks to regulate. But O'Connell's description of the subject, as suggested above, also seemed to advert to the transitional character of the law of succession – as one which seeks to manage a return to some kind of 'normality'. In fact, the idea of State succession as a 'transitional' intervention can be understood in two ways. In the first place it is transitional in the sense that it is less concerned with providing a set of ongoing prescriptions that govern daily life, as much as elaborating a series of rules determining the responsibility of actors for earlier actions or omissions.[73] To the extent that rules of State succession are concerned for the most part with mediating between the 'before' and 'after' of political change, it is obvious that they have very little salience once the terms of the new political settlement have been put in place. In that sense, they seem to be *contingently structural*: structural in the sense that they are effectively 'rules about rules' (governing the conditions for the applicability of substantive rights and obligations, but not stipulating what those rights and obligations might be); contingent in the sense that they come into operation only at the moment at which a 'succession' has taken place, but which otherwise have very little obvious everyday significance.

The contingent character of the rules of succession, of course, adverts to a second way in which they might be seen as 'transitional'. As has often been remarked, State succession is obviously an issue which only irregularly comes to prominence in international law. For the most part it is a periodic concern associated, for example, with the consequences of national unification and colonization in the 19th century, decolonization in the 20th century, and the territorial reconfiguration of Europe after the two World Wars or following the collapse of the Soviet Union in 1989. What is significant, here, however, is not so much the fact that the issue does not gain sustained or continuous attention, but rather that each

---

[73] For an explicit articulation of this view, see K Zemanek, 'State Succession After Decolonization', 116 Hague Recueil (1965) III, 188, p 190.

moment of transition is also in some senses inaugural – marking the beginning
or end of a particular political era or constitutional order – in which each isolated
instance of political change assumes the character of a much broader process of
continuity and change in international society. That scholars, as a result, tend to
speak about the law of State succession in terms of 'eras' [74] is thus to highlight
the discontinuous character of each moment of transitional engagement, and the
discrete, unique, or context-specific nature of the issues arising therein.

During decolonization, for example, a common standpoint that unified both
mainstream international lawyers and those who sought to push through an anti-
colonial reformist agenda, was that the context in which questions of succession
arose was largely distinguishable from that accompanying the practice that had
preceded it.[75] Whatever the reason for this – and as will be shown, there were
conflicting accounts on this score – the idea that decolonization represented a
'new departure', or 'new frame of reference', was almost unexceptionally taken
to be the case. Interestingly enough, however, precisely the same kind of sentiment came to be expressed later in the 1990s when scholars were looking back
at the process of codification during the 1960s and 1970s. Once again, late 20th
century 'transition' looked quite different from 'decolonization' and once again
the normative authority of history was displaced by an enduring sense of nov-
elty.[76] This recurrent theme, of course, has only been such as to hinder the development of an enduring or stable set of rules or principles governing succession,[77]
and has encouraged in its place a continuing practice of contingent restatement
or reformulation.

The debilitating effect of this transitional engagement with the question of succession is evident in two different ways. In one direction, as Lauterpacht noted,
it was to encourage a certain equivocation as to whether any particular position
constituted a 'rule' or an 'exception to a rule'. Thus, as he was to suggest, although
many cases of succession had come to be regulated by treaty (he was thinking, of
course, of the Peace Treaties following the 1914–18 war), this was only to create
an obvious quandary by reason of leaving open the question as to: 'whether treaties providing for the taking over of obligations conform to the rule, or state an
exception; or whether treaties which exclude succession do so as an exception to a
generally recognised principle'.[78]

---

[74] For accounts which speak about various 'eras' of succession see eg, D Vagts', 'State Succession:
The Codifiers' View', 33 Va JIL (1993) 275, pp 277–80; R Mullerson, *International Law, Rights and
Politics* (1994) 137; J Crawford, 'Remarks', 86 ASILProcs (1992) 15.

[75] See below, pp 82–90, 117–19.

[76] See below, pp 210–12.

[77] As the International Court observed in context of maritime delimitation, the very fact that
each and every case appears to be fundamentally dissimilar is such as to 'preclude the possibility of
those conditions arising which are necessary for the formation of principles and rules of customary international law'. *Case concerning the Gulf of Maine Area (Canada/ United States)* Judgment of
Chamber of Court of 12th Oct 1984, ICJ Rep 1984, p 290, para 81.

[78] Lauterpacht, *Analogies*, above, n 67, p 128.

In any particular context, in other words, one would always be faced by the problem not only of interpreting the practice with which one was confronted (was the willingness to continue treaties *here* exemplary of a belief that such continuity was obligatory, or merely convenient?) but also of deciding what the initial starting point should be (was one looking for a rule of continuity, or a rule of discontinuity?). In another direction, the transitional character of the problem was also to render any generic response almost untenable. As O'Connell himself was to observe, for example:

International legal principles are not propounded for one situation or for one occasion, but must, like all principles of law, be capable of generating cogent solutions throughout a span of historical evolution. . . . A proposition of international law which would be expedient for one historical situation only would hardly satisfy the requirements of legal principle because it would lack the capacity to evolve new conclusions for other occasions. If international law were composed only of a series of contingent solutions, apposite only for the resolution of ephemeral issues, it would not be a system but a disorganized aggregation of unrelated instances. It would consist, not of precedent, but of mere fact, and it would not facilitate the adaption of international society to a changing technological and sociological environment, but would help to impel it jerkingly from one state to another without insight or direction.[79]

At stake was the existence of a 'system' of international law as a coherent, univocal, endeavour against which all pleas of special circumstance had to be treated with certain caution. That the law of State succession has routinely been accompanied by such claims is thus to signal either that there is no 'law' as such that may be discerned, or that something else entirely is going on.

3. A Brief History

It has often been suggested that one of the central problems with the idea of state succession has been the misleading nature of the term 'succession'.[80] Speaking about 'succession' seems to suppose that a useful analogy might be drawn between the private law notion of succession as an institution governing the legal consequences of the demise of an individual on the one hand, and those relations in international law that arise as a consequence of what may be referred to as 'changes in sovereignty' on the other.[81] In many respects the two sets of ideas are profoundly different: States are not liable to 'die' in the same sense as

---

[79] O'Connell, above, n 30, p 102.
[80] J Mervyn Jones 'State Succession in the Matter of Treaties', 24 BYIL (1947) p 360.
[81] H Lauterpacht, *Analogies*, above, n 67, p 25; Brierly J, *The Law of Nations*, (6th edn, 1963) p 152.

individuals,[82] and their corporate character is such as to push the salience of any 'domestic analogy' to its extreme. Huber, in his highly influential thesis on State succession of 1898, drew out the formal differences in the following way:

> A civil successor who steps into the place of his predecessor steps into his rights and obligations as though he were himself the predecessor. That is the universal succession of private law in the Roman sense, at least according to prevailing doctrine. But the successor of international law steps into the rights and obligations of his predecessor as though they were his own.... While a person of private law can in law represent more persons than one, and so an heir can continue the personality of the deceased, that is impossible between States. A State is indivisible. Either there are two or more real States or there is only one: one cannot represent another only for a certain part of its dominion. Where a State acquires a dominion, it comes in with its own power as a State and does not succeed to that of its predecessor: its legal personality is extended to its new dominion. It might be otherwise if the notion of a State were a patrimonial one, if the power of the State were a piece of private property in which there could be succession; but that notion is quite obsolete in modern international law.[83]

There can, in other words, be no private law 'inheritance' in the context of sovereign relations. At best, there can be a 'substitution in personality' in which one State is replaced by another in relations of authority and responsibility. This is not to say, of course, that the 'succeeding State' (for want of a better term) will not assume any rights or liabilities as a consequence of its acquisition of territory, but simply that what is, or is not, 'inherited' will be dependent first of all, upon the extent to which it is consistent with that sovereign's existing obligations, and secondly upon its compatibility with the 'facts' of the newly formed political situation. Two objections nevertheless remain: on the one side, there is the 'corporate' character of statehood that appears to deny the reality of 'death', and on the other, the 'indivisibility' of sovereignty that seems to deny the possibility of inheritance.

It is useful, nevertheless, to recall that such a 'domestic' analogy was not always as obscure as it may now seem. As Huber suggests, up until the late 18th century at least, succession was primarily conceptualised in terms of the inheritance of rights and obligations on the part of the 'sovereign', understood as the person of the Monarch, the Emperor or the Prince. Succession, in other words, both recorded the fact of a change of sovereignty (ie the demise of the sovereign) and described the rules governing inheritance. Even if those rules of inheritance themselves were modified to some degree by contractarian philosophy[84] (with

---

[82] Brierly, ibid.

[83] M Huber, *Die Staatensuccession* (1898) pp 18–19. Translation provided by Westlake, 17 LQR (1901) 392, p 396.

[84] Even in the earliest of works, however, there was a palpable tension between an acceptance of the ruler as 'sovereign' and the recognition that that 'sovereignty' derived from the consent of the population. The philosophy of the social contract – to which Grotius at least seemed to adhere – suggested that since the origins of sovereignty were to be found in the willing of individual members of the society over which the 'sovereign' held temporal authority, the ruler could act alternatively in a personal capacity or in the capacity as the 'agent' of the people. There is some

the consequence that 'real' treaties were thought to bind the successor 'in virtue of the interest of the people', or that debts passed to the successor 'through the medium of the State')[85] the fact that the sovereign could be identified as an individual allowed recourse to the Roman law concept of inheritance in civil law, in which the *heres* (the appointed successors) acquire not merely a single *res*, but an aggregate of rights and liabilities called a *iuris universitas*.[86] Prichard explains that at the time of Justinian: 'The universal successor assumes the whole of the legal clothing of the person to whom he succeeds; steps, as it were, into his shoes. He takes over his rights and liabilities of every kind; his property (*res singulae*) and *iura in re aliena*, the debts and other obligations (such as rights of action for damages for breach of contract) owing to him, and the debts and obligations which he owes'.[87]

This idea was employed in rudimentary form in the work of Gentili,[88] Grotius[89] and Pufendorf,[90] and de Vattel,[91] for example, all of whom appeared to take the view that a full complement of rights and duties of the predecessor passed *ipso iure* to a successor sovereign[92] (with the minor exception of those that were strictly 'personal'). What was to become known as the concept of 'universal

dispute as to whether Grotius did actually recognize the sovereignty of the people understood as a corporate entity (a *universitas*, *communitas* or *corpus*). See in the affirmative, O Gierke, *Natural Law and the Theory of Society 1500–1800* (trans E Barker, 1934) pp 45, 55. Contra, H Lauterpacht, 'The Grotian Tradition in International Law', in R Falk, F Kratochwil, and S Mendlovitz (eds), *International Law: A Contemporary Perspective* (1985) 10, p 26.

[85] eg H Grotius, *De Jure Belli ac Pacis*, II, xiv, 10 (between 'favourable' and 'odious' treaties); S Pufendorf, *De jure naturae et gentium libri octo* (1698 translated by Oldfather and Oldfather, 1934) VIII, x, 8; A Gentili, *De Jure Belli Libri Tres* (1612, trans J Rolfe, 1964) Bk III, c xxii, pp 413–16; C Wolff, *Jus Gentium Methodo Scientifica Pertractatum* (1764, trans J Drake, 1934) c IV, ss 413–20, pp 216–18; E de Vattel, *The Law of Nations* (trans J Chitty 1863) Bk II, c xii, ss 183–91, pp 204–8; G de Martens, *Précis du droit des gens moderne de l'Europe* (1788) II, ii, 60–61; For the continuation of this tradition see: H Wheaton, *Elements of International Law* (8th edn Dana, 1866) I, c i, s 22, p 34; J Bluntschli, *Das moderne Völkerrecht der civilisirten Staten als Rechtsbuch dargestellt* (1867) II, c 3, s 43, p 78. Bluntschli cites in that regard the treaties between Louis XIV of France with James II of England, and the Conventions of Napolean III of France with Maximilian of Mexico.

[86] This is what distinguished the heir (the universal successor) from the legatee. H Jolowicz, *Historical Introduction to the Study of Roman Law* (1954), at 127.

[87] A Prichard, *Leage's Roman Private Law* (3rd edn, 1961), at 233. Jolowicz points out that liability for delict was sometimes deemed 'personal' such that it became extinguished altogether. See Jolowicz, ibid, at 128.

[88] Gentili, above, n 85, III, at xxii.

[89] Grotius, above, n 85, II, ix, 10–12, xiv, 1, 10.

[90] Pufendorf, above, n 85, VIII, at xii, ss 1–9.

[91] de Vattel above, n 85, p 172.

[92] D O'Connell, *State Succession in Municipal and International* Law (1967) I, at 9–10; E Feilchenfeld, *Public Debts and State Succession* (1931) ch II. Sir James Marriott, offering an opinion on the change of dynasty in the Kingdom of the Two Sicilies, offered the view that 'all Treaties whatsoever, whether or Pacification, Alliance or of Commerce concluded between Sovereigns of respective States are not *Personal* but *National* and therefore like all other national Rights and Obligations, inseparable from each other, are valid in succession…. The Sovereign contracts not for himself as a private Person (for that idea would be injurious to Sovereignty) but as a public One. In other words he binds himself, his Successors and his People, as the one great Representative of

succession' thereafter survived largely intact until the second half of the 19th century,[93] from which point on it continued to remain an historical point of reference, if not an idea that effectively structured the discipline.[94]

The incipient distinction which Grotius had recognized between real and personal agreements (i.e. a differentiation in the role of the 'ruler' in relation to particular kinds of agreements) was one that subsequently encouraged a separation to emerge between the personality and sovereignty of the 'State' (i.e. the institution and apparatus of governance) and that of the individual ruler. This separation gained ground, theoretically at least, in the work of Pufendorf [95] and Wolff [96] who began to characterize the State as a moral person in itself, endowed with a collective will[97] – a view which was developed most clearly in the work of de Vattel.[98] Although the personification of the State as an entity in itself thereafter gained force, theories of the state remained divided for some time as to the precise locus of sovereignty. Even if the idea of the social contract understood sovereign power as originating in a consensual arrangement on the part of all individuals within a community, the 'government' was generally presumed to possess all of the essential trappings of 'sovereignty'.[99] Gierke argued, therefore,

the whole Kingdom, who neither *dies nor changes* in his national Capacity . . .'. Quoted in A McNair, *The Law of Treaties* (2nd edn 1961) p 669.

[93] cf *The Mechanic*, US-Ecuadorian Mixed Commission of Guayaquil (1862), 2 Moore, Arbitrations (1898) 1574. Later adherents to the doctrine include F Klüber, *Droit des Gens Moderne de L'Europe* (eds); Wheaton, above, n 85, I, s 29; Phillimore, *Commentaries on International Law* (end edn 1871) I, p 168; T Twiss, *The Law of Nations* (2nd edn 1884) p 20; A Rivier *Principes du droit des gens* (1896) I, p 65; D O'Connell, 'State Succession and the Theory of the State', *Grot Soc P* (1972) 23.

[94] Contemporary authors tend to feel obliged to refer to the theory even if coming to the conclusion that it is 'generally discredited today', see, M Malone, 'Succession of States in Respect of Treaties: The Vienna Convention of 1978', 19 Va JIL (1978–79) 885, p 886.

[95] Pufendorf, above, n 85, VII, c 2, s 13 ('C'est une personne morale composée, dont la volonté formée par l'assemblage des volontés de plusieurs, réunies en vertu de leurs conventions, est réputée la volonté de tous généralement, et autorisée par cette raison à se servir des forces et des facultés de chaque particulier pour procurer la paix et la sûreté commune.').

[96] C Wolff, *Jus Gentium Methodo Scientifica Pertractatum* (1764, trans J Drake 1934).

[97] The roots of this 'personification' are to be found initially in the tendency to employ anthropomorphic descriptions of the 'State', see E Dickinson, 'The Analogy between Natural Persons and International Persons in the Law of Nations', 26 Yale LJ (1917) 564. It came to be of particular importance in the philosophy of Hobbes, see: T Hobbes, *Leviathan*, 1651, reprinted 1982 Intro, pp 81–2, and was thereafter employed directly, or indirectly, in the work of later writers eg P Pradier-Fodéré, *Traité de Droit International Public Européen et American* (1985) II, s 447; Bluntschli, above, n 85, s 81, p; Phillimore, above, n 93, II, 45. Dickinson notes that the origin of the notion of 'equal capacity for rights' or 'equal rights' derived *inter alia* from the analogy between natural persons and the separate states in the international society, E Dickinson, *The Equality of States in International Law* (1920) p 6. He argues that this concept was not evident in the work of Grotius (p 34), but came to the fore later in the work of Pufendorf (pp 75–89). Lauterpacht argues similarly that Grotius' employment of the analogy between States and individuals was 'not the result of any anthropomorphic or organic conception of the state as being . . . assimilated to individuals', but simply that States were like individuals, Lauterpacht, 'The Grotian Tradition', above, n 84, p 19.

[98] F Ruddy, *International Law in the Enlightenment* (1975) p 135.

[99] Hobbes, for example, distinguished between the sovereign (government) and the commonwealth, but refused to admit that the latter had any real independent personality: 'For the Soveraign, is the publique Soule, giving Life and Motion to the Common-wealth; which expiring,

that in the 19th century: 'It was only with the elimination of the last traces of a contract of government that it became possible to banish entirely the idea of personality of the Ruler, and to confine the personality of the State, without qualification or reserve, to the sovereign community of individuals'.[100]

The defining moment of this shift in approach seems to be found in enlightenment notions of 'popular sovereignty' in which sovereignty was located in a *volonté générale*, constituting a corporate will distinct from that of the individual members. The idea of the 'corporate will' was not especially new as the two counterpoised notions of the *universitas* and the *societas* had been common currency for some time.[101] But it was the linking of the idea of the corporate will with popular expression, as opposed to the acting and willing of government, that was critical, and was later to develop, through the work of Hegel,[102] and later von Gierke,[103] into the 19th century 'organic' theories of the State which represented the State as a real corporate entity capable of independent and autonomous moral action.[104] As Westlake, a follower of Huber in this respect, was to express it, a State:

is an ideal body, which on the one hand has a certain territory, and on the other hand is a society composed of individual men as its members, and having a corporate will distinct from the wills of its members.... Since the individual men associated in the State are moral beings, and the action of the State which they form by their association is their action, the State must also be a moral being, having a responsibility and a conscience which are of its members. In this character of a moral being, having a corporate will, responsibility and conscience, a State is capable of being a subject of law and having rights.[105]

This changing approach to the idea of the State had certain consequences. To begin with, it led to the emergence of a sharp distinction being adumbrated between the ideas of 'State' and 'government' (the government merely being the momentary 'agent' of the State;[106] the State being the person in which rights

the Members are governed by it no more, than the Carcasse of a man, by his departed (though Immortall) Soule'. Hobbes, above n 97, pt II, c 29, p 375.

[100] Von Gierke, above n 94, p 53. Quadri asserts that the principle of continuity can only be accepted by reference to contractualist doctrine which, to his mind, is unacceptable insofar as it posits and relies upon a non-existent sense of unity among the population of a State, R Quadri *Diritto internazionale pubblico* (1960) p 500.

[101] eg M Oakshott, *On Human Conduct* (1973) pp 198–201.

[102] G Hegel, *The Philosophy of Right* (1821, trans T Knox T 1952) s 331 ('The nation State is mind in its substantive rationality and immediate actuality and is therefore the absolute power on earth.').

[103] O Von Gierke, *Die Genossenschaftstheorie und die deutsche Rechtsprechung* (1887), esp. pp 876–84.

[104] The conception of society as an 'organism', which was prevalent in Europe in the late 19th century may have drawn upon a variety of Hegelian, Comtean, and Darwinian insights. See J Kloppneberg, *Uncertain Victory. Social Democracy and Progressivism in European and American Thought 1870–1920* (1986) 96.

[105] J Westlake, *International Law* (1904), p 3.

[106] This distinction is most clearly seen in the work of Rousseau, and to a lesser extent Locke. JJ Rousseau, *The Social Contract* (trans M Cranston 1968), Bk I, c vi, pp 61–2; Bk III, c i, pp 101–2. An idea of popular sovereignty was, however, evident in the work of much earlier writers, such as

and obligations were vested), and hence also to a distinction between state and governmental succession.[107] If all obligations were concluded in the name of the State, not only would legal relations be immunized from even revolutionary changes in government,[108] but the distinction between 'real' and 'personal' obligations would have to be reinterpreted in terms of a distinction between those obligations that inhered in 'territory' and those which were effectively 'political'.[109] There also emerged a new conception of territorial sovereignty that approximated more closely to the Roman law notions of '*imperium*' or '*jurisdictio*' (the field in which public power is exercised) rather than as '*dominium*' which seemed to invoke a neo-feudal idea of a proprietary entitlement (surviving perhaps only in arguments about 'eminent domain').[110] This had the consequence of broadening the focus of 'succession' to encompass forms of territorial change that did not themselves implicate the 'death of the sovereign' but which nevertheless affected the scope of any claim to sovereignty (including, for example, the cession or annexation of parts of the territory of a State). From here, reliance upon received Roman law conceptions of succession by way of analogy with domestic law, were clearly more difficult to sustain.[111]

The theory of succession thereafter moved in two different directions (sometimes described in terms of their 'Hegelian' or 'Austinian' overtones), each of

Marsiglio of Padua (1324) and St Thomas Acquinas (Summa Theologica, Qu 90, art 3, concl), see generally, Ruddy, above, n 98, p 8. This was also the case with Grotius:

[E]ven if the condition of the State shall be changed into a kingdom, the treaty will continue, for the reason that, although the head has been changed, the body remains the same; and, as we have said above, the sovereignty, which is exercised through a king, does not cease to be the sovereignty of the people.

Grotius, above, n 85, Bk II, c xvi, p 418. For corresponding views in later legal doctrine, see Pradier-Fodéré, above, n 97, ss 82, 146, pp 155, 249; C Gabba, *Quistioni di diritto civile*, (1885) pp 356–92 . cf D O'Connell, above, n 92, p 11. Here the distinction between 'real' and 'personal' oblgiations is transformed into one between 'social' and 'political' commitments.

[107] O'Connell (1972, above, n 93, pp 27–8) suggests that it was Bluntschli who first 'dogmatically distinguished Succession of States and Succession of Governments'. See J Bluntschli, *Das moderne Völkerrecht der civilisirten Staten als Rechtsbuch dargestellt* (1867) II, s 48ff; *Le Droit International Codifié* (trans M Lardy, 3rd edn 1881) pp 76–8.

[108] It was evident, for example, that authors such as Klüber treated the independence of the United States in precisely the same way as he did the French revolution. See J Klüber, *Europäishes Völkerrecht* (1921) p 422.

[109] eg A von Bulmerincq, *Völkerrecht oder intenrationales Recht* (1887) p 195; F Liszt von *Das Völkerrecht* (1898, 12th edn 1925) p 274; S Kiatibian, *Conséquences juridique des transformations territoriales des Etats sure les traités* (1892) pp 13–14. See generally O'Connell (1972), above, n 93, pp 29, 36.

[110] A McNair, 'The Effects of Peace Treaties upon Private Rights', 7 Cambridge L.J, (1939–41) 379, p 381 (summarizing the position in the middle of the 20th century as follows: 'International law recognizes two distinct kinds of interest in regard to immovable property – the *imperium* or sovereignty which belongs to the State, and the *dominium* or property which belongs to the individual, or frequently to the State in its capacity as landowner'.) For a more acute account of the changing conceptions of territory see Lauterpacht, *Analogies*, above, n 67, pp 91–107.

[111] In the work of de Martens, for example, succession was dealt with under the heading 'the territorial modification of States', the principles of which were thought to apply only in cases of total loss of territory (F de Martens, *Traité de Droit International* (1883–7) I, pp 366–77).

which drew upon its own ideas as to the relationship between law/ political institutions and society. On the one hand, there were those who, drawing upon the spirit of nationalism that underwrote the Risorgimento in Italy,[112] were keen to emphasize the idea that a succession of States only really affected the ephemeral 'superstructure' of the State (its political institutions) leaving intact the 'organic' underbed of social relations in which the idea of sovereignty properly lay. Whether, therefore, because of a process of 'organic substitution'[113] or as a consequence of 'popular continuity'[114] it was held that a successor State would assume the legal mantle of the predecessor, taking on thereby the majority of international rights and obligations in what would be tantamount to a new form of universal succession.[115]

On the other hand,[116] there were those who saw in the idea of sovereignty the free-willing expression of communal self-consciousness in which international legal relations could only plausibly be understood as an external expression of sovereign will. The effect of this, of course, was that a change in sovereignty would necessarily involve a legal hiatus in which the sovereignty of one State comes to an end and that of another takes its place. In such a situation, there can be no 'transfer' of rights or obligations between the old and the new State, nor any substitution in sovereignty. Rather, the assumption of rights and obligations in the event of succession was only possible to conceive by means of a positive act on the part of the successor State.[117] Whilst the sense of this emergent voluntarism

---

[112] G Mazzini, 'The Duties of Man', in O Dahbour and M Ishay (eds), *The Nationalism Reader* (1995) 87.

[113] cf eg M Huber, *Die Staatensuccession* (1898), at 18–19; Westlake, above, n 105, p 61, idem, 'The Nature and Extent of the Title by Conquest', 17 *LQR* (1901) 392. Those adopting this position maintained that the successor State (conceived as an organic juridical entity) merely absorbs the factual situation brought about by the predecessor's legal commitments. In doing so, it takes over all the rights and duties of its predecessor, save those which are essentially political. See O'Connell (1972), above n 93, at 40–45.

[114] C Gabba, 'Successione di Stato a Stato', in *Questioni di diritto civile* (2nd edn 1885) pp 356–392. P Fiore, *Traité do droit international public européen et américain* (1885) p 134. Those adopting this position took the view that the State has two forms of personality: the political and the social. In cases of State succession, only the political personality of the State (a fictitious concept) is affected, leaving the social personality (the legal condition of the people) intact. See O'Connell, above n 93, I, at 11.

[115] Huber referred to the idea as *Gesamtnachfolge* (literally 'aggregate' succession) above, n 113, p 24. In truth, it was still far from 'universal' in the sense that, depending on what was taken to be associated with the 'fictitious' element of sovereignty, and what associated with the underlying social element, succession might be more or less extensive. Thus, for example, in Gabba's work succession was negated in respect of most treaties, but affirmed in case of other economic relations.

[116] The organicist notion of sovereignty was always going to be vulnerable to a positivist critique. O'Connell, for example, remarked pithily that '[t]here may be excellent reasons for attributing rights and duties to the successor State in virtue of stability of the social structure, but a legal rule to this effect does not derive merely from the fact of social continuity'. O'Connell, (1972), above, n 93, p 33.

[117] O'Connell (above, n 30, pp 110–11) traces such ideas initially to F Holtzendorff (*Handbuch des Völkerrechts* (1885–1889) II, pp 33 et seq) and through him to K Gareis (*Institutionen des Völkerrechts* (1887) p 61) and A Zorn *Grundzüge des Völkerrechts* (2nd edn 1903).

did not necessarily result in the denial of the possibility of succession (as Jellinek's notion of self-abnegation suggested)[118] it was later deployed by a good number of authors in the early 20th century such as Keith,[119] Gidel,[120] Cavaglieri,[121] and Shönborn,[122] all of whom came close to the apparent conclusion that the 'only law of State succession is that there is no law of succession'.[123]

For the most part, the position formally adopted by scholars at this time was overtly dictated by their approach to a set of related questions such as the relationship between international and municipal law (to what extent was the continuity of international legal obligations contingent upon continuity at the municipal level?), the sources, origin and nature of international law (what role did consent play in succession?), theories of the State (what constituted a succession of States?) or of territory (did it constitute a proprietary entitlement or realm of competence?). Neither positive nor negative theories, however, had any obvious relationship with particular responses to the above questions. Theories of continuity, for example, were adumbrated on the basis of a variety of considerations such as the juristic nature of legal relations (Grotius), the nature of the State (Huber and Fiore), or the nature of international law (Jellinek). Similarly, theories of discontinuity were alternatively based upon rival conceptions of the nature of international law (Schönborn) or upon the results of empirical investigation (Keith). In many cases the theories in question were wholly mutable: Huber's reliance upon von Gierke's theory of corporations as a way of underpinning a thesis of universal succession, was turned by Schönborn in a wholly different direction. Similarly whilst for Jellinek, an imperative theory of law could sustain the possibility of universal succession by way of his supplementary theory of autolimitation, for Keith by contrast it necessarily placed the emphasis upon non-continuity.[124]

Whatever the difficulties associated with the contradictory assertions of international lawyers at this time, it is evident that these two traditions (or perhaps tendencies in thought) have subsequently come to delimit the intellectual domain of state succession in a profound way.[125] On the one hand, their counter position

---

[118] G Jellinek, *Allgemein Staatslehre* (1900) pp 367–75.

[119] A Keith, *The Theory of State Succession with Special Reference to English and Colonial Law* (1907). See also, T Baty, 'The Obligations of Extinct States', 35 Yale LJ (1925–26) 434.

[120] G Gidel , *Des Effets des Annexations sur les Concessions* (1904).

[121] cf A Cavaglieri, *La Dottrina della Successione di Stato a Stato* (1910); 'Regles générales du droit de la paix' 26 *Hague Recueil* (1929) 311, at 364–76.

[122] W Shönborn, *Staatensukzessione* (1913).

[123] Crawford, above, n 74 , p 16.

[124] It is clear, furthermore, that neither positive nor negative theories coped particularly well with questions arising from the partial cession of territory (assuming, for the most part, that the predecessor State will have ceased to exist) and both admitted significant exceptions (dispositive treaties or vested rights in case of the clean slate, personal treaties, or political arrangements in case of universal succession).

[125] Scholars continue to articulate their positions by reference to the two original poles of 'universal succession' and the 'clean slate', even if for the most part, however, the 'modern' approach is taken to be something 'in between'. eg O Udokang, *Succession of New States to International Treaties* (1972); P Menon, *The Succession of States in Respect to Treaties, State Property, Archives and*

encouraged the belief that problems of succession could not be properly addressed until the scourge of Hegelian metaphysics was cast aside. Theories of any 'grand' nature – whether that is theories of the State, sovereignty, or of the basis of obligation – had proved themselves to be far too speculative and too inconclusive to be of much assistance. As Wilkinson was to observe in his study of 'American' practice in 1934, the sheer variety of theoretical models explaining succession was to render none of them plausible, and hence it was 'obvious that there is no secure basis in general theory upon which to speculate concerning the future action of a nation in a given case'.[126]

On the other hand, it suggested that, since one could no longer be sure whether a successor State would 'inherit' obligations of one form or another, a distinction would have to be maintained between the idea of succession as descriptive of a political event (X or Y being a 'successor State'), and the idea of succession as the legal process by which rights and obligations come to be acquired (by means of 'succession' rather than, for example, by consent or 'novation').[127] The distinction between what has become known as succession de facto, and succession *de iure*, in other words, was a means by which international lawyers might circumvent or displace their evident ambivalence as to whether succession was an issue that international law could effectively regulate at all.

Central to the rearticulation of succession doctrine in the early 20th century, however, was the contemporaneous critique of the 'received' notion of sovereignty.[128] As the idea of absolute sovereignty appeared to deny any plausible basis for a law between nations, it came to be reconceptualized, not as the unlimited power of the law-maker, but as the authority of one legally competent to act (and thereafter as a sub-species of the generic idea of 'personality').[129] Whilst this idea of sovereignty as 'competence' or 'personality' offered the theoretical possibility of greater regulation of succession (insofar as the events and

---

Debts (1991); M Malone, 'Succession of States in Respect of Treaties: The Vienna Convention of 1978', 19 Va JIL. (1978–79) 886; D Papenfuss, 'The Fate of the International Treaties of the GDR within the Framework of German Unification', 92 AJIL (1998) 469, p 471.

[126] H Wilkinson, *The American Doctrine of State Succession* (1934) p 15.

[127] See below, pp 64–7.

[128] eg G Scelle, *Précis de Droit des* Gens (1932) I, p 13; For details of the early 20th century critique of sovereignty see, D Kennedy, 'International Law and the Nineteenth Century: History of an Illusion', 17 QLR (1997) 99, p 114 ('To fulfil their polemical mission, to render plausible a legal order among sovereigns, the philosophy which sets this question, which makes sovereigns absolute or requires a sovereign for legal order, must be tempered, if not rejected. As a result, to inherit positivism is also to inherit a tradition of response to the scepticism and deference to absolute State authority, which renders legal order among sovereigns *implausible* in the first place.')

[129] eg *Nationality Decrees in Tunis and Morocco* Case, PCIJ Rep, Series B, no 4 (1923) p 24 ('The question whether a certain matter is or is not solely within the jurisdiction of a State is an essentially relative question; it depends upon the development of international relations.'); *Wimbledon* case, PCIJ Rep, Series A, no 1 (1923) p 25 ('No doubt any convention creating an obligation of this kind places a restriction on the exercise of sovereign rights of the State, in the sense that it requires them to be exercised in a certain way. But the right of entering into international engagements is an attribute of State sovereignty.')

their consequences would be determined by the 'legal order' rather than by mere self-assertion), it was made possible only by a simultaneous reaffirmation of the importance of consent in the form of the *Lotus* doctrine (States being held to enjoy a legally protected freedom of action in relation to all matters to which they have not bound themselves otherwise).[130]

This had an important impact upon the doctrine of succession in two, rather contradictory, ways. On the one hand, it suggested that international law could, and did, govern the way in which international actors were to become members of the international legal community. It allowed the supposition, in other words, not only that the creation of States (ie their recognition) was rule-governed,[131] but also that any such new States would be entering into a pre-established legal order and would be automatically bound, *de minimis*, by the terms of existing customary international law.[132] Once this point had been reached, the task for international lawyers was one of identifying, within the corpus of State practice, relevant rules governing succession to which all new States would be automatically taken to have consented in virtue of their admission to the international community. That they might effectively be rules regulating *entry* into the international community, rather than rules that were otherwise universally applicable within that community was rather conveniently overlooked, as was the idea that 'consent' to such rules was anything more than a theoretical supposition.[133] Importantly, however, international lawyers would no longer have to assume that new States were born with a clean slate, nor would they need to have recourse to 'theories of the State' in order to justify succession.

On the other hand, a continued insistence upon the importance of consent to obligation meant that the assumptions of the clean slate remained hard to shake off. In those circumstances, for the doctrine of succession to survive, distinctions thereafter had to be drawn between different types of political change in terms of how they impinged upon sovereignty. First of all, there were those that affected 'sovereignty' and those that did not: governmental succession was to be distinguished from State succession,[134] and belligerent occupation

---

[130] *Lotus* case, PCIJ Rep, Series A, no 10 (1927) ('International law governs relations between independent States. The rules of law binding upon States therefore emanate from their own free will.... Restrictions upon the independence of States cannot herefore be presumed.')

[131] eg Crawford J, *The Creation of States in International Law* (2nd edn 2005); Guggenheim P, *Traité de Droit International Public* (1953) I, p 190.

[132] See above, pp 13.

[133] See above, pp 14.

[134] For early versions of this principle see Grotius, above, n 85, Bk II, c xvi, p 418. See also, Pufendorf above, n 85, Bk VIII, c xii, s1, p 1360; R Zouche, *Iuris et Iudicii Fecialis sive Iuris Inter Gentes et Quaestionumde Eodem Explicato* (1650, trans J Brierly 1911) pt II, s II, 7, 63; C Wolff, *Jus Gentium Methodo Scientifica Pertractatum* (1764, trans J Drake 1934) ch II, s 243, p 123; Bluntschli, above, n 85, II, c3, s39, p76; C Bynkershoek, *Quaestiones Juris Publici*, II, 25; Rivier, above, n 93, I, p 62; de Martens above, n 111, p 362; Westlake, above, n 103, I, 58; L Oppenheim *International Law: A Treatise* (1905) I, pp 106, 115; Hall, above, n 33, p 22; D Anzilotti, *Cours de Droit International*, (trad & Gidel 1929), p 178; Q Wright, 'The Status of Germany and the Peace Proclamation', 46 AJIL (1952) 299, p 307; A McNair, 'Aspects of State Sovereignty' BYIL (1949)

from annexation.[135] Secondly, there were those that appeared to result in the subsumption or extinction of sovereignty, and those where the sovereignty of the predecessor State remained intact: the former going under the title of 'universal' succession, the latter 'partial' succession.[136] It was no longer possible, as a consequence, to insist upon a single set of rules governing the transmission or inheritance of rights and obligations with respect to all types of territorial change. Even less was it possible to insist upon the possibility of 'universal inheritance' in the sense understood by Grotius. Rather, those rules were necessarily dependent, at the first instance, upon the type of change in question, and the type of change would thereafter dictate the type of rules that were to come into play. Despite the prevailing critique of sovereignty, sovereignty (in its new guise of 'personality') was to remain, as Hall declared, the 'key' to succession.[137]

Whilst the resulting 'relativism' of this emergent doctrinal position was to render subsequent discussion of the law of State succession apparently chaotic, there were those who saw certain patterns emerging. In his analysis of the 'American Doctrine' of succession in relation to public and private law, nationality, public debt, and treaties in 1934, Wilkinson was to highlight two nascent trends. First was the relative lack of utility of the two received 'theories of succession': neither the rule of continuity nor that of the 'clean slate' adequately explained the range of practice under analysis.[138] The principles identified as relevant in the case treaties might not apply with equal vigour in case of public debt. A functional differentiation between different kinds of legal relations needed to be

p 8; J Kunz, 'Identity of States under International Law', 49 AJIL (1955) p 97. A government (the instrumentality through which a State functions) may change from time to time both as to form and as to the head of government without affecting the continuity or identity of the State as an international person. (G Hackworth, *Digest of International Law* (1940) I s 25, p 127). Oppenheim (Jennings and Watts), above, n 39, p 146. ('Mere territorial changes, whether by increase or by diminution, do not, so long as the identity of the State is preserved, affect the continuity of its existence or the obligations of its treaties.... Changes in the government or the internal polity of a State do not as a rule affect its position in international law. A monarchy may be transformed into a republic, or a republic into a monarchy; absolute principles may be substituted for constitutional, or the reverse; but, though the government changes, the nation remains, with rights and obligations unimpaired'. (J Moore, *Digest of International Law*, vol 1, pp 248, 249.)) cf Feilchenfeld, above, n 92, 609–11. See also, *US v Curtiss Wright Export Corp and ors* 299 US (1936) 304, p 316 (J Sutherland): 'Rulers come and go; governments end and forms of government change; but sovereignty survives.'

[135] See below, pp 58–61.
[136] eg A Hershey, 'The Succession of States', 5 AJIL (1911) 285. A useful contrast here is with the work of Wheaton in 1883 who appears to pay no recognition to the distinction.
[137] Hall, above, n 33, p 114.
[138] Wilkinson, above, n 126, p 117 ('None of the doctrines heretofore formulated by the publicists can adequately explain the policy of the United States in regard to both of these categories. It cannot be said that America has assumed all the rights and obligations of ceding states as if it were the preceding sovereign. Neither can it be said that the United States has accepted all of the powers of the ceding state and rejected all of its obligations. Each principle has its usefulness. Each doctrine may explain the action of the United States in regard to one of the two categories of rights and obligations. But, as a blanket explanation of all of the effects of a change of sovereignty, or as a rigid system in which all of the attendant phenomena fit, either principle is manifestly inapplicable.')

recognized. Secondly, and more importantly, Wilkinson suggested that within American doctrine at least, a fault line was emerging as between the two categories of public and private law. In most cases, public laws of a ceding State would cease to have effect, whilst those regulating private rights and relationships (contract, property) would remain in force until altered by the successor State. A change in sovereignty would thus bring an end to the public law of the ceding State (including the public rights of citizens),[139] as it would treaty relations[140] and responsibility for public debt (except insofar as such debt might be hypothecated or otherwise associated with the territory acquired).[141] Private debts, by contrast, would continue to be honoured, as would dispositions of property understood in its widest sense – including grants or concessions of land, rights deriving from patents, licences, copyrights and trademarks, and rights under contract. His general conclusion was thus that there existed 'two distinct categories of rights and obligations, public and private', each of which had quite different implications.[142]

The rationale for this, as far as Wilkinson could discern, stemmed from two sources. One was a general belief that had particular purchase in the US, namely that the protection of private property and private rights was one of the fundamental purposes of the State. As he was to put it: 'To disturb the rights of individuals in their right to property, life, liberty and the pursuit of happiness is to disturb the very foundations upon which America was built.'[143]

The other idea was that the State, as a 'unique legally omnipotent person' was qualitatively different from its territory, population, and political organization. It was because of this distinction between sovereignty and the agencies exercising it, and because also of the fact that 'public laws, obligations, and institutions...are self-imposed limitations of the exercise of sovereign power', that sovereignty when it is transferred, moves without the encumbrance of agencies, institutions, and obligations that derive from the exercise of that power.[144]

Ultimately, Wilkinson had nothing more in mind than to find some way of explaining an obvious incongruity that had emerged between, on the one hand, the general theoretical formulations relating to state succession, and the more complex picture that had begun to develop in US practice through the 19th century. When read as a critique of the redundant formalism of the two opposed doctrines of succession, it said little more than many had already acknowledged in other contexts. When seen, however, as an exposé of an emerging disassociation in the law of succession between public and private legal relations it had, perhaps, more resonance than even Wilkinson himself was prepared to admit.

Interestingly enough, this was a theme also taken up by Carl Schmitt in his final work *Der Nomos der Erde im Völkerrecht des Jus Publicum Europaeum*.[145] As part of his account of the historical decline of European public order, he

---

[139] ibid, 70.   [140] ibid, 116.   [141] ibid, 95.
[142] ibid, 117.   [143] ibid, 118.   [144] ibid, 119–120.
[145] C Schmitt, *The Nomos of the Earth in the International Law of the Jus Publicum Europaeum* (1950, trans G Ulmen, 2003).

sought to unearth, within the 'muddle of contradictory opinions and precedents' relating to State succession in the early years of the 20th century, the core of an 'actual, concrete order'.[146] Like Wilkinson, Schmitt despaired of the 'empty normative generalizations' that had characterized existing doctrine, but at the same time he was to regard its obvious abstractness as essentially 'deceptive',[147] pointing to the existence of some other driving force behind it (which he ultimately took to be the policy of 'land appropriation' sanctioned within the framework of a 'comprehensive spatial order').[148] He began by noting that territorial change when viewed from the standpoint of 'isolated, sovereign, territorial States' was one which denied anything other than 'intentional succession': 'the territory of the state is the theatre of sovereignty; with a territorial change, the agent of sovereignty relinquishes the theatre and another sovereign agent appears on the stage. The projection of sovereignty by the new territorial sovereign over the acquired land…can lead us to think only that the earlier sovereignty over the land had ended and that the new sovereignty had been established.'[149]

Nevertheless, when examined 'within the framework of a comprehensive spatial order' the issue looked quite different. There, the process of territorial change was 'institutionalized' in international law and a continuity thereby established between predecessor and successor ('the earlier and later appropriator of territorial sovereignty') by reason of the fact that both belonged to the '*same space* and its order'.[150] Succession was thus envisaged as a kind of 'derivative appropriation' or 'beneficial construction' in favour of third party States in virtue of the existence of their membership in the spatial order. This did not, ultimately, prevent the continued denial of succession on the basis of other arguments such as customary law or the presumptive will of the State, but was at least to encourage claims to legal succession being directed as against the appropriator of European soil.

Schmitt went on to identify two 'standpoints' which appear to have been decisive in argumentation. The first concerned the existence of this 'spatial order' which he observes as underpinning the League of Nations' Committee of Jurists' opinion in the *Aaland Islands Case*. There, the question arose as to Finland's obligations to abide by the contractual obligations (entered into by Russia in the Paris Peace Treaty of 1856) regarding the non-fortification of the Islands. In consideration of this question, the Committee had concluded that: 'The recognition of any State must always be subject to the reservation that the State recognized will respect the obligations imposed upon it either by general international law or by definite international settlements relating to territory [of which the 1856 settlement was one].'[151]

---

146 ibid, 194.   147 ibid, 193.
148 ibid, 195.   149 ibid, 194.
150 ibid, 195.   151 LNOJ, Special Supp (1920) 16.

In Schmitt's view, this decision clearly confirmed the existence of a *droit commun européen* created by the European Great Powers – which he took to be a concrete juridical-political order of which the provisions of the Paris Peace Treaty formed part. The intangibility of the territorial arrangement (or, in other words, Finland's 'succession' to the commitments in question) was thus premised upon the idea that international law, at that time, was an indissociable part of a regional political order, the existence of which was subsequently put under threat by the very universality of the League of Nations 'framework'.[152]

The second, and for present purposes more significant, 'standpoint' concerned the 'economic side of the spatial problem', namely the existence of a 'common economic space' or 'free market' within Europe that was underpinned by 'a certain relation of public and private law, of State and State-free society'.[153] Schmitt's argument, in this second instance, was that what went unmentioned in the traditional theory and practice of State succession (but yet was quite explicit in the law of occupation)[154] was that all States concerned recognised the existence of a common underlying economic order – that of a 'common free market transcending the political borders of sovereign states'.[155] He was to suggest that it was precisely this order that was presupposed in all arguments and constructions of international law relating to succession:

> Given that state dominion (*imperium* or *jurisdictio*) based on public law, on the one hand, and private property (*dominium*) based on private law, on the other, were separated sharply, it was possible to isolate from juridical discussions the most difficult question, namely that of a total constitutional change tied to territorial change. Behind the foreground of recognized sovereignty, the private sphere, which in this particular case means the sphere of private economy and private property, largely remained undisturbed by the territorial change. With a territorial change, the international economic order – the liberal market sustained by private entrepreneurs and businessmen, which was free in the same sense as free world trade, and the free movement of capital and labour – retained all the international safeguards that it needed to function. All civilized States subscribed to the distinction between public and private law, as well as to the common standards of liberal constitutionalism; for all, property, and thus trade, economy, and industry belonged to the sphere of constitutionally protected private property. This constitutional standard was recognized as fundamental by all states party to the territorial change.[156]

His conclusion was thus that a 'territorial change was no *constitutional change* in the sense of the social order and of property', rather it was a change only in

---

[152] He comments (above, n 145, p 196) that the argument as to the existence of a European spatial order was 'displaced' or rendered 'pothumous and apocryphal' by the League of Nations framework 'because no agreement was to contain any reference to a spatial order, least of all to any European spatial order'.

[153] ibid, 197.

[154] cf. Article 43, Regulations Respecting the Laws and Customs of War on Land, annex to the Convention (IV) Respecting the Laws and Customs of War on Land, The Hague, October 18, 1907.

[155] Schmitt, above, n 145, p 197.

[156] ibid.

the public legal sphere that left unaffected the 'internal currency of private legal property'.[157] This idea provided, as far as Schmitt was concerned, a far better guide to the 'true character of a territorial change' than any 'absolute' formulation of State sovereignty.

There are two key features of Schmitt's account of the law of state succession in the early part of the 20th century that have become, albeit frequently unenunciated, pivots around which much subsequent discussion and debate have hinged. The first relates to the observation that he shared with Wilkinson, concerning the emerging consensus in the early 20th century around the idea that State succession essentially concerned relations of a public, rather than a private nature. Whilst for Wilkinson this was merely a matter of observation, for Schmitt it exposed a crucial underlying assumption that underpinned arguments about succession more generally – namely that they depended, in a contingent way, upon the perceived existence of a stable and relatively homogenous backdrop of economic and political activity. There is no doubt that, by the beginning of the 20th century, legal doctrine was turning in such a direction.[158] As Wilkinson was to note, courts in the US had, for some time, entertained the idea that sovereignty, when it was acquired through the cession of territory or annexation, left intact the private, personal, relations of citizens and subjects in their relations with one another,[159] and this subsequently came to be endorsed, in the form of the doctrine of 'acquired' or 'vested' rights,[160] by the Permanent Court of International

---

[157] ibid, 198. For a later version of this idea of the superficiality of territorial change see below, pp 109–11 .

[158] eg G Kaekenbeeck, 'The Protection of Vested Rights in International Law', 17 BYIL (1936) 1; C Rousseau, *Principes généraux du droit international* (1944) I, pp 901–6; Moore, above n 134, p 98; Hackworth, above, n 134 pp 562–7; A Makarov, 'Les Changements territoriaux et leurs effets sur les droits des particuliers', Annuaire Institut de Droit International (1950) 208; A McNair, 'The General Principles of Law Recognised by Civilized Nations' 33 BYIL (1957) 1, pp 16–18;

[159] eg *US v Soulard* (1830) 4 Peters' Rep 511; *US v Percheman* (1833) 7 Peters' Rep 51; *Otega v Lara*, (1906) 202 US 399; *Vilas v City of Manila* (1911) 220 US 345. Rosenne cites, in addition, cases from Greece, Syria, Danzig, and Germany, see S Rosenne, 'The Effect of Change of Sovereignty upon Municipal Law', 27 BYIL (1950) 267. The authority of the US case law, in this respect, has been treated with some scepticism. Kaekenbeeck cautions, for example, that in case of concessions, practice in the United States has 'consistently subordinated the maintenance of concessions to the proof of a benefit for the territory ceded'. Kaekenbeeck ibid, p 11. See further, in that respect, F Sayre, 'Change of Sovereignty and Concessions', 12 AJIL (1918) 705, pp 712–23. O'Connell remarks, in similar vein, that the US courts' concern was primarily with the question of land tenure, that they frequently resorted to 'exaggerated language' and that 'the term "law of nations" was more often a reference to the natural law basis of the constitution than to international law.' O'Connell (1956), above, n 66, p 80.

[160] Two bases for the doctrine had been identified. One related to the limited nature of governmental competence as expressed in the idea of 'sovereignty'. See CJ Marshall in *US v Percheman*(1833), US SupCt 7 Peters 51, p 86 ('A cession of territory is never understood to be a cession of the property belonging to its inhabitants. The King cedes that only which belongs to him. Lands he had previously granted were not his to cede.... The cession of a territory by its name from one sovereign to another, conveying the compound idea of surrendering at the same time the lands and the people who inhabit them, would be necessarily understood to pass the sovereignty only, and not to interfere with private property.'). The other related to the doctrine of non-retroactivity. In 1908, P Decamps, drawing upon the earlier work of G Gidel (*Des Effects de*

Justice in a series of cases including *German Settlers in Poland*,[161] *German Interests in Polish Upper Silesia*,[162] and *Oscar Chinn*,[163] and in the awards of various arbitral tribunals.[164] Writers such as Lauterpacht were also to observe such developments, concluding in the process that the doctrine of acquired rights was probably the only certain principle in the muddle of confused and contradictory opinion in the doctrine of State succession.[165] McNair went so far as to suggest that it was, in fact, a 'general principle of law'. [166]

This separation between the public and private dimensions of succession was to have certain implications.[167] To begin with, it would seem to suggest that, for all of its radical connotations, a change in sovereignty would largely assume a superficial character – affecting only aspects of public administration and external relations, leaving intact the vast majority of social relations of the affected community with the exception only of rights and obligations of an exclusively public character (as may relate, for example, to questions of nationality

l'annexation sure les concessions (1904) unpublished doctoral thesis, cited in O'Connell) argued that the doctrine of non-retroactivity of law, which he took to be a general principle of law, essentially precluded a successor State from extending its own law into acquired territories in such a way as to extinguish existing legal rights enjoyed by private individuals. P Decamps, 'La definition des droit acquis', 15 RGDIP (1908) 385.

[161] PCIJ, (1923) Series B, no 6, p 36 ('Even those who contest the existence in international law of a general principle of state succession, do not go so far as to maintain that private rights including those acquired from the State as the owner of the property are invalid as against a successor in sovereignty.') The particularly controversial element of this decision concerned the way in which the Court sought to employ the idea of acquired rights as a way of navigating between the German policy of colonization that had underpinned the settlement in Poland, and the Polish policy of de-Germanization which she claimed to have been endorsed by the Treaty of Versailles.

[162] PCIJ (1926) Series A, no 7, pp 22 and 42.

[163] PCIJ, Series A/B, no 63, 65, p 88.

[164] eg *Niederstrasser v Poland*, Arbitral Tribunal of Upper Silesia, 6th June 1931, AD 1931–32, Case no 33, p 667; *Goldenberg v Germany*, German-Romanian Arbitral Tribunal ZAORV (1929) 87; *Sopron-Koszeg Local Railway Company* case, AD 1929–1930, Case no 34; Transvaal Concessions Commission, Cmd. 623 (1901) pp 6–8.

[165] Lauterpacht, above, n 67, pp 129–130.

[166] McNair, above, n 158, p 16–18. It should be noted, nevertheless, that in 1929 a League of Nations preparatory committee entrusted with the task of drawing up bases for discussion for a conference on the codification of international law, asked governments as to whether the 'State becomes responsible through the enactment of legislation infringing vested rights of foreigners?' The replies revealed 'fairly substantial differences of opinion...Some replies admit that the State is responsible. Others say that the rights in question, having been acquired under the law of the State, are liable to be terminated by that law. Some consider a general answer impossible'. League of Nations, doc C75(a) M69 (a) 1929 V, III, p 37. Kaekenbeek suggests (above, n 158, p 14) that 'this is sufficient confirmation that no generally accepted rule of international law is here in existence'. He concludes ultimately (p 17) that 'the principle that a cession of territory does not affect private rights is valid only as long as new legislation is not introduced that affects them; that the introduction of such legislation is not prohibited by international law, and is not in particular made by it dependent on payment of compensation...'.

[167] One obvious implication was that international lawyers would subsequently spend considerable time debating the extent to which particular legal relations were either of a public or private character. See Huber, above, n 83, ss 94–5; Kaekenbeek, above, n 158, pp 11–12.

or allegiance).[168] It would also prompt a reconsideration of the earlier distinction between changes in sovereignty on the one hand and revolutionary changes in government on the other (a reconsideration that appeared particularly apt given the Soviet government's repudiation of the debts of the Tsarist regime in 1919).[169]

Another implication of the separation between the public and private dimensions of succession captured by Schmitt's analysis, is that the central function of the doctrine seemed to be to secure the primacy of capitalist relations of production – or to put it in Marxist terms, the capacity of the 'economic base' to continue to 'determine' the legal and political 'superstructure'[170] – in which the relationship between the West and the periphery could be understood, above all else, in terms of the inclusion or exclusion of those societies that had not yet established the conditions for capitalism.[171] As Schmitt was right to observe, when conceived in a European context, this did not seem to have been the object of much consternation,[172] but when later deployed in the context of decolonization, it was evidently more problematic given the historic role of private individual and corporate interests in the establishment and maintenance of colonial rule.[173]

The second significant element of Schmitt's account of the law of State succession was, thus, his understanding of its limited geographical dimension. As far as he was concerned, when one stepped outside the context of European interstate law, the organizing principles that operated as unspoken presuppositions of juridical doctrine ceased to apply. He explains that, as far as territory in the non-European world was concerned:

This soil was free to be occupied, as long as it did not belong to a state in the sense of internal European interstate law. The power of indigenous chieftains over completely uncivilized peoples was not considered to be in the public sphere; native use of the soil was not considered to be private property. One could not speak logically of a legal succession in an *imperium*, not even when a European land-appropriator had concluded treaties with indigenous princes or chieftains and, for whatever motives, considered them to be binding. The land-appropriating State did not need to respect any rights to the soil existing within the appropriated land, unless these rights somehow were connected with the private property of a member of a civilized State belonging to the order of interstate, international law. Whether or not the natives' existing relations to the soil – in agriculture, herding, or hunting – were understood by them as *property* was an issue to be decided

---

[168] It was arguable that the protection of vested rights only extended as far as foreign nationals were concerned and that, therefore, was only of limited significance.

[169] See below, p 323.

[170] K Marx, *Critique of Political Economy* (1859) Preface, p 20. For a discussion of the place in which 'law' might play in the description of the economic structure of the 'base' see G Cohen, *Karl Marx's Theory of History* (2000) p 216–48.

[171] E Pashukanis, 'International Law' in *Pashukanis: Selected Writings on Marxism and Law* (1980). See generally, C Miéville, *Between Equal Rights: A Marxist Theory of International Law* (2005).

[172] It is possible to read the Permanent Court's advancement of the notion of acquired rights as a polemical reaction against the claims made by the new Soviet government in Russia.

[173] See below, pp 86–7.

by the land-appropriating state. International law considerations benefiting the property rights of natives, such as those recognized in questions of State succession in the liberal age favouring property rights to land and acquired wealth, did not exist on colonial soil. [174]

Of course, much of this would have gone unobserved by most international lawyers at the time. Their focus largely remained upon relations between European powers (or their nationals) and questions concerning the recognition of 'native titles' following the cession or annexation of colonial territory only rarely came to prominence.

But one may speculate much further than this as to the probable impact of colonization upon the developing doctrine of State succession in the early 20th century. Just as it might have seemed obvious that Huber's notion of organic substitution could be linked to, or conditioned upon, a sense of European cultural homogeneity,[175] so also it was evident that the emergent 'positivism' in the work of Keith and Cavaglieri could be linked to the European engagement with the non-European world.[176] The sense of social, cultural, or economic connectedness underpinning Huber's thesis made clear sense in relation to the unification of Germany in the 19th century, but it was by no means self-evident that the same considerations could or should apply in case, for example, of the annexation of Madagascar or Hawai'i. There, the imperatives of establishing effective colonial rule coupled with a continuing uncertainty as to the status of the territory prior to annexation, were to put far greater emphasis upon a principle of discontinuity or non-succession.

This, of course, did not go entirely unnoticed by later commentators. Fielchenfeld, for example, was to observe, that those European States engaged in the acquisition of colonial territories in Africa and Asia, seemed keen to do so under propitious terms, and were hence less inclined to assume any responsibility for the international obligations of those States once acquired.[177] Thus, the US declined to accept any responsibility for the foreign debt of Hawai'i following its annexation and declined to accept any succession to treaty obligations with other powers. A similar position was taken by France in respect of Madagascar, Japan with Korea, and Britain with the Boer Republics.[178] O'Connell, in similar vein, was to castigate Keith, who had defended the position of the British government in relation to its annexation of the Transvaal and Orange Free State, as having written what was effectively 'an academic apologia of the British policy with respect to the debt of the Boer Republics'.[179]

The observations of those such as O'Connell and Feichenfeld were largely directed towards a refutation of the claims of early 20th century 'positivists'

---

[174] Schmitt, above, n 145, p 198.
[175] ibid, pp 198–9.
[176] For an exploration of the relationship between positivism and colonization see Anghie, above, n 65.
[177] Feilchenfeld, above, n 92, p 321.
[178] *West Rand Gold Mining Co v The Queen* [1905] 2 KB 391.
[179] O'Connell, above, n 92, I, p 17.

(against whom they positioned themselves), and were built upon the insight that the earlier doctrinal formations were extraordinarily politically convenient for those seeking to maximize the freedom of the colonizing powers. They did not, as such, suggest that this was anything more than a supplementary gloss. Yet, at certain moments, Schmitt's insights as to the geographical character of doctrine relating to succession were to become fairly explicit. Two examples suffice – one of which concerns the question of succession to torts or delicts, the other to the protection of acquired rights.

In what remain the most significant cases relating to succession as regards 'torts' or 'delicts', first the British and then the US declined to assume responsibility for the putatively tortious actions of governments prior to their annexation of the Transvaal and Hawai'i respectively. In the *Robert E Brown* claim, the arbitral tribunal disallowed (what it otherwise regarded as well founded) claims presented by the United States on behalf of Robert E Brown in respect of losses incurred as a consequence of the tortious acts of the South African Republic, on the basis that such liability did not pass to Britain following its annexation of the territory.[180] There was no evidence, in the view of the tribunal, that such liability would pass in case of succession. In similar vein, the American and British Claims Arbitral Tribunal decided in the *Hawaiian Claims Arbitration* that the US could not be held liable for claims to wrongful imprisonment and 'other indignities' suffered by British nationals at the hands of the Hawai'ian Republic prior to annexation.[181] Any legal liability for such claims was extinguished with the 'termination' or 'extinction' of the international legal entity known as Hawai'i. Apart from the fact that Britain and the US swapped sides in these cases, and were thus forced to argue against their own earlier positions, the significance of these cases lies in how much emphasis was placed upon the distinction between the annexation and cession of territory and the geographic overtones that those processes were thought to have.

The British Agent and Counsel in both of these claims was Sir Cecil Hurst[182] who wrote an account of what he saw to be the current state of play on the question of succession to torts in the British Yearbook of 1924, much of which recounted the substance of the British memorial in the *Robert E Brown* claim. Like Keith before him, Hurst categorically distinguished between the cession of territory and its annexation, and like Keith again, this distinction tended to run along geographical lines: the cession of territory was that which tended to occur in Europe (and North America), annexation was what happened elsewhere (Burma, South Africa, Madagascar). His intuition was that in case of the cession of territory (or the voluntary absorption of one State by another) liability for torts might be admitted because the predecessor continued to exist: '[a]ll that happens is that the channel of diplomatic relations by which the third State approaches the

---

[180] Anglo-American Pecuniary Claims Arbitration, 5 BYIL (1924) 210.
[181] Claim no 84, Nov 10, 1925, in 20 AJIL (1926) 381.
[182] Founding editor of the British Yearbook of International Law, Legal Adviser to the Foreign Office and Judge on the Permanent Court of International Justice.

absorbed Government is altered'.[183] By contrast, in case of annexation, title of
the annexing State is 'founded on might' and title to property 'rests on the fact
of physical control'.[184] What the conqueror annexes, in other words, 'is the territory of the former State, not the State itself, still less its Government'.[185] Once
that is accepted, he suggested, 'it will be seen that in sound theory it is impossible
to hold the conqueror liable for the torts of the Government which he has displaced, because the torts were the torts of the Government and not the torts of the
territory'.[186] He goes on, however, to make very explicit the principle lying behind
this distinction:

> A principle which would render a conqueror liable in damages for all the unliquidated
> claims based on wrongful acts of the State he is driven to subdue would be neither just nor
> reasonable, and would entail consequences which would be fruitful of mischief.
>
> Such a principle would enable a small and backward State to withstand all pressure
> from a better governed and more advanced neighbour, and would act as a direct encour-
> agement to any such backslider among the family of nations to render itself secure from
> intervention and absorption by perpetuating anarchy and misrule within its borders.
> The more the condition of such a State cried aloud for intervention for the sake of the
> inhabitants of the country, whether native or foreign, the more would neighbouring
> Governments be held back from necessary action by the contemplation of the burdens it
> might entail. In short, if there were any such rule of international law, it would merely set
> a premium on misgovernment.[187]

What had been hinted at by the Arbitral Tribunal in the *Robert E Brown* claim,
(in which it suggested that annexation had been forced upon Great Britain as
a matter of 'political necessity' in order to secure the principles of justice, fair
dealing, and the protection of property rights)[188] was thus enunciated as a very
general policy consideration which negated the possibility of succession to delicts
(or 'unliquidated claims' more generally). That it was so obviously to align the
doctrine of non-succession with a justification for the annexation of 'small and
backward' States, can hardly be missed.

The same kinds of considerations also appear to have pertained in the influential case of *Cook v Sprigg* decided by the Privy Council sometime earlier in
1899 – notable, in particular, for its articulation of the peculiarly British
doctrine of 'act of State'.[189] In that case the Privy Council denied the grantees

---

[183] C Hurst, 'State Succession in Matters of Tort', 5 BYIL (1924) 163, p 173.
[184] ibid, 178.
[185] ibid.
[186] ibid.
[187] ibid.
[188] Above, n 180, p 219.
[189] Subsequent cases include: *Forests of Central Rhodopia Case* (1933) 3 RIAA 1407; *Secretary of State for India v Sardar Rustam Khan* 10 AD (1941–42) no 21; *Hoani Te Heuheu Tukino v Aoeta District Maori Land Board* [1941] AC 308; *Raj Rajinder Chand v Mst Sukhi* 24 ILR (1957), p 74; *Dalmia Dadri Cement Co Ltd v Commissioner of Income Tax* 26 ILR (1958) II, p 79; *Thailendrakishoredas v State of Madhya Pradesh* 27 ILR (1958) 30; *Indulkar v State of Bombay* 27 ILR (1958) 32; *State of*

of a concession made by the 'paramount chief of Pondoland' after its annexation by Britain a right to enforce the terms of that concession against the British government.[190] It had concluded, in response to an argument by counsel for the appellants to the effect that private rights and engagements would be left untouched by changes in sovereignty,[191] that:

[i]t is no answer to say that, by the ordinary principles of international law, private property is respected by the sovereign which accepts the cession, and assumes the duties and legal obligations of the former sovereign with respect to such private property within the ceded territory. All that can be properly meant by such a proposition is that, according to the well understood rules of international law, a change of sovereignty by cession ought not to affect private property, but no municipal tribunal has authority to enforce such an obligation.[192]

Some contemporary commentators, such as Westlake, were critical of the apparent 'Austinian' bent to the Privy Council's reasoning in this respect – suggesting that the legality of the claim should not depend upon 'the particular method that ought to be taken in order to enforce it' – but were otherwise content with the conclusions.[193] The significance of the judgment, however, is how far this seemed to take the courts away from a defence of acquired rights – a doctrine to which the government seemed otherwise committed.[194]

The simple explanation, of course, is that this new doctrine was merely a symptom of an emerging 'dualist' approach to international law, the basis for which had already been controversially set out in *R v Keyn (The Franconia)*.[195] But it is also apparent that the doctrine appeared to substantiate Schmitt's contention that the respect or negation of 'acquired rights' in case of the acquisition of non-European territory was largely discretionary. The dualist position advanced by the Privy Council allowed continued fealty to the idea of acquired rights at the same time as avoiding the possibility that the executive might be required to fulfil all the contractual engagements of the deposed government irrespective of its character.[196] It was far better for the Court to leave it to the executive to decide

---

Saurashtra v Memon Haji Ismail Haji Valimohammed 31 ILR (1959) 13. For a critical review of the doctrine in India see, S Agarwala, 'The doctrine of Act of State and the Law of State Succession in India', 12 ICLQ (1963) 1399.

[190] [1899] AC 572.

[191] Citing *US v Percheman* (1833) 7 Peters 51, p 86; *Strother v Lucas* (1838) 12 Peters 410, 435, 438; *Smith v United States* (1836) 10 Peters 326, 330; *United States v Auguisola* (1863) 1 Wallace 352, 358.

[192] [1899] AC 572, 577.

[193] Westlake, above, n 113, p 398.

[194] Report of the Transvaal Concessions Commission, *Parliamentary Papers*, South Africa (1901) Cmd 623, p 7.

[195] *R v Keyn* (1876) 2 Ex Div 63.

[196] It left open the subsequent possibility of enforcement of acquired rights in cases of 'ceded territory'. See *Amodo Tijani v Secretary, Southern Nigeria*, [1921] 2 AC 399, p 407 per Lord Haldane ('A mere change in sovereignty is not to be presumed as meant to disturb the rights of private owners; and the general terms of a cession are *prima facie* to be construed accordingly.').

whose promises should be honoured in such a context. In fact, the counsel for the applicants in the case of *Cook v Sprigg* seemed to make clear that this was precisely the terms under which the issue was to be discussed. As he put it, the question was as follows: 'how far a civilized government on succeeding to the power thereto-fore exercised by a barbarian was bound by all the engagements he [the barbarian] had made'.[197] Even if counsel was subsequently to argue that such engagements were customarily honoured in the United States, one suspects that the Court's refusal to seek protection of his client's interests came as no surprise.

A slightly different mode of evasion (but which directly recalls Schmitt's analysis) is evident in another case coming before the Privy Council in 1919 concerning the right of ownership of the British South African Company of 'unalienated' land in Southern Rhodesia.[198] In seeking to address the question whether title to ownership in that land lay with the company or rather with the British government, the Judicial Committee briefly discussed the possibility that title might actually remain in the hands of the 'natives'. This was obviously an argument that had to be dealt with at some level given the fact that the Crown had never, at that stage, actually claimed to have annexed Matabeleland and Mashonaland, and if there was any dispute over 'unalienated lands' then presumably some examin-ation of a residual title would have to take place. Having heard the evidence, the Judicial Committee confessed to certain doubt as to 'what the rights of the original 'natives' were and who the present 'natives' are',[199] but nevertheless concluded that ownership of the land appeared to be 'tribal' or 'communal' rather than 'private' or personal. This was a fairly critical distinction – so far as the rights were effectively private, it would not automatically have been assumed that they would be extin-guished by the public act of conquest or occupation. But since it took the view that the ownership was 'tribal' in character, it was therefore forced to the conclusion that the maintenance of such rights was 'fatally inconsistent with white settlement of the country' and that the 'aboriginal system gave place to another prescribed by the Order in Council'[200] (under which the Company had been given the right to administer the territory). It was thus the absence of indigenous knowledge of the institution of *private* property that effectively allowed the extinguishment of all native title through the fact of settlement.[201]

From one point of view, the doctrine of succession in the period prior to decol-onization was marked by a shift away from 19th century notions favouring

---

[197]   Above, n 192, p 574 .

[198]   *Re Southern Rhodesia* [1919] AC 211.

[199]   ibid, 233.

[200]   ibid, 234.

[201]   Having concluded that 'further inquiry into the nature of the native rights was unneces-sary', the Judicial Committee continued to argue the alternatives (ibid):

'If they were not in the nature of private rights, they were at the disposal of the Crown when Lobengula fled and his dominions were conquered; if they were, any actual disposition of them by the Crown upon a conquest, whether immediately in 1894 or four years later, would suffice to extinguish them as manifesting an intention expressly to exercise the right to do so'.

succession, to one that prioritised consent on the part of the 'new' sovereign to the inheritance of public obligations, but which secured, at the same time, the rights of individuals in their private capacity. It could thus be recorded as a history written in terms of an on-going contestation over different ideas of statehood or sovereignty within international law, the sense of which could ultimately be displaced, on the one hand by an appeal to the needs of the international community (an innate desire for 'law', 'certainty', 'stability', and 'peace') and, on the other, by a critique of the essentially metaphysical character of debates about 'sovereignty' or the character of the State.[202] Written in such a way, the history was always destined to be one culminating in the triumph of legal continuity – the articulation of a 'new' law of succession that was to be mediated through international institutions (as representative of the 'collective conscience'), and which would seek to ensure a position of maximal succession.

Two observations may be made in respect of such an account. The first is that a standard enunciation of such a history in terms of two rival doctrinal standpoints (those in favour of 'universal succession', those in favour of the 'clean slate') is ultimately extraordinarily thin in the sense that it neither says very much about the kind of explanatory theory in play nor as to the kinds of objectives the authors might have had in mind. Certainly, there were differences in the way in which various scholars approached the question of sovereignty, or as to how they characterized the 'State' for purposes of their articulation of rules of succession, but neither of these factors alone was really determinative of the kinds of conclusions that were ultimately produced. In many ways, such debates merely posed a theoretical/ methodological question as to how one might convincingly proceed to enunciate rules of succession rather than provide anything by way of an answer to what those rules might be.

The second observation is that what appears to have been far more critical in terms of the way in which the law of State succession 'developed' during this period was the context in which such arguments seemed to operate. Schmitt's observations as to the geographical divide between the European and non-European worlds – his identification of rules of continuity with political change in the European heartland, and rules of discontinuity with political change elsewhere – seems hard to dispute, and one may sense in early 20th century doctrine the pervasive influence of a late-imperial ideology. As we shall see in later parts of this book, the continuation of this historical narrative is one that reminds us of both the contextual specificity of doctrine as it was to emerge at various moments in time, and of the significance of geography in the discourse of succession.

---

[202] Brierly argues in 1924, for example, that the principles of international law 'cannot be deduced from what they are so regarded a century ago, and still less from any pseudo-metaphysical notions of what the essential qualities of Statehood ought to be'. (J Brierly, 'The Shortcomings of International Law', 5 BYIL (1924) 13, p 15).

4. Succession, Identity, and Continuity

As already suggested, up until the early part of the 20th century at least, most authors addressed the question of succession through the medium of discourses on statehood and sovereignty. For some it was a question of intuiting certain responses from a general hypothesis about the State (eg that it was an 'organic' entity), for others a matter of understanding the role of international law in relation to States (eg that it is incapable of regulating either the existence or demise of States). In either case, however, the 'State' as a phenomenological entity was largely taken as a professional *a priori* whose identity and existence was largely beyond examination.[203] Treaties could be concluded, disputes resolved, responsibility asserted, and claims instigated, all without reference to the constitution or form of the States concerned, and without concern for the incidental or incremental changes that might affect them. Indeed for most of the time, States could be conceived as fixed points, isolated both in time and space, between which a complex web of legal relations could be constructed.[204] It was only those such as Lauterpacht,[205] Scelle[206] and, in a different direction, Quadri[207] and Arangio-Ruiz,[208] who signally rejected the active 'personification' of States and who, at the same time, disputed the pertinence of the distinction between State and government that seemed to flow therefrom.

For those in the mainstream, however, whatever it was they took the State to mean (a Kelsenian legal order,[209] or a Weberian community monopolizing

---

[203] M Koskenniemi, 'The Wonderful Artificiality of States: Theoretical Perspectives on the Transformation of Sovereignty', 88 Proc ASIL (1994) 22.

[204] J Crawford, *The Creation of States in International Law* (2nd edn 2005) 667 ('Like the communities they encapsulate, States are not static. Yet we assume continuity of our States even as their governments, constitutions, territories, and populations change. International law is based on this assumption.').

[205] Lauterpacht (Analogies), above, n 67, pp 79–81, 129–130.

[206] G Scelle, 'Thèorie et Practique de la Fonction Exécutive en Droit International', 15 Hague Recueil (1936) I, 90, p 93. ('la personnalisation de L'Etat est une pure fiction juridique, qui, dans le domaine des relations internationales, devient particulièrement inacceptable'); G Scelle, 'Règles Générales du Droit de la Paix', 46 Hague Recueil (1933) IV, 331, pp 366, 367. ('il n'y a donc que des individus qui puissent être sujets de droit'. A subject of law is thus 'un individu investi du pouvoir social de créer des situations juridiques'.).

[207] R Quadri, *Diritto Internazionale Pubblico* (5th edn 1968) p 500. ('L'ordinamento internazionale non personifica la nazione entità naturale anorganica incapace di esprimere una individualità propria, ma il *Governo* (in senso lato) inteso come regime, come organizzazione sovrana.'). International legal rights and duties are attached to 'l'entité gouvernementale dont l'essence droit être déterminée en conformité avec l'idée de constitution "vivante" ', R Quadri, 'Cours Général de Droit International Public', 113 Hague Receuil (1964) III, 237.

[208] G Arangio-Ruiz, 'L'Etat dans le sens du Droit des Gens et la Notion du Droit International' 26 OZöR (1976) 3, pp 46–50.

[209] H Kelsen, *The Pure Theory of Law* (2nd edn., trans H Knight, 1964) pp 286–7. ('As a political organization, the State is a legal order.... In traditional theory the State is composed of three elements, the people of the State, the territory of the State, and the so-called power of the State,

legitimate physical violence perhaps)[210] they were continually faced with the problem that, as objects of enquiry, States did not, in fact, remain constant in form or composition over time. The populations of which they were composed would constantly evolve and change on a daily basis.[211] The scope and form of their territory would similarly be affected, not only by the actions of third States, but also by natural geo-physical changes leading, over time, to alterations in frontiers.[212] The personnel of government, including not merely the holders of public office, but those involved in the permanent administration (the civil service and police) would change both incrementally and, at certain points in time, be replaced *en masse*. The constitution of a State, once adopted, would similarly evolve through a continuing process of authoritative interpretation and be subject to amendment and, occasionally, complete overhaul. There was very little, in other words, that lawyers such as Hall could rely upon for purposes of grounding their elaborate legal architecture.

Various techniques have been developed by international lawyers to take account of such changes, of which the doctrines of succession are merely one kind. In the context of treaty law, for example, it has been recognized that a number of types of event might justify the suspension or termination of the agreement in absence of mutual consent.[213] These include material breach,[214]

---

exercised by an independent government. All three elements can be determined only juridically, that is, they can be comprehended only as the validity and the spheres of validity of a legal order.').

[210] M Weber, 'The Profession and Vocation of Politics', in *Weber: Political Writings* (1994) 309, pp 310–11.

[211] As Marek puts it, 'A State, like Heraclitus' river, is in a constant state of flux'. K Marek, *Identity and Continuity of States in Public International Law* (1954), p 4.

[212] 'Mere territorial changes, whether by increase or by dimunution, do not, so long as the identity of the State is preserved, affect the continuity of its existence or the obligations of its treaties.... Changes in the government or the internal polity of a State do not as a rule affect its position in international law. A monarchy may be transformed into a republic, or a republic into a monarchy; absolute principles may be substituted for constitutional, or the reverse; but, though the government changes, the nation remains, with rights and obligations unimpaired'. (Moore, *Digest*, vol 1, pp 248, 249.) cf Feilchenfeld, above, n 92, pp 609–611.

[213] Arts 60 and 62 Vienna Convention on the Law of Treaties. These 'might be considered as a codification of existing customary law', *Gabčikovo-Nagymaros Project* case (Hungary-Slovakia), Judgment of 25 Sep 1997, ICJ Rep 1997, para 46. See generally, K Widdows, 'The Unilateral Denunciation of Treaties Containing no Denunciation Clauses', 35 BYIL (1982) 83; B Simma, 'Termination and Suspension of Treaties: Two Recent Austrian Cases', 21 GYIL (1979) 74; H Briggs, 'Unilateral Denunciation of Treaties: The Vienna Convention and the International Court of Justice', 68 AJIL (1974) 51; S Nahlik, 'The Grounds of Invalidity and Termination of Treaties', 65 AJIL (1971) 736. See also, Second Rep of G Fitzmaurice, UN Doc A/CN4/107, 1957 Yrbk ILC, II (ii), 16; Fourth Rep of G Fitzmaurice, UN Doc A/CN4/120, 1959 Yrbk ILC, II (ii) 37; First Rep of H Waldock, UN Doc A/CN4/144, 1962 Yrbk ILC, II (ii) 27; Second Rep of H Waldock, UN Doc A/CN4/156, 1963 Yrbk ILC, II (ii) 36; Fourth Report of H Waldock, UN Doc A/CN4/177, 1965 Yrbk ILC, II (ii) 3; Fifth Rep of H Waldock, UN Doc A/CN4/183, 1966 Yrbk ILC, II (ii) 51.

[214] Art 60 Vienna Convention on the Law of Treaties. A 'material breach' is defined as 'a repudiation of the treaty not sanctioned by the Convention, or the violation of a provision essential to the accomplishment of the object or purpose of the treaty' (art 60(3)). See, *South West Africa Cases (Ethiopia v South Africa; Liberia v South Africa)*, preliminary Objections, Judgment of 21 Dec 1962, ICJ Rep 1962, 319 at 331 ('One of the fundamental principles governing the international relationship thus established is that a party which disowns or does not fulfil its obligations cannot be

supervening impossibility of performance,[215] and fundamental change of circumstances (*rebus sic stantibus*).[216] War[217] and *force majeure*[218] have also been
considered to be grounds for the suspension or termination of treaties[219] even
if there remains some uncertainty as to which treaties may legitimately be suspended in such circumstances. Similarly, in the context of State responsibility,
a State might plead that a (presumptively unlawful) act or omission was not, in

recognized as retaining the rights which it claims to derive from the relationship'). *Legal Consequences
for States of the Continued Presence of South Africa in Namibia* ICJ Rep (1971) p 47 in which the Court
noted that it was a 'general principle of law that a right of termination on account of breach must be
presumed to exist in respect of all treaties, except as regards provisions relating to the protection of
the human person contained in treaties of a humanitarian character'. See also, *BP Exploration Co
(Libya) Ltd v Government of the Libyan Arab Republic* (1974) ILR 53, pp 297, 332; *Appeal Relating
to the Jurisdiction of the ICAO Council (India v Pakistan)*, Judgment of 18 Aug 1972, 48 ILR (1975)
331; *Gabcikovo-Nagymaros Project* case, ICJ Rep (1997) 7, paras 106–110. For general discussion
see A McNair, above n 92, pp 540–53; Jennings and Watts, above, n 39, pp 1300–3; B Simma,
'Reflections on Article 60 of the Vienna Convention on the Law of Treaties and its Background in
General International Law', 20 OZöR (1970) 18; S Rosenne, *Breach of Treaty* (1985).

[215] Vienna Convention, art 61(1) which refers to the 'permanent disappearance or destruction of
an object indispensable for the execution of the treaty'. See, *Serbian and Brazilian Loans Cases* (1929)
PCIJ, Series A, nos 20–21, pp 40, 120; *Temple of Preah Vihear Case*, ICJ Rep (1961) 32; *Military
and Paramilitary Activities Case (Jurisdiction)*, ICJ Rep (1984) 392; *Gabcikovo-Nagymaros Project*
case ICJ Rep (1997) paras 102–3.

[216] Art 62 Vienna Convention. On which see *Fisheries Jurisdiction* (UK v Iceland), Judgment
of 2 Feb 1973, ICJ Rep 3, at 18 ('International law admits that a fundamental change in circumstances which determined the parties to accept the treaty, if it has resulted in radical transformation of the extent of obligations imposed by it, may, under certain conditions, afford the party
affected a ground for invoking the termination or suspension of the treaty. This principle, and the
conditions and exceptions to which it is subject, have been embodied in Article 62 of the Vienna
Convention on the Law of Treaties, which may in many respects be considered as a codification of
existing customary law on the subject of termination of a treaty relationship on account of changed
circumstances'). See generally, McNair, above, n 92, ch 42; O Lissitzyn, 'Treaties and Changed
Circumstances (*rebus sic stantibus*)', 61 AJIL (1967) 895; A Vamvoukos, *Termination of Treaties in
International Law: The Doctrines of Rebus Sic Stantibus and Desuetude* (1985). The doctrine has been
discussed (albeit indirectly) in a number of cases but has never been found as a justifiable basis for
the termination of an agreement. eg *Free Zones in Upper Savoy and the District of Gex*, (1932) PCIJ
Series A/B, no 46, p 158; *Fisheries Jurisdiction* case ICJ Rep (1973) 3; *Gabcikovo-Nagymaros Project*
case ICJ Rep (1997) para 104 (the Court indicated that 'the stability of treaty relations requires that
the plea of fundamental change of circumstances be applied only in exceptional circumstances'.).
For other cases see Jennings and Watts, above, n 39, p 1307, n 8. Its recognition as a principle of
international law is controversial. Lauterpacht argued for example in 1927, that 'The doctrine has
not become a rule of positive international law; not only because the instances of its application
are highly infrequent, but also because in those rare cases in which it has been invoked it has been
rejected by the other contracting parties against whose interests the denunciation of the treaty was
directed'. Lauterpacht, above, n 67, p 170.

[217] See generally, I Brownlie, 'First Report on the Effects of Armed Conflicts on Treaties', UN
Doc A/CN4/552 (2005).

[218] Jennings and Watts note (above, n 39, p 1304) that since the Vienna Convention does not
mention emergencies or *force majeure* 'they would appear unavailable as a distinct legal justification
for withdrawal from or non-compliance with a treaty'.

[219] It is often pointed out that humanitarian treaties – such as the Hague Regulations of 1899 or
1907 or the Geneva Conventions of 1949 – cannot be terminated as otherwise they could effectively
be rendered nugatory.

fact, unlawful by reason of necessity (or perhaps *force majeure* or distress)[220] if a change in the social environment was such as to prevent fulfilment of the obligation in question.[221] In such cases it is by no means assumed that the agreements concerned are to be regarded as terminated – simply that the events in question entitle individual states parties to suspend or avoid the obligations if they so desire.

Whilst having some obvious relationship to such principles, the law of State succession has developed in relative isolation from other such techniques of legal adjustment – and in many ways can be seen to be antipathetic to the assumptions underpinning them. In the *Gabčikovo-Nagymaros Project* case,[222] for example, Hungary argued, on the one hand, that it had legitimately terminated the treaty of 1977 with Czechoslovakia on the basis of changed circumstances and impossibility of performance whilst, on the other, maintained that such a treaty had never come into force with respect to Slovakia following the dissolution of Czechoslovakia (that, in other words, Slovakia did not 'succeed' to the treaty). In one sense at least, these were part and parcel of the same argument, namely, that changes in the social and political environment either excused Hungary's termination of the treaty, or justified its claim that the obligations in question simply did not survive those changes. But the arguments were also clearly quite different in terms of their effect. The argument concerning changed circumstances was premised upon the idea that, until that moment, the treaty remained in force; the argument concerning succession, by contrast, disputed the existence of any legal relations between the parties on the basis that Slovakia had not itself concluded the agreement with Hungary. The former argument accepted the applicability of the principle *pacta sunt servanda*, the latter disputed it (there being no agreement which must be followed).

Clearly then, whilst the idea of State succession has been developed as a way of dealing with the legal effects of political change, it has come to operate on a very different basis than other forms of 'everyday' legal adjustment. The very invocation of the question of succession is such as to situate the events themselves outside the terms of normal international discourse, and disallows reliance upon otherwise unimpeachable arguments about consent (such as *pacta sunt servanda*) as a way of justifying the existence of legal obligation. This, of course, has not been to prevent some from maintaining that the *boundary* between the two forms of response is a matter of degree, not of kind, or that, in case of treaties, most problems might best be resolved through a process of interpretation. Needless to

---

[220] cf art 23 and 24, ILC Draft Articles on Responsibility of States for Internationally Wrongful Acts (2001), 56 GAOR, supp no 10 (A/56/10) ch IVE1.

[221] According to art 25 of the Articles on State Responsibility, necessity may be pleaded only if the act 'is the only means for the State to safeguard an essential interest against a grave and imminent peril'. The ILC referred, in that respect, to the decision of the ICJ in the *Gabčikovo-Nagymaros Project* Case, ICJ Rep (1997) 7, pp 40–1, which in turn, referred back to the earlier work of the ILC on State Responsibility.

[222] ibid.

say, this has merely been such as to highlight the enduring difficulties associated with defining succession in a way that captures this transition from 'normal' to 'abnormal' states of affairs.

Definitions of succession offered by scholars over the years have ranged from those that tie the issue to the 'transfer' of territory from one State to another,[223] to those that speak about it in terms of the 'replacement' or 'substitution' of one legal subject by another in legal relations.[224] Some have been content to limit the concept to territorial change[225] whilst others have emphasized the importance of the change being one that affects territorial *sovereignty*.[226] Others still have preferred the language of 'responsibility', seeking to avoid, in the process any mention of the contested idea of sovereignty.[227] Two particular issues have informed the choices made, in this respect. The first is the question whether rules of succession are limited to changes that affect territory, or whether they also concern changes to non-territorial legal entities such as international organizations. The second question is whether rules of succession are confined to changes in territorial sovereignty, or whether they may also be cast more broadly to encompass, on the one hand, forms of territorial change that fall short of changes in sovereignty or, on the other, changes of a non-territorial nature. Underlying a response to any of these questions, of course, is the substantive content of the rules of succession themselves – it is only in virtue of the supposition that territorial change may plausibly result in a substantial 'transfer' of competence or responsibility from one legal entity to another, that there is a question to be answered at all.

As regards the first question, there is obviously no particular reason why there should not also be rules governing the responsibilities of international organizations *vis-à-vis* their historical precursors.[228] This was an issue, in particular, as regards the rights and obligations assumed by the United Nations in respect of property and functions for which the League of Nations was initially responsible.

---

[223] Feilchenfeld, above, n 92, p 13. Castrén remarks that '[i]l ne peut s'agir de succession d'Etats que lorsu'a la *perte territoriale* subie par un Etat correspond une *extension territoriale* dont bénéficient un autre ou plusieurs autres Etats'. Castrén, above, n 32, p 387.

[224] M Udina, 'La Succession des États Qant aux Obligations International autre que les dettes Publiques', 44 *Hague Recueil* (1933), at 665 ('la substitution d'un sujet à l'autre dans un rapport juridique donné qui demeure identique'). Kaekenbad, above, n 158, p 10 (succession constitutes a 'substitution of one State for the other as one of the parties to the legal relation'). cf also, Oppenheim, above, n 134, I, p 119. (A succession occurs when 'one or more International Persons take the place of another International Person, in consequence of certain changes in the latter's condition'.); O'Connell (1967) I, above, n 92, p 3.

[225] eg Castrén, above, n 32, p 387.

[226] eg O'Connell, (1967) I, above, n 92, p 3; Menon, above, n x, p 122; Wilkinson, above, n 126, p 16. eg A Lester, 'State Succession to Treaties in the Commonwealth' 14 ICLQ (1965) 476 (succession defined as a 'change in sovereignty in a territory'); W Jenks, *The Common Law of Mankind* (1958) p 72 ('a change of territory through concurrent acquisition and loss of sovereignty'). See also, *Land, Island and Maritime Frontier Dispute (Nicaragua Intervening)*, Judgment of 11th Sept 1992, ICJ Rep 1992, p 598, para 399.

[227] Vienna Convention, 1978, art 2(1)(a) and Vienna Convention, 1983, art 2(1)(a). See also, Zemanek, above, n 73, p 190.

[228] But cf Yrbk ILC (1982) II, p 69 ('strictly speaking, there can never be a "succession" of organizations'.) On this issue generally see P Myers, *Succession between International Organizations* (1993).

It was also at issue in the replacement of inter-war agencies such as the International Commission for Air Navigation, the International Institute of Agriculture and the Office International d'Hygiène by their post-war counterparts (the International Civil Aviation Authority, the Food and Agriculture Organization and the World Health Organization respectively).[229] In the *International Status of South-West Africa Case*,[230] for example, the International Court was concerned with the question whether the United Nations might have assumed responsibility for the supervision of mandated territories as the legal successor to the League of Nations. Its conclusion, in that regard, that it had assumed such supervisory functions, but that such functions 'were neither expressly transferred to the United Nations nor expressly assumed by the organization'[231] appeared, somewhat vaguely, to sustain the idea that there had been a succession in this respect,[232] but the point was certainly not explicit. In any case, what becomes apparent, here, is that organizational succession becomes most acute in contexts in which the organization itself is taking responsibility for the government of territory, and in that context there arise obvious questions as to the extent to which entities under 'international administration' might continue to be bound by the prior acts of the administering authorities after independence.[233] But here, this first question seems to merge with the second – which concerns the question of territorial sovereignty.

As regards the pertinence of the idea of 'sovereignty', the issue is clearly a little more complex. In its work on State succession, the International Law Commission deliberately chose to avoid reference to 'sovereignty' or 'competence' in its definition of succession, choosing rather to define it as the 'replacement of one State by another in the responsibility for the international relations of territory.' The overt reason for this was 'to cover in a neutral manner any specific case independently of the particular status of the territory in question (national territory, trusteeship, mandate, protectorate, dependent territory etc.)'.[234] It was keen, in other words, to extend discussion of succession, within the framework of the Convention, to cases of the gaining of independence of trust or mandated territories, for example, over which the administering power would not necessarily be thought to enjoy 'sovereignty' in its strictest sense.[235] The obvious rationale for this was that it avoided the possibility that the application of principles of succession would become subordinate to a prior debate as to whether the predecessor State actually enjoyed rights

---

[229] Myers, ibid, 13–22.

[230] ICJ Rep (1950) 128.

[231] ibid, 136.

[232] G Fitzmaurice. 'The Law and Procedure of the International Court of Justice: International Organizations and Tribunals' 29 BYIL (1952) 1, p 8; H Lauterpacht, *The Development of International Law by the International Court* (1958) pp 277–81.

[233] This has obvious resonance as regards the international administration of East Timor and Kosovo. On which see generally R Wilde, 'From Danzia to East Timor and Beyond: The Role of International Territorial Administration,' 95 AJIL (2001) 583.

[234] Commentary to Draft Art 2, ILC 1974, II, I, 174, p 175 para 4.

[235] Castrén, above, n 32, pp 386–7; Jennings and Watts, above, n 39, p 316.

of sovereignty in the first place.[236] McNair's remark in his separate opinion in the South-West Africa case to the effect that the Mandate system was an institution in which sovereignty was 'in abeyance'[237] was all too pertinent in this respect.

The difficulty with which the ILC was faced in virtue of this decision, however, was that in leaving the issue of sovereignty out of the equation, it could no longer obviously distinguish between legitimate and illegitimate cases of territorial change. Even if the Charter prohibition on the use of force had led many to the view that annexation did not constitute a lawful means of acquiring sovereignty over territory,[238] and even if Articles 42 and 43 of the Hague Regulations[239] gave expression to the idea that a belligerent occupant only enjoys rights as a 'usufruct',[240] this would not, on the ILC's definition, preclude an occupant of

[236] Wilkinson was to exclude protectorates, mandates and other administrative cessions from the scope of his study for the reason that '[t]he international status of them is as yet so confused and the juristic problems which they cause are so intricate that it is not deemed advisable to include them in a study of State succession'. Above, n 126, p 17.

[237] McNair, Separate Opinion, South-West Africa Advisory Opinion ICJ Rep 146, p 150. ('the Mandate System was a "new institution" – a new relationship between territory and its inhabitants on the one hand and the government which represents them internationally on the other – a new species of international government, which does not fit into the old conception of sovereignty and which is alien to it'.).

[238] See, GA Resn 2625 (XXV) (1970). A significant exception, in this respect, is the Indian 'annexation' of Goa, Daman and Diu. For the attitude of the Indian Supreme Court in this respect see, *Rev Hons Sbastiao Francisco Xavier Dos Ramedios Monterio v State of Goa*, 1970 SCR 100. For a very qualified statement of the effect of this principle see R Jennings, *The Acquisition of Territory in International Law* (1963) pp 52–68.

[239] Art 42 and 43 of the 1907 Hague Regulations state, for example, that:
'Art 42. Territory is considered occupied when it is actually placed under the authority of the hostile army. The occupation extends only to the territory where such authority has been established and can be exercised.
Art. 43. The authority of the legitimate power having in fact passed into the hands of the occupant, the latter shall take all the measures in his power to restore and ensure, as far as possible, public order and safety, while respecting, unless absolutely prevented, the laws in force in the country'.
Regulations Respecting the Laws and Customs of War on Land, annex to the Convention (IV) Respecting the Laws and Customs of War on Land, The Hague, 18 Oct, 1907. The Brussels Declaration of 1874 provided similarly (art 2) that 'The authority of the legitimate power being suspended and having in fact passed into the hands of the occupant, the latter shall take all the measures in his power to restore and ensure, as far as possible, public order and safety'. Oxford Manual on the Laws of War on Land, 1880 provided (art 6): 'No invaded territory is regarded as conquered until the end of war; until that time the occupant exercises, in such territory, only a de facto power, essentially provisional in character.'

[240] For the view that the law of belligerent occupation has not, in fact, 'resolved' the issue of sovereignty, see G Von Glahn, *The Occupation of Enemy Territory: A Commentary on the Law and Practice of Belligerent Occupation* (1957) p 31. See also, *The Manila*, 1 Edw 3 (per Lord Stowell); *The Boletta*, 1 Edw 173; *Fleming v Page*, 9 Howe 603. Some authors have denied the supposition that the occupant acquires any legal 'rights' at all. M Bothe ('Belligerent Occupation' 4 Encyclopedia PIL (1982) 65) for example, argues that 'International law does not grant rights to the occupying powers, but limits the occupier's exercise of its de facto powers'. See also, Q Baxter, 'The Duty of Obedience to the Belligerent Occupant', 27 BYIL (1950) 235, p 243. Contra see, F Morgenstern, 'Validity of Acts of the Belligerent Occupant', 28 BYIL (1951) 291, p 296; J Stone, *Legal Controls of International Conflicts* (1954) 724. Pellet considers (A Pellet, 'The Destruction of Troy will not Take Place', in E Playfair, *International Law and the Administration of Occupied Territories* (1992) p 175) that 'all specialists start from the same observation: occupation constitutes a temporary

foreign territory from either acquiring rights as a successor State or perhaps burdening the territory with obligations which would continue to bind it after its independence. There would, of course, be no doubt that an occupant – whether 'lawful' or otherwise – would remain internationally responsible for its actions in virtue of its control of the territory, but to treat an occupant as either a 'predecessor' or 'successor' State would clearly have the effect of appearing to legitimize what might otherwise be regarded as a form of factual, but not legal, possession.[241]

This particular problem was partially addressed by the inclusion, within the Vienna Conventions, of a provision limiting their application to the 'effects of

situation neither operating nor implying any devolution of sovereignty'. In fact, the range of opinion is far wider than he admits. At one end of the spectrum are those who simply deny any notion of the transfer of sovereignty eg L Oppenheim, 'The Legal Relations between an Occupying Power and the Inhabitants', LQR (1917) 364 ('There is not an atom of sovereignty in the authority of the occupant.'). Others make the same point, but do so more narrowly by focusing upon the issue of territorial title eg G Schwarzenberger, *International Law* (3rd edn, 1957), 179 ('In the abstract, the territorial sovereign remains entitled to dispose of the occupied territory.'). Others agree on the point of title but seem to admit some transfer of sovereign rights, eg, C Rousseau, *Le droit des conflits armés* (1983) p 136 ('On peut ramener l'effet juridique essentiel de l'occupation de guerre (ou *occupatio bellica*) aux deux idées suivantes: 1) cette occupation n'est pas translative de souveraineté; 2) mais elle entraîne une répartiion particulière des compétences dans les rapports de l'Etat occupant et de l'Etat occupé.'). Also, Debbasch, *L'Occupation militaire – Pouvoirs reconnus aux forces armées hors de leur territoire national* (1962) 10 ('l'occupant ... pourra participer au pouvoir souverain. Il ne pourra jamais l'acquérir.'). Others talk of a 'suspension of sovereignty' eg von Glahn, ibid p 31. Oppenheim (Lauterpacht) states (*International Law: a Treatise* (7th edn 1952) ii, pp 436–7): 'the occupant acquires a temporary right of administration over the territory and its inhabitants; and all legitimate steps he takes in the exercise of this right must be recognized by the legitimate government after occupation has ceased'. Dana notes in Wheaton *Elements of International Law* (8th edn 1866) p 337, n 162 that 'Firm possession by the enemy in war suspends the power or right to exercise sovereignty over the occupied place, and gives the enemy certain rights over it of a temporary character which all nations recognize, and to which loyal citizens may submit'. Baty remarks that 'hostile occupation acts as a sterilizing medium to preserve the status quo'. T Baty, *Canons of International Law* (1930) 480. Arbitrator Borel *Ottoman Debt Arbitration* 1 RIAA (1925) 529 at 555 ('Quels que soient les effets de l'occupation d'un territoire par l'adversaire avant le rétablissement de la paix, il est certain qu'à elle seule cette occupation ne pouvait opérer juridiquement le transfert de souveraineté.'). See also, *Lighthouses* case, PCIJ, 17 March 1934, Series A/B, no 62 pp 19, 25.

A version of this approach was adopted by Heyland who took the view that the belligerent occupant did not act as the representative, or *negotiarum gestor*, of the legitimate sovereign, nor as a usufructuary of the occupied territory, but as a legitimate sovereign in its own right. C Heyland, *Die Rechtsstellung de besetzten Rheinlande nach dem Versailler Friedensvertrag und dem Rheinlandabkommen, zugleich ein Beitrag zur Lehre von der Besetzung fremden Staatsgebietes* (1923) p 8. See also E Löning, ('Das Subjekt de Staatsgewalt im besetzten feindlichen Gebiet' 28 *Zeitschrift IR* (1920) 287) who took the more extreme position that the occupant acquired *de iure* sovereignty over the territory.

[241] Certain authors have taken the view that the entire law of occupation is based upon the principle of the 'inalienability of sovereignty through the actual or threatened use of force', E Benvenisti, *The International Law of Occupation* (1992) p 5. This seems to overlook the fact that, in its earliest incarnation, it was not premised upon a concern to eliminate the possibility of acquisition of territorial sovereignty by military force, but simply to regulate it. For a broader enumeration of the purposes of the law of occupation see A Roberts, 'Prolonged Military Occupation: The Israeli-Occupied Territories 1967–1988', in E Playfair, *International Law and the Administration of Occupied Territories* (1992) 25, pp 27–8; D Graber, *The Development of the Law of Belligerent Occupation 1863–1914: A Historical Survey* (1945).

a succession of States occurring in conformity with international law, and, in particular, the principles of international law embodied in the Charter of the United Nations'.[242]

Whilst appearing to confirm the general supposition that 'unlawful' territorial change would not give rise to rights of sovereignty on the part of the 'acquiring State',[243] and hence preventing it from inheriting rights or obligations,[244] the phraseology of this clause was not such as to preclude the application of customary rules of succession to cases of unlawful occupation of territory, or indeed of the Convention itself to putatively 'legitimate' cases of belligerent occupation (occupation pursuant to a war of self-defence perhaps). The apparent hesitancy is further reinforced in Article 40 of the 1978 Convention which stipulates that its terms are not such as to *prejudge* 'any question that may arise in regard to a treaty from the military occupation of territory',[245] even if the ILC's commentary was to make clear that it did not consider 'the military occupation of a territory' to 'constitute a succession of States'.[246]

The real dilemma facing the ILC, in this context, was that to commit itself to a position that limited succession to changes in sovereignty might have forced it to position itself on one side or another of a critical debate as to the 'location' of sovereignty in case of mandates and trusteeships. To the extent that it could not close the door to the possibility of succession in case of 'administered' territories also meant, however, that it could not definitively rule out succession following occupation.[247] At the same time, the recognition that a State emerging from belligerent occupation might be regarded as a 'successor' to the acts of the occupant would seem to validate the legitimacy of the occupation in a way that is more than merely incidental. As an institutional response to a particular set of events, succession seems to imply something more than an ad hoc obeisance to certain 'facts' on the ground (as may be expressed in the maxim *ex factis ius oritur*); it seems to suggest, in addition, that certain consequences will *regularly* ensue from such events and would acquire, in the process, an aura of normality.

---

[242] Art 6, 1978 Convention; art 3, 1983 Convention.

[243] For cases affirming that a 'cession' of territory imposed by the unlawful use of force is effectively 'invalid' see *Amato Narodni Podnik v. Julius Kleinwerth Musikinstrumentenfrabrik* ILR 1957 435; *Ratz-Lienert and Klein v Netherlands Beheers-Institut* ILR, 1957, 536. If the cession were to be the subject of a treaty imposed upon one party, the validity of the agreement itself could be contested by reference to art 52 of the Vienna Convention on the Law of Treaties (1969).

[244] Brownlie, for example, defines State succession as 'a definitive replacement of one State by another in respect of sovereignty over a given territory *in conformity with international law*'. (emphasis added). Above, n 27, p 649.

[245] Vienna Convention 1978, art 40.

[246] Commentary to draft arts 38 and 39, para 2.

[247] For the view that territorial change can be brought about by the 'lawful' use of force see E Lauterpacht, *Jerusalem and the Holy Places* (1968) p 52. Jennings and Watts (above, n 39, p 705) also note, having suggested that title to territory acquired by force may vested in the 'new' sovereign 'after a considerable period of peaceable possession and administration', that '[t]he law often has to take some account of consequences of situations brought about unlawfully'.

As such, the question of 'sovereignty' will always be semi-present, if not an explicit concern.

This general ambivalence concerning the question of sovereignty, in fact, goes somewhat further than a concern about the external *parameters* of the law of State succession (ie a determination of the circumstances in which a 'succession' may be said to have taken place) but also reflects upon the fact that the very conception of territorial sovereignty itself may have certain implications for the internal *content* of rules of succession or the justification thereof. Depending upon how the notion of territorial sovereignty is perceived, different conclusions may follow as regards what rules of succession may be thought to apply to any particular instance of succession. Here, however, one may detect a relationship between the open textured character of the idea of territorial sovereignty, on the one hand, and the determination to avoid its consequences by way of seeking to separate the facts from their consequences on the other (succession de facto being distinguished from succession *de iure*).

a) Three Notions of Territorial Sovereignty

That the concept of territorial sovereignty may appear to have certain implications as regards the substantiation of particular rules of succession may best be appreciated by reference to a relatively simple case: for present purposes the 'cession' of territory from one State to another will be chosen. In such a context there appear to be (at least) three different ways in which that change might be understood, each of which relates to a different conception of territorial sovereignty and each of which will substantiate different conclusions as regards the applicable rules of succession.

To begin with, a cession of territory might simply be regarded as a form of commercial transaction in which property (territory) is passed from one title holder (sovereign) to another. If that were to be the case, one might suppose that what is being acquired is a set of legal entitlements (or relationships) associated with the *res* as are normally determined by existing rules of ownership, and which may also be subject to outstanding liabilities. Reliance upon Roman law principles such as *res transit cum suo onere* or *nemo plus transferre quod non habet*, may thus argue in favour of a limited 'succession' to those rights and obligations that appear to be intrinsically related to the territory in question (and to which the designation 'real rights' might attach).[248] No other effects would necessarily be felt by the two parties concerned as regards their other legal entitlements or liabilities. The difficulty with this, of course, is not only the relative paucity of general rules governing what States may do with territory,[249] but the sense that

---

[248] For a discussion of this point see below pp 173–94.

[249] A Carty *The Decay of International Law* (1986) pp 43–64 (pointing out that the dominant conception of territory since the 19th century has concerned itself with the delimitation of power by reference to territory, rather than its exercise).

such a 'patrimonial' approach to territory[250] is invested with far too many feudal, or absolutist, connotations for it to be entirely acceptable.[251] It marginalizes the importance of 'consent' when it comes to determining the future of territory and grossly underplays the significance of 'territory' in the social and political identity of the individuals and communities that inhabit it.[252] That many have therefore called for the patrimonial theory to be 'generally abandoned'[253] is obviously to question its utility as the starting point for dealing with questions of succession.

An alternative may be to think about the cession of territory as one concerned with the moving of a jurisdictional boundary that is metaphorically 'suspended above' or 'over' the communities and territory subjected to the change.[254] Here, the cession of territory does not automatically implicate any transmission of rights and obligations from one sovereign to the other. Nothing *per se*, is passed or transferred from one State to the other; all that occurs is a simultaneous extension and diminution of sovereign competence on the part of the two States concerned. There are, again, evident problems with this conception of the change. Surely, it might be argued, the successor State does acquire certain substantive rights and obligations 'for example' in relation to public property located within the territory in question, or in relation to agreements with third states delimiting the territory in a particular way? Surely the successor must also accept certain obligations in respect of the population over which it is now assuming

[250] eg, Hall, above, n 33, pp 48, 106 *et seq*; D Donati, *Stato e territorio* (1924) pp 59–117; Arangio-Ruiz, above, n 208, p 57. See generally, M Shaw, *Title to Territory in Africa: International Legal Issues*, (1986), pp 13–14; Lauterpacht above, n 67, pp 91–2. This has sometimes been referred to as the 'object theory' or the 'Eigentumstheorieen'.

[251] Westlake above, n 105, p 86 (the equation between territory and property 'being to confound in a common haze the right of the lord to rule in his manor and the right of our sovereign lord the king to rule in his kingdom.').

[252] Jennings remarks, in that sense, that a territorial change 'means not just a transference of a portion of the earth's surface and its resources from one regime to another; it usually involves, perhaps more importantly, a decisive change in the nationality, allegiance and way of life of a population'. Jennings, above, n 238, p 3. On the latter point, Kratochwil notes that land 'not only provides people with a "place in the world" which forces people to address their common problems and engage in cooperative ventures, but it also becomes a symbol of continuity, and an assurance of transgenerational connectedness'. F Kratochwil, 'The Limits of Contract', 5 EJIL (1994) 465, p 480.

[253] Marek, above, n 211, p 19. See further, Cavaglieri, above, n 121, p 385 (L'anciennne confusion du droit feudal entre *dominium eminens* et propriété privée est contraire à la notion moderne de l'État'); Jennings, ibid, 3 (who doubts the usefulness of the 'analogy').

[254] This broadly correlates to the notion of territory as 'competence'. See generally, E Radnitzky, 'Die rechtliche Natur des Staatsgebiets', 20 Archiv des offentlichen Rechts, (1905) 313; W Henrich, *Theorie des Staatsgebiets* (1922); Guggenheim, above, n 131, p 336; W Schönborn, 'La nature juridique du territoire', 30 Hague Receuil (1929 II) 85. See generally, Shaw, above, n 250, pp 14–15; Marek, above, n 211, pp 20. Kelsen argues, for example, that 'the unity of the State territory, and therefore the territorial unity of the State, is a juristic and not a geographical unity, for the territory of a State is legally nothing but the territorial space of validity of the national legal order called a State'. H Kelsen, *General Theory of Law and State* (1961, trans A Wedberg, 1999) p 208; de La Pradelle, *Nationality Decrees in Tunis and Morocco Case* (PCIJ Rep, Series C, no 2, (1923), pp 106, 108 ('territory is neither an object nor a substance; it is a framework.... The framework within which the public power is exercised ... territory as such must not be considered, it must be regarded as the external, ostensible sign of the sphere within which the public power of the state is exercised.').

authority? Territory is, after all, the subject of claims of public ownership and a space for politics, as much as a domain in which sovereign power may be exercised. Isn't there, furthermore, a question here as to the relationship between territory, understood as the space within which a State may exercise certain legal powers, and territory as forming a part of the legal identity of the State (as a 'criterion of statehood')? It is very difficult to sever, in other words, the abstract idea of territory from that of the State, when the latter is understood as a territorially located political community.[255]

A third alternative, then, is to emphasize the centrality of territory as an idea underpinning a State's legal identity.[256] In such a case the cession of territory might thereby involve the mutual reconstruction of two independent political communities, with the consequence that the legal identity of each is radically altered as a consequence.[257] Here, the survival of legal relations of both the ceding and recipient States would be put in question in virtue of the changes in their identity, and the problem of succession would extend far beyond the confines of rights and obligations pertinent to the territory itself. Apart from the evidently destabilizing effect of such an approach to territorial change, it seems to make too much of the relationship between territory on the one hand and sovereignty, or political identity on the other. It supposes, for example, that even the most superficial territorial change – such as might follow from the delimitation of a boundary in an unpopulated area – will have a necessary consequence upon the identity of the States concerned, providing them with good reason to dissociate themselves from any unwanted obligations incurred prior to the event.

The three conceptions of territory adverted to here – as property, as competence, and as an attribute of a political community – provide radically different answers to the question as to how one might approach the nature and character of State succession. Whilst each may resolve certain problems, it will tend also to generate others. The point is, however, not that one may be preferred above another, or that they can be sequentially ordered in terms of when they acquired greatest resonance, but that each retains to this day a certain explanatory appeal. It is fully apparent, for example, that all three notions of territory continue to find recognition in contemporary discourse: the patrimonial theory in doctrine associated with the 'acquisition' or 'loss' of territory;[258] the competence theory in the doctrine of

---

[255] This is the insight of those advancing what is known as the 'Eigenschaftteorien' or the 'attribute theory' of territory. eg K Fricker, *Vom Staatsgebeit, Gebiet und Gebietshoheit* (1867); Shaw, above, n 250, p 14; Schönborn, ibid, 114–16; P Laband, *Das Staatsrecht des deutschen Reiches* (1911) I, pp 190 ff.

[256] See, Lauterpacht, *Analogies,* above, n 67, pp 93 ('The adherents of this view point out that *imperium* over a lifeless object of nature, such as territory, is impossible. The territory, it is said, is an *element* of the State, and it can no more be regarded as the object of a State's right, than the body of a man can be said to be his property. The territory is the space within which the jurisdiction of the State is exercised, it is the theatre of the State's rule. The State rules *within* the territory, not *over* it.').

[257] A view associated with Fricker, above, n 255. See Schönborn, above, n 254, p 116.

[258] eg Jennings, above, n 238, p 3 (who openly admits that in speaking of territorial title, the main analogy is that with Roman law conceptions of property). In a general sense the patrimonial concept – the idea of sovereignty as a matter of 'title' or 'ownership' of territory – allows for a distinction to be drawn between the *possession* of sovereign rights on the one hand and their *exercise* in practice on the

jurisdiction;[259] and the attribute theory in the doctrines of recognition and state-hood.[260] All three, furthermore, find continued recognition in discussion of State succession,[261] and it is precisely a consequence of the incomplete nature of each account that the meaning and significance of territorial change is able to remain open and contested.

b) Two Notions of Succession

As suggested above, this uncertainty as regards the conclusions that might legitimately be drawn from the notion of territorial sovereignty (and, indeed, the rather inconclusive and speculative character of each of the three 'theories') can be related to a concurrent determination to separate the issue of successsion into two, relatively distinct, sets of problems: the one being the delineation of the circumstances in which succession is thought to take place (often referred to as 'succession de facto'), the other being the legal consequences that are thought to attach to such changes ('succession *de iure*').[262] The rationale for this distinction, as O'Connell made perfectly clear, was that otherwise the phrase 'State succession' appeared to beg the question 'which any investigation of the consequences of change of sovereignty seeks to resolve'.[263] So long as State succession meant

---

other. This distinction between the possession and exercise of sovereignty underlies, and allows for the construction of, concepts such as 'servitudes', 'leases', 'trusteeships', 'mandates', 'protectorates', 'condominia', or 'usufructs'. It also underlies in some degree the distinction between *de iure* and de facto government, and more broadly the distinction between the notions of legitimacy and effectiveness. To take a couple of simple examples: in the case concerning *Lighthouses* in Crete and Samos (1937) the Permanent Court held that sovereignty over the island of Crete had not ceased to belong to the Ottoman Empire despite the fact that according to art 4 of the Treaty of London 1899, the Sultan had ceded 'all rights of sovereignty and other rights which he possessed over that island' to the Allied powers (PCIJ, Ser A/B, no 71, 92 at 103). In other words, 'sovereignty' could be retained simply as a strict question of 'title' or 'ownership' whilst its exercise could be devolved upon other powers. Similarly, in the case of Germany after 1945, although the Four Powers (France, the UK, the USA, and the USSR) assumed 'supreme authority' with respect to Germany, including all powers possessed by a German Government, they maintained simultaneously that Germany continued to exist as a sovereign State. The State of Germany qualified for sovereign immunity, therefore, under the UK State Immunity Act 1978. eg *R. v Secretary of State for Foreign and Commonwealth Affairs, ex p Trawnik* [1985] TLR 18 Apr 1985, and [1986] TLR 21 Feb 1986.

[259] eg *Lotus case* PCIJ, Series A, no 10 (1927) p 23.

[260] J Crawford, *The Creation of States in International Law* (2nd edn 2005).

[261] The patrimonial theory underlies the approach to public property in the 1983 Vienna Convention (arts XX); the competence theory underlies the approach to treaty relations in the 1978 Vienna Convention; and the attribute theory underlies the various distinctions drawn between cases of secession and dissolution, merger and unification. Jennings (above, n 238, pp 7–8) suggests, however, that the law of succession of States 'tends to accept the change of territorial sovereignty as *datum*, and very little if anything seems to hinge on the method by which the change was brought about'.

[262] Kelsen, above, n 209, p 314, 325; Feilchefeld, above, n 92, pp 1–3, 613; Castrén, above, n 32, p 387; Udokang, above, n 125, pp 107–9.

[263] O'Connell, (1956) above, n 66, p 3. Within the ILC Rosenne had proposed discarding the term 'succession' for precisely the reason that it appeared to connote some 'automatic process brought about by operation of law'. Yrbk ILC, 1968, I, p 139, para 8.

something less than a universal substitution in legal relationships, it had to be articulated in terms of events rather than their consequences.[264]

There were several particular advantages of maintaining this distinction between de facto and *de iure* succession. The first, and obvious, benefit was that it liberated scholars from the constraints of thinking about succession in relation to particular theories that sought to explain how and why a succession to rights and obligations might occur. It allowed, thereby, an examination of certain problems under the rubric of State succession, without prefiguring such a discussion by the elaboration of a theory explaining how rights and obligations are 'transferred' or 'assigned', or alternatively how successor States come to be 'substituted' in the legal relations of the predecessor. As the history of the topic suggests, such theories appeared altogether too speculative, and too far enmeshed in particular types of event, to command general support, and the only ready alternative was to adopt a position of agnosticism in relation to them. It is interesting to note, in that regard, that most contemporary accounts of State succession now scrupulously avoid discussion of how or why succession occurs – the intimation being that it is a matter of State practice and little else.[265]

A second consequence of the separation of the two fields of enquiry in this way was that it opened up a much wider range of possible consequences than might be implied by the term succession itself. Once, in other words, the fact of succession was divorced from the particular legal consequences that might be implied by that term, it could be understood as bringing into play a new set of legal relations between the successor State and others in the international community. This would neither demand application of the clean slate, nor require universal succession, but rather allowed a more creative, and nuanced response. On the one hand, for example, this could mean that successor States might be burdened with obligations that were not previously incumbent upon the predecessor State (for example, to grant nationality to stateless individuals who are habitually resident on the territory in question).[266] On the other, it could give rise to a set of intermediate, contingent, or processural rights and obligations, the purpose of which might be to bring about some kind of settlement. Thus, the fact of succession could be understood as bringing into play, for example, a duty to negotiate with other parties as to the passing of State property,[267] or a right of option in case of multilateral agreements,[268] or indeed an obligation to apply principles of equity in the apportionment of debt,[269] without supposing that what is eventually decided would immediately follow from the fact of succession itself.

---

[264] Zemanek above, n 73, p 190 (State succession 'takes place when a legally relevant event causes acts of government in a given territory to be attributed to a subject of international law other than that to which they were attributed before the event'.).

[265] For the ILC's emphasis upon State practice see below pp 114–15.

[266] ILC, 'Nationality of Natural Persons in Relation to the Succession of States', 54 GAOR, Supp no 10 (A/54/10). GA Resn 55/153, 12th Dec 2000, Annex (art 1).

[267] eg art 14, Vienna Convention 1983.

[268] eg art 17, Vienna Convention 1978.

[269] eg art 40 and 41, Vienna Convention 1983.

Despite the evident benefits accruing from the separation of the two sets of issues in this way, there are certain obvious problems. The first difficulty is that if, as would seem to be inevitable, there is no immediate connection between the events giving rise to a case of 'succession', and the legal consequences that are to follow therefrom, there seems to be no clear rationale as to why one designated 'successor' State should assume certain rights and obligations, and not another. Nor, it may be said, are we given any explanation as to why some forms of 'succession' are thought to differ from others. To insist that certain events are classified under the terms of international law as giving rise to a succession of States (the fact, that is, not the consequence) without some consideration as to what the consequences of that assertion might be, appears to be predicated either upon a terminal uncertainty, or upon an unspoken supposition that the consequences themselves are self-evident.

A second difficulty, here, is that the analysis appears to work on the supposition not only that the facts precede their consequences (in both a temporal and conceptual sense) but also that those facts are primarily events extraneous to law (law 'responding' to those events in particular ways, but not being implicated in the events themselves). If it were the case, by contrast, that the terms of succession (the legal consequences) were to impinge upon the 'political' processes that gave rise to the events in question (the 'facts' upon which those consequences depend), the entire domain would fall into self-justification: the reason for the application of a particular rule, being dependent upon the existence of the rule itself.

Whatever dangers this form of self-referential argument may pose for the endeavour, it is a problem that appears difficult to avoid. The claim, for example, that Serbia-Montenegro was the continuation of the former Socialist Federal Republic of Yugoslavia was hard to separate from the obvious consequences of that assertion. The claim itself may generally be regarded as having been inspired by a range of ethno-nationalist, historical, or contextual factors (including, perhaps, an assertion as to where moral or political responsibility for the conflict in Yugoslavia ultimately lay) but it is also hard to ignore the possibility that issues such as access to international institutions and the resources at their disposal, entitlement to overseas property, or liability for international delicts, may also have had some influence here. The rules of succession, which apparently merely concern the consequences of such processes of political change, may thus have had significance for how, and in what way, the protagonists presented those changes, or comprehended their own identities within that process. Koskenniemi notes, in that regard, that the law of State succession seems to provide, 'a conceptual matrix by which one could reproduce in legal terms and in regard to legal relationships the ideas of transformation, collapse, and renewal that lie at the heart of the new political consciousness'.[270]

---

[270] Koskenniemi (Rep), above, n 31, p 66. See also, D Kennedy, 'Turning to Market Democracy. A Tale of Two Architectures', 32 Harv ILJ (1991) 373.

To be a 'successor State', in other words, is to project a certain history or political identity, to insist upon the radical character of change, and to posit a dissociation between the 'present' order of affairs, and that which pertained in the past. The language of succession, in other words, might be such as to generate a unique knowledge of the events in question in such a way as to prevent them being understood as merely 'external' impulses to be received in unmediated form. If that is the case, Hall's suggestion that 'personality' is the key to succession, may be understood to be less of an observation as to the facts, and rather more a prescription for making it so.

c) Continuity and Succession

As the discussion above suggests, traditional approaches to State succession seem to insist upon two relatively contradictory assertions: first that a differentiation must be made between incidents that involve a change in sovereignty and those that do not, for reason that their legal effects are clearly different (the former demanding a justification for legal continuity as a consequence of change, the latter a justification for non-continuity by reference to that change). The second assertion is that the incidents in question are to be contemplated in isolation from, and prior to, the consequences they are to bring to bear upon existing legal relations (succession de facto preceding succession *de iure*). In effect, the first assertion assumes that the consequences determine the event; the second that the event determines the consequences.

At the outset, this relationship between causes and their consequences may be understood by way of recourse to the distinction, often referred to as 'fundamental',[271] between State continuity and State succession. The distinction here, turns upon whether a State may be said to have survived certain changes in its condition, or whether, by contrast, it has 'died' and another State has taken its place. Marek describes the 'practical importance' of this question as follows:

The rights and duties of the new State will initially be derived exclusively from customary international law. The new State will not be internationally responsible for what has taken place on its territory prior to its birth. Its population and frontiers will be undefined and doubtful, pending a final delimitation by way of international agreements. On the other hand, an old State will naturally enough continue to bear its international rights and duties both customary and conventional. It will enjoy the same international status defined by both customary and conventional international law. Its territory and population will remain the same, except in the case of changes which, relating precisely to territory and population, leave the personality of the State unaffected. It will be subject to all legal duties and it will be entitled to claim all legal rights arising out of agreements to which it has been a party. It may be held internationally responsible for what has occurred on its territory....[272]

[271] Crawford, above, n 131, p 667.
[272] Marek, above, n 211, p 2.

In a case of continuity, in other words, it is assumed that there is no succession – no reason for invocation of rules of succession to justify continuity of legal relations – and that legal adjustments to the changing environment would only possibly occur through resort to the general principles of peaceful change (eg *rebus sic stantibus*, necessity, impossibility of performance). In case of succession, by contrast, the 'successor State' will be regarded *prima facie*, as a third party in respect of any pre-existent legal relationships that were associated with the territory subject to succession, and would assume rights and responsibilities only in virtue of consent or by way of a rule of succession.

When seen in this light, the ideas of continuity and succession appear fundamentally opposed.[273] It is clear, nevertheless, that the issue of succession does not merely arise where there is no State continuity. Continuity and succession may evidently be compatible in certain circumstances. On the one hand the category of 'secession', for example, works on the assumption that territorial change does not automatically affect the continuity of the State[274] but clearly gives rise to questions of succession on the part of the seceding entity. One might dispute the logic of this: the secession of territory would nearly always affect the scope of a predecessor State's legitimate claim to territorial sovereignty. The legal identity of Britain before and after the granting of independence to British India was clearly different – in terms, for example, as to what incidents might be thought to threaten its independence or territorial integrity, or as to what action it might take internationally in defence of its legitimate interests. But it is equally evident that in such a case, as in most other cases of 'secession', the 'continuity' of the predecessor State was never called into question in terms of its other legal relationships with the wider world. On the other hand, there may be cases in which a 'continuing State' is simultaneously regarded as a successor. Thus, in case of the 'cession' of the Saar to Germany in 1957, or West Irian to Indonesia in 1962, there was no question that the identity of Germany and Indonesia would be affected by such transfers. They were, however, both potential successors to obligations assumed in relation to those territories by France and the Netherlands respectively.[275] Similarly, the position adopted by Germany in respect of its unification in 1990 was that the Federal Republic of Germany continued its legal identity for international purposes, but that it would succeed to certain rights and obligations of the German Democratic Republic, the territory of which had been absorbed within it.[276]

---

[273] cf Koskenniemi, for example, notes that '[i]f there is identity, then the entity "continues" the rights and obligations of its predecessor – or better, there is no "predecessor" but merely a temporal distinction between the same entity as it was "then" and as it is "now" '. (Koskenniemi, above, n 31, p 120).

[274] eg Marek, above, n 211, p 15; Kunz, above, n 134, 68, pp 71–6; Kelsen, above, n 209, pp 260–4.

[275] O'Connell, above, n 92, pp 41–2.

[276] See below, pp 219–23.

Although the continuity of a State's legal identity may be perfectly compatible with it also being regarded as a successor State, it nevertheless has importance in two different respects. First, the idea of continuity serves to distinguish between those forms of change that do give rise to succession (in virtue of the extinction of the State), and those that do not. Thus, a change in government, albeit of a revolutionary character, has traditionally not been thought to affect the continuity of the State, and hence not give rise to questions of State succession.[277] The same may be said of belligerent occupation and other occupations of putatively 'unlawful' nature.[278] Secondly, the notion of continuity structures the law of succession in a way that requires different scenarios to be treated in a distinct manner. Here, it gives rise to the traditional distinction between 'total' and 'partial' succession: the former occurring in cases in which the predecessor ceases to exist, the latter in cases in which it may continue, albeit in diminished form.[279] The idea of continuity, therefore, serves to differentiate between a case of cession (or secession)[280] and one of dismemberment,[281] between a case of absorption (or annexation) and one of union,[282] and between the birth of a new State and its resurrection.[283]

i) *The Point of Differentiation*

For all the apparent significance of the distinctions adverted to here, it has become very clear that such forms of differentiation raise more questions than

[277] Grotius, above, n 85, Bk II, c xvi, p 418. See also, Pufendorf, above, n 85, B VIII, c xii, s1, p 1360; Zouche, above, n 134, pt II, s II, 7, 63; Wolff, above, n 134, c II, s 243, p 123; Bluntschli, above, n 85, II, c 3, s 39, p 76; Bynkershoek, above, n. 134, II, 25; Rivier, above, n 93, I, p 62; de Martens, above, n 111, p 362; Westlake, above, n 105, I, p 58; Oppenheim, above, n 134, pp 106, 115; Hall, above, n 33, p 22; Anzilotti, above, n 134, Q Wright, 'The Status of Germany and the Peace Proclamation', 46 AJIL (1952) 299, p 307; A McNair, 'Aspects of State Sovereignty' BYIL (1949) p 8; Crawford, above, n 131, p 678; Kunz, above, n 134, p 97; Jennings and Watts, above, n 39, p 146; Feilchenfeld, above, n 92, pp 609–11; Marek, above, n 211, pp 24–51. See also, *US-Ecuador Mixed Commission* 17 Aug 1865 (the Mechanic affair); *US-Venezuela* 1865 (the Day affair); *The Sapphire Napoleon III*, 78 US 164 (1871); *Franco-Chilean Arbitral Tribunal* 7 Jul 1901 (PCA, 11 Oct 1921); *State v Dosso* (Pakistan SC 1958) 27 ILR 22 per CJ Mohamed Munir; *Tinoco Arbitration* 18 Oct 1923 (per Taft CJ), 18 AJIL (1924) 154; *Ottoman Debt Arbitration*, 4 Apr 1925 (per Borel) AD 1925/6, Case no 57; *Roselius and Co v. Karsten and the Turkish Republic (intervening)* Dist Ct of Amsterdam, 21 June, 1926, AD 1925/26, Case no 26, p 35; *Government of France v Isbrandtsen-Moller Co Inc* 48 F Supp 631; *US v Curtiss Wright Export Corp* and ors 299 US (1936) 304, p 316 (J Sutherland); *Trans-Orient Marine Corp v Star Trading and Marine* 731 F Supp 619 (SDNY 1990), affd, 925 F2d 566 (2d Cir 1991); *Carl Marks & Co Inc v USSR* 665 F Supp 323 (SDNY 1987), aff'd, 841 F 2d 26 (2d Cir), 487 US 1219 (1988).

[278] See, Stern, above, n 26, pp 90–1; G Guyomar, 'La Succession d'Etats et le respect de la volonté des populations', *RGDIP* (1963) 93.

[279] eg Fiore, above, n 114; Udokang, above n 125, pp 120–1; Jennings and Watts, above, n 39, p 209.

[280] YBILC (1974), vol II, at 263–6.

[281] eg Austria-Hungary in 1918, see K Marek, n 211, pp 205–10; Federation of Mali, see R Cohen 'Legal Problems arising from the Dissolution of the Mali Federation, 36 BYIL (1960) 375.

[282] eg Yugoslavia 1918, see, Marek, above, n 211, pp 237–62; UAR (1958), E Cotran, 'Some Legal Aspects of the Formation of the United Arab Republic and the United Arab States', 8 ICLQ (1959) 346.

[283] Kunz, above, n 134, 68.

they answer, and that those who continue to employ them do so with a certain hesitancy.[284] Brownlie, for example, suggests that:

> the general categories of 'continuity' and 'State succession', and the assumption of a neat distinction between them, only make a difficult subject more confused by masking the variation of circumstance and the complexities of the legal problems which arise in practice. 'Succession' and 'continuity' are levels of abstraction unfitted to dealing with specific issues. Thus the view that Italy was formed not by union of other States with Sardinia, but by annexation to Sardinia, has the corollary that this was a case of continuity and not, with respect to Sardinia, a State succession. Yet one may wonder if the difference in political procedure should make such a great legal difference.[285]

To Brownlie's example several others might be added: it was never entirely clear whether the Dual Monarchy of Austria-Hungary in 1919 was dissolved or continued to exist in the separate identities of Austria and Hungary.[286] Nor was it clear whether the formation of Yugoslavia had been produced through the absorption of new territories into Serbia or through the creation of an entirely new State.[287] Nor indeed was it clear whether, during the period of union within the United Arab Republic, 'Syria' continued to exist as an independent State.[288] Far from being factual categories whose certainty could at any stage be taken for granted, the ideas of continuity and succession evidently remained wholly disputable.

A recent, and particularly marked, dispute on this point arose in respect of the contrasting approaches adopted in relation to the USSR and the SFRY. In case of the collapse of the Soviet Union, Russia adopted the view, almost from the outset, that it represented the continuation of the 'former' USSR.[289] President Yeltsin thus wrote to the UN Secretary General in December 1991 declaring that membership of the USSR in UN organs was 'being continued by the Russian Federation (RSFSR) with the support of the countries of the Commonwealth of Independent States'.[290] This was confirmed by a Decision of the Council of Heads of State of the Commonwealth of Independent States of 21 December 1991.[291] Whilst the two agreements relating to the dissolution of the USSR were less than univocal on the point (the Minsk accord of 8th December 1991 declared that

[284]   eg Stern, above, n 26, p 40; W Czaplinski, 'La continuité, l'identité et la succession d'Etats', RBDI (1993) 374.

[285]   Brownlie, above, n 27, pp 80–1.

[286]   eg O'Connell, above, n 92, p 4; Crawford, above, n 131, (1st edn 1979) p 404; Feilchenfeld, above, n 92, p 435; Marek, above, n 211, p 204; T Baty, 'Division of States: Its Effect on Obligations', 9 Grot Soc trans (1924) 119.

[287]   Marek, above, n 211, pp 239–44.

[288]   R Young, 'The State of Syria: Old or New?', 56 AJIL (1962) 482.

[289]   R Mullerson, 'The Continuity and Succession of States by Reference to the Former USSR and Yugoslavia', ICLQ (1993) 473; id *International Law, Rights and Politics* (1994) pp 140–5; Y Blum, 'Russia Takes over the Soviet Union's Seat at the United Nations', 3 EJIL (1992) 354.

[290]   31 ILM (1992) 138.

[291]   id, p 151 (in which it declared that 'the States of the Commonwealth support Russia's continuance of the membership of the Union of Soviet Socialist Republics in the United Nations, including permanent membership of the Security Council, and other international organizations'.).

the USSR 'as a subject of international law and a geopolitical reality no longer exists', and the Alma Ata accord of 21st December proclaimed that 'with the establishment of the Commonwealth of Independent States' the USSR 'ceases to exist')[292] no serious objection was ever raised. Russia was allowed, therefore, to continue the membership of the USSR in all major international organizations, and continued its participation in multilateral agreements and took primary responsibility for the outstanding debts of the Soviet Union as a whole.[293] Several other States, such as Finland[294] and the UK,[295] also made explicit their acceptance of this continuity thesis.[296]

In a sharply contrasting case, Serbia and Montenegro's claim to be the continuation of the former Socialist Federal Republic of Yugoslavia was opposed on a broad front. Serbia and Montenegro (known at the time as the 'Federal Republic of Yugoslavia') persisted in the view throughout the 1990s, that the four Republics emerging from the conflict in the former Yugoslavia had effectively seceded from the Federation, leaving it as a 'rump State' continuing the identity of the Federation. The other Republics (Croatia, Bosnia-Herzegovina, Macedonia and Slovenia) by contrast, regarded the conflict as bringing about the dissolution of the Federation such that Serbia-Montenegro was to be considered a successor State alongside the others. Unlike the case of the USSR, there was no mutual agreement (however equivocal) on the point. Other participants in the debate appeared to take the position of the four Republics. Thus, in 1991, the Yugoslav Arbitration Commission (the Badinter Commission) took the view that the SFRY was 'in the process of dissolution' in virtue of the lack of participation of the various Republics in the Federal government. This process was later declared to have been completed in an opinion of 18th May 1992 and the SFRY was pronounced to be no longer in existence.[297] Subsequent to the early opinions of the Badinter Commission in this respect, organs of the UN adopted a similar line. On the 19 September 1992 the Security Council adopted Resolution 777 (1992) in which it noted that 'the State formerly known as the Socialist Federal Republic of Yugoslavia has ceased to exist', and recommended

---

[292] 'Agreement Establishing the Commonwealth of Independent States (Minsk Accord)', 8 Dec 1991, 31 ILM (1992) 143; Alma Ata Declaration, 21 Dec 1991, id, p 148.

[293] In a communication to the UN Secretary General on 24th Dec 1991, it was declared that 'the Russian Federation maintains full responsibility for all the rights and obligations of the USSR under the Charter of the United Nations and multilateral treaties deposited with the Secretary-General'. Multilateral Treaties Deposited with the Secretary-General, Status as at 31st Dec 1993, UN Doc ST/Leg/Sere/12, p 4, n 8.

[294] B Broms, 'The Agreement on the Foundations of Relations between the Republic of Finland and the Russian Federation', 3 Finn Yrbk IL (1992) 615, p 620.

[295] Written Reply of the Secretary of State for Foreign and Commonwealth Affairs to a Parliamentary Question, HC Debs, vol 202, WA, col 384, 24th Jan 1992, quoted in 'UK Materials on International Law', 63 BYIL (1992) pp 639, 652–5.

[296] For a critique see T Schweisfurth, 'Von Einheitsstaat (UdSSR) zum Staatenbund (GUS)', 52 ZaöRV (1992) 541.

[297] Badinter Commission, Opinions 9 and 10, 31 ILM (1992) 1524, 1526.

therefore that Serbia and Montenegro should be precluded from participation in the General Assembly and be called upon to apply for membership in the UN afresh.[298] The General Assembly responded, in Resolution 47/1, by noting that under such conditions Serbia and Montenegro 'cannot continue automatically the membership of the former Socialist Federal Republic of Yugoslavia in the United Nations' and that participation would be contingent upon it applying for membership as a new State.[299] The difficulty, however, as the UN Legal Counsel noted, was that this effectively only prevented Serbia-Montenegro from 'partici- pating' in the UN, but neither terminated nor suspended Yugoslav membership in the organization.[300] As the ICJ was later to note, Serbia-Montenegro appeared to retain a *sui generis* status in respect of UN membership which was only subsequently remedied by its eventual capitulation to the request of the General Assembly when it applied for membership as a new State in 2000.[301] Whilst the approach of the international community to the case of Serbia-Montenegro gave rise to a lively academic discussion (particularly when it was compared to the case of Russia), the significance of the issue was never disputed. Not only did the issue of continuity appear to have significance for membership in international organ- isations, but also for sundry other questions such as responsibility for debt, title to assets,[302] and participation in multilateral agreements.[303]

The contrasting approach to the dissolution of the USSR and that of the SFRY highlighted both the delicacy of the issue, and the absence of any obvious methods of determination. A highly illuminating correspondence in the American Journal of International Law in response to an argument proffered by Blum captures many of the idiosyncrasies of legal argumentation on the questions of identity, continuity, and succession. In his brief note,[304] Blum had argued that the Federal Republic of Yugoslavia had been unjustly excluded from participation in the United Nations and that the weight of practice in case of secession (British India, Pakistan, Bangladesh and the Soviet Union) pointed towards the existence of a right to continued membership on the part of the 'rump State':

In contradistinction to the case of Russia, it cannot be reasonably maintained that, as a result of the events that unfolded in Yugoslavia after June 1991, that country ceased to

---

[298] SC Resn 777 (1992), 19 Sep 1992.

[299] GA Resn 47/1, 47 GAoR, A9 Idem 8, UN Doc A/47/L1 and Add 1 (1992).

[300] UN Doc A/47/485 (29 Sept 1992).

[301] ICJ Rep 2003, 7, p 23, para 50 ('The admission of the FRY to membership of the United Nations on 1 November 2000 put an end to Yugoslavia's *sui generic* position within the United Nations'.).

[302] A Stanic, 'Financial Aspects of State Succession: The Case of Yugoslavia', 12 EJIL (2001) 751; G Acquaviva, 'The Dissolution of Yugoslavia and the Fate of its Financial Obligations', 30 Denv JILP (2002) 93.

[303] eg Resolution VII 30 of the Conference of Contracting Parties to the Convention on Wetlands (1999) (calling upon the Federal Republic of Yugoslavia to submit to the Depositary a notification of succession to the Ramsar Convention). This elicited a response from the FRY in a letter of 1st Sept 1999 declaring the resolution null and void and asserting that the FRY continued to be a contracting party to the Ramsar Convention.

[304] Y Blum, 'UN Membership of the "New" Yugoslavia: Continuity or Break?', 86 AJIL (1992) 830.

exist as a subject of international law. Following the secession of four of the six constituent republics, the two remaining republics of the old federation have continued to assert the continuity of Yugoslavia, albeit in shrunken form. On April 27, 1992, this truncated Yugoslavia adopted a new constitution preserving the name Yugoslavia and its flag (without the red star of the Communist era). The territory of rump Yugoslavia (102,000 square kilometres) comprises 40 per cent of the territory of the old Yugoslavia and its population (10.5 million) is 45 per cent of that of the old Yugoslavia.

Thus, by any objective yardstick – whether factual or legal – it is difficult to deny 'the Belgrade authorities' the right to occupy the seat of Yugoslavia at the United Nations, however reprehensible their policies may seem to some – or even the overwhelming majority – of the Organization's members.[305]

Blum's argument itself was by no means utterly compelling. To begin with, his assertion that four of the six republics had 'seceded' leaving the rump Yugoslavia intact seemed, in light of the Badinter Commission's observations otherwise, more of a conclusion than an argument. The question of secession, after all, was the point in contention. Secondly, his 'factual' indices do little more than revert back to the kind of semi-tautological assertions associated with the idea that a State's identity is not affected unless the territorial change is 'quantitatively very considerable' or if it relates to 'an essential portion of the old State'. These, as Kunz suggested long ago, merely tell us that 'territorial changes do not affect the identity of the State, except when they do'.[306] Blum, nevertheless, had posed a question which seemed to require some kind of principled response.

In the next edition of the Journal, three responses to Blum's argument were published by Degan,[307] Bring[308] and Malone,[309] each of whom sought to refute the argument by different means. Degan argued that Blum had failed to take appropriate cognisance of the opinions of the Badinter Commission which, in its Opinion No 8, had concluded that 'the SFRY no longer exists' and that, accordingly, the FRY was to be regarded as a new State whose existence required recognition.[310] Malone contended that the main distinction between the cases of Russia and Serbia-Montenegro was the existence of an agreement in the case of the former, and its absence in the latter. The de facto termination of the Yugoslav federal structure extinguished the legal personality of an internationally recognized entity and, without an agreement, Serbia-Montenegro had 'no basis to claim a right superior to that of its sibling states' (as Russia had in the case of the USSR).[311] Bring argued that there was effect-

---

[305] ibid, p 833.
[306] Kunz, above, n 134, p 72.
[307] 'Correspondents' Agora: UN Membership of the Former Yugoslavia', 87 AJIL (1993) 240.
[308] ibid, 244.
[309] ibid, 246.
[310] Opinion no 10, para 5. 31 ILM (1992) 1525, p 1526.
[311] Above, n 309, p 247. Interestingly enough Malone effectively asserts that Russia was a successor State, but was nevertheless, in consequence of agreement between members of the CIS, allowed 'to continue membership in the Organization despite the inexistence of the Soviet Union'.

ively 'no operative principle for determining when there is continuity and when succession' and that the matter was therefore to be settled through State practice and an 'evolving *opinio iuris*'.[312] Since no other States had accepted the FRY's claim to continuity, and since it appeared to have been rejected by the United Nations, there was 'not much point in criticizing the outcome of the process as such, since the absence of mandatory legal norms during the process legitimize[d] the result'.[313]

The range and style of these responses and the different conclusions they appear to substantiate, do little more than forefront the evident problems. All insist that an effective distinction may be made between the case of the USSR and that of the SFRY, and that Russia was worthy of being regarded as the continuation of the USSR whereas Serbia-Montenegro was not. None provides, however, any substantive measure by which the two cases may be effectively distinguished (Bring going so far as to suggest that no measure exists). Each author attempts to locate the solution to the problem in a particular idea – institutional practice, recognition policy, judicial decision, or mutual agreement – and each runs up against the limits of those ideas. Institutional practice was clearly equivocal in the case of Yugoslavia. Serbia-Montenegro's status within the United Nations, as the ICJ noted, was thoroughly anomalous: whilst it was formally excluded from participation in various organs of the UN until its admission as a new member state in 2000, no decision had been made to the effect that Yugoslavia's membership in the organization had actually lapsed.[314] This was ultimately to lead to the ICJ putting itself in an embarrassing position by deciding, on the one hand, that it had jurisdiction in relation to the genocide claims advanced by Bosnia against Serbia-Montenegro in 1993,[315] but yet it was incapable of proceeding with the case brought by Serbia-Montenegro against the NATO countries in 1999 by reason of the fact that Serbia-Montenegro was not a member of the United Nations at that moment and hence not a party to the Statute of the Court.[316]

The recognition policy of third States, similarly, was not univocal – although Serbia-Montenegro's claim to continuity was rejected in many institutional *fora*, it neither sought, nor obtained, recognition as a new State, despite the Badinter Commission's intimation that it needed to do so. Even when it acceded to the idea that it was to be regarded as a successor rather than the continuing State, no other States saw fit to offer it recognition as a 'new' State – that conclusion appeared to

[312] Above, n 308, p 244.
[313] ibid, 245.
[314] As the Court noted in the *Legality of the Use of Force* case (ICJ Rep 2004, 279, pp 305–9, paras 65–74) three different positions were taken within the United Nations on the question of the FRY's status within the organization.
[315] ICJ Rep 2007.
[316] ICJ Rep 2004, 279, p 314, para 91. For a review see, M Vitucci, 'Has Pandora's Box been Closed? The Decisions on the *Legality of Use of Force* Cases in Relation to the Status of the Federal Republic of Yugoslavia (Serbia and Montenegro) within the United Nations', 19 Leiden JIL (2006) 105.

flow simply from its admission into the United Nations. Whether, furthermore, its recognition as a successor State was necessary for it to be regarded as one, was a point upon which doctrine concerning recognition was traditionally, and firmly, divided.[317] It is notable that the Badinter Commission itself appeared to waver between the view, on the one hand, that recognition was 'purely declaratory',[318] and on the other, that it also was such as to 'confer' on the entity being recognised 'rights and obligations under international law'.[319] Finally, whilst there was clearly agreement in case of the USSR as regards Russia's claim to continue its membership in the United Nations, it was neither apparent that this represented a *sine qua non*, nor that the absence of an agreement between the parties would necessarily speak against continuity. Bring's contention, then, that there were no operative principles governing the issue appeared fairly close to the mark, even if his conclusion that the outcome effectively 'legitimized' the process was hard to sustain.

ii) From Status to Relations

For all the attention given to the issue in the 1990s, it is apparent that the problems were by no means novel. Indeed O'Connell, writing in the 1960s, was quite clear as to the deficiencies of the received wisdom. He complained that legal doctrine on succession had been derailed by the predominance of Hegelian conceptions of the State, which, from the time of Bluntschli onwards, had placed the issue of identity at the forefront.[320] He argued that from the time at which personality had become the universal touchstone of succession, jurists were forced into the position of assuming that legal relations were generally annulled by change of sovereignty, and that the law of State succession had subsequently 'reached a position of crisis, because evident moral and sociological pressures emphasise the need for continuity and the avoidance of disruption, while theory remains enmeshed in the 19th-century conception of sovereign will'.[321]

O'Connell's particular criticism was directed towards the two-fold distinction 'derived from the post-Hegelian period', between change of sovereignty and change of government on the one hand, and between State continuity and State succession on the other.[322] He was to observe that in many cases the process of

---

[317] Crawford, above, n 131, pp 3–28. (who concludes that (p 28) 'the status of an entity as a State is, in principle, independent of recognition . . . But this conclusion assumes that there exist in international law and practice workable criteria for statehood. If there are no such criteria, or if they are so imprecise as to be practically useless, then the constitutive position will have returned, as it were, by the back door'.).

[318] Opinion no 1, 31 ILM (1992) 1495.

[319] Opinion no 8, 31 ILM, (1992) 1523.

[320] Such an approach, he thought, stood in distinction from the earlier, and better, approach, namely to analyze the effect of change upon the relations concerned, rather than the continuity or otherwise of the parties. O'Connell, above, n 48, p 734.

[321] O'Connell, I, above, n 92, p 34.

[322] ibid, 5. He argues that 'with the abstraction of the concept of sovereignty, however, a conceptual chasm was opened between change of sovereignty and change of government; in the

acquiring independence was a relatively ordered one – preceded by a constitutional devolution of powers and in some cases, a capacity to enter into relations with third States – and concluded that it was absurd to suggest that such cases should be regarded as having a more radical effect than, for example, that which accompanied the revolutionary change of government. Although he did not mention it, no doubt he had in mind the dispute arising as a consequence of the Soviet renunciation of the Tsarist debt in Russia after 1919.[323] For O'Connell, the central issue was not how one might categorize change but of understanding the impact of that change upon existing legal relations: 'If there is any rubric, there-

---

one instance a problem of substitution in the possession of rights and obligations was raised; in the other, continuity of these rights and obligations was presumed in virtue of continuity in the personality of the possessor'. (ibid, at 5–6). This, as Crawford notes, was a departure from his earlier views on the subject. See J Crawford, 'The Contribution of Professor DP O'Connell to the Discipline of International Law', 51 BYIL (1980) 2, p 18. It was presaged in some respects in his earlier work, see, O'Connell, *The Law of State Succession* (1956), p 6.

[323] The Soviet Decree of 28 January 1918 proclaimed: 'All foreign loans are hereby annulled, without reserve or exception of any kind whatsoever'. Quoted by Korovin, 'Soviet Treaties and International Law', AJIL (1928) 763. This was immediately opposed by other States. See Anglo-French joint declaration of 28 Mar 1918: 'aucun principe n'est mieux établi que celui d'après lequel une nation est responsable des actes de son gouvernement, sans qu'un changement d'autorité affecte les obligations encourues; ces engagements ne peuvent être répudiés par aucune autorité quelle qu'elle soit, sans quoi la base même du droit international se trouverait ébranlée', cited in P Fauchille *Traite de Droit International Public* (Rousseau and co, Paris, 1922), I, p 342, n 2. See also communication by British government whilst according *de iure* recognition in 1924, A Toynbee, *Survey of International Affairs* (1924) 491. For US cases, see, Agency of *Canadian Car and Foundary Co. Ltd v American Can Co.* (1918) 253 F 152, aff'd (1919) 258 F 363, AD 1919/22, Case no 14, p 30; *Russian Government v Lehigh Valley Railroad Co* (1919) 293 F 133, aff'd (1927) 21 F 2d. 396 ('The real party in interest is the State of Russia, and that Russia, the State, still lives and is a continuing entity in the contemplation of the law, is true . . .'). British courts assumed continuity (3 AD 35) until *Lazard Bros v. Midland Bank Ltd* [1933] AC 289, 297, 307–8 per Lord Wright. See also *Russian Roubles (Attempted Counterfeiting) Case* (Japan Sup Ct 1919) AD 1919/22, Case no 15, p 31 ('It is of no consequence that Russia internally has been undergoing a political change. The primary consideration is that she has not thereby ceased to exist internationally, as a State'.); *Golovitschiner v Dori* (Cairo Civil Tr, 1923) 1923/24, AD Case no 24 ('Russia, not having been conquered or annexed by a foreign State, has kept her existence as a distinct State'.); *Lowinsky v Receiver in Bankruptcy of the Egyptisch-Türkische Handwerkzigaretten-fabrik 'Jaka' Ltd* (Amsterdam DC 1932) 1931/2, 6 AD no 16 (In conformity with established principle of public international law, changes in the form of government of a State have no influence on its rights and obligations under the Law of Nations so long as its existence as a State and, therefore, as an international person, remains unimpaired. This is the case with the USSR, which has to be looked upon as a sovereign federal State embracing by far the greater part of the territory and the population of the former Russian Empire.'); *N and M Shipoff v Elite,* (Cantonal Court of the Hague) AD 1931/32, Case no 17; *Banque de L'Union Parisienne v Jaudon* (Paris CA 1933) 7 AD no 32; *Weber v USSR* (Amsterdam CA 1942) 11 AD no 74; *In re petition of S* (Hague 1957) 24 ILR 52; *Carl Marks & Co Inc v USSR* 665 F Supp 323 (SDNY 1987), affd, 841 F 2d 26 (2d Cir), 487 US 1219 (1988).

For discussion see O'Connell, (1967) above, n 92, pp 19–20; T Taracouzio, *The Soviet Union and International Law* (1935) pp 21–5, 249–50; Verzijl, above, n 28, p 118; Marek, above, n 211, pp 34–8; Grzybowski, *Soviet Public International Law. Doctrines and Diplomatic Practice* (1970) 92–5; Lagarde, *La Reconnaissance des Soviets*, pp 27–84; P Toma 'Soviet Attitude Towards the Acquisition of Teritorial Sovereignty in the Antarctic', 50 AJIL (1956) 611, pp 614–15; O Lissitzyn, 'Recent Soviet Literature on International Law' 11 American Slavic and East Euroepan Review (1952) 268.

fore, to which one could resort as a touchstone for the solution of all problems of political change over territory it might be this: that the consequences of such change should be measured according to the degree of political, economic and social disruption that occurs'.[324]

Whilst O'Connell did not entirely discard the distinction between succession and continuity,[325] the sense of his thesis may best be perceived in his approach to treaty succession. In that context he argued that the effect of political change (including change of sovereignty) should be determined by existing rules of treaty law rather than by the prior question of 'personality' or 'status'. The 'real question' as he puts it, 'is the extent to which a treaty loses its effectiveness in the changed situation'.[326] In some contexts treaties would survive, in others they would not – much would depend, in that regard, upon the severity of the change in question, and the nature of the agreement in contemplation. Importantly, however, neither the severity of the change nor the nature of the agreement would alone be determinative.

In some respects, O'Connell's critique might be thought to underplay the significance of the question of succession in the political imagination of the protagonists. As Koskenniemi suggests, what the language of succession allows is the articulation in legal terms of the 'character, direction, and limits of political transformation', allowing States to 're-imagine and propagate externally their relationship to the *ancient régime*'.[327] For a State to speak about itself as a 'successor State' or as a 'continuing State' is to provide it with a way in which it can express its own particular view as to its relationship with the past: either one that encourages a neo-natal consciousness as to the distinctiveness of the new order, or one that invests itself in an established tradition, history or culture. Attempting to avoid the issue of status in the law of succession may thus find a significant obstacle in the politics of community identity that may continue to insist upon its significance.

This, however, is perhaps to overstate O'Connell's point. His argument, ultimately, was not such as to change radically the terms of the original debate that structured doctrine relating to State succession. In a general sense, all he does is to erect a presumption that legal relations will continue, and then subject those relations to the possibility of termination on grounds of frustration. Thus, he was to suggest that, '[t]he correct diplomatic stance in modern times is for successor States to serve notice of termination on other parties in respect of those treaties which are no longer useful, and to initiate negotiations for the termination of those which are on their face interminable and which are embarrassing'.[328]

---

[324] O'Connell, above, n 92, I, pp v–vi.
[325] Crawford was to note, once again, that despite O'Connell's critique, the 'traditional structure of the subject was, somewhat precariously, retained'. Crawford, above, n 319, p 20.
[326] O'Connell, above, n 92, II, p 3.
[327] Koskenniemi, above, n 31, pp 66, 68.
[328] O'Connell, above, n 92, II, p 24.

But it is also evident that O'Connell's critique could be developed more broadly than this. His point, in some respects, was that the logic of the early 20th century critique of sovereignty had effectively undercut any obvious insistence upon 'personality' being the key to succession. As he was to put it, personality was not 'a reflection of some prototype sitting on a cloud somewhere, but merely a shorthand expression indicating the faculties of legal action'.[329] If, however, sovereignty merely connoted the 'faculties of legal action', or a 'competence' delegated by a superordinating legal system, then, the ability to distinguish effectively between the 'factual' elements giving rise to a succession of States, and the legal consequences that emanated from those changes (ie between the two different understandings of 'succession'), would become increasingly difficult to articulate.

The problems to which this 'relational' notion of sovereignty give rise are particularly apparent in the work of Krystina Marek. Marek, following Kelsen and Guggenheim, sought to locate the notion of a State's identity in terms of the identity of its legal order. For Marek, however, the 'legal order' of a State comprised not merely the terms of its municipal law, but also the international legal relations (rights and obligations) in which it was embedded. The answer to the question of continuity (understood to be the 'dynamic predicate' of identity) was to be determined, as a consequence, by whether or not those rights and obligations remained relatively constant over time.[330] Despite Marek's own protestation that 'the problem of State identity and continuity bears on the *identity of the subject*' whilst that of succession 'relates to the identity of certain rights and obligations between *different subjects*',[331] the distinction at this point disappears almost entirely. If the continuation of a State is consistent with the continuation of some, but not all, legal relations (by way of *rebus sic stantibus* and associated doctrines), and its discontinuity is equally consistent with the continuation of some, but not all, legal relations (by way of succession), then it becomes remarkably difficult to see how identity may be anything other than a conclusion. If, furthermore, identity is the outcome of decisions *pursuant* to some form of social change, it can no longer be usefully relied upon as an idea that serves to determine the context in which arguments concerning succession may come into play. One is caught, in short, in an essentially circular argument: succession may warrant the continuation of certain rights and obligations in circumstances in which a new State comes into being, but the determination as to whether or not a 'new State' has appeared is dependent upon the continuity of those rights and obligations.

---

[329] D O'Connell argues that: '[t]he concept of "personality" with its Hegelian overtones, seems to have misled the theorists. Modern jurisprudence has assisted us in recognizing that the word "personality" does not stand for something, is not descriptive of anything, and cannot be substituted for by a synonym; it is not, in fact, a reflection of some prototype sitting on a cloud somewhere, but merely a shorthand expression indicating the faculties of legal action'. See O'Connell, 'Independence and Problems of State Succession', in W O'Brien (ed), *The New Nations in International Law and Diplomacy* (1965) 7, at 11.

[330] Marek, above, n 211, p 14 ('The identity of a State is the identity of its international rights and obligations, as before and after the event which called such identity in question, and solely on the basis of the customary norm "pacta sunt servanda".')

[331] ibid, p 10.

Unwittingly enough, however, Marek's argument may appear to lead to a conclusion that is, in some respects, intuitively plausible – that the determination of continuity or succession, in any particular case, operates for the most part *ex post facto* by reference to the acceptance or denial of such assertions on the part of other members of the international community. They are, in that sense, conclusions rather than ideas that initiate enquiry. Koskenniemi observes, in that respect, that:

> We know that the Russian Federation is identical with … the Soviet Union because by and large States and other entities have wished to maintain their old legal relationships with the Soviet Union in force and that the Russian Federation has accepted this. To insist that the transformation has nonetheless been so important to provide no warrant for such a conclusion, or that the States of the Commonwealth of Independent States wrote in the Alma Ata Agreement that the Soviet Union has ceased to exist … is not nonsensical, of course. Such arguments provide relevant reasons for reconsidering the continued validity of old legal relationships. But as stability has returned and old rights and obligations continue to be honoured in practice, there is little point in remaining obsessed by abstract arguments from status.[332]

Koskenniemi's particular criticism, in this respect, was directed towards the assumption that questions of status (State continuity or State succession) should be thought to precede analysis of the consequences of political change. He suggests that, '[t]he view which holds status as prior to relationships thinks of statehood as an autonomous quality possessed by certain entities *ab initio*, prior to and independently of their participation in social life'.[333] This approach, he continues, 'projects a Vattelian domestic analogy that considers States as persons, writ large, and their legal relationships as extensions of their personhood'.[334] Apart from bearing certain 'contestable psychological assumptions' (projecting an idealized, or essentialized, notion of nationhood) this approach, he suggests, also 'undermines the degree to which an entity's "statehood" is constructed in the process of communicative interaction between it and the external world'.[335] When understood as an argument to the effect that identity and difference are primarily relational, and hence incapable of being articulated or maintained as abstract ideas, Koskenniemi's point would seem to be difficult to avoid. By the same token, it is hard to entirely ignore the narratives of identity that protagonists use to justify their positions. However problematic they may be as essentializing (and indeed exclusionary) stories, they nevertheless still enter the debate as a form of justification – even if that is 'through the back door' as Koskenniemi himself puts it.

Thus far, it might be said that problems of identity and status appear both to structure, and be structured by, the law of State succession. As much as

---

[332] Koskenniemi, above, n 31, p 121.
[333] ibid 122.
[334] ibid.
[335] ibid 123.

the distinction between the political matrix of events constituting the idea of succession de facto (or its opposite, 'continuation') and the legal consequences that attend thereto (succession *de iure*) seems to require either the temporal or logical priority of the former, it seems all too evident that they are, in reality, inseparable from the outset. An argument about continuity is always, at the same time, an argument to the effect that certain legal relations will, or will not, be disrupted as a consequence of the change in question. It is thus, not merely an abstract or metaphysical argument about status, but an argument that, at the same time, invokes the implicit consequences (distributional or otherwise) that flow from the fact of succession. There was, thus, nothing accidental about O'Connell's simultaneous dismissal of the categories of identity and continuity and his corresponding advancement of a principle of continuity: the latter *had* to follow the former as otherwise he would be seeking to explain why legal relations may not survive the change. Indeed, his continued advancement of the existence of a law of succession largely proceeded from the fact that he continued to recognize the existence of a residual category of 'personal' obligations that would, indeed, come to an end with a change in sovereignty.

That there is an implicit connection between claims to identity and continuity on the one hand, and the consequences of their denial on the other, is obvious enough. This, after all, was well understood in the context of the debates concerning Serbia's claims to continuity and the effect of its denial in the context of UN membership. But there is a more important point to recognize here: namely that the *meaning* of identity or continuity, or what it appears to *signify*, is largely constituted in its denial. Its importance is determined, in other words, by what consequences seem to flow from the inability to maintain those claims (or from the refusal to admit continuity).

5. Bedjaoui, O'Connell, and the 'End' of Succession

As suggested above, the posited division between the two notions of succession was, in some degree, a liberating initiative insofar as scholars were not thereafter committed to intuiting any particular conclusions from the mere fact of succession. The discipline was thus able to present, and in some ways internalize, rival accounts of succession or non-succession without any obvious need to prioritize one over the other. The two theses of the 'clean slate' and 'universal succession' were just different (albeit wholly opposed) views as to what the law required and, for some at least, were both applicable albeit in different scenarios. It is difficult to think of any other area of international law in which such polarization has been sustained without it being seen, at the same time, as profoundly ideological.

One key factor that has apparently sustained this toleration of mutually antipathetic approaches to the subject has been the absence of any obvious sense of what is at stake. What does the law of State succession ultimately seek to achieve? Security in possession and the protection of rights? Fulfilment of legitimate expectations? The promotion of stability and avoidance of conflict? The promotion of autonomy and independence? All of these, and more, are likely candidates but their very multiplicity makes the identification of any particular orientation hard to discern, let alone be generative of any prescriptive conclusions.

The preamble to the Vienna Convention of 1983 relating to Property, Archives, and Debts makes interesting reading in that respect. It begins by noting the 'profound transformation of the international community brought about by the decolonization process' and that 'other factors' may lead to cases of succession of States in the future, and continues by emphasising the 'need for the codification and progressive development' of the rules relating to succession '*as a means for ensuring greater juridical security in international relations*', [emphasis added]. Here, at least, one is given a preliminary sketch – State succession is about 'juridical security'. But of course in the context of political change, juridical security in the landscape of political organization, may really just come to mean 'having some legal rules', or perhaps being clear about what the consequences are of different kinds of political and territorial transformation. Juridical security, for example, could just as easily be achieved by a rule determining that new States should be burdened by a fair portion of the public debt of the predecessor State as it would by a rule that determined that the entirety of that debt should be shouldered by the latter. Juridical security could mean that movable property be divided amongst the various successors in case of the dismemberment of a State, or that it falls to the State wherein it lies. Certainly one could argue that 'security' would not be promoted were a creditor to be left without agents against which a claim for the return of that property could be pursued, but that still leaves open a remarkably broad range of prescriptive options, and does not begin to provide a basis upon which one might determine where the loss or liability should lie.

Something more than the idea of 'juridical security' is clearly needed for purposes of working out the justice of distributional decisions that follow from changes in sovereignty (and it is for this reason that one finds frequent references in the literature to concepts such as 'equity', 'unjust enrichment' or 'vested rights'), but it is equally apparent that the Vienna Convention eschews enunciation of what those principles might be. What one finds, instead, is a set of general principles – consent, good faith, *pacta sunt servanda*, equal rights and self-determination, sovereign equality and independence, respect and observance of human rights – which, when read together, tend to merely to describe the nature of the problem rather than the kind of solution that appears to be demanded. As a principle *pacta sunt servanda* is fine, so long as one knows whose 'pact' it was; self-determination is helpful so long as one knows who or what may be the subject of that determining, or its consequences. But do these really tell us anything much about what to do with the foreign debt of a country that has suffered political dismemberment?

A common point of departure in most discussions of the question is the idea that the maintenance in force of existing legal relationships is a necessary concomitant to the 'international rule of law'. 'Law abhors a vacuum' as O'Connell was apt to remark – an insight which he read as demanding the enunciation of a presumption of continuity of legal relations in case of succession. Many others join O'Connell in this regard.[336] Shachter speaks about the need for security in expectations and the consequential loss of confidence in an international legal system that might be tempted to ignore the political costs of legal commitment;[337] Jenks speaks about how continuity underpins 'cooperation' and 'participation' in the international community,[338] and Makonnen about how it corresponds to a need to 'minimize disruptions in international legal relations'.[339] In all of these kinds of explanation, cosmopolitan virtue or an abstract commitment to the existence of an 'international legal order' is used as a surrogate for saying that those entities emerging from processes of political change should necessarily continue rather than discard legal obligations assumed by predecessor States. But of course, if it were quite so straightforward, it is unlikely that doctrine would have been so continuously and firmly divided.

A sense of what might really be at stake in case of State succession may be usefully explored through examination of a 'debate' conducted at arm's length (or perhaps 'in parallel') within the lecture theatres of the Hague Academy in 1970 between two highly regarded experts on the subject: DP O'Connell and Mohammed Bedjaoui.[340] O'Connell was probably the most prominent of scholars working on the subject of State succession and had, both before and after the publication of his doctoral dissertation in 1956 (written under the guidance of Hersch Lauterpacht), published a slew of articles on succession during the height of decolonization in the 1950s and 1960s[341] resulting in the production of a monumental, two-volume, monograph in 1967[342] which had been extensively relied upon by the ILC in its work on the Succession of States in Respect of Treaties. He had also been involved, during this time, in the work of the

---

[336] Udokang, above, n 125, p 109.

[337] O Schachter, 'State Succession: The Once and Future Law', 33 Va JIL (1993) 253, pp 259, 260.

[338] W Jenks, 'State Succession in Respect of Law-Making Treaties, 29 BYIL (1952) 105, p 108.

[339] Y Makonnen, *International law and the New States of Africa* (1983) pp 137–9.

[340] D O'Connell, 'Recent Problems of State Succession in Relation to New States', 130 Hague Recueil (1970) 95; M Bedjaoui, 'Problèmes Récents de Succession d'Etats dans Les Etats Nouveaux', 130 Hague Recueil (1970) 463.

[341] His works on succession include: D O'Connell, 'State Succession in the British Commonwealth since the Second World War' 26 BYIL (1949) 454; 'Economic Concessions in the Law of State Succession', 27 BYIL (1950) 93; 'Secured and Unsecured Debts in the Law of State Succession' 27 BYIL (1951) 204; 'Change of Sovereignty and the Doctrine of Act of State', 26 Aust LJ (1952–3) 201; 'Independence and Succession to Treaties', 38 BYIL (1962) 84; 'State Succession and Entry into a Composite Relationship', 39 BYIL (1963) 54; 'State Succession and Problems of Treaty Interpretation' 58 AJIL (1964) 41; 'State Succession and the Theory of the State', Grotian Soc Papers (1972) 23.

[342] D O'Connell, *State Succession in Municipal Law and International Law* (1967) I, and II.

International Law Association's Committee on State succession and had been actively involved in advising various governments on such issues.

Despite his undoubted eminence, and despite the very extensive reliance upon his work as a source of State practice, O'Connell's ultimate influence upon the substantive conclusions of the ILC was largely negligible and must have been a source of some academic discomfort. Bedjaoui, by contrast, had written his doctoral dissertation on *Law and the Algerian Revolution in 1961*[343] and, as one of a new breed of scholars emerging from the developing world, came to assume a position of responsibility within the ILC as Rapporteur on the topic of 'Succession of States in Respect of Matters other than Treaties'. His academic expertise, on this score, judged by reference to his published output, was by no means equivalent to that of O'Connell, but it was evident that he brought a particular perspective to the issue that contrasted sharply with that of other international lawyers in the West.

Quite unusually, both O'Connell and Bedjaoui had been asked to present lectures on precisely the same topic. Even if, as Bedjaoui suggested, there might have been an intended division of labour (with Bedjaoui looking at the problems facing States emerging from decolonization, and O'Connell dealing with the problems facing the metropolitan powers)[344] this was neither a plausible way of approaching the issue, nor was it descriptive of the two accounts that were eventually produced. What was even more surprising, in retrospect at least, was the choice of protagonists. O'Connell was known, at the time, in large part for his advocacy of a general presumption of legal continuity in case of decolonization,[345] and had advanced in his 1956 monograph,[346] the idea that this could be achieved in large measure by resort to the doctrine of acquired rights.[347] Bedjaoui, for his

---

[343] M Bedjaoui, *Law and the Algerian Revolution* (1961).
[344] Bedjaoui, above, n 338, p 467.
[345] This, he made clear was a new departure. See eg, O'Connell, 'Independence' above, n 329, p 86.
[346] O'Connell, above, n 66 and n 340.
[347] Ibid. O'Connell essentially divided the subject of succession into two parts: on one side was the question of succession in respect of treaties which he largely took to be a question of 'treaty law and interpretation' (p 15), on the other side was the question of acquired rights under which heading was included concession, contracts, property, and debt. He explains the doctrine in the following way:

Should the predecessor State have borrowed money . . . two things are created. There is, first, the juridical link between the parties, which exists until either the money is repaid or the State itself has disappeared. There is, secondly, the factual situation which consists in the actual detention by the State of money in which the lender has an equitable interest. When the debtor State is superseded, the legal duty to repay this money is not inherited *ipso facto* by its successor. What is 'inherited' is the state of facts which the now extinguished legal relationship has brought about. The equitable interest which the lender has in this factual situation is described variously as an 'acquired right', 'property right' and 'vested right'. The obligation of the successor State is to respect this interest. It is not an obligation derived from the predecessor, but one imposed *ab exteriore* by international law. It arises when the successor, through its own action in extending its sovereignty, becomes competent to destroy the title-holder's interest. The general principle in which this obligation is embodied, and which underlies the whole problem of State succession, is the principle that acquired rights must be respected.

O'Connell, 1956, above, n 66, p 78 [footnotes omitted].

part, had launched a coruscating attack on the doctrine of acquired rights in his second report to the ILC in 1969,[348] castigating those who defended it, as purveyors of a dubious neo-colonialist enterprise. Bedjaoui and O'Connell, thus, had two very different ideas as to what the international law of State succession should look like, and two very different understandings as to the significance of decolonization for international law.

For Bedjaoui, the central task was that of reforming what he saw to be 'traditional international law' – a tradition that had actively participated, through various doctrinal techniques, in the colonization of Africa and Asia (the standard of civilization, the concept of *terra nullius*, and the authorization of annexation),[349] and which, in the context of decolonization, seemed intent upon perpetuating relations of dependence. The doctrine of acquired rights, in particular, appeared to be fundamentally antipathetic to the realities of decolonization. One could not insist, he suggested, that newly independent States were obliged to honour pre-existent concession agreements allowing foreign corporations to continue to exploit the natural resources of newly independent States, without at the same time placing those States in a condition of continued bondage (as 'probationary' or 'proletarian' States).[350] For O'Connell, by contrast, decolonization was largely an ephemeral or transitional problem – a problem which, at the time of the debate, appeared to have largely run its course – and any undue focus upon the issue would merely obscure the fact that State succession was fundamentally a philosophical, not a political, problem.[351] If thus, Bedjaoui set himself against an imperial tradition that he believed to be represented in the work of O'Connnell, O'Connell set himself against the sort of pointless special pleading that appeared in the work of Bedjaoui.

But there was more to this debate than oppositional rhetoric: here one could also find two finely tuned articulations as to the relative significance of decolonization (and hence, colonialism before it) for the theory and practice of international law. For O'Connell, the issue of decolonization was to be seen as part and parcel of the broader issue of succession. Decolonization, per se, was not interesting, but only as a transitory instance of the more general issue of political change. Any territorial change posed a set of problems for international lawyers that required addressing, and decolonization was no more or less significant in

---

[348] M Bedjaoui, 'Succession of States and Governments: Succession in Respect of Matters other than Treaties', UN Doc A/CN4/216/Rev 1, Yrbk ILC, 1969, II, p 69.

[349] Bedjaoui, above, n 340, pp 471–6.

[350] ibid 470.

[351] O'Connell, 'Recent Problems', above, n 340, p 102 ('The grant of independence to many colonial territories has focused the attention of contemporary international lawyers upon the topic of State succession, but there has been too little recognition on their part of the vast intellectual issues raised by the problem . . . Indeed, one might go further and suggest that never before has international legal scholarship been so barren of philosophical reflection, or so preoccupied with the ephemeral, as it is today.').

that respect.[352] For O'Connell, the ways in which the issue had been traditionally addressed – through on the one hand, theories of the State or notions of State
sovereignty, or on the other by drawing conclusions from extant State practice –
were either too speculative, too reliant upon a redundant metaphysics, or (in the
case of State practice) too inconclusive.[353] The answer, for him, was to view the
question as one of legal philosophy; and it was only through an understanding of
the nature of law that one could grasp the solution to problems of succession.[354]

For O'Connell, therefore, the central problem was related to the survival of the
legal system in time of radical change. Like Kelsen, Verdross, and many others,
he believed that such survival could neither be secured by municipal law itself,
nor by an international law predicated upon State consent. Both were variants of
a kind of boot-straps' argument in which the ultimate 'source of obligation' was
entirely opaque.[355] Rather, it came as a consequence of what he took to be the
social nature of man and the metaphysical character of human society:

> Although the State is the traditional mechanism for the completion of man's social
> nature, the plurality of States finds its existential perfection in the order of the community
> of nations, in the subordination of individual States to the common good of mankind,
> in which political life finds its ultimate terminus. Unless all States are able to place
> minimal reliance upon durable principles of mutual intercourse, the common good,
> which alone gives normative value to human relationships, is apt to be defeated. There
> is, therefore, a sphere of rights and duties that exist, not because States have invented
> or even recognized them, but because they arise immediately from man's social nature
> and personal dignity.... They find their concrete expression in the actual forms of
> inter-State relationships as they may from time to time be contrived, but because they
> are intrinsically antecedent to the State they constitute an objective limitation upon
> sovereignty.[356]

The necessity of protecting, in the interests of the 'greater good of mankind', the
expectations of other States and peoples, necessarily suggested that the central
principle was that of 'minimal disturbance of existing legal situations, consistent
with the actual state of affairs resulting from a succession of States'.[357] It had
to be presumed, in other words, that all law and legal titles that preceded independence would continue in force at least until the time at which they came

---

[352] ibid 103.
[353] He offers the following on State practice (Ibid 117):
The truth of the matter is that this 'practice' is likely to consist of decisions taken by public officials who have not achieved the necessary intellectual penetration of the problem to perceive the
true issues, who may be more influenced by political or other ephemeral considerations than by
juristic logic, who may even be ignorant of the nature of the problem, or of its ramifications, or who
may be equipped with obsolescent literature, or even no literature whatever. Some of the processes
of decision-making respecting matters of State succession that have occurred in recent years can
hardly be dignified as significant contributions to the elaboration of the law.
[354] ibid 119.
[355] ibid, 122–131.
[356] ibid, 119.
[357] ibid 120.

to be repealed.[358] Legal continuity thus preceded sovereignty, and sovereignty could only thus mean a competence or right of decision in relation to the array of legal relations that were already in place. It followed that newly independent States were obliged to respect 'acquired rights'[359] – including the rights of non-nationals under contract or under the terms of concession agreements that had been concluded prior to decolonization,[360] and this extended also to rights arising from torts committed by the predecessor State or obligations to third parties in respect of localized debt.[361] Ultimately, O'Connell was to conclude that there were very few rights and obligations, whether of a strictly municipal or international nature, that did not pass or continue in case of decolonization.

Bedjaoui, by contrast, saw the process of decolonization to be a very particular one – one that differed in many respects from the other older cases of succession in Europe. Decolonization concerned the acquisition of independence of underdeveloped States whose exercise of self-determination had radically re-shaped the economic and political tenor of international law. Whereas formerly international law was a system of law whose content was European, Christian, mercantilist, and imperial, it had been replaced by a system that resisted modes of domination or subordination under the banner of liberty, equality, and universality, in which the principles of self-determination and permanent sovereignty over natural resources were of utmost importance. In that context, the law of State succession had to be similarly re-shaped: the doctrine of acquired rights had to be discarded as an institution of the old imperial order, and newly decolonized States had to be regarded as entirely free to choose whether to honour existing contracts or concessions, whether to recognize the torts of a predecessor State and whether to confer upon those within its territory the benefits of nationality. The character of the right, whether of a public or private nature, mattered little; the ultimate test of continuity was simply whether the continuance of the relationship in question was in the interests of the successor State concerned.

In many senses the difference between the two was a matter of emphasis: where O'Connell saw continuity, Bedjaoui saw change. What Bedjaoui took to be a seminal example – such as the Congolese denunciation of the concession rights of the Belgian Union Minière, or the Zambian rejection of the claims of the British South African Mining Company – O'Connell took to be an exception. As O'Connell explained it, these were isolated instances in which putatively private corporations had been endowed with what was effectively public

---

[358] He comments (ibid, p 141): 'If successor States are to be released from all obligations relating to the interests created by the antecedent legal system, this can only be by virtue of the total evaporation of all law and all titles in the territory affected by change of sovereignty. It is not only the predecessor and successor States or private individuals which would be affected if such a philosophy were to prevail, but the whole community of nations, which has a vested interest in political, social and economic stability'.

[359] ibid 134–46.

[360] ibid, 155–61.

[361] ibid, 162–5.

authority (in the case of the Union Minière, this involved the right to 'appropriate land by police action, exploit it, colonize it at the expense of the native population'; in the case of the British South African Mining Company the right to royalties from all other mining companies).[362] For Bedjaoui, however, they were exemplary of the extractive or exploitative character of colonial rule. Similarly, when O'Connell emphasized the progressive, or evolutionary character of many cases of decolonization,[363] Bedjaoui emphasized the violent disruptive nature of many others. For every case in which O'Connell cited Ghana, Uganda, or British India, Bedjaoui cited his own examples of Algeria, Vietnam, or the Congo. Each took what they could of the diverse experience of decolonization and used it to polemical effect. Each, however, was equally ambivalent as to the significance of that practice.

It is fairly clear that O'Connnell's account of decolonization was problematic. Whilst Bedjaoui was clearly seeking to revitalize what he saw to be an increasingly discredited tradition, O'Connell seemed oblivious to the ideological overtones of what he was advocating. He was quite content to submit that colonial powers had legitimately disowned any responsibility for the contracts, torts, or financial liabilities of the territories over which they had asserted sovereignty in the late 19th century (such as the British disavowal of liabilities in respect of Burma),[364] but when it came for that process to be reversed, he insisted that all interceding liabilities incurred by the colonial masters would continue to burden the newly emergent States.[365] He was also unhesitant in his reliance upon pre-independence arrangements securing acquired rights (whether through constitutional enactment or devolution agreement) as the raw data upon which his conclusions ultimately depended,[366] and similarly oblivious to the political character of his impassioned philosophy of law. The principles that Bedjaoui took to assume a central role in decolonization – namely the principles of self-determination or of permanent sovereignty over natural resources – gain barely a passing reference.

But just as much as O'Connell's account of decolonization might be taken as one infused with a neo-colonial ideology, so Bedjaoui's might be thought equally problematic. It is Bedjaoui, rather than O'Connell, who takes the job of universalizing international law seriously. Bedjaoui is the one who insists that international law is definitively set against colonial ambition or imperial control. It is he who seeks to legitimize decolonization as a process in and of itself, and quite independently of its consequences. Bedjaoui's denunciation of O'Connell ultimately comes in a startlingly traditional form – questions concerning the status, rights, or obligations of the newly emancipated population are simply questions of sovereignty, or consent: it is for the new government to determine the priorities

---

[362] ibid, 142–3.
[363] Above, n 92, II, p 88 ff.
[364] O'Connell, (1956), above, n 66, pp 151–2.
[365] O'Connell, 'Recent Problems', above, n 338, pp 150–4.
[366] O'Connell, (1967) II, above, n 92, pp 352–73.

of development, or the terms of their relationship with the rest of international society. O'Connell's subsequent critique of the views of those such as Bedjaoui emphasizes the limits of this vision:

compared with the situation before 1914, international law today is intellectually anarchic...the first impediment is the argument that international law, being the product of imperialism and Western statecraft, cannot bind new States that have been emancipated from this environment...

The authors offer no better rationalization of this view than the argument that continued subjugation to this alien imposition is inconsistent with accession to sovereignty....The real point is that the argument superimposes the sovereign State on the structure of international relations instead of integrating it in that structure. It repudiates by implication all metaphysical character in the human community and reduces the latter to Hobbes' state of nature, from which Vattel in the 18th century rescued it. It bases law on will, not on subjection to a rational order of behaviour and is to this extent inherently anarchic. Furthermore, the argument is devoid of internal consistency. The sovereign State is an intellectual artefact; its character, its form, and its qualities derive from the theoretical exposition of political organization which is nothing if not Western and has its roots in the Age of Reason as much as has international law. New States can hardly claim the privileges and faculties of States and yet repudiate the system from which these derive; yet this is precisely what the argument involves. It overlooks that a State, when it commences to exist as a State, does so in a structural context which gains its form from law, just as a child when born into society becomes subjected to it by virtue of the order of being in which it is integrated.[367]

In some senses, however, O'Connell's critique itself misses the point. His reliance upon the structural context in which new States emerge to independence is less an argument against Bedjaoui's insistence upon the importance of autonomy, than an attempt to avoid its consequences. But his appreciation that Bedjaoui was advancing not a radical, but rather a reactionary agenda is fairly close to the mark.

To begin with, Bedjaoui clearly embraced what has subsequently been seen as a problematic model of modernization – he missed, in that regard, the deeper implications of colonialism understood not only in terms of European presence, but as the spread of a political order that inscribed in the social world a particular conception of space and time, together with new forms of personhood or social identity, and a range of new disciplinary institutions through which society's sense of self or other might be manufactured.[368] Bedjaoui's decolonization thus implied as much continuity in the form of ideas and institutions of politics and law, as it did rupture. But even if he may be excused his failure to take on board the subsequent insights of post-colonial discourse, the one issue that Bedjaoui's emphasis upon sovereignty left radically unexplored was the constitutive significance of

---

[367] D O'Connell, 'The Role of International Law', 95 Daedalus (1966) 634–6.
[368] For work on this issue see Said, above, n 62; Young, above, n 64.

nationality in the process of self-determination. Who were these aliens whose property could be seized? Who were the colonists and who the colonized?

In laying down the battle lines in terms of 'State micro power' and 'private macro power' he left entirely open the relationships between sovereign and subject, and between race ethnicity and nationality that have always been so fundamentally problematic. Bedjaoui's only response to this problem in his lectures was to suggest that the question of nationality was really one for the metropolitan State.[369] In his earlier reports to the ILC as special rapporteur, however, he makes more explicit his approach to this issue. There he suggested that in point of principle, there could be no succession to nationality: this was, purely and simply a manifestation of a State's sovereignty.[370] He went on to suggest, however, that two expedients could be used to render the principle of non-continuity less rigorous – one would be to allow the successor State to deny certain people its nationality; the other was to allow 'the transfer of populations which the successor State considers undesirable, in order to preserve the homogeneity of the group of people now in its charge'.[371] Even if this was something he recommended the Commission should examine further, he was clearly of the view that one of the possible implications of a newly formed sovereignty was the mass denaturalization of persons or groups of persons resulting in their social exclusion (through loss of guarantees) or their expulsion (through population transfers). It is here, that Bedjaoui's evident authoritarianism emerges.

There is, ultimately, a certain parallelism between their respective positions. Both O'Connell and Bedjaoui seemed to understand themselves working at the limits of their own discipline. Neither was able to rely on the well worn modes of identifying rules of international law, both were concerned that the emergence of new States radically put in question the existing precepts of international law upon which they would normally rely. Both also looked outwards beyond the discipline into other arenas (sociology or philosophy) to provide the basis for their approach to the problem of State succession, and were clear, in that sense, as to the limits of their own engagement with the process as international lawyers. They also had their respective blind spots. O'Connell's prioritization of individual rights could only be justified through the effacement of the social context in which those rights may come to be enforced – and in doing so, his argument assumed a deeply ideological character. It was only, in other words, by refusing to admit that decolonization had changed anything that he could insist upon the continuity of legal rights and obligations. In turn, Bedjaoui's forefronting of the context of decolonization (through arguments of self-determination or permanent

---

[369] Bedjaoui, above, n 340, p 468.

[370] Bedjaoui, 'First Report on Succession of States in Respect of Rights and Duties Resulting from Sources other than Treaties', UN doc A/CN4/204 and Corr 1, Yrbk ILC, 1968, II, p 114, para 133.

[371] ibid. See C Drew, *Population Transfer: The Untold Story of Self-Detemination* (University of London), Unpublished Thesis, 2006).

sovereignty) was only achieved by displacing any consideration as to the question of individual right or justice – and in doing so, his argument not only appeared to revive an 'imperative' concept of law but also denied the possibility of individual rights. The slippage in each case is, of course, evocative – in O'Connell it is the move from individual rights to an imperial ideology, in Bedjaoui from public right to a form of elitist authoritarianism.

6. Conclusions

For those looking back at the history of the topic of State succession in the 1950s just as decolonization was about to enter its most active phase, it seemed to be cut through by several points of contestation that precluded the identification of any coherent doctrine. On the face of it, and most visibly, were two rival conceptions of succession: one associated with a Grotian tradition, in which the continuity of international rights and obligations would be assured (often referred to in terms of the theory of 'universal succession'), the other associated with the emergence of positivism in the late 19th century that denied the possibility of succession to pre-existent rights and obligations (for which the metaphor of the *tabula rasa* was employed). Behind this thin schema of oppositional doctrine – which never accurately captured anything more than a general presumption – were deeper points of contestation associated with differing conceptions of statehood, sovereignty, and territory, and different interpretations of the relationship between international and municipal law.

From one standpoint, the very existence of these divergent traditions was such as to make any further theoretical speculation largely meaningless. One could no more find plausible justification for the argument that sovereignty implied an unfettered right to be free of all inherited obligations, than to assume that rights and obligations would pass in virtue of some underlying sociological continuity in the 'people' or the 'nation'. Too much depended upon the vagaries of legal argument about matters such as statehood (a legal or factual category?), about sovereignty (constituted or constitutive?), about the basis of obligation (from consent or participation?), or about the relationship between municipal and international law (which supported which in time of constitutional change?). If there was to be progress in the codification or development of the law of State succession, then, a healthy scepticism as regards all such constructive assumptions would need to be maintained.

In a moderate form, this scepticism was to form itself around two ideas. The first was the idea that, in essence, the 'problem' could be separated from the 'response'. If one was to adopt a position of neutrality as regards the various contrasting theoretical frameworks that had been advanced in the 19th- and early 20th centuries, it was obvious that the law of succession had to be framed in a way that allowed the possibility of discontinuity of legal relations as much as their continuity. And, in so far as outcomes remained undetermined (await-ing the formation of consistent State practice), the idea of succession had to be separated into two parts: one that concerned itself with the factual changes in the geography of rulership, the other concerning itself with the legal consequences of such facts. In the belief that the 'fact' of succession did not carry with it any par-ticular legal implications, scholars were thus free to scout out State practice and judicial decisions for evidence of rules of succession, without having to engage with deeper philosophical concerns as to the implications of sovereignty, or the notion of statehood.

But this apparent position of neutrality to the 'factual' character of the event also had its *aporia*. It was never entirely clear as to whether what should be sought was a rule confirming the continuity of legal relations, or one denying that continuity. Without knowing what the starting point was, it would have been impossible to read any particular case as one elaborating, as Lauterpacht observed, a rule or its exception. Some initial standpoint had to be assumed in relation to which evidence to the contrary might be asserted. 'But of course, it was never clear, once the assumption had been made that all new States were bound by the terms of existing customary (or 'general') international law, whether resort to the traditional ideas of consent or sovereignty as an initial standpoint would be at all helpful.' The greater the extent to which the idea of sovereignty became understood in terms of constituted, rather than constitutive, authority (delegated rather than original), the more implausible it would be as a way of determining whether the default position would be one of freedom from inherited obligations, or its obverse.

The second idea that appeared to form around the general scepticism to received theory, was that the differentiation between the categories of continuity and succession had to be viewed as a largely problematic one. Whereas Hall had declared that the answer to questions of succession could be effectively structured around the idea of personality (and hence differentiating between 'universal' and 'partial' succession, between multiple secession and dissolution, between unifica-tion and annexation, and between governmental- and state succession) it became all too clear that such categories could not simply be understood as factual ones. No one quite understood how it was that the Kingdom of Italy came to be formed in the 19th century, fewer still could announce with any conviction whether, for example, Austria survived the dissolution of the Austro-Hungarian Empire. Needless to say, the answers to such questions clearly did not come in the form of empirical observation, and scholars thus struggled to delimit the scope of their own endeavour: what did, in fact, constitute a succession of States? And how might such a determination be divorced from the consequences with which it would so evidently be associated?

What does seem clearer than anything, however, is that the arguments about succession or non-succession and the theories advocated to undergird them, seemed to be constructed along typically geographical lines. Whereas in the formation of

European nation-States, the principle of continuity gained ground, underpinned by arguments about national, cultural, or economic homogeneity, the late 19th century imperial expansion into Africa and Asia saw the advancement of a converse tendency. It was simply implausible, as far as many were concerned, to maintain that the colonizing powers should be bound by the acts or obligations of those whom they were coming to civilize. Whilst the association between this advocacy of a positivist or imperative creed and colonial expansion was quickly recognized, the solution to which many adverted by the 1950s was the resuscitation of the old Grotian tradition: in place of an emphasis upon sovereignty or consent, the ideal of legal continuity in time of political change should be taken as the point of departure. That this happened to coincide with decolonization, was only to emphasize, once again, the ideological (*qua* neo-colonial) character of this reactive agenda.

What emerged in the subsequent debates, however, was a clear sense both as to the stakes of the law of succession, and the problems associated with each respective position. On the one side was a commitment to the preservation of existing legal relationships as a means of securing the values and interests of the individual and international community respectively; on the other side was a commitment to promoting decolonization, and the fostering of self-determination through the advancement of autonomous decision-making on the part of the newly emergent elites. That the first position seemed to deny the second was to lend it the aura of a neo-imperial project associated with the continued exploitation of colonial dependencies; that the second position seemed to deny the first, was to lend it an authoritarian aura associated with the promotion of governmental authority at the expense of individual rights. The limits of both positions were in some respects inevitable: what was being promoted, after all, was national self-determination *and* individual rights; the promotion of independence *and* loyalty to the values of the international community. As will be seen, these respective positions remained important underlying terms of reference in the discussion of the question of succession right up until 1989. At that point, the discussion became almost entirely one-sided.

II

Codification and Decolonization
1950–1974

There are few topics of international law that have not, at some stage or other, been mooted as possible candidates for 'codification' and the topic of State succession has clearly been no exception. However, just as various different agencies have involved themselves in the task of articulating rules and principles governing succession, there has remained a strong back-swell of opinion largely opposed to such an initiative. Surprisingly enough, one of those who declared their scepticism on this score was O'Connell, whose involvement in the work of the International Law Association on State succession throughout the 1960s might have indicated a disposition otherwise. In an article penned shortly before his untimely death in 1979, O'Connell was to reflect back upon the achievements of the previous decade, and in particular the drafting of the 1978 Vienna Convention on the Succession of States in Respect of Treaties, with the confession that he was 'unrepentantly doubtful about the merits of codification, which can only arrest the historical development of the law and encapsulate it within a particular time frame and a particular ideological milieu'.[1] State succession, in his view, was a topic 'altogether unsuited to the process of codification, let alone of progressive development'[2] and he saw the demand for codification (recalling Savigny's celebrated dictum) as arising from 'indolence and dereliction of duty on the part of the legal profession'.[3]

Whilst O'Connell's criticism of the Vienna Convention might easily be dismissed as the complaints of one whose views on the subject were almost comprehensively disregarded, he was clearly not alone. In the following year, for example, Crawford defended O'Connell's position in the following terms:

Suitable as it was for extended scholarly treatment of the sort O'Connell had given it, the topic of State succession was not self-evidently 'ripe for codification' at the end of the 1960s, either intrinsically or as a matter of relative priority of importance. In itself it is a rubric containing diverse, diffuse, and difficult issues, many of them solvable only by particular reference to the facts of individual cases. Codification was, at this time,

---

[1] D O'Connell, 'Reflections on the State Succession Convention' ZaöRV (1979) 725, p 739.
[2] Ibid 726.
[3] Ibid 727.

likely to be influenced overwhelmingly by the recent experience of decolonization, an experience not necessarily typical of the cases of succession most likely to occur in future. Various administrative techniques had evolved for coping with discontinuities resulting from succession, and it was arguable that their evolution should be allowed to continue undisturbed by attempts at formulating general rules.[4]

One senses from Crawford's comments, here, a belief not merely that rules of succession remained at that particular time exceptionally ephemeral, but also that it was an issue that might best be left to ad hoc compromise or 'administrative technique' whose 'evolution' would plot a natural course. Writing at the end of the 'era of decolonization' this might have seemed a suitable response to the issue – one could be sure at least that cases of succession as might arise in future, would not assume the same social, political, economic, or cultural dimensions as decolonization, however far parallels might emerge. And to the extent that the surrounding sociology of territorial or political change would inevitably differ from one era to the next (in terms of what might be visibly at stake), codification of the law by reference to one particular set of historical precedents would always be a rather poor surrogate for contemporaneous policy oriented problem-solving.

But at the same time, one is left wondering what this 'evolution' of the law of State succession might entail, and how any such 'progress' might occur if the relevant policy-makers were continually faced with re-framing their engagement with the law.[5] Was it really the case that little was to be gained from the process of codification? Was decolonization really so specific a phenomenon that it has nothing to offer in terms of the way in which State succession is understood today?

1. The Move to Codification

A partial answer to O'Connell's complaint may be found in the terms under which the International Law Commission (ILC) originally came to involve itself with the question of State succession. In 1948 Hersch Lauterpacht had been engaged by the UN Secretariat to produce a 'Survey of International Law in Relation to the Work of Codification of the International Law Commission', which was published in the following year.[6] In that document, Lauterpacht identified twenty-five topics for possible study on the part of the ILC that included, alongside matters such as recognition, jurisdictional immunities, and the law of treaties, one entitled 'Succession

---

[4] J Crawford, 'The Contribution of Professor DP O'Connell to the Discipline of International Law', 51 BYIL (1980) 2, p 31.

[5] Crawford may be said to differ here from O'Connell. See above, p 29.

[6] 'Survey of International Law in Relation to the Work of Codification of the International Law Commission', UN doc. A/CN4/1, (5 Nov 1948), reissued under symbol UN doc A/CN4/1/Rev 1, 10 Feb 1949.

of States and Governments'.[7] Lauterpacht did not offer an unqualified recommendation in this respect. He observed that the issue had historically remained outside the
work of codification because of its association with war and its aftermath. He was also
of the view that certain aspects of the subject – particularly the rules on succession to
treaties – remained largely 'obscure'.[8] Nevertheless, Lauterpacht did identify two particular reasons why the topic might be worthy of codification. The first was that the
ILC had the opportunity of 'giving a precise formulation' to the 'generally recognized'
principle of 'respect for acquired private rights' – clarifying, in particular, its application to the various categories of private rights such as those grounded in the public
debt or concessionary contracts.[9] On this score, O'Connell might have applauded the
endeavour – particularly insofar as his 1956 book on the subject had effectively been
structured around the notion of acquired rights. But at the same time, hindsight suggests that it may not have been the best reason for the move to codification given that
the Commission later decided to eliminate the question of acquired rights from its
work on State succession.[10] The doctrine of acquired rights turned out to be far more
controversial than Lauterpacht ever imagined.

The second reason put forward by Lauterpacht, however, may have had a more
enduring impact. There he noted that: '[c]onsiderations of justice and of economic stability in the modern world probably require that in any system of general codification of international law the question of State succession should not
be left out of account. The law of State succession prevents the events accompanying changes of sovereignty from becoming mere manifestations of power'.[11]

Even, thus, if the subject of State succession might not have been 'ripe for
codification' in the sense outlined by Crawford, it was evident that the kind of ad
hoc approach to succession that had characterised the territorial settlements in
the aftermath of the two World Wars was not one propitious to the development
of principles of law, nor to the constraint of 'power'. The building of international
law as a system seemed to require not only that there should be rules governing
the 'creation of States', as Crawford would, no doubt, attest,[12] but also certain
rules governing the consequences of territorial and political change.

---

[7] His choice of topics in this regard was largely guided by two assumptions. First that the role
of the ILC should not merely be confined to the codification of law where practice is clear and well
established. Rather, it should also seek to codify subjects that were, in his words, 'ripe' for regulation given existing divergences in practice (ibid 60, para 102). Secondly, that the role of the ILC
should ultimately be to codify the 'entirety of international law' (ibid 61, para 102) – not necessarily overnight, but certainly over the period of two decades. The concern here was to introduce
'certainty, precision, and uniformity' in the law which would thereby contribute to the authority
of international law, alleviate the task of international tribunals, and remove one of the traditional
causes of the unwillingness of States to submit disputes to the compulsory jurisdiction of international tribunals (ibid).
[8] Ibid 28, para 46.
[9] Ibid 28, para 45
[10] Yrbk ILC (1969) II, p 228, para 68.
[11] Above, n 6, pp 28–9, para 46.
[12] J Crawford , *The Creation of States in International Law* (2nd edn 2005).

Whatever cautions Lauterpacht may have had about the topic of 'succession of States and governments', the ILC adopted it as one of a list of fourteen topics selected for codification on a provisional basis at its first session in 1949.[13] This, of course, did not result in the subject being addressed with any urgency by the ILC, and it was left on the sidelines until 1961 when the ILC was finally encouraged by the General Assembly to include it on its 'priority list' of subjects to be addressed.[14] The impulse for doing so was fairly self-evident. In the years between 1945 and 1961 the process of decolonization had gathered momentum. Jordan, India, Pakistan, Burma, Ceylon, Israel, and the Philippines had gained their independence in the late 1940s, and were joined by Cambodia, Ghana, Guinea, Indonesia, Laos, Libya, Malaya, Morocco, Sudan, Tunisia, and Vietnam in the 1950s, with Togo, Senegal, Somalia, Nigeria, Niger, Mauritania, Mali, Malagasy Republic, Ivory Coast, Gabon, Dahomey, Cyprus, the two Congos (Brazzaville and Leopoldville), Chad, Central African Republic, and Cameroon all gaining their independence in 1960. The process was to continue apace over the next few years with the independence of Tanganyika in 1961, Algeria, Rwanda, Burundi, Jamaica, Trinidad and Tobago, Uganda, and Western Samoa in 1962, Kenya and Zanzibar in 1963, Malta and Zambia in 1964, Gambia, the Maldives, and Singapore in 1965, Barbados, Botswana, Guyana, and Lesotho in 1966, Equatorial Guinea, Mauritius, Swaziland, and Nauru in 1968, Fiji in 1970, Bahrain, Bangladesh, and Qatar in 1971, the Bahamas and Guinea-Bissau in 1973, and Grenada in 1974.[15] In all such cases, legal advisors around the world were faced with obvious questions as to the extent to which third States could be assured of the continuation of legal rights and obligations that might have existed prior to independence, and resulting pressure from Western governments to find some solution to such issues led to initiatives being taken both within the United Nations and by agencies outside, such as the International Law Association, to 'state' or 'restate' the law.

2. Initial Steps: The International Law Commission Sub-committee

Whilst generally favourable to the idea of codifying the law of State succession[16] the ILC was unsure as to how best to approach the topic. The question of succession seemed to pose a wide variety of problems (from matters of contract, tort, and nationality to questions of ownership and debt, and the survival of treaties) and it was not entirely apparent what had been happening over the past decade in the context of decolonization. The ILC decided, therefore, on the one hand to

---

[13] Yrbk ILC (1949) p 281.

[14] GA Resn 1686 (XVI) 18 Dec 1961.

[15] Suriname, Mozambique, and Angola (1975), Djibouti (1977), Dominica (1978).

[16] Several members of the ILC were, however, sceptical about the existence of rules of State succession, see eg, Verdross, 632 mtg, 30 Apr 1962, Yrbk ILC (1962) I, p 27, para 52; Waldock, ibid, para 57.

request the Secretariat to put together several studies on contemporary practice and, on the other, to establish a Sub-committee composed of ten members[17] with a view to making recommendations to it, as to the scope of the subject and the method to be adopted. Having studied and discussed the various working papers drafted by its members[18] together with three 'studies' on the subject produced by the Secretariat,[19] the sub-committee drafted a report the main points of which were subsequently endorsed by the ILC at its fifteenth Session in 1963.[20]

The Sub-Committee's report consisted of a series of brief papers composed by each of its members and a set of recommendations that were drafted consequent to its discussions. Four of the recommendations found in the Sub-committee report appear to have had considerable significance in terms of how the ILC subsequently addressed the topic of succession. The first of these was the decision to 'prioritize' examination of the question of State succession and to de-emphasize, by contrast, the question of governmental succession. Several members of the Sub-committee (such as Briggs,[21] Tabibi,[22] and Castrén[23]) were initially quite clear in the view that questions of State and governmental succession were entirely distinct. For them the issue could be addressed at the level of 'personality': since a change in government did not 'affect the identity of a State', nor necessarily involve a change in territory, there was no need to conflate it with the question of State succession, which involved changes in legal identity and hence necessitated corresponding changes in the legal environment.[24] State succession, apart from anything else, was much more important. Others, however, were more cautious in this respect. Rosenne, for example, adopting a position later to become associated with O'Connell,[25] cautioned against the employment of such 'technical' and 'artificial' distinctions:

In some instances the acquisition of independence may have taken the form, technically, of a change of government, such change being the product of due constitutional

---

[17] Manfred Lachs (Chairman); Milan Bartoš, Herbert Briggs, Erik Castrén, Abdullah El-Erian, Taslim Elias, Chieh Liu, Shabtai Rosenne, Abdul Tabibi, and Grigory Tunkin.

[18] Tabibi A/CN4/SC2/WP2; Rosenne, A/CN4/SC2/WP3; Castren, A/CN4/SC2/WP4; Bartoš, A/CN4/SC2/WP 5; Elias, A/CN4/SC2/WP6; Lachs, A/CN4/SP2/WP7.

[19] 'The Succession of States in Relation to Membership in the United Nations', UN Doc A/CN4/149 and Add 1 (1962); 'Succession of States in Relation to General Multilateral Treaties of which the Secretary-General is the Depositary', UN Doc A/CN4/150 (1962); 'Digest of the Decisions of International Tribunals Relating to State Succession', UN Doc A/CN4/151 (1962).

[20] Rep of Manfred Lachs, Chairman of the Sub-Committee on Succession of States and Governments, UN Doc A/CN4/160 and Corr 1 (1963), Yrbk ILC (1963) II, Annex II, p 260.

[21] Summary Record of 4 mtg, 18 Jan 1963, Yrbk ILC (1963) p 265.

[22] Tabibi, UN Doc A/CN4/SC2/WP2 (1963), Yrbk ILC (1963) II, 284.

[23] Castrén, UN Doc A/CN4/SC2/WP4 (1963), Yrbk ILC (1963) II, 290, p 291.

[24] Ibid 291.

[25] In 1963 O'Connell had first set out his scepticism as to whether the issue of 'personality' should be regarded as the 'key' to succession (D O'Connell, 'State Succession and the Effect upon Treaties of Entry into a Composite Relationship', 39 BYIL (1963) 54, pp 56–8). By 1965 this had been extended into a direct attack upon he 'State-government' distinction (D O'Connell, 'Independence and Problems of State Succession' in W O'Brien *The New Nations in International Law and Diplomacy* (1965) 7, p 11).

process. . . . In others, the process of emancipation and independence of colonial territories has clearly created a new international personality. In some cases the transition was peaceful, in others it was accompanied by the use of force and acts of warfare, sometimes with, and sometimes without, the co-operation of the metropolitan State.[26]

As Rosenne was to explain,[27] a difficulty with the distinction between State and governmental succession was that there appeared to exist two categories of colonial territories with which they would have to deal: those which had been formally annexed by the colonial powers and those which had not.[28] Territories annexed as 'colonies' would begin life as entirely 'new' States; those merely placed under a régime of 'protection' or 'trusteeship' enjoyed a distinct legal identity prior to independence and hence were not entirely 'new'. Whereas in case of the acquisition of independence of Kenya or Ghana, for example, there was no doubt that one was faced with a case of State succession. That conclusion, however, was not so obvious in the cases of Jordan, Lebanon, or Morocco on the termination of the respective mandates and treaties of protection.[29]

To some extent this argument was clearly persuasive for members of the Sub-committee, but there was a simultaneous reluctance to address the issue of governmental succession in its entirety. It was clear to the Sub-committee, for example, that questions of succession to acts of insurgents[30] or responsibility for ultra vires acts of previous governments[31] were not subjects with which the ILC should involve itself. It was therefore suggested that the Commission should initially concentrate upon the topic of State succession, and address succession of governments 'in so far as necessary to complement the study of State succession'.[32] The equivocation of the Committee on this point was, in some respects, quite understandable given the fact that the ILC was only just embarking on its first study of the topic, but it was also to highlight a point of continued prevarication that was to mark the work of the Commission thereafter. How was it to deal with the intermediate category of 'quasi' or 'residual-sovereignty' within the framework

---

[26] Rosenne, UN Doc A/CN4/SC2/WP3, Yrbk ILC (1963) II, 285, p 286, para 3.

[27] Summary Record of 5 mtg, 21 Jan 1963, Yrbk ILC (1963) II, pp 267–8.

[28] Reference was made, in this respect, to the case law of the PCIJ and ICJ in *Mavrommatis Palestine Concessions Case* PCIJ, Series A, no 2 (1924); *Nationality Decrees in Tunis and Morocco* case PCIJ, Series B, no 4 (1923); *Case Concerning Rights of Nationals of the United States of America in* Morocco Judgment of 27 Aug 1952, ICJ Rep 1952, 176; and *International Status of South West Africa*, Advisory Opinion, ICJ Rep 1950, 128.

[29] See further below pp 149–52.

[30] Examples existed, eg *US v Smith*, 1 Hughes 347 (concerning the right of the Federal government to collect on a debt owing to the Confederate government). There were several cases which dealt, in similar manner, with the question of succession to 'puppet' regimes. eg *Socony Vacuum Oil Co Claim* ILR (1957) 55.

[31] Art 11, Articles on State Responsibility (2001), UN doc A/56/10.

[32] Yrbk ILC, (1963) II, p 261.

of State succession? Were the various templates of colonial authority really that significant in light of the imperative of self-determination?

The second recommendation of the Sub-committee was again a matter of prioritization. In several of the working papers before the Sub-committee, members had suggested that the central question for the ILC would be the extent to which 'traditional' rules and principles governing State succession adequately covered the situation of colonial independence. In his paper, for example, Elias suggested that whilst existing rules and past State practice were not necessarily inapplicable, a 'deeper kind of legal analysis and adaptation is called for'.[33] One could neither apply the principle of universal succession, nor that of the *tabula rasa*, to newly independent States. What was needed, rather, was a close and painstaking study and analysis of the policies and practices of States and depositaries concerned.[34] Elias's emphasis upon the study of practice rather than redundant doctrine or 'theories of succession' was echoed by several others in the Sub-committee,[35] but it was Bartoš who presented the contemporary problem most clearly. Bartoš pointed out that 'traditional' approaches to the question of succession predicated upon general rules of continuity or discontinuity of legal relations were far too categoric, and insufficiently attuned to the 'material and legal status of the independent or emancipated State':

The absolute repudiation of such treaty relations by the new State would appear at first sight to ensure that there will be no acceptance of passive succession, ie acceptance of unfavourable treaties which may have been concluded by a foreign master without regard to the needs or interests of the liberated territory and its population. Such a situation, however, would put the newly created State in difficulties, at least for a time, for it would have no treaty relations with other States, perhaps not even its neighbours, with the consequence that even its frontiers, transit requirements, water supply, use of waterways, etc. could be called into question. On the other hand, if the old rule is maintained that treaties termed *traités internationaux réels* – ie treaties relating to the status of territory, to territorial servitudes and to privileges granted with regard to investments – continue in force, then the right of self-determination and the unrestricted sovereignty of the emancipated people is challenged once more as, consequently, is also the inalienable right of that people to the sources of its national wealth.... [I]f such treaties are recognized as remaining in force, the question arises whether the people concerned have really gained their freedom, or whether these treaties do not represent the vestiges of colonialism and the basis for what is now called 'neo-colonialism' – one of the phenomena contrary to the principle of decolonization which, deriving as it does from the right of self-determination, has become one of the guiding principles of the international practice established by the will of States within the framework of the United Nations. Here, as in many other

---

[33] Elias, UN Doc A/CN4/SC2/WP6, Yrbk ILC (1963) 283.

[34] ibid 284. Elias concluded, however, with the suggestion that a 'presumption' in favour of State succession 'with proper qualifications and exceptions' might provide 'a more rational basis for the continued integrity of international law and the facts of international life'.

[35] Tabibi, above, n 22, p 285.

branches of public international law, traditional rules must necessarily be intermingled with modern concepts; or rather it is necessary to bring these traditional rules into accord with the principles of the United Nations Charter and with the gradual evolution resulting from its development and application.[36]

For Bartoš then, the problem was one of adapting, or modifying the traditional rules of succession (such as existed) in order to bring them into 'harmony' with the law of the newly created State and the right of its people to self-determination. The ILC was thus urged to commit itself to the progressive development of the law of State succession 'in the spirit of the policy of decolonization' and in line with the principles within the UN Charter.[37] What was left to be discovered was how to translate these ideas into a framework of clear and consistent rules and/or principles.

There were several obvious consequences associated with Bartoš's approach to the issue. One was that emphasis would clearly have to be placed upon an analysis of contemporary, rather than historic, practice[38] and the 'progressive development' of the law of succession rather than its mere codification;[39] another, that the most appropriate outcome in such circumstances might be the adoption of a draft agreement rather than a set of general principles or model rules.[40] Although mooted, neither of these suggestions found their way in to the final report. What did, however, was a clear direction to the Commission to the effect that it should 'pay special attention to problems of succession arising as a result of the emancipation of many nations and the birth of so many new States after World War II' and that 'the whole topic should be viewed in the light of contemporary needs and the principles of the United Nations Charter'.[41] This direction was subsequently reinforced by several General Assembly Resolutions[42] which instructed the ILC to concentrate, above all else, upon the practice of decolonization and

---

[36] Bartoš, above, n 23, p 293.

[37] ibid 296.

[38] See eg Rosenne, 634 mtg., 2 May 1962, Yrbk ILC (1962) I, p 33, para 6 ('He...doubted the advisability of over-stressing the significance of the precedents of the 19th century, and of concentrating on material deriving from such events as the unification of Italy and of Germany. Those precedents and the literature dealing with them were not strictly germane. The Commission was concerned with the problems of the second half of the 20th century. The 1919 peace treaties had given rise to a number of instances of succession, and the resulting jurisprudence had been intimately connected with those treaties and in part with the question of membership of the League of Nations. The practice and the jurisprudence fell into two categories: that concerning the cession of territory as between pre-existing countries, and that concerning the cession of territory to another country brought into existence as the result of the war, such as Poland. The experience had been quite different since 1945, being characterized by the creation of new states where none had formerly existed.)

[39] Cassin (Acting Chairman), Yrbk ILC (1963) II, p 276.

[40] Rosenne, above, n 18, p 268.

[41] ibid.

[42] GA Resn. 1902 (XVIII) of 18 Nov 1963 (recommending that the Commission 'continue its work on the succession of States and Governments, taking into account the views expressed at the eighteenth session of the General Assembly, the report of the Sub-Committee on the Succession of States and Governments and the comments which may be submitted by Governments, with

became, as we shall see, a central motif in the rules finally articulated by the ILC. Paradoxically, however, this emphasis upon the experience of decolonization, was also to become the most persistent point of criticism of the 1978 Vienna Convention.[43]

The third decisive recommendation of the Sub-committee concerned the topics to be addressed. In his initial memoranda concerning the delimitation of the topic,[44] Elias suggested that there were four main fields that the ILC might consider addressing: State succession in respect of treaties, contracts (including debts and concessions), torts, and State property. Rosenne, for his part, was not convinced that all such matters fell within the remit of an 'international law of State succession', particularly given the terms of Article 2(7) UN Charter:[45]

The effect of identifying and applying the concept of domestic jurisdiction would be, broadly speaking, to exclude all questions appertaining to the legal relationships between the new State and its nationals when those relationships are a continuation of identical relations previously subsisting between the former Government of the dependent territory and the same individuals who were then subjects of that Government.... Questions analogous to succession may arise in those relationships. However, these are not questions of succession under international law.[46]

It thus appeared to Rosenne that a whole host of questions could be excluded from the ILC's work at the outset, including for example; questions relating to the continuity of the legal system; the enjoyment of private law rights and obligations; the continuation or otherwise of rights of officials on becoming nationals of the new State; the status of contracts, internal debts, tax liabilities, and franchises; and the question of torts.[47] Consideration of such issues would only arise in the case of aliens. In the discussion, however, members of the Sub-committee were less than convinced about this a priori exclusion of such matters. Briggs, for example, reiterated the point that Feilchenfeld[48] had made to the effect that one of the central questions in case of succession was the extent to which international law required a successor State to assume or revivify the municipal law

---

appropriate reference to the views of States which have achieved their independence since the Second World War.').

[43] See below, pp 199–201.

[44] Elias, UN Doc. ILC(XIV)/SC2/WP1, Yrbk ILC (1963) II, 282.

[45] Art 2(7) UN Charter provides: 'Nothing contained in the present Charter shall authorize the United Nations to intervene in matters which are essentially within the domestic jurisdiction of any state or shall require the Members to submit such matters to settlement under the present Charter...'.

[46] Rosenne, above, n 18, p 287.

[47] ibid. Rosenne had already laid his position out, in this respect, in an article in the British Yearbook of International Law. See S Rosenne, 'The Effect of Change of Sovereignty upon Municipal Law', 27 BYIL (1950) 267, p 290. ('After a change of sovereignty, however caused, the law in force in the territory affected by the change in sovereignty is, regardless of its substantive content, the law of the new sovereign, from whom alone its validity is derived. This is the necessary result of the intimate connexion that exists between law and sovereignty.')

[48] E Feilchenfeld, *Public Debt and State Succession* (1931) p 602.

obligations of its predecessor.[49] What was, or was not, within a State's domestic jurisdiction was thus a conclusion, not a point of departure, and could only be established once the appropriate study of the matter had been undertaken.[50] It was thus decided to include within the remit of the subject all matters that might plausibly be affected by a succession of States,[51] and, by way of organization, the Subcommittee suggested that the ILC divide the topic into three 'headings': succession in respect of treaties; succession in respect of rights and duties resulting from other sources than treaties; and succession in respect of membership of international organizations.[52] It suggested, furthermore, and in light of the fact that it was still engrossed in its work on the law of treaties, that priority be given to the first of these topics.

As with other recommendations of the Sub-committee, this decision initially structured the ILC's approach to succession. At its 1967 session, the Commission adopted the headings advanced by the Sub-committee and appointed two Special Rapporteurs to deal with succession to treaties and succession to rights and duties resulting from sources other than treaties respectively. The question of membership in international organizations, however, was left to one side and eventually abandoned a few years later.

The final recommendation of significance adopted by the Sub-committee was its suggestion that the question of succession in respect of treaties 'should be dealt with in the context of succession of States, rather than in that of the law of treaties'.[53] As suggested above, at the time at which the Sub-Committee was meeting the ILC was mid-way through its work on the Law of Treaties. Whilst Fitzmaurice had dealt with the question of succession in passing in several of his reports,[54] there was no indication at all that the question of succession to treaties would be addressed in sufficient detail[55] (as it turned out, of course, Article 73 of the 1969 Vienna Convention specifically reserved the application of the Convention as regards questions of succession).[56] The obvious question that had

---

[49] Briggs, Lachs Report, Appx I, above, n 20, p 269.

[50] Elias, loc cit.

[51] These included: treaties; territorial rights; nationality; public property; concessionary rights; public debts; 'other' questions of public law; property rights, interests and relations under private law; and torts. Lachs Report, above, n 20, p 261, para 15.

[52] ibid, para 13. There was considerable discussion as to whether procedures for dispute resolution should also be addressed. In the event, the Sub-commission merely recommended the matter be referred to the Special Rapporteur concerned.

[53] ibid 261, para 10.

[54] First Rep art 6, UN Doc A/CN4/101, Yrbk ILC (1956) II; Second Rep art 17(I)(A)(i) and 21(3), UN Doc A/CN4/107, Yrbk ILC (1957) II; Fourth Rep art 2(1)(c), 6, 21, 28, UN Doc A/CN4/120, Yrbk ILC (1959) II ; Fifth Rep art 15, 27, UN Doc A/CN4/130, Yrbk ILC (1960) II.

[55] Waldock, the new Rapporteur on the law of treaties had expressed doubts as to whether 'a general doctrine of State succession could be said to exist', and had suggested that the issue could largely be addressed, as McNair had done, by reference to the principle *rebus sic stantibus*. Waldock, 630th mtg, 26 Apr 1962, Yrbk ILC (1962) I, p 9, para 12.

[56] Art 73 Vienna Convention on the Law of Treaties (1969) ('The provisions of the present Convention shall not prejudice any question that may arise in regard to a treaty from a succession of

to be addressed was whether the issue of succession in respect of treaties should be dealt with as part of that ongoing project, or rather as part of a separate project on State succession.[57] The issue was not merely one of organization, but appeared to have both methodological and substantive dimensions. Rosenne, for example, pointed out in his working paper that whilst the ILC had already established in its work on the law of treaties that it should eschew classification of treaties by reference to their subject matter, that was far less easy in case of State succession. Practice and opinion in case of succession, he suggested, frequently discriminated between different types of treaties (for example by postulating the survival of 'dispositive treaties', or treaties creating local obligations in case of change of sovereignty). This was such as to leave open the question whether the Commission could effectively deal with the problem of border stability, for example, within the framework it had chosen for the law of treaties.[58] Further to this, the question of treaty survival in case of succession also posed a series of questions additional to those currently under investigation – particularly as regards the third party effects of devolution agreements – which again pointed to the need to address it in relative independence of its work on the law of treaties.

Whilst Rosenne's points were such as to suggest that the full range of issues relating to succession might not be suitable for incorporation within the work on the law of treaties (delaying, perhaps, the completion of that project), the full implications of the Sub-committee's recommendation were not entirely clear. Did this merely mean that the Commission should adopt a set of articles as a supplement to those drafted on the law of treaties (taking the rules on treaty law as its starting point)? Or were there further implications associated with addressing the issue within the context of 'State succession'? In part, at least, the decision might be read as implying that the main emphasis would be upon developing a 'law of State succession' in which the various material elements (treaties, contracts, torts, property, and debt for example) would be united within a single conceptual and methodological framework, and which would not necessarily conform to the approach adopted in respect of the law of treaties. Once again, the Sub-committee appears to have struck upon an issue which was to become quite significant for the Commission's subsequent work on State succession.

Although the Commission had approved the report of the Sub-Committee at its session in 1963 and had appointed a Special Rapporteur (Manfred Lachs) to examine the issue, no further progress was made in the following three sessions (1964–6) owing to its continued work on the law of treaties and special missions. At its session in 1967 the Commission reviewed its programme of work and decided to expedite study of the question of State succession in respect of treaties.

States or from the international responsibility of a State or from the outbreak of hostilities between States.').

[57] eg Rosenne, above, n 18, p 287, para 12.
[58] ibid 287–8, para 14.

Since Manfred Lachs had resigned from the Commission on his appointment to the International Court of Justice, Sir Humphrey Waldock was appointed as Special Rapporteur.[59] Mohammed Bedjaoui was also appointed as Special Rapporteur to deal with the adjacent questions of succession in respect of rights and duties resulting from sources other than treaties.

Waldock was to produce five reports on succession in respect of treaties in the years 1968–1972.[60] The first of these consisted largely of a discussion of methodological and conceptual issues, but also included draft articles relating to the definition of succession, the scope of the provisions, the question of constituent instruments of international organizations, and succession to boundaries. In the second report, Waldock produced a draft article relating to consequences of the cession of territory and addressed the respective status of devolution agreements and unilateral declarations. In his third, he produced eight draft articles with commentary relating to the position of 'new States', which he supplemented in his fourth report with an additional five articles mainly dealing with bilateral agreements and other related provisions. In his final fifth report, Waldock sought to deal with all outstanding issues including those relating to protectorates, trusteeships, and mandated territories, the formation and dissolution of unions of States, and the dismemberment of States, concluding with two final provisions relating to boundary and territorial settlements. To assist him in his work, the Secretariat produced a series of studies relating to past and contemporary practice that supplemented those produced for the Commission's Sub-committee.[61]

Waldock himself came to the project on State succession having recently completed the work of the ILC on the law of treaties. Shortly after starting his work, the Vienna Conference on the Law of Treaties had been convened resulting in the adoption of the Vienna Convention of 1969 which itself represented something of a triumph for the ILC and, more specifically, for Waldock himself who had assumed the role of chairman in 1967. Waldock was an international lawyer steeped in practice. His formative years had been spent in the British Admiralty from where he began to acquire a prominence and reputation such that by the 1950s he was regularly employed as counsel by the British government in cases before the ICJ (*Corfu Channel* case, *Anglo-Norwegian Fisheries* case, *Anglo-Iranian Oil Company* case). This also led him to a variety of wider engagements such as

    [59] Rep of 19 Session, UN Doc A/CN4/199, paras 38–41, Yrbk ILC (1967) II, p 368.
    [60] Waldock, First Rep on Succession of States and Governments in Respect of Treaties, UN Doc A/CN4/202, Yrbk ILC (1968) II, 87; Second Rep on Succession in Respect of Treaties, UN Doc A/CN4/214 and Adds 1 & 2, Yrbk ILC (1969) II, 45; Third Rep on Succession in Respect of Treaties, UN Doc A/CN4/224, and Add1, Yrbk ILC (1970) II, 25; Fourth Rep on Succession in Respect of Treaties, UN Doc A/CN4/249, Yrbk ILC (1971) II, 143; Fifth Rep on Succession in Respect of Treaties, UN Doc A/CN4/256 and Add 1–4, Yrbk ILC (1972) II, p 1.
    [61] In addition to those cited above (n. 19) the Secretariat produced five studies on the succession of States to multilateral treaties, UN Docs A/CN4/200/Rev2 & A/CN4/200/Add1 & 2, Yrbk ILC (1968) II, and a volume of information provided by member states entitled *Materials on Succession of States* ST/LEG/SER.B/14.

acting as legal advisor to Secretary-General Hammaskjold in his critical mission to Peking in 1955. It is evident that Waldock brought this practical orientation to his work in the ILC. In his review of Sir Humphrey Waldock's life and work, Brownlie repeatedly refers to Waldock's practical aptitude: Waldock possessed a 'rare combination of legal scholarship, practical sense and diplomatic skill';[62] he was always keen to 'make things work'[63] and foster consensus; he was a 'man of common sense'[64] and one constantly seeking to hammer everything out 'on the anvil of practice and principle'.[65] His orientation, Brownlie suggests, was one of 'non-sectarian positivism';[66] yet this was not a theoretical position as he appears to have had 'no deep interest in theory as such'.[67] In fact, one of his strengths 'lay in his capacity to reconsider his first view',[68] to 'draw together a diversity of views' and seek solutions through compromise. This was a view echoed by Paul Reuter in the ILC itself, who praised Waldock's work on succession for his 'reliance on experience and the facts and the avoidance of premature formulations and over-generalizations'.[69] His was the not the voice of an ideologue, but that of 'logic' and experience.

It is difficult to overestimate the influence of Waldock's approach to codification upon the articles of succession. Throughout, his commitment to the development of formulations, worked out on the back of a detailed examination of State practice, is more than evident. Equally, his unwillingness to hamstring the project by making grand deductions from theoretical premises is also clear: at times he was utterly strategic in his adoption of particular theoretical postures. Although many subsequently criticized the draft articles for their apparent obsessive attention to the question of self-determination, this was not, in fact, a principle that Waldock had focused upon at the outset. Rather, it was an idea that he appeared to adopt halfway through his work as a way of organizing what might otherwise have been an inconsistent array of practice. As Brownlie suggests, it was Waldock's fealty to State practice that was the key to his work, and his reports to the ILC on State succession are indicative of both the possibilities and limits of that approach.

3. The International Law Association

Whilst Waldock was undoubtedly the key figure in developing the work of the ILC relating to succession, it would be wrong not to make note also of the work undertaken by the International Law Association in relation to the same subject.

---

[62] I Brownlie, 'The Calling of the International Lawyer: Sir Humphrey Waldock and his Work', 54 BYIL (1984) 7, p 41.

[63] ibid 57.   [64] ibid 66.
[65] ibid 41.   [66] ibid 63.
[67] ibid 73.   [68] ibid 41.
[69] Reuter, Yrbk ILC, 1970, I, p 137, para 57.

The ILA had begun its work on State succession shortly before the ILC in 1961 when it established a Committee of fourteen members under the chairmanship of Charles Rousseau with DP O'Connell as Rapporteur. The Committee began by producing a volume entitled *The Effect of Independence on Treaties* published in 1965, and continued its work until 1972 by which time it had drafted four reports, and had adopted several significant resolutions concerning State succession.[70]

Whilst all of the ILA's work on State succession was evidently influential in terms of the attention given to it in the Commission's work, at the early stages it was the 'handbook of practice' which gained most attention.[71] The conclusions of the handbook (if one can call them that) gave a fairly clear indication as to the direction of the ILA's subsequent work, and in many respects reflected the work and opinions of its Rapporteur, O'Connell.[72] The 'handbook' begins, very significantly, by providing an account of two different 'processes' by which independence may be attained.[73] The first was said to be an 'orderly, and sometimes progressive, transfer of constitutional power to dependent territories', the second 'that of secession when no regular grant of power is involved'.[74] This distinction between the constitutionality or otherwise of the process of acquiring independence served as a way of distinguishing, as far as the ILA Committee was concerned, between two categories of practice. On the one hand were the disorderly processes that accompanied the acquisition of independence in the 19th and early 20th centuries, exemplified by the separation of Iceland from Denmark in 1918, Brazil from Portugal in 1825, the dissolution of Colombia in 1828–31 and the dissolution of the union between Norway and Sweden in 1905.[75] On the other hand, and by contrast, were the cases of decolonization after 1947, which

---

[70] Committee on the Succession of New States to the Treaties and Certain other Obligations of their Predecessors, 'Interim Report', 52 ILA Rep Conf 14–20 Aug (1966) p 574; 'Interim Report and Draft Resolutions', 53 ILA Rep Conf 25–31 Aug (1968) 596; 'Report', 54 ILA Rep Conf 23–29 Aug (1970) 101; 'State Succession and Governmental Contracts', 55 ILA Rep Conf 21–26 Aug (1972) 654.

[71] International Law Association, *The Effect of Independence on Treaties* (1965), pp xiii–xiv. The Committee noted that it would be 'premature . . . to formulate definitive principles to govern the solution of this problem. . . . While refraining, therefore, from commitment at this stage to a statement of rules of law, the Committee offers a statement of the problems raised and an analysis of the possible attitudes towards them.' It was fairly evident, however, where the ILA's ultimate sympathies lay.

[72] One may note, in particular, the similarity between the approach to treaties in the ILA handbook and that adopted by O'Connell in *State Succession in Municipal Law and International Law* (1967) II, p 88 ff. This had been preceded by several lengthy articles in which most of the arguments had already been rehearsed. eg D O'Connell, 'Independence and Succession to Treaties', 37 BYIL (1962) 84; D O'Connell, 'State Succession and the Effect upon Treaties of Entry into a Composite Relationship', 39 BYIL (1963) 54; D O'Connell, 'State Succession and Problems of Treaty Interpretation', 58 AJIL (1964) 41.

[73] The handbook thus echoes the distinction made by Rosenne above, p 97–8 .

[74] Above, n 71, p 1.

[75] Other possible cases include the secession of the United States from Britain, the secession of Texas from Mexico in 1840, Greece from the Ottoman Empire in 1830, Cuba from Spain in 1898, and Panama from Colombia in 1903.

were largely marked by an orderly and constitutional 'transfer of authority' (the exceptions specifically mentioned being Israel and Guinea).[76] As a consequence, the ILA Committee observed that:

[t]he implication is that independence of colonial territories at the present time is a process constitutionally and sociologically distinguishable from the traditional forms of secession, and that the problem of State succession to treaties, which arises from the fact of independence, is contextually novel. It follows that the precedents afforded by previous instances of succession cannot be regarded as completely relevant.[77]

This distinction was to have certain practical consequences as far as the ILA Committee was concerned. In its examination of 'previous cases of independence' it was observed that in several of them, the new State had denied the continuance of pre-independence agreements with third powers (citing the United States, the Spanish American colonies, Greece, Panama, Finland, Czechoslovakia, and Poland). This was not a uniform practice[78] but was sufficient to suggest that a principle of automatic succession to treaty obligations would be hard to sustain. By contrast, the Committee was to observe in practice relating to Commonwealth countries such as Australia, Canada, New Zealand, India, Pakistan, and Ceylon, a general commitment to the continuity of pre-independence treaties of various kinds (evidenced in public pronouncements,[79] 'devolution agreements',[80] and the treaty lists of various States).[81] This seemed to flow, in the view of the Committee, from the gradual, evolutionary, process by which each of the Commonwealth States acquired its independence (moving through stages of internal self-governance to external autonomy) in which treaty continuity seemed to follow, as a natural consequence, from the fact of continuity of the local legal order. As far as the ILA Committee was concerned, therefore, decolonization was to be perceived to be far less of a radical, or traumatic, experience than that which had marked the dissolution of various unions within Europe and elsewhere in the 19th century, and its implicit conclusion was that no great reliance could therefore be placed upon those earlier precedents as a way of

---

[76] G Fischer, 'L'indépendance de la Guinée et les accords franco-guinéens', 4 *AFDI* (1958) 711.

[77] Above, n 71, p 2.

[78] Three different examples suffice: I. In *The Mechanic* the Ecuadorian Mixed Claims Commission had upheld in an award of 1862 the US contention that the US-Spanish treaty of 1785 had been inherited by Colombia. J Moore, *Digest of International Law(1906)*, V, p 341. II O'Connell, above, n 72, pp 92–95; II. Whilst Finland was generally regarded as not having inherited treaty obligations from Russia, exceptions existed in respect of certain boundary agreements between Russia and Sweden. See further, O'Connell, ibid 99–100; III. Whilst Czechoslovakia generally adopted a negative attitude to inheritance of the treaties of Austria-Hungary, it undertook to adhere, under the terms of the Treaty of St Germain 1919, to a range of agreements specified in Annex I of the Treaty. O'Connell, ibid 179–180; McNair, A, *The Law of Treaties* (1962, 2nd edn), p 604.

[79] On unilateral declarations, see below pp 128–31.

[80] On devolution agreements see below pp 122–7 .

[81] It is notable that the treaty lists referred to are principally those of European and North American States together with Australia and New Zealand.

sustaining the idea that States emerging from colonialism might begin life free of any inherited treaty obligations.

The ILA Committee's emphasis upon the evolutionary nature of the independence process during decolonization was, in some respects at least, a product of the somewhat selective nature of its appraisal of practice. The Committee devoted considerable space to the elucidation of the constitutional arrangements and practice of Commonwealth Dominions in their gradual acquisition of independence.[82] The cases of Australia, Canada, New Zealand, and India took pride of place, and by contrast far less consideration was given to the more sudden, and less gradual, process of decolonization in parts of Africa,[83] or indeed of the much more ambivalent position adopted in the case of the Irish Free State.[84] Very little was made of the various initiatives in Tanganyka and Uganda 'amongst others' to maintain in force pre-independence treaties on a provisional basis,[85] and its discussion of the effect of devolution agreements was extremely cursory. The Committee's emphasis upon the internal constitutional processes that preceded independence was to render the description of practice extremely complex[86] (it was observed, for example, that in British practice, treaties came to be applicable

---

[82] Crawford explains that in the work of O'Connell, he saw the Dominions as acquiring 'an intermediate form of legal personality to which treaty obligations could be attributed and which could be regarded as continuing in the eventual State personality of the Dominion after independence'. This idea was then extended to cover not only the period in which the Dominions had a degree of distinct international personality, but also to the period of 'separate internal competence for treaty *performance* in an internationally undivided Empire'. Crawford, above, n 4, p 7. K Roberts-Wray, *Commonwealth and Colonial Law* (1966) pp 247–301

[83] The discussion in the handbook concerning the incremental process of dominion independence clearly emphasized the 'factors assimilating the newly independent Commonwealth countries in the Older Dominions' such as the specific application of treaties to overseas territories, their separate administration (in the guise of the doctrine of the divisibility of the Crown), and the participation of local legislatures in implementation of agreements. Handbook, above, n 71, pp 111–17.

O'Connell was somewhat ambivalent as to whether the position of newly independent states could fully be assimilated to that of the Dominions. See O'Connell, 'Independence' above, n 72, p 105.

[84] In a famous address to the Dáil, de Valera made clear that:

the present position of the Irish Free State with regard to treaties and conventions concluded between the late United Kingdom and other countries is based upon the general international practice in the matter when a new State is established. When a new State comes into existence, which formerly formed part of an older State, its acceptance or otherwise of the treaty relationships of the older State is a matter for the new State to determine by express declaration or by conduct (in the case of each individual treaty) as considerations of policy may require. The practice here has been to accept the position created by the commercial and administrative treaties and conventions of the late United Kingdom, until such time as the individual treaties and conventions themselves are terminated or amended. Occasion has been taken, where desirable, to conclude separate engagements with the States concerned.

Irish Free State Debates, 11 July 1933, cited in J Mervyn Jones, 'State Succession in the Matter of Treaties', 24 BYIL (1947) 360, p 367.

[85] On unilateral declarations see below, pp 128–31.

[86] Ago was to remark that the work of the ILA 'though useful, left an impression of excessive complexity and a disappointing lack of clarity'. Yrbk ILC, 1970, I, p 149, para 3.

to dependent territories in eight different ways),[87] but the underlying assumption remained clear enough. The key element for purposes of determining the continuity or otherwise of international agreements was the development of a local legal identity prior to independence[88] whose survival in the transition to independence would largely ensure the continuity of international agreements (if only because many such agreements will have been 'localized' within the legislative order.)[89]

Behind this judgment, was an account of the nature and effect of succession which can only fully be understood by reference to the work of O'Connell. By this stage, O'Connell had already made clear that, in his view, 'traditional' approaches to the question of treaty succession (for which read those in the late 19th and early 20th century) were problematic for two main reasons.[90] The first was the limited nature of the practice upon which they were based. Not only was it clear that the typical instances of succession were limited to either the transfer of territory from one colonial power to another or the annexation of new colonies, but it was also evident that the treaties in question tended to be confined to bilateral treaties of alliance, peace, commerce, and extradition. The second concern was that the authors in question had tended to try to deal with the problems of succession in terms of a pre-formed, but undoubtedly problematic, conception of 'personality' in which their conclusions hinged almost entirely on a finding as to whether or not a State was 'new' or 'old'. He was to observe, in this respect, that:

hidden in the word 'personality' is an assumed definition which is nothing more or less than the conclusion to the argument being pursued. If an author chooses to interpret personality as meaning capacity to contract, and predicates continuity of treaties upon personality, then he will argue that treaties survive only if the States retain the treaty-making power; and if he chooses to interpret it as meaning capacity to legislate to carry out the treaty internally, then he will argue the irrelevance of the treaty-making power.[91]

O'Connell thus advocated an approach that took into account 'sociological as well as juridical factors'. Taking as his starting point a notion of the 'harmonization' of international and municipal law,[92] he was to suggest that in case of succession, a presumption of treaty continuity could be found on the one hand in the juridical survival of the legal order and, on the other, in the sociological identity of

[87] Above, n 71, pp 37–8. These included, at one end of the scale, treaties applying to all colonies in virtue of British signature or through territorial application clauses to those, at the other end of the scale, which were concluded directly between the colonial government and a foreign country.

[88] O'Connell, II, above, n 72, p 113 ('One of the decisive factors promoting [the continuity of treaties upon independence] ... is the embodiment of imperial treaty relationships in the local and separate legal orders of the dependent territories.').

[89] This is asserted as being the case in respect of French, Belgian and Dutch law with the obvious implications as regards their colonies, above, n 71, pp 120–7.

[90] O'Connell, (Independence) above, n 72, p 84.

[91] O'Connell, (Composite Relationship), above, n 72, p 57.

[92] O'Connell, I, above, n 72, p 31; II, above, n 72, p 89.

the territory and the people affected by a treaty.[93] Treaty survival, in other words, hinged upon the prior implementation of international agreements in local law: if local law survived, so also would those international agreements that had become 'localized' through legislative or other enactment.[94] If, furthermore, incorporated treaties were to survive, one could then establish a general presumption of treaty continuity in case of succession. This was evidently the case, on his analysis, as regards the phenomenon of decolonization. [95]

The implicit subordination of the question of treaty continuity to the continuity of the domestic legal system was obviously a convenient shortcut, but it seemed to open out as many questions as it answered. Apart from the very real difficulties associated with postulating the survival of a legal system or its *grundnorm* at the same time as supposing that the newly emergent State enjoys full rights of sovereignty (revisiting the classic argument as to the relationship between the continuity of law and the identity of the 'sovereign' or the 'legal order',)[96] this was always going to be an unsatisfactory argument. If the answer to the question as to whether treaties have survived the transition to independence was merely to be found in the degree of legal continuity at the domestic level, the matter would no longer be one with which international lawyers could effectively engage (unless, of course, they were to take the far more radical step of arguing that international law requires the continuity of local law, both public and private, in case of succession).[97] It might have made sense in the context of decolonization (insofar as continuity of local law was frequently maintained) but it would have

[93] ibid 117.
[94] O'Connell, (Independence), above, n 72, pp 88–9 explains as follows:

In all the cases assembled under the heading of evolutionary independence there occurred a process, more or less extended in time, whereby the territories concerned acquired their own legal orders separate from the metropolitan legal orders, and whereby they were only exceptionally affected either by metropolitan legislation or by metropolitan treaty-making....As local autonomy grew, so the relevant legal orders became ever more detached from metropolitan influence, until...treaties were not extended without local decision, and survived locally even when terminated with respect to the metropolis. This process of 'localization' of treaties has its mysterious aspects, but it presents no insuperable puzzle to jurisprudence. The *grundnorm* was shifted imperceptibly from the metropolis to the territories by attrition of constitutional links, and resulted in a concretization of treaties in the local legal orders, so that these gained a new and modified validity from a new centre of legal gravity.

[95] ibid p 84–5. ('The problem of succession raised by this phenomenon is novel, inasmuch as the process is not one of sudden fragmentation of a political entity, but evolution through various intermediate stages of internal autonomy to full maturity, the process extending over varying periods of time, but tending to be constant in character. The treaties affected are not, generally speaking, treaties of the parent State contracted without specific relation to the maturing territories, but treaties expressly applied territorially and, on the whole, autonomously administered; they are thus, in a sense, "localized". Furthermore, they deal with subject matters utterly novel and immeasurably complex, and they are mainly multilateral in form and technical in character. The structure of the modern world is dependent upon their continuity.').

[96] A discussion of problems as matters of analytical philosophy is to be found in J Raz, *The Concept of a Legal System* (2nd edn, 1980).

[97] The only explicit defence of this position is to be found in the work of O'Connell, discussed above, pp 85–6.

clearly opened up the question of treaty survival in case of revolutionary changes in the legal order.[98] O'Connell also evidently failed to appreciate the distinction between treaties requiring legislative action and those that could be performed executively – if the latter did not survive (by reason of not being 'localized') then any postulated presumption of continuity would be both highly relative and far less general than might otherwise be supposed.[99]

But there was also a more obvious problem associated with the ILA Committee's account of decolonization as an orderly, constitutional process, more akin to a change in government than anything else. However far the colonial powers might have wanted to 'manage' decolonization to ensure a stable and orderly process of transition in which British or French commercial and other interests were secured in the process, that was not necessarily how the subaltern populace would have seen the process, nor indeed the emergent elites themselves. Not only were there the cases in which the Committee's picture simply did not fit (Algeria, Israel, Upper Volta, and Vietnam being the obvious examples), but it overlooked the very real process of resistance, struggle, and incipient nationalism that pushed forward the move towards decolonization. In many cases, the final managerial arrangements concerned with 'handing over' the reins of government were preceded by violent conflict between the administration and incipient national liberation movements.[100] In many others, furthermore, independence was followed by the outbreak of civil conflict the causes of which could be traced directly or indirectly to the political settlement that structured the decolonization process.[101] For all the evidence pointing towards an orderly, constitutional transition, there is also much to suggest that in many cases it was nothing of the sort.

Further to this, O'Connell's argument seemed to be all too convenient. In many colonial territories, the 'local law' upon which O'Connell was to place such great store, was in large measure not an indigenous 'legal order' or one that in any great respect reflected local culture or values, but a law frequently 'transplanted' as part of the colonial project of 'civilization'.[102] Whilst it was not necessarily the immediate desire of the newly formed governments that all 'colonial' law should be discarded or abandoned, neither was it obvious that local implementation of, for example, an extradition agreement with a Western government should determine the survival of the treaty. This was surely a case of the tail wagging the dog.

As far as the ILA Committee was concerned, however, the arguments in favour of treaty continuity in case of succession did not merely flow from what it observed in State practice, but were also of a prudential character. In surveying

---

[98] eg Russia 1919, Yugoslavia, 1945.
[99] Crawford, above, n 4, pp 12–13.
[100] eg in Kenya, Algeria, Malaya, Guinea-Bissau, Vietnam, Angola, Mozambique, Zimbabwe, Namibia, and Madagascar, to name but a few. See generally, R Young *Postcolonialism: An Historical Introduction* (2001) pp 161–81.
[101] eg Congo, Angola, Nigeria.
[102] Roberts-Wray, above, n 82, pp 534–7.

the various 'policy options' available to new States the Committee was to indicate its implicit preference for a presumption in favour of treaty continuity. Not only would it avoid the problems of selection that other policies might involve, but it would also avoid the objection of undue constraint; 'almost all' of the treaties inherited could easily be 'got rid of', if politically inconvenient, by utilization of denunciation clauses, or by negotiation'.[103] Further to this, the Committee emphasized that:

a relevant factor tending towards continuity rather than discontinuity of treaty relationships is the role which the modern treaty plays in stabilising the economic environment of States; a great and complex structure of world relationships, involving fundamental human interests, is contingent upon the survival of some categories of treaties. The successor States themselves will be as much prejudiced as other States, in their relations *inter se*, by the collapse of this system....

Whilst the handbook itself drew no explicit conclusions, the suggestions implicit in the above analysis became the subject of a series of recommendations put before the ILA conference in 1966[104] and again in 1968.[105] In the 1968 session, eight resolutions were adopted without amendment relating to succession in respect of treaties (reproduced in Waldock's second report),[106] the main thrust of which were to articulate a presumption of continuity of treaty obligations in all cases of succession. The first resolution provided that, in case of a newly independent State, it 'may invoke and have invoked against it a treaty that was internationally in force with respect to the entity or territory corresponding with it prior to independence' so long as it was notified of the existence of the treaty and had not declared within a 'reasonable time' after the attainment of independence that it does not regard the treaty to be in force.[107] The second resolution provided that in case of unification, treaties would continue 'within the regional limits prescribed at the time of their conclusion to the extent to which their implementation is consistent with the constitutional position established by the instrument of union', and that in case of the dissolution of a union, 'the separate components of the composite State may invoke or have invoked against them treaties of the composite State to the extent to which these are consistent with the changed

---

[103] Above, n 71, p 2.

[104] In 1966 the ILA Committee concluded its work with four recommendations, the first of which demonstrated a clear preference for treaty continuity: 'In all decisions and actions concerning the applicability of pre-existing treaties to newly independent States, weight should be attached to the advantages of achieving the maximum degree of continuity in treaty relations'. ILA Report of the 52 Conference, Helsinki, 1966, p 585.

[105] ILA, Rep of the 53 Conference, Buenos Aires, 1968, p 589.

[106] Above, n 60, p 48.

[107] ibid, Resn 1, para (b)(iii) and (iv). Continuity would also be presumed in cases in which the parties concerned expressly so agree or where the terms of the agreement have been applied *inter se* (paras i and ii). In case of bilateral agreements, the other contracting party may also have a right to denounce the agreement (para iii).

circumstances resulting from the dissolution.'[108] The other resolutions largely concerned associated matters such as the question of termination, reservations, signature, and the effect of succession on the entry into force of an agreement. A notable inclusion, however, was a provision relating to agreements delimiting boundaries in which it was provided that if the agreement had been executed (in the sense that the boundary had already been delimited) then 'what is succeeded to is not the treaty but the extent of national territory so delimited'. Otherwise, succession would be governed by the principles in the first resolution or to 'other legal principles as may prove to be relevant'.[109]

4. A Change in Focus: The Waldock Reports

Whether or not as a direct consequence of the ILA's work in this field, Waldock was quick to change the focus of the Commission's work on succession in respect of treaties in several important ways. In his first report[110] Waldock began by revisiting two of the decisions that the Commission had apparently made in 1963. The first of these concerned the Sub-Committee's recommendation that the general framework governing its approach to the issue should be that of the 'law of State succession'. Waldock begins his report by asserting, in line with the approach taken by O'Connell,[111] that 'the solution of the problems of so-called "succession" in respect of treaties' is to be sought, not within 'any general law of "succession"', but rather within the framework of the law of treaties.[112] His rationale, to begin with, was that the sheer diversity of 'modern practice' seemed to preclude the possibility of dealing with the issue of treaty continuity in terms of any general principle of succession. Neither the principle of universal succession nor that of the clean slate was helpful. He was, furthermore, deeply sceptical as to whether 'any specific legal institution' of succession had actually been recognized in international law – a point which seemed to be demonstrated by the variety of theories on the point found in the writings of past and contemporary jurists.[113] He suggested, in that vein, that: '[i]f any one specific theory were to be adopted by the Commission, it would almost certainly be found to be

---

[108] ibid, Resn 2.

[109] ibid, Resn 8.

[110] Waldock, First Rep, above, n 60.

[111] In 1956 O'Connell had suggested that '[t]he effect of change of sovereignty on treaties is not a manifestation of some general principle or rule of State succession, but rather a matter of treaty law and interpretation'. D O'Connell, *The Law of State Succession* (1956) p 15. O'Connell later suggests, in somewhat modified form, that: 'International law...does not have a special rule respecting either the inheritance or lapse of treaties in the event of State succession; it utilizes the ordinary rules for the termination of treaties, and leaves it to judicial, or judicious, appreciation in each instance whether a treaty, upon interpretation, is applicable in the new context'. O'Connell, above, n 72, II, p 6, and generally, pp 1–9.

[112] Waldock, First Report, above, n 60, p 89, para 9.

[113] ibid.

a strait-jacket into which the actual practice of States, organizations, and depositaries could not be forced without inadmissible distortions either of the practice or the theory'.[114]

Waldock's determination to address the issue as a 'sequel' to the rules on treaty law[115] rather than as a question of succession, was thus formed upon two intuitions: the first was that many of the issues could be addressed merely through the extension of existing rules of treaty law to problems of succession; the second was that the main concern should be to ensure fidelity to State practice rather than indulge in a Procrustean desire to force it within some *a priori* theoretical framework.[116]

As regards Waldock's second intuition, it is evident that the attempt to avoid theory would always be difficult. Even adopting a firmly empirical stance, Waldock would still have to try to organize the practice under observation within the frame of some general rubric in order to differentiate between the 'rules' and their 'exceptions'. In doing so he would also have to decide upon the relevant considerations. Would the key be the nature of the agreement, the intention of the parties, or even, perhaps, the nature of the events giving rise to succession?[117] Other members of the Commission were alert to the possibility of a slight of hand here. Albónico, for example, suggested that Waldock's proposal would have the effect of affirming a principle of continuity:

If the problem were approached from the point of view of the law of treaties, the general principle would be that, subject to certain exceptions that confirmed the rule, a party that consented to be bound by a treaty did so both on its own behalf and on behalf of its successors.... If the problem were approached from the standpoint of succession, however, the emphasis would be on the change which took place when the sovereignty of the predecessor State was replaced by that of the successor State. Since the successor State was a separate legal entity, the rule would be exactly the opposite to that which would apply

---

[114] ibid, para 10. This was echoed by several others in the Commission. See eg Cassin, Yrbk ILC (1968) I, p 134, para 5 ('The different theories on the subject could hardly provide guidance for the Commission, let alone solutions for the difficult problems involved. It would therefore be better to rely on practice, diverse though it may be.'); Castañeda, Yrbk ILC, 1968, I, pp 136–7, para 34; Ramangasoavina, Yrbk ILC, 1968, I, p 142, para 35.

[115] He explains that his intention was to draft articles 'designed as a sequel to the draft articles on the law of treaties rather than as one section of a single comprehensive codification of the several branches of the law applicable to succession of States and Governments'. ibid, para 11. The draft articles on the Law of Treaties had included a provision (draft art 69) providing that the rules should not be read as 'prejudging' any question of succession. This was ultimately to become art 73 of the Vienna Convention on the Law of Treaties (1969).

[116] Waldock was to return to this problem quite consistently in the course of his work on succession. The longer he pursued the question in terms of the law of treaties, the more improbable it became for any institution of succession to be generated in the ILC's work. He thus commented, in the discussion of his second and third reports that the ILC might have to take a very different stance in relation to matters such as public property than in relation to treaties, Waldock, Yrbk ILC, 1970, I, p 135.

[117] cf Ushakov, Yrbk ILC, 1968, I, p 138, para 54.

under the law of treaties: there would be no transfer of obligations and rights to a State which had not been a party to the negotiation, signature or ratification of the treaty.[118]

Despite Albónico's concerns, it was not at all obvious that the alternative would have been any different: after all, the doctrinal separation between the 'fact' of succession and its 'consequences' had been articulated primarily as a result of the perception that to speak of succession was to imply legal continuity. In any case, it was still not entirely clear as to what would be entailed by a decision to approach the matter from the standpoint of the law of treaties in the way Waldock suggested, and it was certainly not obvious that his alternative starting point would actually make the issues any more tractable.[119]

Whilst treaty interpretation may suffice to establish the position of contracting parties as regards the extension of rights to successor States (ie allow, in certain cases, the participation of successor States), it would do little to substantiate how or why the fact of succession itself may lead to the assumption of treaty obligations on the part of a non-signatory State.[120] Ultimately the central problem seemed to be that treaty law has as its defining characteristic the assumption of legal obligations by explicit and intentional acts of consent by identifiable parties. The institution of the treaty as a *'pactum'* or 'agreement' seems to require as much, and the supposition that a State may become party to a treaty without intending or wishing to do so can only be regarded as a signal exception to this basic principle. The idea of succession thus seems to fall foul, in particular, of the *pacta tertiis* rule (as was to be embodied in Article 34 of the Vienna Convention on the Law of Treaties)[121] which provides that a treaty cannot, by its own force alone, create obligations for third parties.[122] Since treaties are deemed to be effective only as between the parties in their relations *inter se*,[123] it would seem to follow that successor States cannot be bound by their terms merely in virtue of the fact

[118] Albónico, Yrbk ILC, 1968, I, p 135, paras 20–21. He added that there would be three exceptions to the latter rule: one relating to treaties governing the status of territory; another relating to treaty provisions which have become binding as part of customary international law; and a third relating to multilateral treaties which laid down rules for a group of states and which were binding on their successors.

[119] See, Yaseen, Yrbk ILC, 1968, I, pp 142–3, para 44 ('If it were decided to refer only to the law of treaties, all problems would be solved if it were possible to give a categorical answer to the question whether the successor State was a third State with respect to the treaty or whether it was a party to the treaty; but that was impossible.').

[120] Castañeda, Yrbk ILC, 1968, I, p 137, paras 38–40.

[121] W Beckett, 'Decision of the Permanent Court of International Justification Points of Law and Procedure of General Application', 11 BYIL (1930)1.

[122] It is accepted that obligations may be assumed by third parties in respect of treaties to which they are (definitionally speaking) not a party, but only insofar as they explicitly consent. See art 35 Vienna Convention.

[123] *German Interests in Polish Upper Silesia*, PCIJ, Ser A, no 7, pp 28–9 (a treaty 'only creates law as between the States which are parties to it; in case of doubt, no rights can be deduced from it in favour of third States'); McNair, above, n 78, pp 309–21.

that the State formerly exercising sovereignty over the territory subject to succession was itself a party to that treaty.[124]

If a strict application of the *pacta tertiis* rule would appear to eliminate any possibility of *de iure* 'succession' to treaties (in the sense that the successor State would automatically assume rights and obligations under the instrument as a matter of law and irrespective of consent), two alternative approaches may be used to preserve the continuity of treaty obligations. The first is to understand State succession as a limited exception to the application of the *pacta tertiis* rule so as to provide for the assumption of obligations on the part of States which would otherwise be regarded as third parties.[125] If so, then clearly there is a need to look beyond the standard framework of the law of treaties. The second alternative is to deny that the changes in question are such as to make successor States third parties at all.[126] In such a case, however, one necessarily turns back to the theories of succession and sovereignty that Waldock seemed so keen to avoid. That neither here, nor at any later stage, did Waldock seek to explain what the consequences of his approach might be, or the theoretical framework that lay behind it,[127] was largely typical of his stance. He was concerned, above all else, to elucidate rules that appeared to him to be practical – both in terms of how far they seemed to be readily cemented in existing practice, and in terms of how appealing they might be to any future clientele. He was not, by contrast, overly concerned with putting together a coherent theoretical framework for understanding the relationship between treaty relations and notions of sovereignty, and his resistance to the existence of a 'law of succession' must be seen in that light.[128]

---

[124] Nor indeed, is there evidence that those obligations can arise by means of an 'assignment' from one State to another. As Waldock pointed out in his Second Report: 'An assignment is by its very nature a transaction which purports to impose an obligation on a third party – an obligation on the third party to accept a different form of performance of its contract than that to which it is entitled; and in international law the rule seems clear that an agreement by a party to a treaty to assign either its obligations or its rights under the treaty cannot bind any other party to the treaty without the latter's consent.'
Waldock, Second Report above, n 60, p 56, para 10.

[125] For such an approach see, McNair above, n. 78; G Fitzmaurice, 'Fifth Report on the Law of Treaties' Yrbk ILC (1960) II, p 94, para 55. R Jennings and A Watts *Oppenheim's International Law* (9th edn, 1992) I, 1263, suggest that both the League Covenant and the UN Charter must 'be regarded as having set a limit, determined by the general interest of the international community, to the rule that a treaty cannot impose obligations upon States which are not party to it'. See as regards the 'objective' personality of the UN, *Reparation for Injuries Suffered in the Service of the United Nations*, Advisory Opinion ICJ Rep, (1949) 174, p 185.

[126] eg the ILC suggested that 'if a succession of States occurs in respect of the territory affected by the treaty intended to create an objective regime, the successor State is not properly speaking a "third State" in relation to the treaty. Owing to the legal nexus which existed between the treaty and the territory prior to the date of succession of States, it is not open to the successor State simply to invoke art 35 of the Vienna Convention under which a treaty cannot impose obligations upon a third State without its consent.' Yrbk ILC, 1974, II, p 204, para 30.

[127] For his attempt to locate the idea in the notion of a 'legal nexus' see below, pp 141–7.

[128] For the view that Waldock ultimately relied upon the law of succession rather than the law of treaties in his approach to 'new States' see Bedjaoui, Yrbk ILC, 1972, I, p 79, paras 7–9.

The second issue revisited by Waldock concerned the suggestion of the Sub-committee that the Commission should pay special attention to the problem of succession arising as a result of the emancipation of States since World War II. As we have seen, the ILA also seemed to insist, in this respect, that older precedents were of limited value as a way of framing a response to the problems raised by decolonization.[129] Waldock, for his part, was happy to affirm that an emphasis on problems of new States needed 'no justification or explanation'.[130] He took the view, nevertheless, that problems of succession affect old States as much as new and doubted whether 'any purpose would be served by distinguishing at all sharply between the value of earlier and later precedents'.[131] The basic elements of earlier cases of succession were much the same as in modern cases and to attach no value to those precedents would be somewhat arbitrary. He concluded by reminding the Commission that: 'the basic problem in regard to succession remains what it has always been: to discuss with sufficient clearness how far the practice is an expression of policy and how far and in what points an expression of legal right or obligation.'[132]

The implication of this, of course, was to put in question the agenda that had been set by Bartoš in the Sub-committee. Bartoš had emphasized the importance of addressing the question of succession by reference to 'modern' principles of international law, and particularly those established in the UN Charter (including, in particular, the principle of self-determination).[133] For him, historical precedents – such as those concerning the permanence of territorial servitudes and other 'privileges of investment' – were undoubtedly problematic insofar as they appeared to allow the persistence of neo-colonial conditions of exploitation and subordination that were directly in conflict with the right of self-determination. This, in turn, suggested that the problem was less one of 'identifying' the law and distinguishing it from policy; rather it was a question of working out the most appropriate legal solutions that accommodated both the legitimate interests of the newly independent States, and those of other members of the international community.[134] Law and policy, practice and principle, were thus inextricably inter-twined.

One thus finds between Bartoš, Waldock, and the ILA Committee three different ideas as to the relationship between the phenomenon of decolonization and historic instances of State succession. Both Bartoš and the ILA Committee emphasize the relative marginality of earlier precedents – insisting that the experience of decolonization was quite different from, for example, the separation of

---

[129] See above, pp 106–8.
[130] ibid 90, para 14.
[131] ibid, para 15.
[132] ibid, para 16.
[133] These he referred to as 'norms of jus cogens relating to decolonization' which represented 'the fundamental laws of the international community'. Bartoš, Yrbk ILC, 1968, I, p 138, para 57.
[134] For similar see, Yasseen, Yrbk ILC, 1968, I, p 143, para 47.

Belgium from the Netherlands, or Finland from Russia. Their reasons for this conclusion differed of course. For the ILA Committee it was a question of the non-revolutionary character of decolonization, for Bartoš by contrast a question of the application of the principle of self-determination. But both were happy to endorse the particularity of decolonization and of course in doing so, put in question the longevity of the project. Waldock, by contrast, seemed to deny that decolonization was in any respects a novel phenomenon – responding, perhaps, to the intuition that all cases of secession past and present were cases of self-determination[135] – and seemed to deny in the process that there was any separation between the 'modern' and 'traditional' law on the subject. In his second report, Waldock was to make this position even more explicit. There, he was to note that the position adopted by Bartoš amongst others was problematic given the nature of the ILC's work:'decolonization is approaching completion, and the adoption of rules governing it will not satisfy future needs; attention should therefore be devoted mainly to the cases of succession most likely to occur in the future, eg dissolution, merger, economic integration, and not only to the important but transitory problems of decolonization'.[136]

But yet he was also to note, with no obvious sense of self-contradiction, that apart from the resort to devolution agreements in the context of decolonization, State practice actually:

contains comparatively little evidence suggesting, so far as concerns the present topic, a need to treat decolonization as a specific category of succession. Equally it contains little evidence to suggest that decolonization, as such, calls for recognition as a specific element in the legal rules applicable to the succession of new States. The points mentioned [in discussion] . . . appear for the most part to be points which, if valid, will be valid also in the case of a new State arising from a dismemberment outside the process of decolonization.[137]

The practice surrounding decolonization could thus be addressed, but it would have to be shorn of any ideological or other connotations associated with a process of resistance to 'colonialism.'[138]

Waldock's refusal to acknowledge the singularity of decolonization – and perhaps, at the same time, any emphasis upon the UN Charter as having ushered in a new era of international law – was in some respects predicated upon his obvious empiricism. He seemed to share with the ILA Committee (and indeed with many other members of the ILC) a belief that the problem of State succession could only properly be understood once an exhaustive survey of State practice and judicial decisions had been undertaken. The volumes of material produced by the Secretariat and the ILA, were thus a necessary prelude to any process of legal

---

[135] Briggs, Yrbk ILC (1963) II, p 276.
[136] Waldock, Second Report, above, n 60, p 49. This point was echoed by others in the Commission, see, Reuter, Yrbk ILC (1968) I, p 135, para 16.
[137] Waldock, Second Report, above, n 60, p 49.
[138] By his Fifth Report, one may sense that Waldock had changed his attitude on this score, see below, pp 166–73.

restatement or policy prescription (an orientation to the subject which has never quite been shaken off). Deductions from abstract principle, whether that be 'succession' or 'self-determination', were only to be admitted insofar as the 'weight' of practice and opinion would bear. By way of justifying his proposed draft article ensuring the continuance of boundaries established by treaty, for example, Waldock simultaneously excluded the pertinence of self-determination by way of arguing that in its Charter formulation it was an 'independent principle', whilst maintaining that the majority of both practice and opinion seemed 'clearly to be in favour of the view that boundaries established by treaties remain untouched by the mere fact of succession'.[139] Rather than see such practice as standing in a position of tension with the emergent principle of self-determination (as might be understood, perhaps, in Judge Dillard's sense of a people determining the destiny of territory),[140] Waldock re-defined the latter so as to exclude conflict. Whilst he was careful to make clear that his position, in this respect, 'in no way excludes the independent operation of the principle of self-determination in any case where the conditions for its application exist',[141] his reworking of the principle was such as to suggest that the 'conditions of application' would only ever be found to exist by way of conclusion.

It is to be noted, nevertheless, that for all of Waldock's empiricism,[142] he was ultimately far more willing to give expression to the notion of self-determination in his draft articles than the ILA Committee before him. In his Second Report, for example, Waldock was to dismiss the ILA's presumption of treaty continuity in case of succession. He suggested that it was one thing to 'admit as a matter of policy the general desirability of a certain continuity in treaty relations upon the occurrence of a succession and another thing to express that policy in terms of a legal presumption. On this point, quite independently of the question whether such a presumption is compatible with the modern State practice, the Commission may have to consider the possible relevance in this regard of the principle of self-determination'.[143]

Waldock's position, in this respect, differed quite sharply from that of O'Connell whose volumes on succession barely give any mention to the possible salience of self-determination. As we shall see, however, Waldock saw self-determination as a kind of pragmatic guide to be resorted to as a way of avoiding the more uncomfortable conclusions that would result from an absolute deference to 'sovereign consent', but his journey to that conclusion was nevertheless an interesting one.

[139] Waldock, Second Report, above, n 60, p 92.
[140] Separate Opinion of Judge Dillard, *Western Sahara* Advisory Opinion, ICJ Report 1975, 12, 116, p 122 ('It is for the people to determine the destiny of territory and not the territory the destiny of the people.').
[141] Waldock, Second Report, above, n 60, p 93, para 2.
[142] cf G Schwarzenberger, 'The Inductive Approach to International Law', 60 Harv L Rev (1946–47) 539.
[143] Waldock, Second Report, above, n 60, p 50, para 22.

5. The Law of Treaties and Beyond

As suggested above, Waldock initially started with the view articulated by O'Connell in his monograph of 1956 to the effect that the problem of succession to treaties should be approached from the perspective of treaty law rather than by reference to a putative 'law of succession'. For O'Connell this initial standpoint had led him to reject (at that time at least) the idea that treaties should automatically continue in case of succession. Much depended upon the character of the agreement. In case of personal treaties (which he took to be by far the largest category) they will expire with the disappearance of a State party[144] and will only bind successors insofar as some element of personality is continued in the successor.[145] In case of dispositive agreements, these will continue, as will provisions of multilateral 'legislative conventions' by reason of their 'objective' character.[146] Whilst O'Connell soon moved away from this position[147] (even though he was to continue to insist upon the significance of treaty interpretation),[148] Waldock proceeded to work through some of the initial implications of this decision in his first two reports.

The first implication identified by Waldock related to the scope of application of the articles on succession to treaties. Just as the ILC had excluded from its work on the law of treaties, agreements between States and 'other subjects of international law' and agreements 'not in written form', so also, Waldock proposed that these be excluded from the scope of articles on succession to treaties. No particular controversy surrounded such decisions.[149] In similar vein, Waldock suggested that reservations be attached as regards the application of the articles to constituent instruments of international organizations[150] and 'boundaries resulting from treaties'.[151] In respect of the latter, the ILC had already excluded from the rule regarding a fundamental change in circumstances the case of treaties 'establishing a boundary'[152] and it seemed quite obvious to Waldock that the same rule should apply, *mutatis mutandis*, to cases of succession.[153] Although in appearance this might seem to have cemented a rule of automatic succession to boundary agreements, Waldock was

---

[144] O'Connell, (1956) above, n 111, p 15.

[145] ibid 28, 32, 36, 43.

[146] ibid 64.

[147] O'Connell (Independence), above, n 72, pp 85–7. Where he both argues in favour of treaty continuity and doubts the relevance of the distinction between 'personal' and 'real' treaties.

[148] O'Connell (Interpretation), above, n 72.

[149] That this may have brought into question the application of the principles to treaties concluded by 'semi-sovereign' States was not fully appreciated.

[150] The ILC followed, in this respect, the terms of art 5 of the Vienna Convention on the Law of Treaties. Very little discussion of the matter followed the proposal within the Commission. See, Yrbk ILC, 1972, I, pp 150–2.

[151] Waldock, First Report, above, n 60, p 92.

[152] Later to become art 62, Vienna Convention on the Law of Treaties (1969).

[153] Waldock, First Report, above, n 60, p 92.

careful in his explanation. This decision was informed by the idea that what was in question was not the treaty itself, but rather the boundary established pursuant to the treaty – the boundary represented, in other words, merely the legal situation resulting from the execution of the agreement and could not be affected by any subsequent rules governing the application of treaties.[154] This was an issue, however, to which the ILC was to return at a later stage.

In his second report, Waldock continued to try to 'clear the decks' by tackling the question of the cession of territory (entitled rather clumsily 'area of territory passing from one State to another'). Here, like many before him, Waldock identified the relevant rule to be that of 'moving treaty frontiers':

Shortly stated, the rule provides that, on a territory's undergoing a change in sovereignty, it passes automatically out of the treaty régime of the predecessor sovereign into the treaty régime of the successor sovereign. It thus has two aspects, one positive and the other negative. The positive aspect is that the treaties of the successor State begin automatically to apply in respect of the territory as from the date of succession. The negative aspect is that the treaties of the predecessor State, in turn, cease automatically to apply in respect of the territory.'[155]

As he admitted, the rule appeared to exclude any succession in respect of treaties – its applicability being relevant only insofar as it involved the consequences of a change in sovereignty. More to the point, however, was the fact that the rule appeared to be an extension of Article 25 of the Vienna Convention on the Law of Treaties which provided that unless intended otherwise, 'a treaty is binding upon each party in respect of its entire territory'. For Waldock this meant not only that treaties had to be extended to any new territory acquired (even if acquired after the conclusion of the agreement), but also that treaty obligations of the ceding State in respect of that territory would cease, owing simply to the loss of sovereignty. Rather than rely simply on the acquisition or loss of sovereignty by way of justification, however, Waldock emphasized that this was a conclusion that could be drawn, as a matter of treaty interpretation, from the intentions of the parties. Even if those intentions were insufficiently clear, the rule would still be established in virtue of the principles of impossibility of performance or fundamental change in circumstances (*rebus sic stantibus*).[156]

In relying upon existing rules of treaty interpretation for this purpose, Waldock clearly felt less need to conduct the kind of detailed analysis of State practice that he was undertaking in respect of other parts of the project. In a rather half-hearted attempt to locate his principles in existing State practice, Waldock cited a number of examples many of which, however, related to cases concerning the extension of treaties to annexed territory (Algiers, Madagascar, Hawai'i, and Goa).[157] That annexation was understood, in certain quarters at least, as giving

---

[154] ibid, p 93.
[155] Waldock, Second Report, above, n 60, p 52, para 2.
[156] ibid.
[157] Some of his other examples – such as the extension of Serbian treaties to Yugoslavia in 1919 – may also be thought a somewhat suspect basis for his doctrine.

rise to title in virtue of factual control rather than by means of voluntary grant[158] perhaps explained why a consistently negative attitude was adopted towards the survival of treaties of the territory so acquired. But at the same time, it put in question the assumption that such practice would sustain the same conclusion in case of the cession of territory.[159] Needless to say, few other members of the Commission were to object to the rule enunciated by Waldock,[160] in this context, and his apparent assumption that it was a relatively uncontroversial doctrine appears to have been sustained.

a) Devolution Agreements

Thus far, Waldock had managed, through the consistent extension of the law of treaties to questions of succession, to exclude a great deal. He had also managed to do so without reliance upon any overt engagement with the more obvious problems posed by the idea of succession. It was only when he came to deal with devolution agreements and unilateral declarations in his second report, that he was forced to work at the margins of what the law of treaties itself might tell him. Since the UK-Iraq agreement of 1931,[161] the settled practice of the UK had been to propose a devolution agreement to all its overseas territories shortly before or after their independence the effect of which was to ensure that all rights and obligations under relevant international agreements would pass to the latter.[162] Such practice had also encouraged other States such as New Zealand,[163]

---

[158] eg, J Westlake, 'The Nature and Extent of Title by Conquest', 17 LQR (1901) 392.

[159] Other members of the Commission also pointed out counter-examples illustrating the continuity of certain treaties relating to ceded territory. eg, Bedjaoui, Yrbk ILC(1972) I, p 47.

[160] See discussion, Yrbk ILC, 1972, I, pp 152–4; 156–8 (where the main point of discussion concerned the question whether some explicit reference to the legality of the transfer should be included).

[161] UKTS no 15 (1931); cmd 3797. Art 8 of that agreement provided that:

The High Contracting Parties recognize that upon the entry into force of this Treaty, all responsibilities devolving under the Treaties and Agreements referred to in Article 7 hereof upon His Britannic Majesty in respect of Iraq will, in so far as His Britannic Majesty is concerned, then automatically and completely come to an end, and that such responsibilities, in so far as they continue at all, will devolve upon His Majesty the King of Iraq alone.

It is also recognized that all responsibilities devolving upon His Britannic Majesty in respect of Iraq under any other international instrument, in so far as they continue at all, should similarly devolve upon His Majesty the King of Iraq alone, and the High Contracting Parties shall immediately take such steps as may be necessary to secure the treansference to His Majesty the King of Iraq of these responsibilities.

[162] Devolution agreements were concluded in respect of the following: Transjordan, 6 UKTS 144; Burma, 70 UNTS 184; Ceylon, 86 UNTS 28; Malaya, Cmnd 346; Cyprus, Cmnd 1252; Nigeria, 384 UNTS 209; Sierra Leone, Cmnd 1464; Ghana, 287 UNTS 233; Jamaica, Cmnd 1918; and Trinidad and Tobago, Cmnd 1919. See generally, O Udokang, *Succession of New States to International Treaties* (1972), pp 186–99; O'Connell (1967) II, above, n 72, pp 352–73; McNair, above, n 78, p 650; A Lester, 'State Succession to Treaties in the Commonwealth', 12 ICLQ (1963) 475, pp 503 et seq.

[163] With Western Samoa, 476 UNTS 3.

Malaysia,[164] the Netherlands,[165] and France[166] to follow suit, and by the time at which Waldock was writing (1969) some twenty devolution agreements had been concluded in connection with the emergence of a territory to independent statehood.[167] The character of such agreements varied. Some had been concluded in the immediate aftermath of independence; many however had been signed shortly before and on the advice of colonial officials. Some provided for a definitive passing of rights and obligations, others were somewhat more ambivalent on that score.[168]

The key concern of Waldock was the extent to which such devolutions might be thought effective as bringing about a succession to the treaties of the predecessor State. In his paper for the ILC's Sub-committee, Milan Bartoš had suggested that devolution agreements had an ambivalent character. Viewed from one perspective, they were agreements thrashed out through a process of political negotiation with the representatives of a newly independent State and which secured, in many cases, the interests of third States rather than those of the predecessor State. Their rejection would thus constitute a breach of the principle *pacta sunt servanda*. From another perspective, however, they also seemed to represent 'the price of independence',[169] the terms of which were largely dictated under conditions of inequality, and were frequently oppressive (continaining, for example, obligations concerning military alliances and the maintenance of foreign bases). Upholding their validity, in other words, would run counter to the principles of the UN Charter.[170] Bartoš's equivocation, on this score, was to result in the suggestion that they be regarded neither as effective nor as void, but rather as a special class of 'voidable' agreements whose terms could be successfully attacked if they could be shown to be incompatible with the status of the newly independent State (a point to be adjudicated by the ICJ).[171]

Waldock was somewhat less ambivalent on this point. The validity of devolution agreements, in his view, could largely be determined by Articles 42–53 of the Vienna Convention and he doubted the need for any special rule to be articulated in the context of State succession.[172] He was to note, in passing, that

---

[164] Agreement Relating to the Separation of Singapore from Malaysia as an Independent and Sovereign State, 4 ILM (1965) 932. See also, S Jayakumar, 'Singapore and State Succession: International Relations and Internal Law', 19 ICLQ (1970) 398.

[165] Indonesia, 69 UNTS 208.

[166] France signed devolution agreements with India (in relation to Chandernagore) 203 UNTS 155; Morocco, 51 AJIL (1957) 679; Laos, Cambodia and Vietnam (see O'Connell, above, n 72, pp 363–4).

[167] Waldock, Second Report, above, n 60, p 54.

[168] For a critical review see O'Connell, above, n 72, p 120.

[169] Tabibi, Yrbk ILC, 1972, I, p 56, para 47.

[170] Bartoš, above, n 18, p 297.

[171] This was later echoed in Bedjaoui's remarks that examination had to be given to the 'périod suspecte' during which such agreements might have been concluded, and evaluated in light of the principle of self-determination, Bedjaoui, Yrbk ILC, 1972, pp 53–4, para 21.

[172] Waldock, Second Report, above, n 60, p 56, para 8. One may note the exclusivity clause within art 42 of the Vienna Convention 1969 ('The validity of a treaty or of the consent of a State to be bound by a treaty may be impeached only through the application of the present Convention.').

the legal effects of a devolution agreement 'cannot be completely separated from that of its effects *vis-à-vis* third States',[173] but on that score took the view that such agreements could only be read as making provision for the transfer of treaty obligations from the predecessor to the successor State rather than as a vehicle for the establishment of rights and obligations in relation to third parties (in the sense provided by Articles 35 and 36 of the Vienna Convention). He thus saw the issue as one of determining the effect of such agreements by reference to their apparent intention: that of assigning treaty rights and obligations to the successor State. When viewed in that light, however, devolution agreements appeared to have very little substantive value:

> It is ... extremely doubtful whether such a purported assignment *by itself* changes the legal position of any of the interested parties. The Vienna Convention on the Law of Treaties contains no provisions regarding the assignment either of treaty rights or of treaty obligations. The reason is that the institution of 'assignment' found in some national systems of law by which, under certain conditions, contract rights may be transferred without the consent of the other party to the contract does not appear to be an institution recognized in international law. An assignment is by its very nature a transaction which purports to impose an obligation on a third party – an obligation on the third party to accept a different form of performance of its contract than that to which it is entitled; and in international law the rule seems clear that an agreement by a party to a treaty to assign either its obligations or its rights under the treaty cannot bind any other party to the treaty without the latter's consent.'[174]

The most he was thus able to admit, was that devolution agreements represented a 'formal and public declaration of the transfer of responsibility for the treaty relations of the territory from the predecessor to the successor State'[175] the effect of which was: a) to confirm what occurred anyway under general principles of law (the cessation of responsibility of the predecessor State as regards the implementation of treaty obligations in the territory concerned);[176] and b) to indicate the intentions of the new State in respect of the predecessor's treaties.[177] He thus

---

[173] ibid, para 9.

[174] ibid, p 56, para 10. Waldock appears to have taken this view from F Mann, 'The Assignability of Treaty Rights' 30 BYIL (1953) 475; E Lauterpacht, 'The Contemporary Practice of the United Kingdom in the Field of International Law: Survey and Comment, VI 7 ICLQ (1958) 515, pp 523–30 and McNair (1967), above, n 78, pp 340–2. See also, *Case Concerning the Temple of Preah Vihear* ICJ Rep 1961, 17, Oral Proceedings (Thailand), p 27.

[175] ibid.

[176] K Zemanek, 'State Succession After Decolonization', 116 Hague Recueil (1965) III, 188 pp 213–15; Sette Câmara, Yrbk ILC, 1970, I, p 152, para 30.

[177] Lauterpacht comments in this respect that inheritance agreements if not legally effective, are not entirely purposeless:

> They assist, in the early days of independence, in focusing the attention of the authorities of the new State upon the need to clarify the range and extent of their treaty commitments. They provide a basis on which third States can take the initiative in proposing the maintenance or novation of pre-existing bilateral treaties. Finally, if the practice persists, it may help to establish a true concept of succession, under which the successor State assumes the rights and duties created by every treaty

proposed the adoption of a draft article the effect of which was largely to deny any legal effect to devolution agreements.[178]

Waldock's reliance upon the law of treaties, thus, was to avoid the ambivalence that characterised Bartoš's response to the problem, but it did raise questions in its own right. Was it really correct to say that devolution agreements were not intended to create rights in favour of third parties in the sense of Article 36 of the Vienna Convention? From one perspective, the answer was 'no' – their concern was merely to allocate responsibility for existing treaty relations between the parties, not to create any new rights and obligations *vis-à-vis* third States.[179] From another perspective, however, the purported assignment could also be seen as one in which third States were intended (whether or not explicitly) to be endowed with newly enforceable treaty rights as against the successor State (as opposed to those which may continue to subsist in relation to the predecessor).[180] That such agreements may also purport to involve, at the same time, the imposition of new obligations on third States (insofar as there was a new person with which to engage) was only to suggest that something more than mere acquiescence on their part would be required for the agreement to have effect.[181]

In order to sustain his position (and in contrast to his approach in relation to the cession of territory), Waldock undertook a detailed and fastidious examination of State practice in which he demonstrated a consistent unwillingness to take anything at face value. He noted, for example, that the UN Secretary General, in his role as depositary of multilateral treaties, had appeared to assign

which is closely linked with its territory and which cannot be regarded as of so odious a nature politically as to terminate upon the change in sovereignty.

Lauterpacht above, n 173, pp 525–30. O'Connell (1967) was to conclude that, in practice, devolution agreements 'have permitted a presumption of continuity to arise', above, n 72, p 365. See also F Vallat, 'Some Aspects of the Law of State Succession' 41 Trans Grot Soc (1956) 123, p 134; H van Panhuys, 'Las succession de l'Indonesie aux accords internationaux conclus par les Pays-Bas avant l'independence de l'Indonesie', 2 NILR (1955) 67.

[178] The text of draft art 3(1) was as follows:
A predecessor State's obligations and rights under treaties in force in respect of a territory which is the subject of a succession do not become applicable as between the successor State and third States, parties to those treaties, in consequence of the fact that the predecessor and successor States have concluded an agreement providing that such obligations or rights shall devolve upon the successor State.
The general terms of this provision were retained in what was to become art 8 of the Vienna Convention of 1978.

[179] Rosenne suggested that since Waldock's draft seemed to suggest that devolution agreements were merely 'statements of policy' there may not be any particular need for the article, Rosenne, Yrbk ILC, 1970, I, p 155, para 67.

[180] Kearney, Yrbk ILC, 1970, I, p 165, paras 23–25; Yasseen, Yrbk ILC, 1972, I, p 53, para 11 ('The main danger was that the devolution agreement might be considered to contain not an offer depending on the will of the offering State, but a final offer.').

[181] Several of those who are sceptical as to the third party effects of devolution agreements, are nevertheless of the view that the possibility exists for the agreements in question to be brought into effect by way of novation. eg, McNair, above, n 78, p 142. For a more positive endorsement of the possibility of assignment see O'Connell, II, above, n. 72, p 352, also Kearney, Yrbk ILC, 1970, I, p 165, para 23. Contra, Sette Câmara, Yrbk ILC, 1972, I, p 55, para 39.

automatic effects to devolution agreements by registering States as having succeeded to treaties merely in virtue of being notified of the terms of the agreement. Waldock, however, regarded this practice as being fundamentally in error. The Secretary-General did not, he suggested, act as depositary when receiving a devolution agreement under Article 102 of the Charter, but 'in his capacity simply as registrar and publisher of treaties'.[182] As such, he could not be thought to have the authority to attribute to a devolution agreement the effect of constituting the successor State as party to the agreements in question. That was a different role to be performed once he had received the appropriate notification as depositary to the various agreements. In the same vein Waldock was studiously attentive to the apparent inconsistency in practice of those States that customarily attached an automatic effect to devolution agreements. Thus he was to note that the UK, which had been at the forefront in terms of promoting the conclusion of devolution agreements, had appeared to reject any automatic effect to the devolution agreement concluded between Laos and France in 1953, and the US had similarly taken the general view that the continuity of particular agreements would be subject to its consent.[183]

That Waldock was clearly of the view that devolution agreements did not, in themselves, create a legal nexus between the successor State and third parties did not, ultimately, appear to flow inexorably from his analysis of the problem in terms of the law of treaties and/or State practice. He had to work quite hard to explain why it was that third States might not rely upon such agreements in determining their treaty position with new States and why, for example, the UN Secretary-General was wrong to construe such agreements as constituting a notification of succession on the part of the successor State. The impression one gains, the closer one looks at his report, is that he had decided almost from the outset that any other conclusion was unsustainable to the constituency of newly emergent States. One senses also, that Waldock saw this conclusion as representing an application of the principle of self-determination (albeit the case that he studiously avoided any mention of it).[184]

But there was also a more significant underlying consideration here. Had Waldock pursued the line of argument apparently favoured by the UK and US to the effect that devolution agreements were the basis for the establishment of treaty relations with new States, he would, no doubt, have to have considered Bartoš's concerns as to the conditions of inequality underlying the conclusion

---

[182] Waldock, Second Report, above, n 60, p 59, para 19.

[183] ibid, pp 59–61, paras 21–23.

[184] Two causes of his unwillingness to engage in an open discussion of self-determination may have been a) the appreciation that his position effectively denied newly independent States the opportunity to rely upon devolution agreements for purposes of securing their 'treaty heritage' (See, in that respect, Quintin-Baxter, Yrbk ILC, 1972, I, p 54, para 29); and b) that it was unclear as to whether the provision might have applicability outside the context of decolonization e.g. in relation to the separation of Singapore from Malaysia (Waldock, Yrbk ILC, 1972, I, p 56, para 56).

of such agreements.[185] This, as Waldock was aware, was an issue that had been controversial in the drafting of the Vienna Convention on the Law of Treaties[186] and had led to the adoption of a separate resolution at the Conference on the topic of economic coercion.[187] Waldock's silence on matters such as self-determination, sovereign equality, and coercion may be read, thus, as an attempt to leave uninterrogated the carefully constructed edifice of rules on the law of treaties even if, in the process of doing so, he was forced to conclude that the agreements to which he had applied those rules were ultimately of negligible legal value.[188] In excising the questions of politics or ideology that appeared to lie behind the conclusion of devolution agreements, he was also forced to regard the agreements themselves as extraneous to law (a point which was emphasized, in part, by the fact of calling them 'agreements' rather than 'treaties').[189] For the most part, members of the Commission were satisfied with Waldock's approach to devolution agreements and concurred in his view that they were essentially *res inter alios acta*, incapable of creating a legal nexus between the successor State and third parties.[190] Several members of the Commission did stress, however, that such agreements constituted an 'expedient and effective' means by which new States might conclude the treaties indispensable for their everyday life, and that their use should not be discouraged.[191]

---

[185] This was recognized explicitly by certain members of the Commission. eg, Yasseen, Yrbk ILC, 1970, I, p 161, para 52.

[186] On unequal treaties generally see, F Nozari, *Unequal Treaties In International Law* (1971) 286; I Detter, 'The Problem of Unequal Treaties', 15 *International and Comparative Law Quarterly* (1966) 1069, pp 1081–2; A Lester, 'Bizerta and the Unequal Treaty Theory', 11 *International and Comparative Law Quarterly* (1962) 847; L Caflisch, 'Unequal Treaties', 35 *German Yearbook of International Law* (1992) 52.

[187] 'Declaration on the Prohibition of Military, Political or Economic Coercion in the Conclusion of Treaties', See *Official Records of the United Nations Conference on the Law of Treaties, First and Second Sessions, Documents of the Conference* (United Nations publication, Sales no. 70V5), doc A/CONF39/26.

[188] There is another side to the position adopted by Waldock, however. As he seemed to admit (alongside O'Connell and Lauterpacht) the use of devolution agreements could, nevertheless, be a medium through which State practice might be shaped or formed to the point at which a rule of continuity might emerge in customary international law. That O'Connell clearly believed that such a rule had already appeared was really merely a difference in the evaluative weight that each attributed to the existing practice.

[189] cf Rosenne, Yrbk ILC, 1970, I, p 155, para 67 (in which the point is made that if the agreements are not, strictly speaking, 'treaties', then other States are not to be regarded as 'third parties' within the sense of the Vienna Convention on the Law of Treaties). There was a certain equivocation, however, in the Commission's subsequent discussion as to whether a devolution agreement might give rise to obligations between the successor and predecessor States. eg, exchange between Waldock, Ushakov and Ago, Yrbk ILC, 1972, I pp 50–2, paras 41–75. Ago, was clearly of the view that, irrespective of the status of the party concluding the agreement (ie whether it was a provisional government or insurgent movement) they were nevertheless to be taken as 'international agreements', Yrbk ILC, 1972, I, p 55, para 35.

[190] eg, Albónico, Yrbk ILC, 1970, I, p 152, para 41; Castañeda, Yrbk ILC, 1970, I, p 157, para 15.

[191] eg, Sette Câmara, Yrbk ILC, 1970, I, p 152, para 30; Castañeda, Yrbk ILC, 1970, I, p 158, para 18.

b) Unilateral Declarations

As with the case of devolution agreements, Waldock was to face several difficulties in the application of the law of treaties to unilateral declarations. The practice of using unilateral declarations as a means of dealing with the problem of succession to treaties had begun in 1961 following Tanganyika's rejection of the United Kingdom's offer to enter into a devolution agreement by exchange of letters.[192] Fearing that it would be bound by the agreements specified, yet unable to enforce them as against third parties, Tanganyika resolved instead to write to the UN Secretary-General declaring that it would continue to apply bilateral treaties on its territory, on the basis of reciprocity for a period of two years, and would examine each multilateral agreement in order to decide which steps to take 'whether by way of confirmation of termination, confirmation of succession or accession'.[193] In the following years, similar declarations were made by a number of other newly decolonized States (including Botswana, Lesotho, Nauru, Uganda, Kenya, Malawi, Zambia, Guyana, Barbados, Mauritius, Swaziland, Rwanda, and Burundi)[194] the terms of which subtly varied depending upon whether the presumption was to continue the treaty relations in question on a provisional basis[195] or to decide within a particular period as to whether or not the treaties had survived.[196] A number of others (Cameroon, Congo (Brazzaville), Cote d'Ivoire, Niger, and Malagasy Republic) merely communicated their desire to continue existing agreements and conventions.

The purpose of such declarations appears to have varied. In one sense they appeared to be an expedient by which new States sought to maintain the benefits to which they may have been entitled under prior agreements (such as access to cocoa markets under the terms of existing Cocoa agreements). In another sense, however, they also represented a right of freedom of action in relation to existing agreements whose content and significance were yet to be determined.[197] In the latter sense, of course, they were to provide new States with the opportunity to examine existing treaty commitments and understand their implications as regards future policy, without necessarily committing themselves to such agreements on a permanent basis. As, in some cases, new states were not always in possession of information as to which treaties had formerly been applied to their territory, this was clearly a prudential step.

---

[192] 'Problems of State Succession in Africa: Statement of the Prime Minister of Tanganyika', 11 *ICLQ* (1962) 1210.

[193] *Materials on Succession of States* ST/LEG/SERB/14, pp 177–8.

[194] For a discussion of this practice see Y Makonnen, *International Law and the New States of Africa* (1983) pp 210–60.

[195] eg Malawi, Tanzania, Kenya, Burundi and Uganda, Handbook, above, n 71, pp 117–18.

[196] eg Zambia. See, Makonnen, above, n 194, p 220–3

[197] Quentin-Baxter, Yrbk ILC, 1972, I, p 60, para 22.

The particular problem Waldock faced with this practice was that it 'did not fall neatly into any of the established treaty procedures'.[198] To begin with, the declarations themselves, albeit addressed to members of the international community as a whole, were not communicated to the UN Secretary-General as Depositary, nor were they communicated directly to other depositaries of relevant agreements. Rather, they appeared to have been merely disseminated to the UN Secretary-General as a means of making public their declared position. The declarations, furthermore, envisaged the application of treaties on a provisional basis – the possibility of which found no formal recognition in the Vienna Convention on the Law of Treaties.[199] Observing that, as unilateral acts, such declarations could not possibly give rise to binding treaty relations between the successor State and other third States, Waldock concluded that they must be treated merely as furnishing: 'the basis for a collateral agreement in simplified form between the new State and the individual parties to its predecessor's treaties for the provisional application of the treaties after independence'.[200]

He explained that, in his view, the declarations effectively invited an agreement for the provisional application of the treaties in question pending the determination as to whether each individual treaty was to be considered in force with respect to the new State either by virtue of succession or by way of novation.[201] Since the legal effect of those declarations would be dependent upon their express or tacit acceptance on the part of other States, and since they generally envisaged only the provisional application of treaty obligations, they fell some way short of providing for the definitive participation of successor States in the treaties concerned.[202] That was a point to be determined by the general rules that Waldock was in the process of drawing up. Waldock did, nevertheless, propose the inclusion of certain clauses to govern the provisional application of treaties pending either their entry into force or their termination within the period specified.[203]

As with his position on devolution agreements, Waldock approached the question of unilateral declarations with the idea in mind that newly emergent States

---

[198] Waldock, Second Report, above, n 60, p 66, para 13.

[199] The nearest proximate provision, was art 25 of the Vienna Convention 1969, which dealt with provisional application of treaties prior to their entry into force.

[200] Waldock, Second Report, above, n. 60, p 67, para 18.

[201] ibid, para 19.

[202] Waldock was to note that the declaration of Zambia was somewhat closer to a proclamation of succession than others insofar as it began with the acknowledgement that 'many treaty rights and obligations of the Government of the United Kingdom in respect of Northern Rhodesia were succeeded to by Zambia upon independence by virtue of customary international law', and continued by providing that '[i]t is desired that it be presumed that each treaty has been legally succeeded to by Zambia and that action based upon this presumption until a decision is reached that it should be regarded as having lapsed'. ibid, p 64, para 6.

[203] These were ultimately excised from the text of art 9 of the Vienna Convention which simply recorded that obligations or rights under treaties in force 'do not become the obligations or rights of the successor State or of other States parties to those treaties by reason only of the fact that the successor State has made a unilateral declaration providing for the continuance in force of the treaties in respect of its territory'.

essentially stood outside the existing array of treaty relations formerly applicable to their territory. Neither could they be assumed to be parties to those relations in virtue of the mere fact that the treaties were formerly applicable to that territory, nor could third States be regarded as either acquiring rights or obligations as a consequence of such acts. There was, as Waldock continued to insist, no 'legal nexus' between the successor State and other States parties to treaties that formerly applied to its territory. Whereas the thinking behind his conclusions on devolution agreements appears to have been influenced – indirectly or otherwise – by the possible taint of inequality, this of course did not go to the same extent with respect to unilateral declarations.[204] But having effectively set out the proposition that successor States could not insinuate themselves in the treaty relations between the metropolitan State and third States by agreement with the former, so also it would seem to follow that no more could be achieved by unilateral act.

To the extent that Waldock's approach to this question was informed by the idea that successor States were effectively 'third parties' in relation to existing treaties that extended to the territory in question,[205] it was to work on two assumptions both of which had been disputed in recent years. The first was that, for the most part at least, the treaties in question were 'personal' rather than 'territorial' in character (ie that they were contingent upon the 'identity' of the participants) – a point which Jenks, amongst others, had disputed in case of the emergent category of law-making treaties.[206] The second was that the legal 'person' to whom those obligations attached after independence was radically different from that which existed prior to that moment – a point, again, which those such as O'Connell had suggested might be erroneous in case of many Commonwealth countries.[207] But Waldock's position was not, in fact, quite so clear cut. Insofar as he had drafted a series of clauses relating to the continuance of treaties on a provisional basis that would be effective through the tacit acceptance, by other parties to those agreements, he had implicitly accepted that continuation of the *status quo* was an option.[208] As Reuter pointed out in the subsequent discussion, however, Waldock's general premise seemed to allow no scope for the 'application of the original treaty' provisional or otherwise. Rather, and in his view, it was a case of an entirely new 'collateral' agreement coming into effect by way of

---

[204] eg Yasseen, Yrbk ILC, 1970, I, p 161, para 52; Tabibi, Yrbk ILC, 1972, I, p 62, para 46. There was some discussion as to whether unilateral declarations and devolution agreements might be dealt with together, but it was the view of Waldock and others that they were distinct to the extent to which they were addressed to different audiences. Waldock, Yrbk ILC, 1972, I, p 57, paras 68–69.

[205] In contemplation of this issue, a considerable degree of doubt was expressed as to whether Waldock's proposals were applicable in relation to other categories of succession, such as in case of the union of States or cession of territory. eg, Reuter, Yrbk ILC, 1972, I, p 62, para 48.

[206] W Jenks, 'State Succession in Respect of Law-Making Treaties', 29 BYIL (1952) 105, See also, Tsuruoka, Yrbk ILC, 1972, I, p 63, para 53.

[207] O'Connell, II, above, n. 72, p 131.

[208] He was not proposing, for example, that new States could make a similar declaration in respect of treaties which were not formerly applicable to the territory concerned.

offer and acceptance.[209] Waldock's simultaneous denial of any real connection between new States and treaty relations pre-existing their independence, and his insistence that those agreements could nevertheless be 'continued' albeit by way of a 'collateral' arrangement, was thus in some respects inconsistent. Crucially, however, it was to give succour both to those who believed that new States should be entitled to exercise their sovereign rights in choosing which agreements might become binding on them,[210] and those who believed in the principle of the 'stability of international treaty relations' and saw in this provision an important means by which treaty continuity might be maintained.[211]

6. New States

By far the most significant aspect of Waldock's work on succession in respect of treaties was undertaken in his Third report in which he drafted a series of articles relating to the position of 'new States'.[212] He had, in some respects, already set the scene for his work on this topic in his treatment of devolution agreements and unilateral declarations the main practice in relation to which was drawn from the period of decolonization. But it was evident that in case of each of those phenomena, Waldock had determined to render his conclusions subordinate to the more general rules governing succession to treaties. And it was the elaboration of general rules on succession in respect of new States that would assume greatest importance.

In his introduction to his Third Report, Waldock had indicated that he intended to use the term 'new State' as a 'term of art'[213] which would describe 'a succession where a territory that previously formed part of an existing State has become an independent State'.[214] Whilst this appeared remarkably broad,[215] Waldock was to suggest that he understood it in more narrow terms:

It thus covers a State formed either through the secession of part of the metropolitan territory of an existing State or through the secession or emergence to independence of a colony; but it excludes a State formed by a union of States, by a federation of a State with an existing State, by the termination of the protection of a protected State or by the emergence of a trusteeship or mandated territory to independence.[216]

Three elements of this stand out. Firstly, and in line with the views adopted by many other scholars working in the field, Waldock clearly took the view that the

---

[209] Reuter, Yrbk ILC, 1972, I, p 58, para 84.
[210] *eg,* Reuter, ibid.
[211] eg, Ago, Yrbk ILC, 1972, I, p 62, para 42.
[212] Waldock, Third Report, above, n 60.
[213] ibid, p 27, para 8.
[214] Draft art 1(d), ibid 28.
[215] There were those who suggested that the definition was, in fact, too narrow. eg, Ushakov, Yrbk ILC, 1972, I, p 33, para 24.
[216] Waldock, Third Report, above, n 60, p 27, para 9.

unification, or 'federation' of States was to be regarded as a separate category albeit the case that unification in such contexts could plausibly be understood as giving rise to the emergence of an entirely new State. Secondly, Waldock excluded from the term the position of Protected States, Mandates, and Trusteeships. His point, here, was not that these categories of dependent territories were necessarily to be treated in a different way, but that it was convenient to identify the basic principles applicable to new States in their 'purest form before considering the possible effect of special factors in particular cases of succession'.[217] He was perfectly aware, given the discussion in the Sub-committee, that the position of 'semi-sovereign' states may well be slightly different given the ICJ's stance in relation to the effects of the protectorate established in relation to Morocco. But that was a matter he left until his final, fifth report.[218] Finally, and most significantly, Waldock made no differentiation in his definition between States emerging from a context of colonialism, and any other State seceding from the metropolitan territory (that was a distinction to emerge at a very late stage in proceedings).[219] He appeared, in other words, to understand the category purely in terms of the nature of the process rather than in terms of the putative effect of self-determination upon the rules of succession.[220] Had he adopted the latter strategy, he might have inclined not only to distinguish, in line with UN practice, between decolonization and other cases of secessionary independence, but also to address, at the same time, the possible alternative modes of exercising the right of self-determination (by free association or integration with another State).[221] As we saw above, however, this was an approach to the topic that Waldock had emphasized from the outset.[222]

i) *Treaties providing for Succession*

The first draft article set out in Waldock's report governed the position in respect of treaties which specifically provided for the participation of 'new States'.[223] In one sense, of course, most multilateral agreements provide for means by which non-States parties may become participants in the treaty regime in question, but Waldock's concern was to deal with the position in respect of those agreements that contained clauses purporting to regulate in advance the application of the treaty on occurrence of succession. There were, of course, not many agreements that purported to do so,[224] and Waldock relied, in that regard, upon the terms

---

[217]   ibid, p 28, para 9. Also, Yrbk ILC, 1970, I, p 134 (Waldock).
[218]   See below, pp 147–55.
[219]   See below, pp 166–73.
[220]   For similar views see Castrén, Yrbk ILC, 1970, I, p 137, para 56; Ago, Yrbk ILC, 1970, I, p 149, para 4.
[221]   GA Resn 1541 (XV), (1960) Annex Principle VI.
[222]   See above, pp 117–19.
[223]   Waldock, Third Report, above, n 60, p 29 (art 5).
[224]   An early example cited was the Treaty of Berlin, 69 BFSP 749.

of Article XXVI (5)(c) of the General Agreement on Tariffs and Trade of 1947, Article XXII (6) of the Second International Tin Agreement of 1960, Article 67 (4) of the International Coffee Agreement of 1962, and Article 66 (2) of the International Sugar Agreement of 1968.[225]

The terms of each of these agreements varied insofar as they dealt with the process by which dependent territories might become contracting parties.[226] In case of Article XXVI, paragraph 5(c) of GATT, a customs territory acquiring full autonomy in the conduct of its external commercial relations would 'upon sponsorship through a declaration by the responsible contracting party' be deemed a 'contracting party'.[227] By contrast, the Second International Tin Agreement envisaged that territories participating in the agreement would automatically become 'contracting governments' on independence,[228] and the 1962 Coffee Agreement provided for a procedure by which such territories could become contracting parties by notification within a period of 90 days.[229] As Waldock was to note, only in relation to the GATT had any newly independent States become contracting parties by means of the provision in question, and in that case practice had developed in quite a complicated way. Some States (Israel, Tunisia, and Cambodia) had deliberately chosen not to avail themselves of the clause and became contracting parties rather by way of accession[230] and others had decided

---

[225] Waldock, Fifth Report, above, n 60, pp 29–31. He cited, in addition, art VIII of the Geneva Agreement of 1966 between the United Kingdom and Venezuela, which provided that '[u]pon the attainment of independence by British Guiana, the government of Guiana shall thereafter be a party to this Agreement, in addition to the Government of the United Kingdom of Great Britain and Northern Ireland and the Government of Venezuela'.

[226] J Lissitzyn, 'Territorial Entities other than Independent States in the Law of Treaties', 125 Hague Recueil (1970) 64.

[227] 'If any of the customs territories, in respect of which a contracting party has accepted this Agreement, possesses or acquires full autonomy in the conduct of its external commercial relations and of the other matters provided for in this Agreement, such territory shall, upon sponsorship through a declaration by the responsible contracting party establishing the above-mentioned fact, be deemed to be a contracting party.' This clause was originally art XXVI para 4, 55 UNTS 274. It became para 5(c) pursuant to the Protocol of 1957 (278 UNTS 204). It was originally drafted to deal with the somewhat unusual situation presented by the cases of Burma, Ceylon, and Southern Rhodesia in 1947 which possessed, at that time, autonomy in external commercial relations but not full independence. See T Kunugi, 'State Succession in the Framework of the GATT', 59 AJIL (1965) 268, p 270.

[228] Art XXII (6) reads: 'A country or territory, the separate participation of which has been declared under Article III or paragraph 2 of this Article by any Contracting Government, shall when it becomes an independent State, be deemed to be a Contracting Government and the provisions of this Agreement shall apply to the Government of such State as if it were an original Contracting Government already participating in this Agreement.' 403 UNTS 76.

[229] Art 67(4) provided: 'The Government of a territory to which the Agreement has been extended under paragraph (1) of this Article and which has subsequently become independent may, within 90 days after the attainment of independence, declare by notification to the Secretary-General of the United Nations that it has assumed the rights and obligations of a Contracting Party to the Agreement. It shall, as from the date of such notification, become a party to the agreement.' 469 UNTS 238.

[230] Kunugi attributes the lack of enthusiasm for participation by means of accession to the 'cumbersome and disadvantageous' nature of negotiation for 'underdeveloped new states' and upon the

simply not to become parties at all. A third category had become parties merely through the sponsoring of their participation by the predecessor State,[231] and a fourth category had undergone a period of provisional *de facto* application, prior to choosing to become a party.[232]

In light of this practice, Waldock identified two basic rules. The first was that where an agreement provided for the participation of new States by some means (whether that be ratification, accession, signature, or mere notification) fulfilment of those specified conditions would be sufficient in order for the State to become a party to the agreement. This, in itself, was an obvious implication of the existing terms of the Vienna Convention on the Law of Treaties and said very little, in itself, about the institution of succession.[233] The second, and somewhat more significant rule, however, was that in cases where a treaty purported to lay down that a successor State would automatically become party to the agreement on its independence (ie that there was not merely a right of participation, but an obligation) then the terms of Article 35 of the Vienna Convention would become relevant such that any participation would be dependent upon the written consent of the State concerned.[234] It was thus not possible, as far as Waldock was concerned, for a successor State to be automatically regarded as party to an international agreement in virtue only of the terms of the agreement itself. Once again, he appears to have taken the view that successor States were third parties in relation to any such existing treaty arrangements.

ii) A Right of Participation

Waldock's approach to this particular question was indicative of his more general approach to treaty succession in relation to new States. In drafting the subsequent provisions (draft Articles 6 and 7), Waldock was to begin by distinguishing two aspects of the problem of succession: one being the question whether a new State is under an *obligation* to continue to apply treaties to its territory after independence; the other being the question whether it has a *right* to consider itself as

---

fact that it would entail a complete lapse of the previous application of GATT instruments in the territory of an acceding State'. Kunugi, above n 227, p 271.

    [231] The list includes: Gambia, Ghana, Indonesia, Jamaica, Kenya, Malawi, Malaysia, Malta, Nigeria, Sierra Leone, Tanzania, Trinidad and Tobago, Uganda, and Zaire.

    [232] Including Burundi, Cameroon, Central African Republic, Chad, Congo, Cyprus, Dahomey, Gabon, Ivory Coast, Kuwait, Madagascar, Mauritania, Niger, Rwanda, Senegal, Togo, and Upper Volta.

    [233] cf art 11 Vienna Convention (1969), which provides that the consent of a State to be bound by a treaty may be expressed in a number of different ways, including by 'any other means if so agreed'.

    [234] Waldock did note that an exception might exist in cases such as that of the UK-Venezuela agreement in which representatives of the successor State were consulted as regards the terms of the agreement. Waldock, Third Report, above, n 60, p 31, para 12.

a party to such agreements. For Waldock, too many commentators had failed to distinguish these two elements of the equation:

> If a successor State were to be considered as automatically bound by the treaty obligations of its predecessor, reciprocity would, it is true, require that it should also be entitled to invoke the rights contained in the treaties. And, similarly, if a successor State were to possess and to assert a right to be considered as a party to its predecessor's treaties, reciprocity would require that it should at the same time be subject to the obligations contained in them. But reciprocity does not demand that, if a State should be entitled to consider itself a party to a treaty, it must equally be bound to do so.[235]

This distinction between rights and obligations of participation had been initially mooted by Waldock in his earlier reports but it was only in the context of draft Articles 6 and 7 that it was fully explained. In essence, draft Articles 6 and 7 (to become Articles 16 and 17 of the Vienna Convention) laid down the proposition that new States would not be bound by treaties simply by reason of the fact that the treaty was in force in respect of its territory prior to independence, but they would enjoy a right to become party to multilateral agreements by means of notification of succession. This envisaged 'right of participation' existed independently of the faculty of participation that may be laid down in the final clauses of a multilateral agreement, and would not be subject to the approval or consent of other contracting parties.

In order to establish this position, Waldock initially had to address the question whether a newly independent State could be regarded as being 'under a legal obligation to consider itself bound by its predecessor's treaties'.[236] Only if the answer to this was in the negative would his distinction between rights and obligations stand up. Waldock was confronted, here, by a new stream of scholarship from the likes of O'Connell,[237] La Forest,[238] Jenks,[239] and the ILA,[240] all of whom expressed a clear preference for a rule of treaty continuity in case of succession (at least in respect of multilateral agreements). For such authors, the developing practice of States in the middle of the 20th century, whilst not entirely consistent and certainly still emerging, underscored in a general sense the desirability of avoiding a 'legal vacuum' in the wake of territorial change. As Jenks was to put the case, for all the 'political and psychological' factors involved in the gaining of independence, it was wrong to consider obligations of multipartite legislative instruments as bearing the badge of continuing servitude. Rather,

---

[235] ibid 31, para 1.
[236] ibid 32, para 1.
[237] O'Connell, above, n 72, pp. 88–9.
[238] G La Forest, 'Towards a Reformulation of the Law of State Succession', 60 Proc Am Soc IL (1966) 103.
[239] Jenks complained that the 'traditional view' is 'indefensible in principle, unreasonable in practice, and inconsistent with the long-term development of international law and international organisation'. Jenks, above, n 206, p 107.
[240] See above, pp 105–13.

they were, in his view, 'a necessary part of full cooperation in the international community and participation in them must therefore be regarded as one of the hallmarks of emancipation'.[241] It was not, he concluded, a case of 'perpetuating the dead hand of the past, but of avoiding a legal vacuum'.[242]

Without engaging directly with such work, Waldock's starting point was to establish what he saw to be the 'traditional view'. This he took to be that espoused by McNair in the following terms:

> In spite of some evidence to the contrary, emanating mainly from diplomatic rather than legal sources, it is submitted that the general principle is that newly established States which do not result from a political dismemberment and cannot fairly be said to involve political continuity with any predecessor, start with a clean slate in the matter of treaty obligations, save in so far as obligations may be accepted by them in return for the grant of recognition to them or for other reasons, and except as regards the purely local or 'real' obligations of the State formerly exercising sovereignty over the territory of the new State.[243]

McNair, for his part, had based this conclusion upon practice following the emergence to independence of the United States, the Spanish American Republics, Belgium, Poland, Czechoslovakia, Finland, the Baltic States, Panama, and Pakistan, and had clearly not engaged in consideration of the practice arising from decolonization. Waldock was to claim, however, that McNair's position was actually reinforced in significant part by the practice of States and depositaries since 1945[244] and was also supported by the 'majority of writers, at any rate until quite lately'.[245] He made no direct reference in his reports to the work of O'Connell or the ILA[246] (in some senses his disagreement with their analysis

---

[241] Jenks, above, n 206, p 108.

[242] ibid 109.

[243] McNair, above, n 78, p 601. There is a subtle difference in phraseology in respect of the 1961 edition when compared to that of his original volume of 1938. In the latter McNair makes clear that this is 'believed to be the view of the United Kingdom Government'. See A McNair, *The Law of Treaties* (1938) p 450.

[244] Waldock, Third Report above, n 60, pp 34–7.

[245] ibid 32, para 2.

[246] His one note of criticism of advocates of continuity was directed towards Jenks' argument that 'law-making treaties' represented a significant exception to the 'traditional view' – an argument which Waldock took to confuse the categories of conventional and customary law. O'Connell shared this view (above, n 72, p 213):

> The description of a multilateral treaty as "legislative" serves a useful purpose in explaining the process of law-making on a large scale, but it is misleading as a touchstone of transmissibility. A treaty, no matter what its form or its subject matter, is always a contract, and the problem is one of succession to contractual rights and duties rather than birth into a legislative régime. In the sense in which the term is used, all multilateral treaties are legislative, and Jenks apparently admits this in his reference to some 927 treaties ranging in subject matter from renunciation of war and peaceful settlement of international disputes, through copyright and counterfeiting, to weights and measures. Clearly not all of these treaties are transmissible; no State has yet acknowledged its succession to the General Act for the Pacific Settlement of Disputes. Hence treaties devolve, not because of their legislative characteristics, but because of their subject matter, and if subject matter

of contemporary practice had already been set down in his treatment of unilateral declarations and devolution agreements) but he was to conclude that whilst 'continuity' was a 'desirable' and 'progressive policy' there was scant evidence in practice of any legal presumption in favour of continuity and, in any case, 'the principle of self-determination militated against such a presumption'.[247]

The differences between Waldock's and O'Connell's approach to this issue is quite stark. Whereas O'Connell had identified the inconsistency of State practice in relation to treaty succession as a reason for the advancement of a policy of legal continuity (policy being a supplementary category), Waldock had not found anything in practice that seriously contradicted the 'traditional view'. In this regard, of course, Waldock was always on more solid ground insofar as any instance in which a newly independent State agreed to continue the treaties of the predecessor State could be interpreted just as easily as an act of consent as one driven by a belief that such continuity was obligatory. But the disagreement, of course, went beyond the practice itself and extended also to the question of policy. Much as O'Connell had insisted that there was a range of both ethical and prudential reasons for a commitment to treaty continuity, Waldock could always fall back on the principle of self-determination which, in his view, was largely supportive of the clean slate.

Waldock's concern, however, was not to embrace McNair's 'tradition' without qualification. Having established the inadmissibility of any notion of automatic succession, he could now safely distance himself from advocates of the 'clean slate' by reference to his distinction between rights and obligations:

The metaphor of the clean slate is a vivid and convenient way of expressing the basic concept that a new State begins its international life freed from any *obligation* to continue in force treaties previously applicable with respect to its territory simply by reason of that fact. But even when that basic concept is accepted, the metaphor appears in the light of the existing State practice to be at once too broad and too categoric. It is too broad in that it suggests that, so far as concerns the new State, the prior treaties are wholly expunged and are without any relevance to its territory. The very fact that prior treaties are often continued or renewed indicates that the 'clean slate' metaphor does not express the whole truth. The metaphor is too categoric in that it does not make clear whether it means only that a new State is not *bound* to recognize any of its predecessor's treaties as applicable in its relations with other States, or whether it means also that a new State is equally not *entitled* to claim any right to be or become a party to any of its predecessor's treaties.[248]

Even if many were keen to maintain that new States were not bound to honour their predecessor's treaty commitments, this did not, as far as Waldock was concerned, lead to the conclusion that those States were thereby precluded from

---

is the relevant aspect the fact that a treaty is multilateral and not bilateral, or vice versa, would seem theoretically to be of little moment'.

[247] Yrbk ILC, 1970, I, p 135 (Waldock).
[248] Waldock, Third Report above, n 60, p 33, para 6.

doing so. The position he was to assume, in other words, clearly veered towards the idea of the clean slate, but in reality sat somewhere between that idea and the opposed notion of treaty continuity. Although clearly not a 'compromise' solution, it was one that perfectly befitted the analytical exactitude of its author.

The really 'new' idea that Waldock had to establish was that new States enjoyed a right to become parties to existing treaty arrangements 'independently of the consent of the other parties to the treaty' and independently of the terms of admission laid down in the treaty concerned.[249] This was clearly problematic, not least because up to this point Waldock had largely been running through the consequences of his insight that new States were (or in a position analogous to) third parties to any existing treaty relations. If they were to be so regarded, and absent any intent to confer upon them special privileges, it would be just as difficult to establish that new States enjoyed a right of participation as it would to suggest that they were automatically bound by existing agreements. Before developing his argument in this direction, however, Waldock felt compelled to make an initial distinction – whereas, in his view, one could sustain the idea of a right of participation in multilateral agreements, that was not the case in respect of bilateral agreements.[250] Quite why this distinction existed, Waldock did not fully explain other than to remark that the practice of multilateral treaty depositaries appeared to allow new States to participate in treaties by means of notification and irrespective of the views of other parties.[251] In case of the UN Secretary-General, for example, Waldock pointed out that:

> whenever a former dependency of a party to multilateral treaties of which the Secretary-General is the depositary emerges as an independent State, the Secretary-General addresses to it a letter inviting it to confirm whether it considers itself to be bound by the treaties in question. This letter is sent in all cases.... The Secretary-General does not consult the other parties or await their reactions when he notifies them of any affirmative replies received from the new State. He appears, therefore, to act upon the assumption that a new State has the right, if it chooses, to notify the depositary of its continued participation in

---

[249] ibid 37, para 1. This position, of course, was not entirely 'new' in the sense that several other scholars had advocated just such a position. eg, Zemanek, above, n 174, p 232.

[250] Waldock, Third Report above, n 60, p 37, para 1. In subsequent discussion Waldock elaborated further on the difference in practice Yrbk ILC, 1970, I, p 134 ('Succession to bilateral treaties was a very important part of the present subject, and for purposes of codification it suffered from one disadvantage in comparison with multilateral treaties. The absence of a depositary meant that the practice was less formal and looser, so that much depended on interpreting the attitudes of the States concerned. The machinery of the depositary, on the other hand, imposed a certain discipline an depositary practice provided valuable guidance for the identification of rules relating to succession to multilateral treaties. The position was different in the case of bilateral treaties, where it was more difficult to reduce the law relating to them to clear-cut rules.')

[251] In rejecting the idea that the consent of other participating States should be required (as for bilateral treaties) Waldock remarked that such an approach would be 'unrealistic, unduly conservative and unprogressive', Yrbk ILC, 1970, I, p 135.

any general multilateral treaty which was applicable in respect of its territory prior to the succession.[252]

The same held good in respect of other depositaries such as the practice of the Swiss Government, the Swiss Federal Council, and the United States.[253]

Turning to the rationale for this practice, Waldock considered, but ultimately rejected, the idea that it depended upon the prior application of the treaty in respect of the territory concerned.[254] The determinant was not, in his view, whether the agreement had been given force in the municipal law of the territory, but rather whether or not it was in force internationally in respect of that territory. The right of participation, in other words, was based upon the idea that the predecessor State, through its various actions in respect of treaties, had created a 'legal nexus of a certain degree between the treaty and the territory'.[255] The existence of this 'legal nexus' created between the treaty and the territory by the acts of the predecessor State, was to have certain implications that went beyond the right of new States to participate in multilateral treaties irrespective as to whether provision was made for such participation in the final clauses of the agreement in question.[256] It would also mean, as far as Waldock was concerned, that new States would be capable of asserting their right of participation in multilateral agreements not yet in force,[257] and competent to maintain or reject reservations entered by the predecessor State.[258] It was these incidental considerations that largely differentiated the process of succession from that of accession to multilateral agreements.[259]

Waldock was to propose three exceptions to this general principle, the effect of which was to inject a sense of flexibility into its operation and which thereby deflected the concerns of some of its more persistent critics. The first was where the admission of the new State was incompatible with the 'object and purpose' of the treaty; the second where the treaty was a constituent instrument of an international organization and subject to an admissions procedure; and the third

[252] Waldock, Third Report, above, n 60, p 37, para 2.
[253] The US had communicated the following view of its practice: 'The depositary practice of the United States with respect to newly independent States has been, in general, to recognise the right of such States to declare themselves bound uninterruptedly by multilateral treaties of a non-organizational type concluded in their behalf by the parent State before the new State emerged to full sovereignty.' UN Legislative Series, *Materials on Succession of States* (1967) p 224.
[254] cf Zemanek, above, n 174, pp 229, 231. See also ILA, above, n 71, pp 36–8. See also, O'Connell's idea of 'localization', above pp 109–10.
[255] Waldock, Third Report above, n 60, p 39, para 6.
[256] ibid 39, para 8.
[257] ibid 43–46. For discussion see Yrbk ILC, 1972, I, pp 87–91. Cf. ILA, *Interim Report of the Committee on Succession of New States to the Treaties and Certain Other Obligations of their Predecessors* (1969) pp 602–3.
[258] Waldock, Third Report above, n 60, p 47. For discussion see Yrbk ILC, 1972, I, pp 92–9.
[259] Waldock, Yrbk ILC, 1972, I, p 86, para 3. A principal difference, of course, was the temporal one concerning the moment at which a notification of succession would have effect. See discussion in Yrbk ILC, 1972, I, pp 103–12.

where the 'limited number of negotiating States and the object and purpose of the treaty' dictated that the participation of an additional State would require the consent of all parties.[260] Not all members of the Commission were happy with these exceptions,[261] but for the most part they seemed to recognize the importance of not trying to articulate a rule that was excessively rigid.

In the subsequent discussion within the ILC, a good many of its members endorsed Waldock's approach, particularly as regards his rejection of the ILA's presumption of continuity,[262] and in his dismissal of Jenks's thesis concerning 'law making treaties'.[263] Some applauded his formula as an expression of the principle of self-determination,[264] or the notion of 'free will';[265] others for its 'realism' and fidelity to State practice.[266] Others still were impressed by Waldock's apparent 'moderation' in advancing a solution that stood somewhere between the two extremes of continuity and self-determination.[267] There were, of course, voices of doubt particularly as regards the apparent lack of reciprocity as far as third States were concerned,[268] and the extent to which the rule seemed to establish a right of participation going beyond the terms of the treaty itself.[269] There was also concern as to how far this principle might also extend to 'new' States formed by way of fusion,[270] but these were very much contested views.[271]

As this suggests, in all of its discussions concerning the issue, the Commission remained largely divided as to whether the rule was a by-product of the principle of self-determination (and hence limited, perhaps, to the experience of

[260] Yrbk ILC, 1972, I, p 76.
[261] El-Erian opposed the mention of constituent instruments believing the example of Pakistan to be problematic. Yrbk ILC, 1972, I, p 83, para 56. Nagendra Singh opposed the debarring of succession by reason of the 'object and purpose' of the agreement, Yrbk ILC, 1971, I, p 84, para 71.
[262] See eg, Eustathiades, Yrbk ILC, 1970, I, p 136, para 42; Castañeda, Yrbk ILC, 1970, I, p 156, para 4 (describing the ILA's approach as 'reactionary') and p 157, para 13; Bartoš, Yrbk ILC, 1972, I, p 72, para 57; Rossides, ibid, para 47; Ruda, Yrbk ILC, 1972, I, p 82, para 35; El-Erian, Yrbk ILC, 1972, I, p 83, para 53.
[263] eg Yasseen, Yrbk ILC, 1972, I, p 70, para 24; Ago, ibid 71, para 39; Bedjaoui, ibid 72, para 49; Castañeda, ibid 74, para 14. Contra, Alcívar, ibid 74, para 10. For a discussion of this issue following in light of the comments of several governments see Vallat, First Rep, UN doc A/CN4/278, and Add 1–6, Yrbk ILC, 1974, II, pp 43–5.
[264] eg Castrén, Yrbk ILC, 1970, I, p 136, para 50; Albónico, Yrbk ILC, 1970, I, p 152, para 35; Castañeda, Yrbk ILC, 1970, I, p 157, para 14; Thiam, Yrbk ILC, 1970, I, p 162, para 72.
[265] eg Ushakov, Yrbk ILC, 1970, I, p 140, para 23.
[266] eg Eustathiades, Yrbk ILC, 1970, I, p 136, para 42; Ruda, Yrbk ILC, 1970, I, p 150, para 14; Sette Câmara, Yrbk ILC, 1970, I, p 151, para 24; Rosenne, Yrbk ILC, 1970, I, p 154, para 58; Yasseen, Yrbk ILC, 1970, I, p 161, para 53; El-Erian, Yrbk ILC, 1972, I, p 73, para 3 (specifically maintaining that it reflected customary international law).
[267] eg Ramangasoavina, Yrbk ILC, 1970, I, p 141, para 39; Castrèn, Yrbk ILC, 1970, I, p 160, para 42.
[268] eg Bartoš, Yrbk ILC, 1972, I, p 70, para 27;
[269] eg Reuter, Yrbk ILC, 1972, I, p 77, para 52; Ago, Yrbk ILC, 1972, I, p 82, para 46.
[270] eg Reuter, Yrbk ILC, 1972, I, p 71, paras 35–6.
[271] For strong affirmations as to the customary status of the provisions in this respect see Yasseen, Yrbk ILC, 1972, I, p 78, paras 62–65; Bilge, Yrbk ILC, 1971, I, p 81, para 30.

decolonization) or rather a principle that was concerned with the position of all new States irrespective of their circumstances prior to independence.[272] Some members of the Commission emphasized the importance of the newly adopted Declaration on Friendly Relations the terms of which had significantly provided that under the Charter the territory of any colony or non-self-governing territory had 'a status separate and distinct from the territory of the State administering it'.[273] Others emphasized, by contrast, the similarities between decolonization and other cases in which new States had come into being. In some respects the impressive achievement of Waldock's work on this issue was the way in which he managed to give the impression of adhering to the principle of self-determination without expressly doing so. He thus managed to satisfy those who were keen to maximize the freedom of movement of States emerging from colonialism at the same time as mollifying those who regarded the implications of self-determination (with its rigidly consensualist attitude towards sovereignty) as in some senses antipathetic to international law or the interests of the international community. But, as Waldock probably would have recognized in any case, the choice was not between self-determination and something else, but of working out what, precisely, self-determination might mean in the context of succession. Many members of the Commission were of the view that self-determination implied a complete freedom of choice in respect to the treaty actions of the former colonial masters. Many were equally clear, however, that for all the benefits that might be gained from freeing themselves from inherited commitments, new States might also positively benefit from being able to rely upon an existing network of agreements rather than have to conclude all afresh. Denying the possibility of succession in the name of self-determination was not necessarily an emancipatory initiative.

iii) The Legal Nexus

The real point of difficulty, however, concerned Waldock's use of the idea of the 'legal nexus' as a way of justifying the existence of a right of participation. Several members of the Commission were left unpersuaded by his argument on this point. Ushakov, for example, suggested that it 'seemed an unsatisfactory solution to make the exercise of the rights of the successor State depend on an act of will

---

[272] For two contasting views on this see Ago, Yrbk ILC, 1970, I, p 150, para 5; Castañeda, Yrbk ILC, 1970, I, p 156, paras 6–7.

[273] GA Resn 2625 (XXV), 24 Oct 1970, Annex ('The territory of a colony or other Non-Self-Governing Territory has, under the Charter, a status separate and distinct from the territory of the State administering it; and such separate and distinct status under the Charter shall exist until the people of the colony or Non-Self-Governing Territory have exercised their right of self-determination in accordance with the Charter, and particularly its purposes and principles.').

based on reasons which might become obsolete after a change of sovereignty'.[274] Castañeda was similarly unconvinced:

Every treaty, of course, applied to a specific territory but, except for treaties establishing rights *in rem*, there was no special connexion between a treaty and a territory.[275]

The central problem with Waldock's notion of the 'legal nexus' was that it appeared to have persuasive content only in so far as it concerned the actual application of treaties in former colonial territory.[276] This was, of course, the position adopted by Zemanek amongst others, from which Waldock had explicitly distanced himself. But if the 'legal nexus' was not to be found in the local application of an international agreement, how otherwise might it be established? If it was created through the mere 'extension' of a treaty to the territory concerned without any local application, was that really sufficient to establish a 'legal nexus' enabling new States to participate in international agreements absent the consent of other parties? If, by contrast, it was nothing to do with the 'territorial' application of a treaty, then might it not be the case that a new State would enjoy a similar right of participation in any open multilateral agreement? [277] But at that point, the ILC would clearly have moved far away from understanding the issue as one of succession *per se*.

Apart from the opaque nature of his reference to the 'legal nexus', Waldock was also faced with an apparent internal inconsistency in his approach to the issue. In dealing with unilateral declarations, Waldock had insisted upon the lack of a 'legal nexus' between the successor State and other States parties to agreements formerly applicable to its territory. Unilateral declarations, he had declared, could not be effective in inserting the new State into treaty relations with third parties without the latter's consent. But of course, if that were true, would the position be any different in respect of a notification of succession?[278] Would it not always remain open for third States to object that their consent was needed for the participation of another State in an agreement, particularly when it meant sidestepping the prescribed procedures for participation laid down in the agreement itself?[279] That this may only infrequently have occurred in practice, and that existing States parties might have been generally enthusiastic about ensuring continuity of treaty relationships (and hence tolerant of participation through notification of succession) did not really avoid the issue. As it stood, Waldock's idea of the 'legal nexus' seemed to be something of a moveable feast.

The sheer mutability of the idea of the 'legal nexus' was to become particularly apparent when the ILC dealt with the question of bilateral treaties. During

---

[274] Ushakov, Yrbk ILC, 1970, I, p 140, para 25.
[275] Castañeda, Yrbk ILC, 1970, I, p 158, para 27.
[276] Albónico understood the 'legal nexus' to be generated in virtue of the treaty being applied to the territory and thus saw it only as applying in cases of general multilateral agreements already in force. Albónico, Yrbk ILC, 1970, I, p 153, para 47.
[277] Ustor, Yrbk ILC, 1970, I, p 153, para 55.
[278] Bartoš, Yrbk ILC, 1972, I, p 70, para 27.
[279] Ustor, Yrbk ILC, 1970, I, p 153, para 54.

discussions within the Commission, it was very clear that members were initially sharply divided upon the question whether a right of participation existed in respect of bilateral as well as multilateral agreements. Some had insisted that no proper distinction could be drawn between multilateral and bilateral agreements,[280] others had argued that very real differences existed.[281] Waldock, himself, had made clear that as far as he was concerned the rule permitting participation by notification only applied in case of multilateral agreements,[282] and in his subsequent Fourth Report, he proposed the adoption of a distinct set of arrangements for bilateral agreements. According to draft Article 13 (later to become, with little change, Article 24 of the Vienna Convention) a bilateral treaty would be considered in force between the new State and the other State party only when they 'expressly so agree', or when such agreement may be inferred from their conduct. This emphasis upon mutual consent, of course, was to deny the successor State the right to determine unilaterally whether bilateral agreements should continue in force, and was to suggest that their survival would ultimately be brought about by a process most closely analogous to 'novation'.[283]

Waldock offered two initial reasons for differentiating between bilateral and multilateral treaties in this respect. The first was that the 'personal equation' (the identity of the other contracting party) played a far more significant role in bilateral treaty relations than it did in multilateral treaties. Since the 'very object' of bilateral treaties was to regulate mutual rights and obligations by reference to their own 'particular relations and interests', it was not possible to 'infer from a State's previous acceptance of a bilateral treaty as applicable in respect of a territory its willingness to do so after a succession in relation to a wholly new sovereign of the territory'.[284] Secondly, it was apparent to Waldock that the effect of succession to a bilateral agreement was of a more limited nature. It could only give rise to the establishment of new treaty relations between the successor and the other contracting party, and would not extend for example to relations between the

---

[280] Tabibi, Yrbk ILC, 1970, I, p 140, para 27; Ustor, Yrbk ILC, 1972, I, p 116, para 48.

[281] Ushukov, Yrbk ILC, 1970, I, p 139, para 13 (who saw the differences between treaties in terms of their content rather than their form); Tammes, Yrbk ILC, 1972, I, p 113, para 10; Ruda, Yrbk ILC, 1972, I, p 114.

[282] Waldock, Yrbk ILC, 1970, I, p 134, paras 19–21.

[283] Having established this principle, Waldock was to extend it in various other ways. First of all, he dealt with the question of the duration of bilateral treaties – particularly so as to address the problem of 'provisional application' (draft art 14) and went on to establish that the survival of any bilateral treaties would not, in itself, have any implications as regards the relations between the predecessor and successor States (draft art 15). That the 'continuance' in force of bilateral agreements through agreement gave rise to a distinct legal relation between the successor State and the other contracting parties, also meant that the continuance in force of those agreements would be unaffected by the termination or amendment of the original relations between the predecessor State and the other State party (draft art 17).

[284] Waldock, Fourth Report above, n 60, p 146, para 3.

successor and the predecessor States[285] (in contrast to the position in respect of multilateral agreements).[286]

Waldock was very aware that, in proposing this solution, he was to depart once again from the position emerging in contemporary scholarship. The ILA Committee had undertaken quite a detailed survey of different kinds of agreements and had observed that a considerable degree of continuity was evident in relation to a range of bilateral treaties[287] including air transport agreements, extradition treaties, technical assistance agreements, commercial agreements, boundary or territorial agreements, and to a lesser extent with double taxation agreements.[288] Similar findings were evident in the Secretariat reports on succession in respect of extradition agreements,[289] air transport and trade agreements,[290] and in its *Materials on Succession of States*.[291] In contemplation of this practice, however, Waldock was to observe that the 'prime cause of the frequency with which some measure of continuity is given to such treaties' seemed to be the 'practical advantage of continuity to the interested States in present conditions'.[292] But in that respect he was to go on to conclude that 'it may be doubted whether the practice justifies the conclusion that continuity derives from a customary legal rule rather than the will of the States concerned'.[293]

The main evidence produced by Waldock to sustain this conclusion was the fact that continuity of bilateral agreements had largely been achieved by means of an exchange of Notes or Letters, the very existence of which seemed to indicate that the continuance of bilateral treaties was 'a matter not of right but of agreement'.[294] In other cases – instanced in particular by the practice of the US, UK, and Canada – emphasis appeared to have been placed upon the need for mutual agreement (in the form of express or tacit consent) in arriving at a

---

[285] But cf K Keith, 'Succession to Bilateral Treaties by Seceding States', 61 AJIL (1967) 521, p 525 (indicating that a number of bilateral taxation agreements had been concluded prior to independence between the government of the 'seceding' State and the predecessor State).

[286] The fifth ILA Resolution adopted at its 1968 Conference read as follows:
'Unless multilateral treaty otherwise provides, a newly independent State which succeeds to it becomes a beneficiary of the rights and becomes affected by the obligations thereof vis-à-vis all parties thereto, including its own predecessor and other succeeding States, whether they are successors to the same predecessor State or to other parties'.

[287] Japan, for example, claimed the right to the continuance of its traffic rights into Singapore, which had been granted to it in the Agreement between Japan and the United Kingdom for Air Services (1952) on the basis of continuity pure and simple. I Tabata, 'The Independence of Singapore and her Succession to the Agreement between Japan and Malaysia for Air-Services', 12 Jap Ann IL (1968) 36.

[288] ILA, Rep, of the 52 Conf, Helsinki, 1966, 557 at pp 576–7.

[289] 'Succession of States in Respect of Bilateral Treaties', UN Doc A/CN4/229, Yrbk ILC, 1970, II, 102.

[290] 'Succession of States in Respect of Bilateral Treaties – Second and Third Studies', UN Doc A/CN4/243 and Add 1, Yrbk ILC, 1971, II, 111.

[291] UN Publication, Sales no E/F68V5.

[292] Waldock, Fourth Report above, n 60, p 146, para 5.

[293] ibid 148, para 10.

[294] ibid 148, para 11.

decision as to whether a bilateral treaty has survived, and hence a solution based upon the idea of 'contracting in' rather than 'contracting out' appeared to be the most appropriate.[295]

There was something clearly disingenuous about Waldock's approach to this issue. To begin with, he evidently did not seek to dispute the practice of continuity. He might, for example, have made reference to the largely negative practice of Algeria, Israel, and Upper Volta, amongst others, or the objections of Thailand to Cambodia's claims in the Temple case.[296] He might also have denied any general assertion of continuity by reference to the more uncertain practice in relation to categories of agreement such as treaties of alliance, military base agreements, or agreements providing for arbitration or judicial settlement.[297] That he did not pursue any of these avenues, but instead sought to attack the presumption of continuity on the basis that however consistent the practice, actual or tacit consent was necessary, only put in question whether there might ever exist sufficient evidence to persuade him otherwise.

One of the authors to which Waldock referred, and who had made a strong case for the continuity of certain categories of bilateral treaties in case of secession was Keith.[298] Keith's argument was that a range of both legal and 'non-legal' factors pointed towards the existence of a rule of succession. As regards the non-legal factors, these included the fact that, in many cases, the agreements will have been concluded by the 'local government' of the nascent State rather than the metropolitan government (he cited, for example, the Defence Areas Agreement between the government of the Federation of the West Indies and the United States of 1961).[299] Many furthermore will have been implemented by domestic legislation which would continue after independence, and the attainment of independence itself would frequently be of little significance for the continued application of the agreement in question.[300] As regards the 'legal factors', Keith

---

[295] ibid 149, paras 13–14. The UK Foreign Office, for example, in reply to a request made by the Norwegian Government concerning the continuity of the Anglo-Norwegian Double Taxation Agreement of 1951 with respect to newly independent States, offered the view that: 'the Inheritance Agreements concluded between the United Kingdom and those countries now independent were thought to show that the Governments of those countries would accept the position that the rights and obligations under the Double Taxation Agreement should still apply to those countries but that the question whether the Agreement was, in fact, still in force between those countries and Norway was a matter to be resolved by the Norwegian Government and the Governments of those countries'. (*Materials on Succession of States*, above, n 291, p 192).

[296] 1 Pleadings, pp 145–8, 164–6; 2 Pleadings, pp 31–40, 74–83, 106–9.

[297] eg, note of Senegal to France, quoted in J Gautron, 'Sur Quelques Aspects de la Succession d'Etats au Sénégal' AFDI (1966) 836, p 857.

[298] Keith, above, n 285, p 545.

[299] 409 UNTS 67.

[300] He argues, for example, that independence 'is of no significance to the customs official administering tariffs, to the tax officer granting a tax rebate to a foreign resident, to the Treasury official repaying a loan, to the civil aviation officer clearing a flight by a foreign aircraft, to the postal official cashing a money order'. Keith, above, n 285, p 543.

merely observed that the practice of continuing bilateral agreements was both consistent and indicative of a 'sense of obligation':

for one thing, many of the actions recorded above were made in ignorance of the others. Much of the practice consists of a large number of separate, independent acts of government. And, as already noted, States have not, on the whole, attempted to reserve their position, to say that they are merely conceding a privilege. For these reasons it is submitted that the two requirements of consistent practice and *opinio iuris* are met and that new States are to remain bound by certain categories of bilateral treaties.[301]

Waldock, of course, was not just one, but two steps away from this position. Not only did he deny the continuity thesis (a position, as shown above, premised upon the legal irrelevance of devolution agreements and unilateral declarations of continuity), but he also denied the possibility that a new State might, by its own actions alone, ensure the continuity of bilateral agreements formerly extended to its territory. His rejection of the latter position, however, was determined by an approach to State practice which foreclosed the possibility of a customary rule of continuity at the outset.

Interestingly enough, both Waldock and Keith relied upon the principle of self-determination as supporting arguments for their respective positions. Waldock was clear in the view that his solution seemed to be 'more in harmony with the principle of self-determination' than that which insisted upon a presumption of continuity. The principle of self-determination warranted the conclusion that 'the conduct of the particular States in relation to the particular treaty should be the basis of the general rule for bilateral treaties', and should displace any general presumption built upon the admittedly 'considerable' measure of continuity found in State practice.[302] Keith, by contrast, understood self-determination as having quite different implications. First of all, the principle of self-determination appeared to stress the identity of the dependent territories 'as separate entities of which international law takes cognizance *before* independence'.[303] If colonial territories, as the UN Declaration on Friendly Relations seemed to suggest, enjoyed a 'status separate and distinct from the territory of the State administering it', then there was no reason to treat as legally negligible the treaty actions of the government of that territory prior to independence. Further to this, Keith saw within the principle of self-determination the idea that the acquisition of independence was a 'process' rather than a sudden occurrence, and took the form of a progressive legal devolution of authority, rather than a radical 'break from the past'.[304] Any postulate of non-continuity, he implied, was countermanded by the fact that prior to independence, local governments were already enjoying a certain measure of self-determination. Keith's position, in this respect, neatly prefaced some

---

[301] ibid 545.
[302] Waldock, Fourth Report above, n 60, p 150, paras 18 and 19.
[303] Keith, above, n 285, p 544.
[304] ibid. This general approach was shared with that of O'Connell, see above, pp 109–10.

of the subsequent difficulties the ILC was to have in its approach to the various categories of 'semi-sovereign' entities.

7. Semi-Sovereignty: Mandates, Trusteeships and Protectorates

As noted above, in discussing the relationship between State and governmental succession, the ILC's Sub-committee had decided to defer final judgment on the issue for the reason that in case of the granting of independence to territories under Mandates, Trusteeships, and Treaties of Protection, it was not entirely clear as to whether they would constitute cases of State succession in its strict sense, or rather some other form of succession. The matter was to arise again in the Commission's discussion of Waldock's draft article on the 'use of terms' in his first report.[305] There, Waldock had deliberately avoided any use of the word 'sovereignty' in his definition of 'succession', defining it rather as 'the replacement of one State by another...in the possession of *competence* to conclude treaties with respect to a given territory' [emphasis added].[306] This was applauded by certain members of the Commission who emphasized that the question of the passing of treaty competence encapsulated situations that would not necessarily be understood in terms of a change of sovereignty[307] – particularly the case, as Waldock made clear, of the termination of Mandates, Trusteeships, and Treaties of Protection. On the other hand, however, there were those who regarded the question of sovereignty to be a key element in any case of succession. Rosenne, for example, was to point out that dependent territories occasionally enjoyed a competence to conclude treaties, and that the devolution of that 'competence' to them by a metropolitan State could hardly be regarded as an instance of succession.[308] There was also concern that omission of the word 'sovereignty' would have the potential of bringing within the frame of the draft articles, situations of military occupation. On this latter point, Waldock's immediate response was to suggest that issues raised in virtue of military occupation could be dealt with by a separate provision 'reserving' it from the draft, but that decision, of course, did not entirely dispose of the issue posed by the category of 'semi-sovereign' States.

As noted above, in his Third Report of 1970, Waldock had begun drafting substantive articles relating to the position of 'new States', which were defined in a way that did not include States formed through union or federation, or those formed 'by the termination of the protection of a protected State or by

---

[305] Yrbk ILC, (1968) II, doc A/7209/Rev1, p 127, paras 47–50.

[306] Waldock, First Report above, n 60, p 90.

[307] eg, Tammes, Yrbk ILC, 1968, I, p 137, para 43; Bedjaoui, ibid 141, para 23.

[308] Rosenne, Yrbk ILC, 1968, I, p 141, para 19; Bedjaoui, ibid, p 141, para 24. He was also to note, as a consequence, that the ILA's distinction between evolutionary and revolutionary succession was, as a consequence, to be treated with caution.

the emergence of a trusteeship or mandated territory to independence'.[309] The reason for this, as far as Waldock was concerned, was to allow separate consideration of the latter issue at a later date to determine whether or not separate provisions were required (or whether, by contrast, they might otherwise be treated in the same way as 'new States').[310] He finally returned to the issue in his Fifth Report in 1972, albeit with some hesitancy. It was evident, as he made clear, that such cases were largely exceptional given the 'progressive disappearance of dependent territories and of the modern law regarding self-determination'.[311] But he was also to note that the process of emancipation 'was not yet absolutely complete' and that, in any case, 'it could be relevant historically to determine the law in existence at the moment of independence in order to ascertain whether at that time a treaty was in force'.[312] Yet, having examined the practice, he was ultimately to conclude that the 'special characteristics' of this category of case 'do not appear to call for different rules' except as regards one or two minor points.[313]

As regards the position of Protected States, Waldock began by sharply distinguishing between two categories of case – the case of the 'protected State', and that of the 'colonial protectorate'. Protected States differed from colonial protectorates insofar as they 'retained in some measure a separate international personality during the period of their dependency upon another State'.[314] He admitted that this distinction was a difficult one to draw in many cases, and the point at which protection gave way to annexation was frequently one of 'nice appreciation'.[315] These doubts aside, he was clear in the view that the category of protected States was a distinct one, and that the defining point seemed to be found in a recognition of its continued personality as an independent State, even though the authority to conduct external relations might have been invested in another State. That, of course, was a position that had been established by the International Court of Justice in the *Case concerning rights of nationals of the United States of America in Morocco*.[316] There, the ICJ had declared that, despite

---

[309] Waldock, Third Report, above, n 60, p 27, para 9.

[310] ibid 28, para 10.

[311] Waldock, Yrbk ILC, 1972, I, p 133, para 51. Echoed by El-Elerian, Yrbk ILC, 1972, I, p 134, para 58; Alcívar, Yrbk ILC, 1972, I, pp 135–6, paras 80–82; Yasseen, Yrbk ILC, 1972, I, pp 136–7, paras 2–4.

[312] ibid, pp 133–4, para 51.

[313] Waldock, Fifth Report, above, n 60, p 4, para 3.

[314] ibid 4, para 4.

[315] ibid. He referred, in that regard to the remark of the PCIJ in the *Nationality Decrees in Tunis and Morocco Case*, (PCIJ, Series B, no. 4, p 27) in which it remarked that the extent of powers enjoyed by a protecting State 'depends, first, upon the treaties between the protecting State and the Protected State establishing the Protectorate, and secondly, upon the conditions under which the Protectorate has been recognized by third Powers as against whom there is an intention to rely on the provisions of these Treaties'. It continued by remarking that whilst many protectorates may have common features, 'they have individual legal characteristics resulting from the special conditions under which they were created, and the stage of their development'.

[316] ICJ Rep 1952, 172, p 188.

the terms of the Treaty of Fez establishing a French Protectorate over Morocco, the latter 'remained a sovereign State' and had merely undertaken a contractual arrangement by which France 'undertook to exercise certain sovereign powers in the name and on behalf of Morocco'.[317] Although Waldock was of the view that calling Morocco a 'sovereign State' in such circumstances was rather too strong,[318] he was nevertheless happy to accept that Morocco 'retained its personality as a State in international law'.[319]

From this initial, albeit hesitant, presumption, Waldock then went on to address the question whether this 'special status' had any effect as regards the rules regarding succession. Two questions stood out: first whether the treaties concluded by the protected State prior to its entry into protection would continue in force, notwithstanding its change in status? And secondly whether treaties concluded by the protecting power on behalf of the protected State would continue to bind the latter after independence? The answer to the first question seemed to flow logically from the fact of the continued personality of the protected State. Thus, in the *US Nationals in Morocco* case, the Court had concluded, in virtue of the fact that Morocco remained a sovereign State that the protecting power (France): 'is bound not only by the provisions of the Treaty of Fez, but also by all treaty obligations to which Morocco had been subject before the Protectorate and which have not since been terminated or suspended by arrangement with the interested States'.[320] The United States, as a consequence, was entitled to rely upon the provisions of the Treaty with Morocco of 1836 for purposes of exercising consular jurisdiction in all disputes between its citizens or protégés.

In respect of the second question concerning treaties concluded by the protecting power, the answer appeared to be a little more difficult. The 'logic' of this attitude towards the continued sovereignty of the protected State might suggest that if treaties were concluded on its behalf, or in its name, they should continue to bind it after independence (so far as circumstances permit), but if treaties were merely 'extended' to that territory by the protecting power under some 'colonial clause', no such continuity could be presumed. Whilst there was some support for this conclusion in academic writings[321] and in practice[322] Waldock was sharp in identifying inconsistencies and discrepancies. Whereas

---

[317] ibid, p 188.

[318] Zemanek, above, n 174, p 195.

[319] Waldock, Fifth Report, above, n 60, p 4.

[320] ICJ Report 1952, 176, p 188. Further support was found in *British Claims in the Spanish Zone of Morocco (Rio Martin) Arbitration* (per Max Huber), *RIAA* II, (1949) 725 and in the Tongolese notification to the UN Secretary General concerning the position of existing treaties after independence, UN Doc A/CN4/263. Further examples are to be found in McNair, above, n 78, pp 622–9 concerning Tunis, Madagascar, Korea and Morocco.

[321] eg Zemanek, above, n 174, pp 196–202.

[322] eg practice of Morocco after independence. Waldock, Fifth Report, above, n 60, pp 5–6, para 12. This was also the position adopted by the Legal Committee of the French Union in 1950, cited in O'Connell, II, above, n 72, p 145.

Morocco[323] and Tonga[324] appeared to have taken the view that they were obliged to take over treaties concluded on their behalf by former protecting powers (France and the UK respectively) this was evidently not the case in respect of Tunisia, Laos, Vietnam, and Kuwait.[325] The conclusion also seemed to rest, in Waldock's eyes, upon an excessively 'formal' reading of the distinction between treaties concluded on behalf of, or in the name of, a protected State and those merely extended to it: was the difference in method really intended to have significance as regards their potential heritability?[326] Waldock doubted this and, as a consequence, concluded that there were really no grounds for treating protected States any differently from former colonies as regards succession to treaties, except as regards the continuity of treaties concluded prior to entry into protection. Similar conclusions were drawn in respect of Mandates, Trusteeships, colonies, and associated States.[327]

The position adopted by Waldock, in this context, stands in contrast to that of Zemanek writing only a few years earlier. Zemanek, as suggested above, had taken the position that treaties concluded in the name of a protected State would continue in force after independence, but his reasons for concluding as much were somewhat novel. For Zemanek, the ICJ was simply wrong in its conclusion that the Treaty of Fez encroached only upon Morocco's competence in external relations. In reality French administration 'reached down to all levels': French courts enjoyed extensive jurisdiction both *ratione personae* and *materiae*, the 'Commissaire Résident général' enjoyed a right to veto any legal enactment, and the Sultan was rarely if at all consulted in the conclusion of treaties.[328] This, however, was not such as to warrant the conclusion that the protectorate was illusory, but simply demonstrated that the question as to whether protectorates retained their status as sovereign States was 'beside the point'.[329] What was of importance for Zemanek was the question of imputability: which acts are, in law, attributable to the personality of Morocco as distinct from that of France? The answer to that question was to be determined simply by whether or not France had 'validly' acted in the name of Morocco, and the key to validity in that sense was to be found in the terms of the Treaty of Fez.[330] The treaty, in other words, delineated

---

[323] For a discussion of the US base agreement in Morocco see O'Connell, II, above, n 72, pp 257–8.

[324] See comments of government of Tonga, cited in Vallat, First Report, above, n 263, p 25, para 103.

[325] Waldock, Fifth Report, above, n 60, pp 6–10.

[326] O'Connell makes the argument in case of Tunisia that even if the Bey may not have participated in the negotiation of an agreement 'the implementation by the Bey, coupled with the specific localization of the treaty, was sufficient under the treaty of protection to preserve the international status of Tunisia and imply its consent to France's agency in treaty making'. O'Connell, II, above, n 72, p 144.

[327] See below, pp 151–5.

[328] Zemanek, above, n 174, pp 196–7.

[329] ibid, p 199.

[330] This conclusion is, in part, premised upon Zemanek's concept of 'functional succession' which concerns the attribution of responsibility to a different 'subject' of international law on the basis of a change that affects only 'part of the supreme power'. ibid 189.

the terms under which the government of France could act as the government of Morocco for purposes of treating with other States internationally.

The reasoning and conclusions of Waldock and Zemanek on these points are quite curious when placed alongside one another. Whereas Zemanek initially appears to suggest that the formal terms of the Treaty of Fez were largely illusory insofar as they purported to guarantee the continued 'sovereignty' of Morocco, his conclusion is predicated solely upon the delimitation of responsibility under the terms of that agreement (which ultimately determined whether France or Morocco would be responsible for any acts in question). Waldock, for his part, begins with the assumption that a protected State will, depending upon the terms of the treaty, continue its personality, but then proceeds to avoid the conclusions that such an assumption would produce by suggesting that it would be unduly formalistic to suggest that the treaty could have the effect of delegating responsibility for external affairs to a third party. In some respects the conclusions of each would have been more consistent with the arguments of the other. Zemanek's anti-formalist position in respect of the Treaty of Fez might have led to the argument that Morocco, for all intents and purposes, ceased to exist as a subject of international law, and that any agreements concluded during that period would be subject to rules of succession as might apply to 'new States'. This, in essence, was the position later adopted by Bedjaoui in the Commission's discussion of the issue.[331] Waldock's argument, by contrast, to the effect that the Treaty of Fez did ensure the continued personality of Morocco, might have led to the more obvious conclusion that any agreements concluded in the name of that person would continue to bind it after the restrictions on its competence were lifted. This, in fact, was the position of Bilge who concluded that since there had been no replacement in sovereignty, there could be no succession.[332] Both Waldock and Zemanek, however, were clearly of the view that the question of sovereignty did not take the matter very far: Zemanek avoided the problem by his focus upon the idea of 'responsibility', Waldock, by dint of his unswerving reliance upon what practice seemed to tell him.

Waldock's approach to Mandates and Trusteeships largely followed that relating to protected States. He began by observing that the nature of Mandates and Trusteeships was one in which the external relations of the territory concerned were temporarily administered by a sovereign State on behalf of the international

---

[331] Bedjaoui, Yrbk ILC, 1972, I, p 137, paras 6–12 ('The whole idea underlying article 18 was false because it was based on a legal fiction. There had never been a pure protectorate where the protecting Power solemnly respected the sovereignty of the protected State.... In point of fact, there had often been a twofold and genuine succession of States: one at the time of the establishment of the protectorate, and the other at the time of the second independence. The question whether the treaty remained applicable was thus pointless, since it had ceased to be applied during the period of the protectorate.').

[332] Bilge, Yrbk ILC, 1972, I, p 139, para 27 (suggesting that since, in case of 'genuine protectorates' there had been no 'replacement in the sovereignty or competence to conclude treaties', and since the protectorate retained its 'sovereignty', there could be no 'succession').

community and under a trust for the people of the territory. In neither case did the administering power enjoy sovereignty as such, but it did assume responsibility for the international relations of that territory.[333] Having reviewed the various Mandate and Trusteeship agreements, Waldock drew two initial conclusions: first that treaties previously applied in respect of the territory were no longer generally considered applicable (with certain qualifications concerning what he called 'dispositive treaties');[334] secondly, that although the mandatory power did not acquire sovereignty, it was vested with the authority both to extend its own treaties to the territory, and conclude new treaties on its behalf. The precise terms of this varied from one agreement to another (and differed as regards the different classes of Mandates)[335] but it is apparent that, in practice, mandatory powers frequently merely extended their own agreements to the territory concerned.[336]

The central question, however, concerned the effect of independence upon the treaty obligations of the mandated and Trusteeship territories. Zemanek had concluded, in line with his position on protected States, that the question was one concerning the extent to which the acts in question were attributable to the 'personality' of the mandated territory[337] (and hence a differentiation between treaties entered into on behalf of the territory, and those merely extended to that territory was significant). O'Connell was to take a similar line in his book of 1967: 'It would seem clear that the doctrine of international representation in respect of mandated territories requires that on expiration of the Mandates the former mandated territories are bound by international engagements validly concluded by their Mandatories during their infancy.'[338]

Waldock, however, was less than convinced that this was actually evidenced in practice. On the one hand, it was perfectly clear that, at the time, the League of Nations and the various Mandatory powers believed that international agreements would continue to bind the mandated territories on their independence. The Council of the League of Nations had adopted a resolution as early as 1931 to the effect that one condition for the termination of a Mandate would be the 'maintenance in force...of the international conventions, both general and

---

[333] Waldock, Fifth Report, above, n 60, p 10, para 24.

[334] The exception here concerned the capitulation agreements with Western Powers which were only 'suspended' by the terms of the Mandates over Palestine, Transjordan, Syria, and Lebanon. See generally Q Wright, *Mandates under the League of Nations* (1930) pp 482–4.

[335] In case of Class A Mandates, it was provided that the Mandatory 'shall adhere on behalf of...[the territory concerned] to any general international conventions already existing, or which may be concluded hereafter with the approval of the League of Nations, respecting the slave trade, the traffic in arms and ammunition...etc.'. See Art 9 Mandate for Palestine and Transjordan, Art 9 Mandate for Syria and Lebanon in case of Class B and C Mandates, the general formula provided that the Mandatory shall apply to the territory any general international conventions 'applicable to his contiguous territories'. eg art 8 British Mandate for Togoland and the Cameroons; art 8 French Mandate for Togoland and the Cameroons and art 9 of the Belgian East African Mandate. Wright, above, n 334, pp 600–18.

[336] Zemanek, above, n 174, p 204; Wright, above, n 334, pp 467–9.

[337] Zemanek, above, n 174, p 206.

[338] O'Connell, II, above, n 72, p 151.

special, to which during the mandate, the mandatory power acceded on behalf of the mandated territory'.[339] This was reproduced in the Declaration made by Iraq at the moment of her admission to the League, and a similar provision was to be found in the Treaty of Alliance with Britain of 1930.[340] Although the League had effectively ceased to function at the time at which Jordan, Syria, and Lebanon became independent, Britain and France maintained the view that treaty obligations would continue in those cases as well.[341] The UN General Assembly had also recommended, in its original partition plan for Palestine, that each State be bound by all international agreements 'to which Palestine has become a party'.[342]

On the other hand, and despite the obvious concurrence of views on the part of Western powers, the practice of the territories themselves was far less clear. Israel, of course, took the view that it was an entirely new State and not a successor to the Mandate, and consistently maintained the position that international agreements concluded on behalf of the Mandate of Palestine were not legally effective in relation to it.[343] In the cases of Jordan, Syria, and Lebanon, practice was extremely varied. Whereas Syria and Lebanon appeared to have acceded to the view that multilateral agreements for which the UN Secretary-General acted as depositary continued in force,[344] only a handful of bilateral agreements seemed to have been continued.[345] Jordan, for its part, merely acceded to some of the multilateral agreements formerly applicable to its territory and evidence as to the continuity of bilateral agreements was sparse. As regards Trusteeship territories, although several had entered into devolution agreements (Western Samoa, Somalia, and British Togoland) these were merely 'bilateral acts between the Administering Authority and the territory rather than an expression of United Nations policy',[346] and Tanganyika (together with Burundi and Rwanda) had resisted any supposition of automatic inheritance of agreements entered into on its behalf by the British authorities. Indeed, it was precisely because of the lack of competence of the mandatory power that led

---

[339] LNOJ (1931) Minutes of the Council at its 64 session, 2055–6. See further L Evans, 'The General Principles Governing the Termination of a Mandate', 26 *AJIL* (1932) 735.

[340] 132 BFSP, 1930, I, 208, art 8.

[341] In case of Jordan this was expressed in art 8 of the Treaty of Alliance with Britain (1946). 6 UNTS 146. In case of Syria and Lebanon, General Catroux, on behalf of the Free French, had proclaimed their independence in 1941 and in doing so had made clear, in the case of Syria, that it would 'naturally' succeed to rights and obligations undertaken in its name. See Waldock, Fifth Rep, above, n 60, p 12, para 29; O'Connell, II, above, n 72, pp 158–9; R de Murault, *The Problem of State Succession with Regard to Treaties* (1954) p 122.

[342] GA Resn 181 (II), 1947.

[343] UN doc. A/CN.4/19, I, para 26, Yrbk ILC, 1950, II, p 216. O'Connell notes, however, that various pieces of implementing legislation were maintained in force by Israel (above, n 72, p 157).

[344] UN doc A/CN4/150, paras 11–13, Yrbk ILC, 1962, II, p 108.

[345] de Muralt concludes that 'the Syrian and Lebanese States do not, generally speaking, continue the obligations of the treaties concluded by the Mandatory', above, n 347, p 124. Waldock, for his part, identifies only six bilateral agreements that appear to continue in force for those countries. Fifth Rep, above, n 60, pp 13–14, para 34.

[346] Waldock, Fifth Report, above, n 60, p 15, para 38.

Tanzania to reject the continuance of the Belbases agreements.[347] Waldock thus came to the conclusion that Mandates and Trusteeships, so far as they remained a category of significance, could be addressed largely in the same way as protected States, and hence as new States – i.e. that there could be no standing assumption of any automatic succession to treaties.[348] In the event, these conclusions were such as to encourage the Commission finally to abandon the idea of giving any special reference to Mandates, Trusteeships, or protected States in the draft articles.

Ultimately, the issue that structured discussion in respect of all these cases – and indeed which underlay the difference in approach of various authors to the question of decolonization more generally – was the relationship between sovereignty and representation. On one side were those willing to adduce from the fact that mandatory powers did not exercise sovereignty in relation to the territory concerned, the conclusion that there was simply no possibility of there being any automatic inheritance of treaty obligations. This could be extended to the case of 'Protected States' insofar as the ICJ had maintained that such regimes of protection did not eclipse the sovereignty of the State falling under protection, and extended also to straightforward 'colonies' on the basis that they enjoyed something approximating a 'right of independence' under the terms of the Declaration on Friendly Relations (1970). For such authors, the entire issue could be structured around the idea of 'sovereignty', which they appeared to take as a fixed category. On the other hand, there were those who saw the various arrangements of governance – whether they be Mandates, Trusteeships, Protectorates, or protected States – as effectively making redundant the category of sovereignty as a way of understanding the imperatives of succession. To say, as McNair put it in the *South-West Africa* case, that in the case of mandated territories, sovereignty was 'in abeyance', was only to make apparent the limited utility of arguments about sovereignty for purposes of deciding the future of treaty obligations. It neither affirmed nor refuted the possibility of succession.

If the idea of formal 'sovereignty' seemed to raise more questions than it answered, one could always look behind it to the question of representation: to what extent had the local population and local elites been involved in the conclusion of the treaty or in its application and localization through legislation? How far, in other words, might one infer consent on the part of the local population (through the local administration), notwithstanding the fact that they were in no formal sense independent? One senses, however, that for those relying upon the category of sovereignty for their resistance to colonial inheritance, the arguments about representation were largely self-interested ones. Just because the British authorities had begun to rely upon the notion of the divisibility of the Crown, emphasizing in the process the relative autonomy of local regimes of governance in the various parts of the Empire, this was not sufficient reason for intuiting to

---

[347] See below, p 190.
[348] Waldock, Fifth Report, above, n 60, p 14, para 35; p 15, para 40.

the 'colonized population' its consent to international arrangements concluded on their behalf. Bedjaoui, for example, insisted that 'the Commission should take into account the anti-colonial philosophy of the United Nations'[349] and recognize in the process that:

The problem of representation in international law arose not in the case of protected States, mandates or trusteeships, or dominions, which were all survivals of colonial or semi-colonial situations condemned by the Charter, but perhaps more fruitfully in the case of unions or dismemberments of States.[350]

Representation, in other words, appeared to be a consideration that could only effectively be brought to the fore once the scourge of colonialism had been eviscerated. The subtle and deeply embedded nature of colonial rule meant that it was neither possible nor legitimate to search for assent to international obligations on the part of the colonized population. As suggested above, however, this radical critique of colonialist ideology was also one that only really went so far as to empower the elites that were to assume responsibility for governance after independence: the cost of resistance being the authorization of a new authoritarianism.[351]

8. Other Categories of Succession

It was only in Waldock's final Fifth Report, that he belatedly came round to dealing with categories of succession other than the cession of territory or the acquisition of independence of new States to which he had devoted most attention up to that point. Here, he distinguished three different categories of case. The first concerned the 'formation of unions of States', the second the 'dissolution of a union of States' and the third 'other dismemberments of a State into two or more States'.[352] The categories identified by Waldock said a great deal about his approach to the project of codification.

In his book published only several years earlier, O'Connell had identified nine different categories of succession each of which, in his view, was distinct in terms of the rules that would serve to be applicable to it. These included: annexation and cession (Chapter 2), protection and suzerainty (Chapter 3), entry into a federation (Chapter 4), unification (Chapter 5), reconstruction (Chapter 6), secession (Chapter 7), grants of independence (Chapter 8), protectorates and trust territories (Chapter 9) and dismemberment (Chapter 10).[353] For Waldock's purposes, several of these categories were combined. No real distinction was to be drawn between protection and suzerainty, protectorates and trust territories, and grants

---

[349] Bedjaoui, Yrbk ILC, 1972, I, p 138, para 17.
[350] Bedjaoui, Yrbk ILC, 1972, I, p 138, para 18.
[351] See above, pp 88–91.
[352] Waldock, Fifth Report, above, n 60.
[353] O'Connell, II, above, n 72, pp 25–230.

of independence or (indeed, as it turned out) secession. The category of 'entry into a federation' was dealt with either under the heading of unification (if it involved States) or under the rubric governing new States (if it involved territories), and Waldock clearly believed the categories of 'annexation' and 'reconstruction' to be largely redundant or insignificant. Apart from Waldock's obvious desire to avoid an excessively complex typology of succession, the difference in attitude may be traced to the relative emphasis given to domestic constitutional arrangements.

As suggested above, in O'Connell's case, his general approach to succession had been predicated upon the idea that succession was a problem of general legal philosophy rather than one specifically of concern to international lawyers. He rejected any dogmatic compartmentalization of international and municipal law, preferring instead to attack the issue of succession as one for which a uniform response was needed and which could only be constructed by reference to what he saw to be the concrete legal sociology of political change. Local responses to the question of succession in the form of judgments of courts concerning the continuity of law (as may relate, for example, to legislation or contract) were not merely 'material sources' of State practice to which the international lawyer might, or might not, refer, but rather the repository of legal insights into the same general problem of legal continuity to which both municipal and international lawyers had to address themselves. His search for a uniform response to this general problem (through the harmonization of international and municipal law)[354] was thus to necessitate taking into account the particularities of constitutional arrangements both in terms of their structure and evolution such that differences between federal and unitary arrangements, between forms of 'protection', 'trusteeship', or 'suzerainty', or between the modes of 'revolutionary' and 'evolutionary' independence had to be recognized.

Waldock, by contrast, saw the problem exclusively as one of international law, and one that was to be determined as a matter of deduction from State practice rather than one of general legal philosophy. Certain distinctions had to be maintained – one could not realistically posit the same rule for a case of secession as for a case of unification or conflate the categories of universal and partial succession – but it was evident to Waldock that different types of constitutional arrangement were of little concern, given the general bar of domestic jurisdiction. Thus, whereas O'Connell had reacted against Hall's prescription that everything depended upon international 'personality', Waldock had firmly internalized the structural constraints of the latter and effectively took it as his consistent point of departure. That this did not entirely explain Waldock's retention of a distinction between the dissolution of unions of States and the dissolution of unitary States was to be explained only perhaps because of his uncertainty as to which analogy was appropriate.

---

[354] D O'Connell, *International Law* (2nd edn, 1970) I, p 43–6.

a) Unions of States

Until well into the 20th century, international lawyers were apt to lapse into classification when describing the principal actors in international law. This characteristically extended beyond the identification of various non-State agencies (such as individuals, corporations, and intergovernmental institutions) to a classification of States themselves. Although the overriding concern with 'legal personality' (defined in terms of the criteria for statehood) might have been such as to efface any effective distinctions between 'types' of State[355] – except, perhaps, in those limited cases in which the constituent units of a federal State enjoyed power to enter into agreements with other States[356] – the tendency to differentiate between unitary States and 'unions of States' (with a further internal distinction between 'real' and 'personal' unions) appears to have been a habit difficult to shake off, even if its significance was admitted to be limited.[357] The background to this residual categorization, however, was not premised upon any real differentiation in the status of such States (in terms of their abstract legal capacity), but in terms of the perceived relevance of unification as a mode of State formation for the consequential rules of succession that were deemed to apply. Precisely why that might be the case was something that obviously required some investigation, and Waldock took up the challenge.

By way of trying to define the remit of his draft articles dealing with unions of States, Waldock began by making some fairly self-evident distinctions. To begin with, there was a distinction between 'unions' of States that brought into being 'a new political entity...on the plane of international law and organization' (eg the United Nations or its specialized agencies), and those that also created a new political entity on the plane of internal constitutional law (eg the United Arab Republic, the United Republic of Tanzania, or the Union of Iceland and Denmark). This distinction also extended to 'hybrid unions' such as the EEC which, whilst bearing some of the hallmarks of a 'quasi-federal association of States', nevertheless assumed the character of a 'regional international organization' for purposes of succession.[358] A second distinction, for Waldock's purposes, was to be made between a union of mere territories (or a territory with a State), and a union of two independent States. The rationale, here, was that in the case of a union of territories (such as Ghana, formed from the amalgamation of the

---

[355] Kunz argued, for example, that 'Les conceptions des différents liaisons d'États ne sont pas conceptions normatives, ne sont pas des conceptions du droit, mais des conceptions de classification fournies par la doctrine.' J Kunz, 11 RDILC (1930) 835, p 849.

[356] cf ILC Commentary to art 4, Articles on State Responsibility, Yrbk ILC (2001) II, 59, p 84.

[357] eg, Crawford, above, n 12, pp 479–500.

[358] Waldock pointed out, for example, that art 234 of the Treaty of Rome 'unmistakably approaches the question of the pre-community treaties of member States with third countries from the angle, not of succession or of the moving treaty frontier rule, but of the rules governing the application of successive treaties relating to the same subject matter'. Waldock, Fifth Report, above, n 60, pp 18–19, para 3.

colony of the Gold Coast, Ashanti, the Northern Territories Protectorate, and the Trust Territory of Togoland) there would be no question of the continuity of the international personality of the component territories, and they could therefore be treated on the same lines as any other newly independent State.[359] Similarly, the uniting of a territory with a pre-existing State (such as Newfoundland's entry into the Dominion of Canada) was most closely analogous to a case of cession and therefore appeared to be governed by the moving treaty frontiers rule.[360] Only in case of the uniting of two independent States would a new rule of succession have to be identified.

This second distinction between unions of States and unions of territories was not one that was uniformly adhered to by other scholars. The ILA, in its work on succession, had not sought to distinguish in any categorical sense between the formation of 'composite States' by reference to the status of the original component units.[361] In its commentary to its resolution concerning succession in case of 'unions or federations of States', the ILA indicated that the rule of continuity of treaties within their original treaty limits would apply both to unions of States and to unions of territories (citing, in support, the case of Somalia).[362] Its position on this point, however, was largely dictated by the fact that it had already determined that, in case of newly independent States, a presumption of continuity would operate. If treaties survived the creation of a new unitary State, it would be very strange to suggest that they would not similarly survive the formation of a federal union (with the obvious qualification that survival might depend upon the consistency of the treaty with the constitutional position established by the union/ federation), and therefore the distinction between the unification of States and the unification of territories could not be sustained.

That Waldock had proceeded on a different basis in respect of newly independent States meant that drawing a parallel between the unification of States and the unification of territories would only make sense if he was to come to roughly the same conclusions in each case. In an abstract sense, of course, it would have

[359] ibid, p 19, para 7. For more detailed discussion of the cases of Nigeria, Malaysia, Ghana, and Somalia see ibid 32–5.

[360] ibid, para 8.

[361] In its second resolution of the 53 Conference of the ILA in 1968 it adopted the following resolution:

In cases of unions or federations of States, treaties, unless they otherwise provide, remain in force within the regional limits prescribed at the time of their conclusion to the extent to which their implementation is consistent with the constitutional position established by the instrument of union or federation

In such a case where the treaty remains in force, the question whether the union or federation becomes responsible for performance of the treaty is dependent on the extent to which the constituent governments remain competent to negotiate directly with foreign States and to become parties to arbitration proceedings therewith.

[362] Note 2, Interim Report, of the Committee on the Succession of New States to the Treaties and Certain Other Obligations of their Predecessors, ILA, Rep, of 53 Conference, Buenos Aires, 1968 (1969) pp 600–1.

been open for Waldock to insist that a union of States was such as to create a 'new' legal person and hence that rules governing unification were the same as those governing the acquisition of independence. But Waldock appeared to regard the issue of pre-existent personality as a primary point of distinction. As he was to explain: 'A sovereign State, when it joins a federation or union of States, has an existing treaty regime of its own – an existing complex of treaties to which it is a party in its own name. A mere territory may have an existing complex of treaties formerly made applicable to it by its administering Power; but in general these treaties are not treaties to which it is itself a party at the moment when it joins the federation'.[363]

Again one finds Waldock rejecting any suggestion that mere 'territories' might have entered into international agreements in their own name rather than that of their colonial masters, and seems to have assumed that the type of devolution of treaty-making competence prior to independence that had been so influential in the development of the ILA's prescriptions, were of little legal significance. His quali-fication that this was only 'in general' the case, was perhaps added in light of his acceptance that in certain cases (specifically the class of 'Protected States') the terri-tory concerned may actually remain party to certain treaty arrangements contracted prior to the imposition of colonial administration.[364] In any case, he subsequently proposed, and had endorsed, a provision whereby the unification of territories would be governed by the same principles as those relating to newly independent States.[365]

Having thus narrowed down the topic to the unification of pre-existent States, Waldock cast around for relevant precedents. The problem was that remarkably little relevant practice existed. The Unions of Norway and Sweden (1814–1905) and Denmark and Iceland (1918–1944) were of little apparent interest since neither Norway nor Iceland had been independent States prior to the union.[366] In similar vein, whilst the Republic of Somalia, formed through the union of Somalia and Somaliland, was technically a union of independent States,[367] their separate existence prior to unification was 'very short lived' and largely preliminary to the formation of the union itself.[368] Other examples of practice

---

[363] Waldock, Fifth Report, above, n 60, p 27, para 32.

[364] See Quentin-Baxter, Yrbk ILC, 1972, I, p 162, para 24.

[365] See Excursus A, Yrbk ILC, 1972, I, p 172.

[366] Oddly enough, Waldock was later to note in the context of the dissolution of unions that 'there existed some pre-union treaties which had continued in force for the union with respect to Iceland' indicating that, in some respects at least, there were legal issues to be explored. See Waldock, Fifth Report, above, n 60, p 38, para 8.

[367] In general, Somalia did not recognise its succession to many treaties. No notification was made as regards multilateral treaties to which the Secretary-General is depositary, and evidence is scarce as regards other treaties. In case of certain ILO conventions, however, Somalia accepted some as being applicable in relation to the entirety of its territory, others it deemed to apply only in relation to the territory of Somaliland or that of the Trust Territory. Waldock, Fifth Report, above, n 60, p 35, para 9. O'Connell pointed out that the general attitude of the Somalia government was that 'treaties, when continued at all, apply only to the areas in which they territorially applied before independence'. O'Connell, above, n 72, p 101.

[368] Waldock, Fifth Report, above, n 60, p 34, para 9.

from the late 19th and early 20th centuries, furthermore, appeared difficult to interpret.[369] The formation of the German Federation in 1871 (with the possible exception of the annexation of Hanover and Nassau) was marked by the survival of most treaty obligations[370] including those concerning commerce,[371] consular relations,[372] and extradition.[373] The same was the case as regards the Swiss Federation formed in 1848,[374] the Greater Republic of Central America formed in 1895,[375] and (in the next century) the formation of the USSR on 23rd July 1923.[376] Nevertheless, whilst such precedents appeared to endorse a general principle of continuity,[377] what was less clear was whether treaties survived within their original limits, or whether they were subsequently extended to the entirety of the territory. In the case of the Swiss Federation and the USSR it was evidently the case that pre-federation treaties of the individual Cantons/Republics would survive only within their respective territorial limits after federation. Evidence in the case of the German Federation, by contrast, was somewhat mixed.[378] Ultimately, the problem seemed to depend upon whether treaty survival was premised upon the Federal State being a successor to the States within their respective regional limits, or rather upon the continued legal

[369] ibid, p 27, para 33.
[370] O'Connell, II, above, n 72, pp 58–60; E Castrén, 'On State Succession in Practice and Theory', 24 Nord TIR (1954) 67; McNair, above, n 78, pp 629, 632–3.
[371] eg *Flensburger Dampfercompagnie v United States*, AD 1931–2, no 38.
[372] *Bertschinger v Bertschinger*, 22 ILR 141.
[373] eg *In re Thomas* (1874) 12 Blatchford 370; Moore, above , n 78, pp 354–6.
[374] O'Connell, II, above, n 72, pp 60–1.
[375] Formed by a Treaty of Federation signed by El Salvador, Nicaragua, and Honduras, was extended in 1897 to include Costa Rica and Guatemala which expressly provided that '[f]ormer treaties entered into by the States shall still remain in force in so far as they are not opposed to the present treaty'. Waldock, Fifth Report, above, n 60, p 28, para 35.
[376] It was declared that the existing treaties of the Russian, White Russian, Ukrainian, and Transcaucasian Republics 'shall remain in force in the territories of the respective Republics'. O'Connell, above, n 72, II, p 60, n 7.
[377] The obvious exceptions concern the admission of Texas and Hawaii into the United States. In case of Texas the US took the view that Texas's pre-federation treaties had lapsed and that the treaties of the United States extended to her. See eg Statement of US Secretary of State 1876 'the union between the United States and Texas... necessarily cancelled the treaties between Texas and foreign powers, so far, at least, as those treaties were inconsistent with the Constitution of this country.' F Wharton, *Digest of International Law* (1887) I, p 24. Both Britain and France objected, arguing that Texas could not, by voluntary merger, exonerate herself from her own existing treaties. Dodson, Kings Advocate, FO 83 2207 and 2382, in A McNair, *The Law of Treaties* (1938) pp 391–3. British law officers, however, changed their position in 1857. It was accepted that arguing for the existence of a separate treaty of commerce and navigation with Texas was incompatible with the US federal constitution. Since Britain had recognised the 'annexation' of Texas it was concluded that 'the separate Treaty merges in the general Treaty of Commerce (if any) subsisting between such Foreign Country and the Federal Union'. For text see McNair, above, n 78, pp 630–2. This, it must be said, seems to have been a pragmatic resolution of a problem that related more closely to the highly ambiguous nature of Texas' entry into the federation, and the apparent difficulty commentators had in deciding whether it was a case of unification or a case of annexation
[378] Practice was certainly mixed on this point. See O'Connell (Composite Relationship), above, n 72, pp 68–77.

personality of each member State.[379] On this latter point, the ILA had clearly rejected the view that treaty continuity depended upon the retention of a measure of international personality on the part of the constituent entities, with the simple observation that in practice 'continuity has occurred even in the absence of such faculties'.[380]

When it came to it, Waldock gave greatest attention to two recent cases of unification: that of Egypt and Syria to form the United Arab Republic in 1958,[381] and of Tanganyika and Zanzibar to form Tanzania in 1964. Superficially, both of these cases appeared to establish the same precedent, namely that the 'successor' States would continue to be bound by existing treaty obligations within their existing territorial sphere of applicability.[382] In the case of the UAR, a communication of the UAR Foreign Minister was directed to the United Nations indicating that 'the Government of the United Arab Republic declares that the Union is a single Member of the United Nations, bound by the provisions of the Charter, and that all international treaties and agreements concluded by Egypt or Syria with other countries will remain valid within the regional limits prescribed on their conclusion and in accordance with the principles of international law.'[383]

Following this notification, the Secretary-General proceeded to list the UAR as party to all the treaties to which Egypt and Syria had been parties before the union, but indicated, in each case, whether Egypt or Syria had taken action in respect of the treaty in question.

In the case of bilateral treaties, the UN Secretariat's studies on extradition treaties,[384] air transport treaties,[385] and trade agreements,[386] suggested that the treaties remained in force unaffected by the fact of unification.[387] Like the

---

[379] The latter view is preferred by McNair, above, n 78, p 629.

[380] Interim Rep, of the Committee on the Succession of New States to the Treaties and Certain Other obligations of their Predecessors, ILA Rep, of the 53rd Conference, Buenos Aires, 25th–31st Aug 1968, 596, p 600. For the opposed view see E Castrén, 'La Succession d'États', 78 Hague Recueil (1951) 385, p 443, (proffering the idea that the loss of treaty making capacity of a component part of a federal union, would result in the conclusion that the treaties of such a member would expire with its entry into the federation).

[381] See E Cotran, 'Some Legal Aspects of the Formation of the United Arab Republic and the United Arab States', 8 ICLQ (1959) 346; R Young, 'State of Syria: Old or New', 56 AJIL (1962) 482; C Rousseau, 'Syrie: Sécession de la Syrie et de la RUA' 66 RGDIP. (1962) 413.

[382] The provisional Constitution of the United Arab Republic envisaged the creation of a unitary State comprised of two 'regions', but with a single legislative body and a centralised executive possessing treaty making powers (art 56). Art 69 of the Provisional Constitution provided, however, that: 'The coming into effect of the present Constitution shall not infringe upon the provisions and clauses of the international treaties and agreements concluded between each of Syria and Egypt and foreign Powers. These treaties and agreements shall remain valid in the regional spheres for which they were intended at the time of their conclusion, according to the rules and regulations of international law'.

[383] Yrbk ILC (1962) II, p 113, doc A/CN4/150, para 48.

[384] Yrbk ILC (1970) II, p 89, doc A/CN4/225, para 108.

[385] ibid, (1971) II, p 148, doc A/CN4/243/Add 1, paras 149–166 and 181.

[386] ibid, 179–181 and 184, doc A/CN4/243/Add 1, paras 149–166 and 181.

[387] This seems to have been reflected in the treaty lists of other States, see, O'Connell, II, above, n 72, pp 72–3.

UAR, the uniting of Tanganyika and Zanzibar into the Republic of Tanzania in 1964 involved the unification of two independent States under a common Head of State and a common organ responsible for international relations.[388] In a note resonant of that issued by the UAR, the Republic of Tanzania informed the Secretary-General on 6th May 1964 that:

the United Republic of Tanganyika and Zanzibar declares that it is now a single member of the United Nations bound by the provisions of the Charter, and that all international treaties and agreements in force between the Republic of Tanganyika or the People's Republic of Zanzibar and other States or international organizations will, to the extent that their implementation is consistent with the constitutional position established by the Articles of the Union, remain in force within the regional limits prescribed on their conclusion and in accordance with the principles of international law.[389]

As far as membership in the UN, was concerned, the Secretary-General seems to have dealt with this communication in the same manner as that of the UAR,[390] as indeed did the organs of the UN and specialised agencies.[391]

Whilst superficially similar, the cases of the UAR and Tanzania were, in many respects quite different. As regards the UAR, it was held to be entitled to take the seats of Egypt and Syria within the United Nations (and organs thereof) without requiring it to undergo admission as a member State (this process was later reversed with no greater difficulty).[392] The continuity of treaties within the original territorial scope of validity, therefore, seemed to follow from the idea that the UAR did not so much 'replace' the personalities of the two Republics in international relations, but continued them albeit under the guise of a single agency.[393] As O'Connell pointed out, however, this conception of the union was difficult to understand within the framework of traditional conceptual categories: 'It was not a real union because the Republic was a State; nor was it a personal union, because whatever international personality of the constituent States

---

[388] E Seaton, and S Maliti, 'Treaties and Succession of States and Governments in Tanzania', *African Conference on International Law and African Problems* (1967) paras 26–28.

[389] *Multilateral Treaties* (1968) p 7, n 6.

[390] ibid.

[391] Membership of GATT, the FAO and ITU seems also to have followed from Tanganyika's prior membership in those organizations.

[392] The same approach was adopted *mutatis mutandis* by the specialized agencies. M Whiteman, *Digest of International Law* (1963), II, pp 987–90; O'Connell, II, above, n 72, pp 193–6. Waldock concludes that: 'the Secretary-General and the other organs of the United Nations, acted on the basis that the United Arab Republic united and continued in itself the international personalities of Egypt and Syria'. Fifth Report, above, n 60, p 21, para 14.

[393] As the ILC pointed out, one of the major characteristics was the fact that 'the process of uniting was regarded not as the creation of a wholly new sovereign State or as the incorporation of one State into the other, but as the uniting of two existing sovereign States into one'. Commentary Draft Art. 32, Yrbk ILC (1974) II i, 171, 1974, p 258, para 24. Crawford, in discussing the case under the title 'unusual formations' suggests in similar vein that 'despite the recognition of the Republic as a unitary State, it appears to have been a loose association the existence of which was not inconsistent with the continuing international personality of its component parts'. Crawford, above, n 12, p 489.

survived was of very limited character. At the same time it was not a federation since there was no classical distribution of legislative powers'.[394]

The only conclusion O'Connell felt able to draw, therefore, was that the union was entirely *sui generis* albeit one which had certain analogies with other types of association. Even if, as Waldock argued, O'Connell was relying upon a rather spurious distinction between real unions and 'States',[395] the evident difficulty was that, whilst for certain purposes the United Arab Republic was treated as a single entity (as evidenced, in particular, by the centralization of legislative and treaty making powers under the Provisional Constitution[396] and by its unitary membership in international organizations) in many other respects it remained a loose federation of two separate entities.[397] Whether this was to make it a *sui generis* entity, or rather, emblematic of the inevitable contortions that accompany the attempt to rationalize the formation of political unions in terms of a unitary concept of governmental authority, is open to question.

For all the equivocation over the characterization of the UAR, the formation of Tanzania was far less obviously a union of two equally positioned States. Tanzania was listed as party to those multilateral treaties to which Tanganyika had been party prior to unification and on the basis of the date at which Tanganyika had notified its act of acceptance, ratification or accession.[398] No mention was made of their applicability within pre-existent territorial limits, nor was any mention made of Zanzibar. This point was later made explicit in a note to the Secretary-General who was informed that the United Republic of Tanzania 'continues to be bound by multilateral treaties . . . which had been signed, ratified, or acceded to on behalf of Tanganyika'.[399] The somewhat 'lopsided' arrangement that resulted was, it seems, largely due to the fact that Zanzibar had also only just achieved independence as a former colonial protectorate (in 1963) and had taken the view that pre-independence treaties had terminated following the revolution in 1964.[400] Zanzibar had not, therefore, either notified other States of its acceptance of multilateral or bilateral agreements,[401] nor had it apparently concluded any

---

[394] O'Connell, II, above, n 72, p 74. See also Ago, Yrbk ILC, 1972, I, p 160, paras 73–4. (who speaks about the 'poverty of the legal language' in this context).

[395] Waldock, Fifth Report, above, n 60, p 22, para 16. He takes O'Connell as relying upon Oppenheim's 'mystical' view that a real union was 'not itself a State . . . but a composite international person'. L Oppenheim, *International Law: A Treatise* (Lauterpacht, 8th edn 1955) I, p 171.

[396] 8 ICLQ (1959), pp 374–80.

[397] eg position in respect of the IMF. See generally, K Bühler, 'State Succession, Identity/Continuity and Membership in the United Nations' in M Koskenniemi and P Eiscmann, *State Succession: Codification Tested Against the Facts* (1997) p 187.

[398] eg, 1946 Convention on the Privileges and Immunities of the United Nations; 1947 Convention on the Privileges and Immunities of the Specialized Agencies; 1961 Vienna Convention on Diplomatic Relations.

[399] *Multilateral Treaties*, 1999, I 2, n 31.

[400] Waldock, Fifth Report, above, n 60, pp 24–5, paras 22–24.

[401] But cf Parcel Post Agreement and Regulations of Execution, (1959) 11 UST 293.

further such agreements before unification.[402] The continuity of pre-unification treaties, therefore, appeared to be a matter of little practical significance as far as Zanzibar was concerned.

Despite the evident peculiarities of each of these cases, Waldock was to suggest, largely in line with the position adopted by the ILA, that such practice appeared to indicate 'a rule prescribing the continuance in force *ipso jure* of the pre-union treaties of the individual States within their respective regional limits and subject to their compatibility with the constitution of the Union'.[403] However, two points of caution were evident. First of all, Waldock was not entirely confident that the principle of *ipso iure* continuity was adequately established in practice, and whilst he clearly preferred it, ultimately offered the Commission a choice between two formulae, one of which provided for automatic continuity, the other for continuity through express or tacit agreement.[404] His second concern related to the 'compatibility' criterion which had been particularly evident in the practice of Tanzania, and which had been discussed in the work of the ILA.[405]

In its provisional report, the ILA had not taken a view on the question whether treaty survival depended upon the constitutional competence to give effect to the agreements in question after the formation of the new entity. Its ambivalence on the issue was explained in the following terms:

On the one hand, it may be argued that a State, if it may be exonerated from treaty obligations by being annexed to another State, may also be exonerated if its relationship with that other State is less than total absorption. On the other hand, it may equally cogently be argued that, since a State may not plead constitutional incapacity as an excuse for non-compliance with a treaty, escape from treaties is not achieved by a new constitutional relationship with another State'.[406]

For Waldock this was really to go too far in 'introducing internal constitutional provisions into a rule of international law, and in a manner which takes insufficient account of the rights of the other States parties to the treaty'.[407] But even rejecting the hypothesis that continuity depended upon the continued treaty-making capacity of the component units of the union/ federation (for which the

---

[402] It is reported that in case of bilateral treaties concluded by Tanganyika after independence but before unification, practice appears to have been that they continued in force but only in relation to the territory concerned. Waldock, Fifth Report, above, n 60, p 25, para 24.

[403] ibid pp 25, 29, paras 25, 39.

[404] Yrbk ILC, 1972, I, pp 158–9.

[405] The ILA formula allowed the continuity of pre-union treaties 'to the extent to which their implementation is consistent with the constitutional position established by the instrument of union or federation', Resolution 2, above, n 105. In its report, however, the ILA indicated that 'it had not taken a position on the question whether treaty continuity depends upon consistency of a treaty with the constitutional position established by the instrument of union or federation, or whether treaties continue in force irrespective of the constitutional competence to give effect to them after the formation of the new entity'.

[406] Interim Report, (1968) above, n 70, p 600.

[407] Waldock, Fifth Report, above, n 60, p 30, para 43.

UAR and Tanzania were good examples) he was still to struggle with the possibility that the continuance in force of a treaty might in practice be incompatible with the terms of the union. If a trade agreement, for example, cut across the unified economic regime envisaged for the union, its continuity could surely not be secured.[408] The only answer, as far as Waldock was concerned, was to introduce a qualification by which continuity of an agreement would be conditional upon the compatibility of its object and purpose with the constitution of the union. If laid down as an 'objective legal test' and applied in good faith, it would represent a 'reasonable and practical rule'.[409]

As ever, Waldock's eye for the pragmatic solution, largely obscured the underlying rationale for his proposal.[410] The key conundrum was that Waldock neither wanted to conceive of unification as bringing into being an entirely new State,[411] nor was he willing to accept that continued treaty-making competence on the part of the component units of a federation might be the rationale for local treaty continuity. The historic international personality of the units of union/ federation was thus important in his mind for purposes of discriminating between a case of union, and the merger of former colonial territories into a new State, but he was unwilling to attribute to that personality any role in the rule thus articulated. If local treaty continuity did not follow from the fact of personality, nor by way of tacit agreement, then one was left casting around for a rationale for his proposal. Indeed, when pushed on the matter during discussions within the Commission, Waldock replied rather lamely that his conclusion was merely 'in conformity with what he had found in State practice'.[412]

Waldock's equivocation on this point was to encourage a quite extensive discussion of the matter within the Commission. Certain members, emphasizing the radical nature of unification, took the view that they should be placed in the same position as 'new States'.[413] Others by contrast, emphasized the essential difference between States emerging from decolonization and those from the unification of two independent States, and advocated as a consequence a general rule of continuity on the basis that it would be the best means of protecting the interests of third States.[414] Nearly all, however, emphasized the 'novel' nature of the proposals,[415] and the absence of clear examples from practice.[416] In the event, a majority of the ILC preferred a rule conserving the continuity of treaties

---

[408] ibid, p 31, para 46.
[409] ibid.
[410] Ushakov, Yrbk ILC, 1972, I, p 159, para 71.
[411] Waldock, Fifth Report, above, n 60, p 32, para 50.
[412] Yrbk ILC, 1972, I, p 159, para 72.
[413] eg Hambro, Yrbk ILC, 1972, I, p 164, para 47; Castañeda, Yrbk ILC, 1972, I, p 166, para 76.
[414] eg Ushakov, Yrbk ILC, 1972, I, p 164, para 43. Reuter located the principle in the law of treaties: a State could not, by means of concluding a new treaty (of union) dispense with its responsibility under existing treaties, Reuter, Yrbk ILC, 1972, I, p 176, para 47.
[415] eg Reuter, Yrbk ILC, 1972, I, p 165, para 58; Ustor, Yrbk ILC, 1972, I, p 166, para 77.
[416] eg Ago, Yrbk ILC, 1972, I, p 165, para 66.

within their territorial limits in case of unification, and did so for the most part for reasons of policy.[417]

In the final stages of drafting in 1974, a brief but significant discussion took place concerning the relationship between the rule governing the transfer of territory on the one hand (the moving treaty frontiers' rule) and that governing the uniting of States. Tammes had suggested that the rule governing unification was premised upon the idea that a new State had come into being, and that this therefore gave rise to questions as to what rule would apply in cases in which one State was to be entirely absorbed by another (referring to the classic conundrum as to whether Italy was formed through a succession of incorporations into the Kingdom of Sardinia, or by the establishment of a new State through unification).[418] For the most part, members of the Commission were unwilling to engage with the problems to which this appeared to give rise. Some argued, for example, that 'absorption' was no longer a legitimate category, given the general prohibition on annexation. Others maintained that it would be inappropriate to allow a State to avoid its international obligations by means of entering into a union with another State.[419] Others still, suggested that there was a need to maintain the formal boundaries between the cession of territory and unification (in other words between 'partial' and 'total' succession).[420] Ultimately the Commission maintained its commitment to the rule of continuity but included, within the commentary to the draft articles, a note to the effect that it would 'cover the case where one State merges with another State even if the international personality of the latter continues after they have united'.[421]

b) The Dissolution of States

Having set out to distinguish unification from other modes of State creation for purposes of succession, Waldock continued to employ this distinction in the context of State dissolution. He put forward two separate sets of articles for consideration by the Commission, one dealing with the dissolution of unions of States, the other with 'other dismemberments of a State into two or more States'. On an abstract level, this seemed to make perfect sense. If unification resulted in the continuity of treaties within the territorial confines of the component parts of the union, then dissolution of such a union, would presumably result in the reversal of that position. Each component part would be bound by treaties applicable

---

[417] Had they been in a position to examine practice relating to the unification of Vietnam in 1976, the picture might have been far more complex. H Bokor-Szegő, 'Identity and Succession of States in Modern International Law', in Bokor-Szegő (ed), *Questions of International Law: Hungarian Perspectives* (1986) 15.

[418] Tammes, Yrbk ILC, 1974, I, p 177, paras 13–16.

[419] eg, Reuter, Yrbk ILC, 1974, I, p 184, para 3.

[420] eg, Pinto, Yrbk ILC, 1974, I, p 178, para 26.

[421] Commentary to arts 30–32, para 1.

to that territory. If, however, a unitary State were to dissolve through, for example, the secession of various territorial components, then the question would arise as to whether the best analogy should be that governing the dissolution of a union, or that concerning the emergence to independence of a new State? In the event, Waldock's proposals veered towards the latter. In case of the dissolution of a union he thus proposed either a rule of *ipso iure* continuity or one that envisaged the possibility of novation by consent. In the case of 'other dismemberments', the rules elaborated for 'new States' were to apply.[422]

In case of the 'dissolution of unions' Waldock appeared to have plenty of practice to support his preferred presumption of continuity. He began with the dissolution of the Union of Colombia in 1829–31,[423] the Union of Norway and Sweden in 1905[424] and continued with the dissolution of the Austro-Hungarian Empire in 1919,[425] the union of Iceland and Denmark in 1944,[426] the United Arab Republic[427] and the Mali Federation in 1960.[428] In nearly all cases, he identified a willingness on the part of the States concerned to continue existing treaties applicable to the territory concerned after dissolution. Even judged by the standards of the material relied upon by Waldock himself, the picture was evidently somewhat more complex. Britain had disputed Sweden's unilateral proclamation as to the continuance in force of all Union treaties, claiming for itself the right to examine those relations anew.[429] Austria had frequently demonstrated an unwillingness to continue automatically Dual Monarchy treaties as was evidenced in the Secretariat studies on extradition treaties,[430] trade agreements.[431] and multilateral agreements.[432] Iceland had adopted the rather curious position of continuing bilateral agreements but not multilateral agreements. The so-called 'dissolution' of the United Arab Republic was clearly a matter of dispute given Egypt's retention of that title and general silence on the question of treaty continuity, and the Mali Federation was, even in Waldock's own terms, something of an anomaly.[433]

[422] Waldock, Fifth Report, above, n 60, pp 35–44 (draft art 21). He articulated two rules here: one that seceding States would be dealt with in accordance with the provisions relating to newly independent States; the other that the 'predecessor' State would remain bound by existing treaty obligations so far as not incompatible with the new situation.

[423] ibid, p 36, para 3. See also McNair, above, n 78, pp 606–11; O'Connell, above,(Composite Relationship), n 72, pp 117–21.

[424] ibid, p 36, para 4. See also O'Connell, (Composite Relationship), above, n 72, pp 122–3; R de Muralt, above, n , pp 87–8.

[425] ibid 37, paras 5–7.

[426] ibid 37–8, para 8.

[427] ibid 38–9, paras 9–11.

[428] ibid 39, para 12.

[429] 98 BFSP (1909) 833–934; reproduced in McNair, above, n 78, p 614.

[430] UN Doc A/CN4/229, Yrbk ILC, (1970) II, 102, p 123, para 116.

[431] UN Doc A/CN4/243, Yrbk ILC, (1971) II, 117, p 136, para 110.

[432] ibid, paras 110–112.

[433] Waldock comments as regards Senegal's proclamation of treaty continuity, and Mali's denunciation of the cooperation agreements that 'succession was accepted by the State which might

Predictably enough, in light of the debate over unions of States, the Commission was once again divided on this point. Some took the view that States emerging from a union were effectively 'new States' insofar as they enjoyed no independent personality whilst part of the union.[434] Others, by contrast, saw the dissolution of unions to be simply the obverse of their formation and therefore a rule of continuity would be appropriate.[435] Whilst the latter view ultimately prevailed, serious questions were raised concerning Waldock's methodology at this point. Quentin-Baxter, for example, observed that the question whether the component parts of a union had previously existed as separate States was probably less important than the particular circumstances surrounding the dissolution of the union:

Assuming, for example, that the State of Pakistan, East and West, had continued to exist in the old shape for a very long time, maintaining its unity by a process of devolution, by balancing the interests of the two parts, and had then, in the changed circumstances of the 21st century, decided that the remaining ties must be dissolved, could it fairly be said that the law governing the dissolution of the union should be determined almost solely by the situation which had existed before the formation of the union?[436]

Waldock, no doubt, would have taken the example of Bangladesh to be beside the point, insofar as he was dealing with the dissolution of unions of States rather than, as he put it, 'the ordinary case of dismemberment of territory'.[437] But this was really just to expose the rather rudimentary nature of the distinction he had drawn between the dissolution of unions and 'other dismemberments of a State'.[438] Was the separation of Bangladesh from Pakistan really so different from the dissolution of the United Arab Republic, and could one place such great significance upon the 'trace of international personality' that Waldock saw to be the hallmark of unions as distinct from unitary States?

When Waldock then proceeded to deal with 'other dismemberments' of States, it quickly became evident that he was not really speaking about the 'dismemberment' of States at all, but rather a separate category of 'secession' in

have been expected to deny it and denied by the State which might have been expected to assume it'. Waldock, Fifth Report, above, n 60, p 39, para 12. See generally, R Cohen, 'Legal Problems Arising from the Dissolution of the Mali Federation', 36 BYIL (1960) 375.

[434] eg, Tammes, Yrbk ILC, 1972, I, p 174, paras 21–22; Nagendra Singh, Yrbk ILC, 1972, I, p 174, para 30.

[435] eg, Ramangasovina, Yrbk ILC, 1972, I, p 175, para 37; Ustor, Yrbk ILC, 1972, I, p 176, para 55; Bilge, Yrbk ILC, 1972, I, p 177, para 59.

[436] Quentin-Baxter, Yrbk ILC, 1972, I, p 178, para 5.

[437] Waldock, Yrbk ILC, 1972, I, p 179, para 11.

[438] Tabibi, Yrbk ILC, 1972, I, p 180, paras 20–21 (in which he argued that the separation of East and West Pakistan should be viewed as the dissolution of a union of States). It is notable that the ILA only dealt with the dissolution of unions of States. In its second resolution of the 53rd Conference of the ILA in 1968 it adopted the following resolution: 'In cases of the dissolution of unions or federations, the separate components of the composite State may invoke or have invoked against them treaties of the composite State to the extent to which these are consistent with the changed circumstances resulting from the dissolution'

which the precedents he had cited earlier concerning the 'traditional view' were all applicable.[439] He thus ran over, once again, the historic practice relating to the secession of American colonies from Britain and France, that of Belgium from the Netherlands (1830), Cuba from Spain (1898), and the formation of Czechoslovakia and Poland in 1919. Additional material was produced in relation to the Irish Free State (1922), Pakistan (1948), the dismemberment of the Federation of Rhodesia and Nyasaland (1963), the independence of Singapore in 1965, and the secession of Bangladesh from Pakistan (1972), all of which seemed to confirm his thesis that in the case of a dismemberment of a State 'as distinct from the dissolution of a union of States' the emergent States are treated in precisely the same way as other 'newly independent States'.[440] Again there was a certain selectiveness in terms of his choice of example (no real mention was made, for example, of South Africa, Canada, or Australia), but the real problem was where to place this practice? Were these really cases of dismemberment, or were they rather simply cases resulting in the emergence to independence of a new State?

A clue to Waldock's prevarication on this point is found in the final paragraphs of his commentary to draft Article 21. There, he was to note that:

in most cases of dismemberment one or other part is recognized as, or claims to be, the continuation of the State that has suffered the dismemberment; and if any part is treated as still representing the former State, the other part or parts are correspondingly treated as having become independent States by secession.... Ought the draft articles, however, to envisage the case of the total disappearance of the previous State and its replacement by two or more States? In other words, do the categories of succession include, as a special case, the mere division of a State into two or more States? And in that event is the international personality of the former State to be considered as extinguished and the state replaced by two or more *new* States, or as continuing in a divided form in the international personalities of the States resulting from the division?[441]

Having entitled his draft article 'Other dismemberments of a State', Waldock makes clear in this passage that he had not really addressed the total disappearance of the previous State at all, and that he had largely just concentrated upon secession, reiterating in the process the work already undertaken in respect of new States.[442] The presence of this article, however, was significant insofar as it seemed to draw an implicit line between the acquisition of independence of colonies on the one hand, and other cases of secession on the other even if, in fact, the rules were to be the same for each category.

It was only at a fairly late stage that members of the Commission picked up on this apparent tension within Waldock's approach. Ago had started the ball rolling in the discussion of draft Article 6 (relating to new States) in remarking

---

[439] See above, pp 136–7.
[440] Waldock, Fifth Report, above, n 60, p 43, para 13.
[441] ibid, p 43, para 15.
[442] Ushakov, Yrbk ILC, 1972, I, p 216, para 65.

fairly innocently, that the rule appeared equally applicable to 'cases of secession in general' and not just to decolonization. 'Whether what seceded was a former colony or a metropolitan province of the State itself', he suggested 'made no difference'.[443] Ustor responded vigorously by arguing that in cases of secession, partition or dismemberment:

the new States could not say that treaties previously concluded were not their treaties, since their parliaments might contain members who had actually participated in the ratification of those treaties. Such States would obviously not enjoy the same status as a former colony, which entered the international forum as a completely new State.[444]

At this point other members of the Commission joined the fray with examples and counter-examples traded to and fro. Bartoš, in support of Ago, pointed out that the union of Norway and Sweden had broken up precisely because the Norwegian parliament opposed the foreign policy then pursued by the Stockholm government and that for it to have inherited treaties as a consequence would have been perverse.[445] Ushakov replied in support of Ustor, with the suggestion that if Tanganyika and Zanzibar were to separate, there would be no justification for them to claim to be freed from treaty obligations concluded on their behalf by Tanzania.[446] Decolonization, in his view, ought to be treated as a separate category. [447]

At this stage Waldock's carefully constructed typology of succession started to unravel. On the one hand if unification were to be subject to a general rule of treaty continuity (within the respective territorial limits) it would seem dangerous to admit, in light of the fleeting unions that had marked the period shortly after decolonization, that the reversal of that process would allow those States to free themselves from inherited treaty obligations. If, furthermore, the dismemberment of a union was to attract a rule of continuity, surely that should apply with equal force to the dismemberment of unitary States?[448] Differentiating between the two categories seemed to be extremely problematic when one considered cases such as Bangladesh or (potentially at least) Tanzania.[449] On the other hand, the argument could obviously be run in the opposite direction. If new States were under no obligation to continue existing treaty arrangements, then surely the same rule should apply in case of secession, and equally so in case of the dismemberment of States whether or not they be unions?[450] Was not any State emerging from such processes a 'new State'? Clearly some way of discriminating between

---

[443] Ago, Yrbk ILC, 1972, I, p 71, para 37.
[444] Ustor, Yrbk ILC, 1972, p 74, para 20.
[445] Bartoš, Yrbk ILC, 1972, I, p 75, para 27.
[446] Ushakov, Yrbk ILC, 1972, I, p 75, para 29.
[447] Quentin-Baxter, Yrbk ILC, 1972, I, p 233, para 27.
[448] eg, Ushakov, Yrbk ILC, 1972, I, p 231, para 11; Reuter, Yrbk ILC, 1972, I, p 232, para 13 (arguing that a union of States was purely a construction of internal law).
[449] Ushakov, Yrbk ILC, 1972, I, p 175, para 32; Waldock, Yrbk ILC, 1972, p 32, para 11.
[450] eg, Tammes, Yrbk ILC, 1972, I p 174, para 22; Nagendra Singh, ibid, p 174, para 30.

the various categories seemed to be necessary, but it was not immediately obvious how this might be done.

As the discussions proceeded in 1972 and 1974, the Commission inched its way towards the conclusion that the only way of resolving these tensions was by treating decolonization as a discrete category.[451] This was certainly not something that explicitly structured the draft from the outset, but an idea that crept up almost unheeded.[452] Indeed in his original formulation, as suggested above, Waldock was prepared to accede to the idea that in case of dismemberment or secession, the rules applicable to new States should apply with the proviso that the rump State (if it continued) would remain bound by any existing treaty obligations. This also remained the case until the end of the 1972 session and provided, paradoxically enough, the justification for a circumscribed definition of 'newly independent States' (applying only to 'dependent territories'). There, it was debated as to whether the definition should also include non-colonial secessions, but it was reasoned that since the rules were the same in each case, nothing of great significance was thought to hang on what did, or did not, constitute a newly independent State.[453]

The Commission's response to such issues was to emerge only at a very late stage. By the beginning of its 1974 meeting, with Vallat at the helm, it had abandoned the distinction between the dissolution of unions and unitary States and was left with two articles: one dealing with the 'dissolution of a State' and another with the 'separation of part of a State'.[454] In the former case, which included the dissolution of both unions and unitary States, a rule of continuity was articulated; in the latter case the successor State would be governed by the same principles as those pertaining to newly independent States.

The responses received from governments in 1974, however, were to put all Waldock's categories under renewed scrutiny.[455] For some, the question was that of working out the implications of self-determination. The Swedish government, for example, queried why 'the principle of self-determination should require a clean slate for newly independent States and for States emerging by separation ... but not

---

[451] eg, comments of Reuter, Yrbk ILC, 1972, I, p 135, para 73. See also comments of Swedish government, Vallat, First Report, UN doc A/CN4/278, and Add 1–6, Yrbk ILC, 1974, II, p 5, para 12 ('The General Assembly's wishes might better be met by seeking a separate solution to treaty problems related to succession connected with decolonization, ie., by an ad hoc settlement of an ad hoc situation.')

[452] It was clear half way through the session in 1972 that members of the Commission were still undecided as to whether the term 'newly independent States' included cases of secession occurring outside the context of decolonization. Ushakov, Yrbk ILC, 1972, I, p 183, para 70.

[453] The matter was raised again in 1974 following a UK proposal to define a 'newly independent State' as one whose territory was, prior to the succession of States, 'part of the territory of the predecessor State'. Cited in Vallat, First Report, above, n 263, p 30, para 137.

[454] ibid 68–72 (draft art 27 and 28).

[455] The Soviet States were unhappy that no mention had been made concerning the application of the principle of the clean slate in cases of 'social revolution' (exemplified by the position adopted by the Soviet Union after the October Revolution) and hence sought to re-open the State-government distinction. eg, Comments of USSR, cited in Vallat, First Report, above, n 263, p 14.

for States created by uniting of States or dissolution of a State'.[456] For others, however, the problem existed irrespective of what one might read into the problem of self-determination. The Belgian government, thus, suggested that the notion of the clean slate was, in reality, linked to the concept of sovereign autonomy rather than self-determination and therefore the distinctions drawn by Waldock between 'newly independent States' and other cases of succession were largely 'artificial'.[457] The US, in similar vein and on a related issue, suggested that the distinction between the 'dissolution of a State' and the 'separation of part of a State' was 'quite nebulous' and 'nominal' and that the latter could be brought within the frame of the category of 'newly independent States'.[458] In presenting these views, Vallat himself merely reiterated the formal importance of differentiating between the dissolution of a State, on the one hand, and the separation of parts of a State on the other, but did not commit himself to a view as to whether the operative rule in the latter case should be one of continuity or consent. He was to remark, however, that:

> Where there is dissolution of a State, a treaty concluded by the predecessor State will have been made on behalf of the State as a whole. It may be presumed to have been made with the consent of the people of all parts of the State and, so long as the State remains in existence, to be binding on the entire State. This is a very different situation from that of a dependent territory which, although it may be consulted about the extension of the treaty, does not normally play any part in the actual government of the State concerned, and cannot therefore be regarded as responsible for the conclusion of the treaty as such. The same observation may be made about the position of a part of a State that breaks away and becomes independent. However, in this case, it is more likely that the part will have been in a position more akin to that of a dependent territory. Indeed, it is quite possible that the attempt to impose the application of a particular treaty may be the cause of the secession of part of the State.'[459]

The nub of the issue, thus, was the condition of 'dependency' from which one might intuit a right to be freed from inherited obligation. In a formal sense, all were clear as to the distinction between an overseas colony and a contiguous territory in terms of their putative involvement in the 'actual government of the State', clear also that this was a distinction that underpinned UN policy relating to self-determination. But when it came to determining the consequences of the gaining of independence, the absence or otherwise of territorial contiguity did not explain a great deal. What seemed to be more important was the 'consent' or 'will of the population',[460] but as Waldock had already observed, '[s]uch factors were not really susceptible of codification, despite their relevance as underlying considerations'.[461]

---

[456]   ibid 8.
[457]   Oral comments of Belgium, cited in Vallat, ibid 65, para 364.
[458]   Written comments of the United States of America, cited in Vallat, ibid 69, para 391.
[459]   Vallat, ibid 71, para 401.
[460]   eg Kearney, Yrbk ILC, 1972, I, p 234, para 40.
[461]   Waldock, Yrbk ILC, 1972, I, p 234, para 45.

Nevertheless, the matter was referred to a drafting Committee chaired by Hambro, which sought to overcome the problems adverted to above through the adoption of a single rule of continuity for both cases of dissolution and separation (secession).[462] It was reasoned that most of the examples produced by Waldock and others, justifying a negative provision 'concerned the separation of a State of what would now be called a dependent territory'.[463] In order to put this insight into place, therefore, a third paragraph was to draft Article 27 (later draft Article 33) providing: 'if a part of the territory of a State separates from it and becomes a State in circumstances which are essentially of the same character as those existing in the case of the formation of a newly independent State, the successor State shall be regarded for the purposes of the present articles in all respects as a newly independent State'.[464]

This 'essentially similar circumstances' clause thus became the means by which the Commission could overcome an otherwise rigid formula for differentiating between dependency understood in the colonial/non-colonial sense, and dependency understood in terms of representation or participation in government and foreign affairs. The form of expression, however, was far from ideal – bringing to mind the old problematic distinction between evolutionary and revolutionary secession[465] – but it was clearly designed to address cases such as that of Bangladesh. As it was to turn out, however, this clause was finally removed at the Conference in 1978, leaving the impression that the problem of dependency and alien rule was really one confined to the context of salt-water colonialism.

9. Dispositive Treaties

As we have seen, Waldock had begun his work on succession with the idea in mind that the draft articles should represent a 'supplement' to the ILC's work on the law of treaties, and that, so far as possible, its approach should mirror that adopted in the draft articles on the latter. As Rosenne had already pointed out in the Commission's Sub-committee, this was to have certain implications as regards the articulation of functionally specific rules for different categories of treaties. In its work on the latter, the ILC had largely taken the position that it should concentrate, as far as possible, upon the formal elements of treaty-making, maintaining in the process a general distinction between the form and substance of such agreements. The law of treaties, understood as those rules that governed the entry into force and effect of treaty relations, was to be distinguished from 'treaty law' understood as the substantive commitments that come to be framed

---

[462] Draft Articles 27 and 28. Hambro, Yrbk ILC, 1974, I, pp 257–8.
[463] ibid 258, para 7.
[464] Draft Art 27(3). ibid, p 258.
[465] See above, pp 106–13.

within the terms of those agreements. The law of treaties was properly part of customary international law and putatively universal in scope; treaty law, by contrast, bound only those States party to the agreement (except, and insofar, as the content of the treaty might later come to reflect, or be expressive of, the position in customary law). Such an approach was largely reinforced by a series of bifurcations in general legal doctrine between primary and secondary rules (or 'structural' and 'substantive' rules), formal and material sources of law, and in some degree at least, between peremptory and dispositive norms.

In contrast to the ILC's general stance in relation to the law of treaties, the tradition of scholarship addressing the question of succession, had long distinguished between categories of treaties by reference to their subject matter. Vattel's original distinction between 'real' and 'personal' treaties,[466] whilst understood to be premised upon a largely redundant conception of sovereignty,[467] had been re-packaged and re-deployed over the years as a convenient analytical tool for avoiding some of the more uncomfortable consequences that might ensue from an all or nothing approach to treaty succession. The doctrine of universal succession thus went hand in hand with the recognition that certain agreements were essentially 'personal' or 'political' and hence not susceptible to inheritance, the clean-slate doctrine, by contrast, was normally qualified by the recognition of a category of 'dispositive', or 'real' treaties whose inheritance was unavoidable.[468] To the extent, then, that a putative law of succession might distinguish between categories of agreements by reference to their content rather than their form, this seemed to put in question Waldock's original commitment to the terms of the Vienna Convention of 1969.

For all the differences between the general approach to the law of treaties on the one hand, and State succession on the other, it was also apparent that the ILC's stance in relation to the former was not quite as univocal as the above description might suggest. In two contexts, in particular, it had deliberated quite extensively as regards the possibility that certain kinds of substantive commitment might warrant the elucidation of special treaty rules. The first such context

---

[466] E De Vattel, *The Law of Nations* (trans J Chitty. 1863) II, xiii, 203 ('We must not confound those treaties or alliances which, since they impose the obligation of repeated acts on both sides, cannot remain in force except through the continued existence of the contracting powers, with those contracts by which a rights is once for all acquired, independently of any subsequent acts of either party. If, for example, a Nation has granted in perpetuity to a neighbouring prince the right to fish in a river or to keep a garrison in one of its fortresses, the prince does not lose his rights even though the Nation from which he has received them should happen to be conquered by, or in any other way subjected to the control of, a foreign Power. His rights do not depend upon the continued existence of the State from which he received them, for the latter alienated them, and its conqueror could only take over what is actually possessed.')

[467] O'Connell notes that the original distinction was largely one between 'bargains personal to the displaced rulers and bargains made with respect to the "private rights of citizens" '. In the 20th century, however, this became a distinction between 'political treaties and territorial settlements'. O'Connell, II, above, n 72, pp 232–3.

[468] eg, H Kelsen, *Principles of International Law* (1952) p 418 ('There is no succession to treaty obligations and rights, apart from such succession that may result from dispositive treaties').

which eventually resulted in the adoption of a specific rule within the Vienna Convention of 1969 was in relation to the applicability of the principle *rebus sic stantibus*. There, having established the general principle that a 'fundamental change in circumstances' might be invoked as a ground for terminating or withdrawing from an agreement, the ILC went on to introduce a specific exception in case of treaties 'establishing a boundary'.[469] This was, in its view, supported by the dictum of the ICJ in the *Free Zones* case and reflective of the opinion of 'most jurists'. In response to those maintaining that the total exclusion of boundary treaties from the rule might appear to conflict with the principle of self-determination, the Commission suggested that they had to be made an exception 'because otherwise the rule, instead of being an instrument of peaceful change, might become a source of dangerous frictions'.[470] Self-determination was an 'independent principle' whose application in the context of the law of treaties might only 'lead to confusion'.[471]

The other context in which the ILC had deliberated upon the significance of particular substantive obligations was as regards draft Article 34 (later to become, in amended form, Article 38 of the Vienna Convention) concerning the third party effects of treaty rules 'through international custom'. This was an issue discussed extensively by Fitzmaurice in his Fifth Report of 1960[472] and subsequently by Waldock himself in his Third Report of 1964[473] in which a central point of contention arose as regards the question whether treaties establishing 'objective regimes' – understood to be those creating rights and obligations *erga omnes* – could be treated as a special category. Certain members of the Commission had argued that 'objective regimes' such as 'treaties for the neutralization or demilitarization of particular territories or areas, and treaties providing for freedom of navigation in international rivers or maritime waterways' had, by their very nature, *erga omnes* effect.[474] Others, by contrast, understood that such effects were not, in any way, premised upon the particular character of the agreement, but rather came about either through processes of tacit consent and/or acquiescence, or by way of the 'grafting of an international custom upon a treaty'. In the event, being sharply divided upon the issue, the ILC declined to assume a particular stance in this regard, admitting merely that certain treaty rights and obligations might have *erga omnes* effect without specifying how or why that might be the case.[475] Both of these earlier discussions, however, had clear significance for the development of rules of succession.

---

[469] eg, Commentary to draft art 59(2). Draft Articles on the Law of Treaties, Yrbk ILC (1966) II, 177, p 259.

[470] ibid.

[471] ibid.

[472] G Fitzmaurice, 'Fifth Report, on the Law of Treaties', Yrbk ILC, 1960, II, p 69.

[473] H Waldock, 'Third Report, on the Law of Treaties', UN doc A/CN4/167, Yrbk ILC, 1964, II, p 26.

[474] Commentary to draft art 34, Yrbk ILC (1966) II, 177, p 231.

[475] ibid.

a) Boundary Treaties

It seemed to be fairly self-evident to Waldock, that if the terms of Article 38 of the Vienna Convention (immunizing boundary treaties from pleas of changed circumstances) had their basis in considerations of public order, it would follow that such agreements should also enjoy immunity in case of changes in sovereignty. Presumably a change in sovereignty would, at the very least, constitute grounds for pleading that a 'fundamental change in circumstance' had occurred, and the possibility, then, that boundary agreements might not survive independence or unification would constitute not only a significant threat to the territorial *status quo*, but also a surprising erosion of the principle enunciated in Article 38.[476] Such reasoning undoubtedly weighed heavily upon Waldock who had himself been involved in the development of the rule in Article 38, and had already put forward a draft article in his very First Report to the effect that boundaries established by treaty should be unaffected by changes in sovereignty.

It was evident, nevertheless, that Waldock was treading on sensitive ground. In the General Assembly's Sixth Committee, the matter had come to debate, and a groundswell of critical opinion had led to the adoption of the following reservation in respect of the Commission's work:

boundary treaties imposed by colonial Powers against the wishes of the people of subject territories should be regarded as contrary to the rule *pacta sunt servanda,* to the fundamental principle of self-determination, which was a principle of *jus cogens,* and to General Assembly resolutions 1514 (XV) and 1654 (XVI).... It was believed that since boundary questions were highly political issues, the Commission should refrain from making legal pronouncements when the particular situations involved fell within the competence of other organs of the United Nations'.[477]

The sense of this, of course, was all rather confused: having argued that the Commission was wrong in its legal conclusions concerning the implications of self-determination, the Sixth Committee then suggested that the issue was not legal at all, but rather one of politics. Reading through this, one may sense that some members of the Sixth Committee were unwilling to have the ILC pronounce upon the legal validity of all inherited boundary agreements in circumstances in which there were ongoing disputes between neighbouring States on precisely that point. Needless to say, this analysis of self-determination was merely such as to encourage Waldock to a further degree of caution when he returned to the topic in his Fifth, and final, Report. There, he provided alternative formulations for two different articles, one dealing with 'boundary settlements', the other with 'treaties of a

---

[476] cf Tabibi, Yrbk ILC, 1972, I, p 248, para 78 (stressing that art 62(2)(a) of the Vienna Convention 'in no way impeded the independent operation of the principle of self-determination' and that it referred only to 'lawful boundary treaties'.).

[477] 23 GAOR, Annexes, vol. II, Ag Item 84, UN doc A/7370, para 58.

territorial character'.[478] In each case, he proposed a rule of continuity (the difference in formulation hinging upon whether it was the treaty which continued, or rather the regime of rights and obligations established pursuant to the agreement) but he was also to make perfectly clear that this was not to sanctify borders the location of which was subject to dispute.

The significance of identifying the category of 'dispositive' agreements (referred to alternatively as 'real' or 'localized' treaties, or as 'servitudes')[479] issued from Waldock's stance as regards the heritability of treaties more generally. As O'Connell had pointed out in his 1967 monograph on succession to treaties, the necessity of isolating 'the touchstone of succession to treaties' only really arose if one began with a presumption of non-succession. If one commenced, rather, from a presumption of continuity one could exclude by way of construction, those that were inapplicable in the changed circumstances. One would then be left with a residue of surviving treaties that would probably include those traditionally classified as 'real' or 'dispositive', but in their case continuity would not be dependent upon their *a priori* categorization as such.[480] This was largely the position adopted by the ILA in its work on succession. Having established a general principle of treaty continuity in case of independence or unification, it thereafter avoided the necessity of dealing with the status of dispositive agreements. This was reflected in its resolution on treaties delimiting national boundaries in which it was observed that the question of succession to the treaty as such (as opposed to the executed parts of the agreement) was dependent upon the same general rules of succession.[481]

---

[478] Waldock, Fifth Report, above, n 60, p 44.

[479] The ILA defined 'dispositive treaties' as treaties which are 'in the nature of objective territorial regimes created in the interests of one nation or the community of nations; are applied locally in virtue of territorial application clauses, (and) touch or concern a particular area of land'. ILA, *The Effect of Independence on Treaties*, (1965) p 352. O'Connell offers the following comment: 'In the effort to cast the net more widely than the servitude conception permits, therefore, the term 'dispositive' has come to be employed to designate a wide spectrum of treaties which create real rights. The criterion of dispositive character...is that a territory is impressed with a status which is intended to be permanent (or relatively so), which is independent of the personality of the State exercising the faculties of sovereignty.... [R]eal rights in international law are those which are attached to territory, and which are in essence valid *erga omnes*. The restrictions imposed by the treaty are less of a contractual character than equities in favour of the beneficiary, States. A dispositive treaty is thus more of a conveyance than an agreement and as such is an instrument for the delimitation of sovereign competence within the impressed territory.' O'Connell, II, above, n 72, pp 14–15. McNair doubted whether the term dispositive was appropriate given its association, for French speakers, with the operative part of a judgment. He suggested by contrast, that they be referred to as 'treaties creating purely local obligations', (McNair, above, n 78, pp 655–6).

[480] O'Connell, II, above, n 72, p 12. O'Connell was to note, however, that since there were cases in which a general presumption favours lapse of treaties (specifically annexation) 'the search for the touchstone cannot be abandoned', ibid, p 13.

[481] Resolution 8, 53 ILA Rep Conf 25–31 Aug. (1969) xiv–xv ('When a treaty which provides for the delimitation of a national boundary between two States has been executed in the sense that the boundary has been delimited and no further action needs to be taken, the treaty has spent its force and what is succeeded to is not the treaty but the extent of national territory so delimited; but where a boundary treaty provides for future action to delimit it, or provides for future reciprocal

Waldock, of course, in adopting a largely negative stance as regards *ipso iure* succession on the part of newly independent States, was forced to return to the issue by way of ensuring that the consequences of non-succession to treaties would not put in jeopardy the boundary settlements that had largely delineated the pattern of decolonization. The real question for both O'Connell and Waldock, however, was how much further this could be taken – did it include, for example, treaties relating to transport, fishing, demilitarization or neutrality, or treaties providing for freedom of navigation on international waterways? How, furthermore, might one construct a rationale for such a rule of inheritance? Would it depend upon the purpose served by the agreement, the degree to which the obligations concerned were associated with land,[482] the extent of 'localization',[483] the acceptance or aquiescence by third parties,[484] its executed/ executory[485] character, or something else?

Contemporary practice and opinion as regards the broad category of dispositive agreements were fairly disparate in nature. McNair, in his volume on Treaty Law, had made some rather elusive comments on the subject in the chapter entitled the 'effect of succession on treaties creating local obligations':

It is not easy to State the legal doctrine which attaches to this kind of treaty obligation its peculiar effect. For most of them it would suffice to say that the instrument from which they originate created rights *in rem*, against the whole world, whoever the sovereign of the territory affected might be, but this would not cover capitulations or semi-legislative provisions made as part of an international settlement. . . . In many cases it suffices to invoke such principles as *nemo dat quod non habet, nemo plus iuris transferre quam ipse habet*, and *res transit cum suo onere*, for when a State cedes a piece of territory over which it has granted to another State a right of transit or a right of navigation on a river, or a right of fishery in territorial or national waters, it cannot cede that territory unencumbered by that obligation.[486]

McNair's concern, of course, was to provide some kind of explanatory framework for the various instances of specifically British practice relating to boundaries, rights of navigation,[487] demilitarization[488] and capitulations.[489] His broadly inductive

---

rights in relation to the boundary, the question whether the treaty is succeeded to or not is a question to be answered by reference to the principles in s 1 above [concerning the continuity of treaties subject to denunciation]').

[482] eg R Jennings, *The Acquisition of Territory in International Law* (1963) 11; Oppenheim above, n x, (1955) I, p 159; Kelsen, *Principles of International Law* (1952) p 417.

[483] For those emphasizing 'localization' see W Hall, *A Treatise on International Law* (8th edn 1924) 115; O'Connell, (1956), above, n 111, p 63; F Váli, *Servitudes of International Law* (1958) p 321.

[484] eg, Q Wright, 'Conflicts between International Law and Treaties', 11 AJIL (1917) 573.

[485] W Schönborn, *Handbuch des Völkerrechts* (1913) II, 32.

[486] McNair, above, n 78, p 656.

[487] eg survival of rights conferred upon Britain under the Treaty of 1825 with Russia following the cession of Alaska to the United States. ibid 657–9.

[488] eg Aaland Islands under the Treaty of Paris 1856, ibid 659–660.

[489] eg Survival of Turkish capitulations in relation to Cyprus following the cession of Cyprus to Britain under the Convention of Constantinople of 4 Jun 1878, ibid 662–4.

approach,[490] however, was to leave rather too many questions unanswered. As Fitzmaurice subsequently noted, McNair's reliance on the *res transit* doctrine merely begged the question as to whether the 'onus does in fact burden the actual *res* itself, or whether it is merely in the nature of a personal obligation incumbent on a particular State'.[491] For him, the key to the issue was whether or not the treaty was intended to be one affecting the *status* of the ceded territory rather than merely creating *personal* obligations for a given country in respect of that territory. His suggested test, therefore, was whether the treaty obligations in question were 'of such nature, intended to be effective universally or quasi-universally as to impress the territory or something in it with a character henceforth inherent in the territory and irrespective of whether any personal obligation in the matter has been assumed by the local sovereign'.[492]

O'Connell was to put a further gloss on this distinction between 'personal obligations' and obligations relating to 'status', by concluding that dispositive agreements were thus a peculiar kind of legal transaction:

The criterion of dispositive character ... is admittedly elusive, but at least it can be agreed that the fundamental notion underlying the expression is that a territory is impressed with a status which is intended to be permanent (or relatively so), which is independent of the personality of the State exercising the faculties of sovereignty ... The restrictions imposed by the treaty are less of contractual character than equities in favour of the beneficiary State. A dispositive treaty is thus more of a conveyance than an agreement, and as such is an instrument for the delimitation of sovereign competence within the impressed territory.[493]

For all their differences, however, McNair, O'Connell and to a lesser extent Fitzmaurice, saw this category as representative of a broadly similar set of 'agreements', which included not merely boundary treaties, but also international servitudes and capitulations.[494]

However conceptually coherent their position, advocates of this largely affirmative scholarship in relation to dispositive agreements were clearly vulnerable to the argument, in case of dispute, that the agreement in question was *in fact* contingent upon the identity of the contracting party (ie that it simply did not attach to the *res*).[495] In his Hague lectures of 1951, Castrèn had highlighted this point, suggesting that the tendency to regard as immaterial the person of the sovereign

---

[490] Schwarzenberger, above, n 142, (who cites McNair's approach with approval).

[491] G Fitzmaurice, 'The Juridical Clauses of the Peace Treaties', 73 Hague Recueil (1949), 255 at p 298.

[492] ibid 298.

[493] O'Connell, II, above, n 72, pp 14–15. See also, O'Connell, 1956, above, n 111, pp 49–50.

[494] ibid, 1956, 50–63. In his 1967 volume, O'Connell dispensed with the terminology of 'servitudes' which he saw to be largely misleading (ibid, II, 17–23) and included, in its place, 'particular dispositive situations' and 'dispositive international settlements'.

[495] Thus the view that the element of localisation merely indicates a higher probability of succession M Marcoff, *Accession à l'indépendence et succession d'Etats aux traits internationaux* (1969) pp 205–6.

or the identity of the population in arguments about the dispositive character of territorial agreements formed a largely 'unsatisfactory' basis for continuity.[496] 'Are there any treaties' he asked, 'in which the sovereign of a territory or its population can be ignored?.'[497] Territorial agreements,[498] like any other, were at least partly 'personal' in the sense of being linked to a particular State, and any differentiation on this score was to overlook this obvious ambiguity. Practice, furthermore, was largely uncertain, and the favourable attitude of States in such cases to treaty continuity could be attributed just as easily to *'raisons d'opportunité'* as to a sense of legal obligation.[499]

Castrèn, however, did not distance himself entirely from the position adopted by McNair in relation to frontier agreements, but his reasoning was again quite different. Whilst admitting that doctrine was favourable to the idea that successor States be bound by existing frontier agreements, he took the view that these constituted no exception to the general rule (of the 'clean slate'). Treaties relating to frontiers, in his view, were effectively 'executed agreements', and having established *'une situation juridique déterminée'* had to be respected by the successor State as much as by any other foreign power.[500] It was not the case, thus, that frontier agreements themselves would be subject to automatic succession, but the situation resulting from their implementation which gave rise to continuing obligations on the part of the successor.[501] Castrèn's view in this respect was later echoed by the ILA, which generally endorsed his approach to executed agreements. The ILA noted, nevertheless, that boundary agreements may also have non-executed provisions, or provisions relating to 'future action' (such as, one may suppose, provisions relating to the settlement of disputes) the continuance of which would depend upon the general rules of succession otherwise articulated.[502]

Having surveyed much of this opinion, and concluding that the 'diversity of opinion' amongst writers made it virtually impossible to discern whether, to what extent, and upon what basis, 'international law today recognizes any special

---

[496] Castrén, above, n 380, p 437. See also, Lester, (1963), above n 162, p 475; A Esgain, 'Military Servitudes and the New Nations', in W O'Brien (ed) *The New Nations in International Law and Diplomacy* (1965) p 42; A Keith, *The Theory of State Succession* (1907) p 22.

[497] Castrén, ibid ('Existe-t-il des traits permettant de faire abstraction du souverain du territoire et de la population?').

[498] It became clear that what Castrén understood by 'territorial agreements' included, but was not limited to, treaties relating to transport, fisheries and hunting. ibid.

[499] ibid. Zemanek was to run precisely the same argument in the opposite direction. He suggested that '[d]eviations from the rule of automatic succession to dispositive treaties seem to be due more to political considerations or to the operation of the *clausula rebus sic stantibus* than to a rejection of the rule of automatic succession'. Zemanek, above, n 174, pp 242–3.

[500] ibid. See also, Sette Câmara, Yrbk ILC, 1972, I, p 250, para 9.

[501] Ago, Yrbk ILC, 1972, I, p 251, 13 (emphasizing that the creation of a 'real right' was not related, in any direct way, with the question of succession to treaties. Once the treaty had been executed 'the treaty was terminated, and was nothing more than evidence of the legitimacy of the transfer'.).

[502] Above n 109.

category or categories of treaties of a territorial character which are inherited auto-matically by a successor State'[503] Waldock turned to the proceedings of inter-national tribunals.[504] This was not, however, to clarify substantially the position. He noted that in the *Free Zones of Upper Savoy and the District of Gex case* [505] the Permanent Court had decided that the Treaty of Turin of 1816, which fixed the frontier between Switzerland and Sardinia and imposed restrictions on the levy-ing of customs duties in the Zone of St Gingolph was to be viewed as a stipulation 'which France is bound to respect, as she succeeded Sardinia in the sovereignty over that territory'.[506] But it was less clear whether this was a consequence of the territorial character of the agreement (as had been emphasized by Switzerland in its pleadings)[507] or as a consequence of general rules of succession.[508] Similarly in the *Aaland Island* case, the League of Nations Committee of Jurists, having dismissed the 'existence of international servitudes', nevertheless concluded that Finland was under an obligation to maintain the demilitarisation of the Islands as had been stipulated under the terms of the 1856 Aaland Islands Convention between Britain, France and Russia. It suggested, in that vein, that:

The recognition of any State must always be subject to the reservation that the State rec-ognized will respect the obligations imposed upon it either by general international law or by definite international settlements relating to territory [of which the 1856 settlement was one].[509]

Again, however, the reasoning here was to suggest that the continuity of obli-gations derived less from their territorial character, and rather more as a conse-quence of the dispositive authority of the powers involved in the peace settlement itself. [510] Apart from the obvious imperial overtones of this reasoning (a con-cern that the Committee only partially allayed in its dismissal of the concept of servitudes) it was evident that, if everything constituting part of a 'definite

---

[503] Fifth Report, above, n 60, p 49, para 9.
[504] ibid 50–2.
[505] Order of 6 Dec 1930, PCIJ, Series A, no. 24.
[506] ibid, p 17.
[507] Case of the *Free Zones of Upper Savoy and the District of Gex*, PCIJ, Series C, no. 17–1, vol III, p 1654.
[508] Waldock insisted that the 'territorial character' of the arrangement was quite clear all along and that the case could therefore be 'accepted as a precedent in favour of the principle that certain treaties of a territorial character are binding *ipso jure* upon a successor State', (Fifth Rep, above, n 60, p 50, para 14). But it might equally be inferred that, given the circumstances, the Court's failure to make that point clear was indicative of the doubts it may have had about the category of 'territorial treaties'.
[509] LNOJ, Special Supp (1920) 16.
[510] cf also Separate Opinion of Judge McNair in the Advisory Opinion on the *International Status of South West Africa*, ICJ Rep 1950, 128, p 153 ('From time to time it happens that a group of great Powers, or a large number of States both great and small, assume a power to create by a multi-partite treaty some new regime or status, which soon acquires a degree of acceptance and durability extending beyond the limits of the actual contracting parties, and giving it an objective existence. This power is used when some public interest is involved and its exercise often occurs in the course of the peace settlement at the end of a great war.').

international settlement' was included, virtually nothing would be left on the outside.[511]

The other two cases to which Waldock referred provided only indirect support for a hypothesis of automatic succession to territorial treaties. In the case concerning the *Temple of Preah Vihear*,[512] Thailand and Cambodia had both presented arguments in their pleadings concerning the question of whether Cambodia had succeeded to the rights of France in relation to the provisions on pacific settlement under the Franco-Siamese Treaty of 1937. Cambodia had argued that those were ancillary ('*accessoire*') to the terms of the earlier treaty of 1904 delimiting the boundary between Thailand and Cambodia.[513] Thailand, for its part, argued that they were effectively 'political provisions' quite independent of the terms of the earlier agreement.[514] Although both States appear to have been in agreement that the terms of the 1904 Treaty demarcating the boundary between them remained binding notwithstanding Cambodia's independence from France, the Court itself did not address the question of succession. Similarly, in the case concerning the *Right of Passage over Indian Territory*,[515] concerning Portuguese claims to a historic right of passage between its territory of Damão and the enclaves of Dadrá and Nagar-Aveli, the Court felt unable to rely upon the terms of the Treaty of Poona of 1779 concluded with the Marathas or indeed any of the other agreements concluded between Portugal and Britain. It resorted rather to the idea that practice had created a local custom that was 'unaffected by the change of regime...when India became independent'.[516] As a precedent for the survival of territorial treaties or even the regimes created thereby, this was fairly insubstantial.

It was only when, finally, Waldock turned to State practice that he appeared to find himself on somewhat firmer ground – at least in respect of boundary treaties. He began by noting that in the *Temple* case, both Thailand and Cambodia had taken as their point of departure the continued validity of the Franco-Siamese Treaty of 1904 which demarcated the boundary between them. This was expressive of a stance adopted more generally in relation to States emerging to independence. In 1964, for example, the Assembly of Heads of State and Government of the Organization of African Unity had adopted a resolution declaring that 'all Member States pledge themselves to respect the borders existing on their achievement of national independence',[517] and the view of the former colonial powers such as Britain was firmly in favour of the continuance of executed clauses of

---

[511] One only has to examine the extensive terms of the Treaty of Versailles of 1919 to understand the implications of this reasoning. See Castrén, above n 370.
[512] ICJ Report 1962, 6.
[513] ICJ Pleadings, Temple of Preah Vihear, 1959, I, p 165.
[514] ibid 145–6.
[515] ICJ Report 1960, 6.
[516] ibid 40.
[517] OAU doc AHG/Res16(1). A similar resolution was adopted by the Conference on Heads of States and Governments of Non-Aligned Countries in 1964. Waldock, Fifth Report, above, n 60,

agreements delimiting boundaries. There were, of course a number of ongoing boundary disputes – including, in particular, a dispute between Ethiopia and Somalia concerning the former's unilateral suspension of grazing rights that had formed part of the original boundary delimitation between Britain and Ethiopia in 1897,[518] and one between Afghanistan and Pakistan relating to the Treaty of Kabul of 1921 concluded between Great Britain and Afghanistan.[519] But these were not, in Waldock's eyes, sufficiently serious to be taken as challenges to the general proposition. Indeed, he was to note that in quite a number of the disputes, such as those between Morocco and Algeria,[520] between Surinam and Guyana,[521] between Venezuela and Guyana, and between China and several of its neighbours (including Burma, India and Pakistan)[522] the point in contention was either that the boundary treaty in question left the course of the boundary in doubt, or that its validity was questionable (owing to inequality, incapacity of the parties etc).[523] Waldock was thus able to conclude that the 'weight of evidence of State practice and of legal opinion' was clearly 'in favour of the view that in principle a boundary settlement is unaffected by the occurrence of a succession of States', and that boundary settlements had thus to be excepted from the moving treaty-frontier rule and from the clean-slate principle.[524] That the practice was probably equally amenable to the conclusion that boundary agreements survived only with the actual or tacit acceptance on the part of the States concerned was carefully avoided.[525]

Having thus assumed a position which, for most purposes, was in line with nearly all contemporary scholarship, Waldock proceeded to add two notes of caution. First of all, in maintaining that boundary settlements were 'unaffected' by a succession of States, he made it clear (perhaps in deference to the concerns expressed in the General Assembly's Sixth Committee)[526] that this did not have implications as regards 'any other ground of claiming the revision or setting aside of the boundary settlement, whether self-determination or the invalidity or termination of the treaty'.[527] The 'mere occurrence' of a succession of States would

---

p 52, para 22. See generally, M Shaw *Title to Territory in Africa: International Legal Issues* (1986) 185–7.

[518] The grazing rights had initially been secured by exchange of letters shortly after the 1897 Treaty (89 BFSP 36) but had been re-affirmed in an agreement between Britain and Ethiopia in 1954 (161 BFSP 93). See generally, UN, *Materials on State Succession*, above, n 291, p 185; O'Connell, II, above, n 72, p 283.

[519] UN, Materials on State Succession, above, n 291, pp 1–5; O'Connell, II, above, n 72, pp 275–7; Tabibi, Yrbk ILC, 1972, I, p 249, paras 80–1.

[520] O'Connell, II, above, n 72, pp 289–91 (commenting that the Moroccan claim 'is based upon spiritual rather than a legalistic principle'.).

[521] ibid 274–5.

[522] ibid 277–282.

[523] Waldock, Fifth Report, above, n 60, pp 53–4, para 25.

[524] ibid 54, para 27.

[525] Tabibi, Yrbk ILC, 1972, I, p 248, para 76.

[526] Tabibi, Yrbk ILC, 1972, I, p 248, para 75.

[527] Waldock, Fifth Report, above, n 60, p 54, para 27.

be considered thus, 'neither to consecrate the existing boundary if it is open to challenge nor to deprive it of its character as a legally established boundary, if such it was at the date of the succession of States.'[528]

Just as much as a fully delimited boundary would be unaffected by a succession of States, so also would the various claims in relation to a disputed boundary remain untouched by the same event.[529] Whilst there was some undoubted sense in this, there was also a degree of equivocation in relation to the issue of self-determination which, however politically appealing it might have been to various sections of his potential audience, could also be seen to be fatal to his argument. If the principle of border stability was open to challenge on the basis of self-determination, inequality, lack of capacity, or anything else, then precisely what was being guaranteed? Certainly one might argue, in an abstract sense, that a change in sovereignty *in itself* was not reason enough to warrant the overturning of boundary settlements, but the real issue as many saw it, was that in the context of decolonization at least, a change of sovereignty *meant* self-determination. Guaranteeing the intangibility of border settlements at the same time as recognizing the possible validity of challenge by reference to the principle of self-determination was really to re-enact (albeit within a formal framework of presumption and rebuttal) the old opposition between peoples determining the future of territory or vice versa.

A potential explanation for Waldock's attitude, in this respect, was that he was thinking of border settlements in a particular way. A border, of course, can be understood in at least three different ways: one as a physical line on the ground, policed and maintained by agents of coercion; another as a jurisdictional limit demarcating the formal legal parameters of sovereign power; yet another as delimiting the outer limits of a political order the compass of which defines the identity of the 'sovereign' (in the sense of who may participate in that political order).[530] For Waldock, the border seemed to represent either the first or second of these conceptions – it was something largely incidental to the question of identity and whose location could plausibly be argued about in terms of the ethnic, religious, or cultural identity of the inhabitants on either side (ie self-determination), but which did not in any obvious way, put in question the identity of the 'sovereign' whose authority it apparently delineated. Had he considered, however, that the border also had significance as regards deciding 'who the people were' for purposes of articulating claims of sovereignty (even if only by reference to the doctrinal significance of territory as a formal 'condition' for statehood), the

---

[528] ibid.

[529] K Kaikobad 'Some Observations on the Doctrine of Continuity and Finality of Boundaries', 54 BYIL (1984) 119, p 129 ('The fact is that a State succeeds not only to all the territorial rights of her predecessor, but also to all the limitations and liabilities that are connected therewith. Therefore, all claims in relation to the status and location of the boundary existing prior to succession will also be deemed to continue'.).

[530] See above, pp 61–4.

incompatibility between self-determination and border stability might have been more evident. In any event, however, it may have been the case that Waldock ultimately believed that self-determination arguments (as with arguments concerning inequality in relation to colonial treaty-making) were unlikely to find much legal or political purchase in the newly decolonized world. The open arbitrariness that underpinned many of the border settlements in Africa and Asia (about which few people really disagreed) was such as to offer nearly every newly emergent government a potential grievance against its neighbours; and in the process was also to create a continuing sense of insecurity.[531] Only the most brave or foolhardy of the emergent elites were to wage a campaign seeking to redraw the map of Africa or Asia.[532]

The second point Waldock was to make in respect of the principle of boundary inviolability was that he was unsure whether the rule should be framed in terms relating to the boundary treaty rather than the 'legal situation established by the treaty'. As suggested above, it was the view of some (Castrèn for example) that the rationale for boundary continuity was related to the fact of treaty-execution (evidenced, perhaps, in the presence of border guards, immigration officials, customs regimes and the paraphernalia of border control). For such scholars, there would be no question of succession to the treaty itself, but only to the facts pursuant to its implementation. Whilst seeing some merit in this point of view, Waldock was also concerned that it could also be 'somewhat artificial'.[533] In certain cases, he suggested, a boundary in thinly populated territory may not have been 'fully demarcated' and in which context recourse would have to be made to the treaty for purposes of ascertaining the boundary. Further than this, some boundary treaties might also have ancillary provisions intended to form a 'continuing part of the boundary régime' suppression of which would materially change the boundary settlement (he had in mind, perhaps, the example of the Somali grazing rights in its dispute with Ethiopia).[534] Although Waldock clearly

---

[531] Tabibi, Yrbk ILC, 1972, I, p 248, para 79 (although African boundaries had been established to serve the interests of the colonial Powers, to alter them 'would shatter the whole fabric of the African States'.). This is echoed by the ICJ in the case concerning the frontier dispute, (*Burkina Faso/ Republic of Mali*) ICJ Report 1986, 554, at 567, para 25 ('the maintenance of the territorial status quo in Africa is often seen as the wisest course, to preserve what has been achieved by peoples who have struggled for their independence, and to avoid a disruption which would deprive the continent of the gains achieved by much sacrifice. The essential requirement of stability in order to survive, to develop, and gradually to consolidate their independence in all fields, has induced African States judiciously to consent to the respecting of colonial frontiers, and to take account of its in the interpretation of the principle of self-determination of peoples'.).

[532] cf M Mutua 'Why Redraw the Map of Africa: A Moral and Legal Inquiry', 16 Mich JIL (1994–05) 1113.

[533] Waldock, Fifth Report, above, n 60, p 54, para 29.

[534] Váli above, n 483, p 321 ('If a right in foreign territory is the result of territorial settlement, it is nothing but just and equitable that the State which succeeds to the political boundaries of the grantor State should also be burdened by the obligations which are equally the effect of a territorial arrangement.').

thought that the idea of a boundary régime should not be confined merely to the fact of 'demarcation', he left the matter open in his report to the Commission.

In the Commission's discussion, the majority expressed its almost unanimous support for a rule securing the continuity of boundaries established by treaty,[535] albeit that there was disagreement as to whether one might effectively sever the boundary from the legal framework within which it was secured.[536] For some, the issue would be best expressed in the form of a 'savings clause'[537] preventing reliance upon the clean-slate principle as a way of undermining the validity of 'executed' boundary settlements. Others, however, emphasized the importance of the treaty as evidence of title[538] or were concerned with what fate the pre-existent treaty might be said to have.[539] In the event, the Drafting Committee convened during the 1972 meeting, produced the final text of a savings clause (later to become Article 11 of the Convention) which largely satisfied the different constituencies of opinion. It provided, in brief, that a succession of States should not affect 'a boundary established by a treaty' or indeed rights and obligations established by treaty relating to the régime of a boundary.[540]

Predictably enough, the matter was to become the subject of heated discussion when States themselves were consulted on the issue. Some, such as Afghanistan,[541] Romania,[542] Zambia,[543] Morocco,[544] and Somalia[545] opposed the draft article on the basis that, since most such boundaries had been constructed for the convenience of the Colonial powers rather than by reference to geographic or ethnic considerations, their preservation infringed both the right to self-determination and the contractual freedom of new States. Others, by contrast, saw the principle as indispensable for the preservation of international peace and tranquillity, and regarded the question of self-determination as strictly irrelevant.[546] As expressed by Guyana '[t]he principle of self-determination could not be extended to the point of removing the very foundation of the existence of the new State from the moment of its creation'.[547] Vallat, pursuing the general line of Waldock's argument was not persuaded to reconsider the draft. For him, the point was not whether a coherent rationale could be agreed upon for purposes of justifying the

---

[535] eg Hambro, Yrbk ILC, 1972, I, p 251, para 11.

[536] eg Sette Câmara, Yrbk ILC, 1972, I, p 251, para 10. For the concern that the boundary would often have to be severed from the treaty see Quentin-Baxter, ibid 258–9, para 60.

[537] eg Ushakov, Yrbk ILC, 1972, I, p 251, para 12; Ago, ibid para 13; Elias, ibid p 252, para 25; Tsuruoka, ibid p 253, para 26; Ustor, Yrbk ILC, 1972, I, p 253, para 33.

[538] eg Yasseen, Yrbk ILC, 1972, I, p 251, para 15; Ramangaosavina, ibid 252, para 18; Alcívar, ibid 258, para 55; Waldock, ibid p 260, para 72.

[539] Waldock, Yrbk ILC, 1972, p 253, para 31.

[540] Yrbk ILC, 1972, I, p 275.

[541] Yrbk ILC, 1974, II, p 73, para 417.

[542] ibid 75.

[543] ibid 76.

[544] ibid.

[545] ibid 77.

[546] Australia, Greece, India, Liberia, Kenya, and Poland, ibid.

[547] ibid 76.

continuity of boundary treaties,[548] or a matter of seeking to reconcile the principle of self-determination with border stability.[549] Rather, it was simply a case of recognizing the great 'disturbance to international relations that might follow from … a right of unilateral repudiation' of existing borders.[550] This argument of general policy, or 'practical politics' was the one that ultimately won the day, and Waldock's draft survived largely intact to become Article 11 of the 1978 Vienna Convention.

b) Territorial Agreements

In some respects, Waldock's thinking as to the character of boundary régimes led him naturally into the broader topic of 'territorial treaties', but on this subject he was clearly moving into more troubled waters.[551] An evident problem in this respect, and one that had exercised international lawyers for some considerable time, was the historic association of this kind of agreement with the Roman law doctrine of 'servitudes' (which foresaw specific rights in a 'servient' estate being impressed in the owner of a 'dominant' estate).[552] For many, the language of servitudes was problematic. On one part, it relied rather too heavily upon the 'domestic analogy' assuming, in the process, a neat equation between the power exercised by a sovereign in relation to territory, and that exercised by an individual in relation to property.[553]

[548] Vallat, First Report, above, n 263, p 83, para 431. ('The underlying principle of continuity of boundary … rights and obligations may be expressed in different ways. It may be said that a successor State can only acquire such rights as it was within the power of the predecessor State to give and that the territory of the successor State must be subject to such limitations and obligations as adhered to the territory before the succession of States. It may be said that some treaties create real rights and obligations which are valid as against all the world …. [I]t may well be said that the successor State cannot inherit a larger territory than fell within the boundaries enjoyed by the predecessor State. A successor State which, for example, emerges to independence by seceding from another State cannot by that act automatically enlarge its boundaries and acquire territory at the expense of a third State.').

[549] ibid 84, para 437 ('If the principle of self-determination is to be applied, it should surely be applied equally with respect to the part of the territory of the neighbouring State which is claimed by the newly independent State.').

[550] ibid, para 435.

[551] This is evidenced, in particular, in the ILC's earlier stalemate on the question of objective regimes. See above, p. 175.

[552] In its international sense, a servitude has been understood as denoting 'exceptional restrictions made by treaty or otherwise on the territorial supremacy of a State by which part or the whole of its territory is in a limited way made to serve a certain purpose or interest of another State.' R Jennings, and A Watts. *Oppenheim's International Law* (9th edn 1992) I, pp 670–1. See generally, H Lauterpacht, *Private Law Sources and Analogies of International Law* (1927) 119–124; H Reid *International Servitudes in Law and Practice* (1932); Váli, above, n 483; A Esgain, 'Military Servitudes and the New Nations' in W O'Brien, *The New Nations in International Law and Diplomacy* (1965) 42.

[553] eg, A McNair, 'So-Called State Servitudes' 6 BYIL (1925) 111, p 121; O'Connell, II, above, n 72, p 18 and 'A Re-consideration of the Doctrine of International Servitude' Can Bar Rev (1952) 807; P Guggenheim, *Traité de Droit International Public* (1953) I, pp 394–7; J Brierly, *The Law of Nations* (1963) pp 190–4; I Brownlie, *Principles of Public International Law* (5th edn 1998), pp 377–80.

On another, the ideas of 'dominance' and 'subservience' upon which the concept relied, appeared incompatible with the UN Charter's commitment to sovereign equality.[554] Even for those somewhat sympathetic to the idea, the term was 'ugly' on the ear.[555] In those cases in which the issue had been discussed before international courts and tribunals, furthermore, recognition of the existence of 'servitudes' as such had been studiously avoided. Thus, in the *North Atlantic Fisheries* case, the Tribunal rejected the US contention that fishing rights granted to it by Britain under a Treaty of 1818 amounted to a servitude; they were, rather, economic rights of a personal nature. Similarly, but to different ends, the Permanent Court refused to rely upon the concept in both the *Wimbledon* case[556] and the *Free Zones* case,[557] as did the Committee of Jurists in the *Aaland Islands* case.[558] In the latter, as noted above, the Committee went so far as to say that 'the existence of international servitudes, in the true technical sense of the term, is not generally admitted'.[559]

But for all the evident objections to the concept of 'international servitudes', international lawyers were apt to regard the underlying problem as fundamentally linguistic.[560] The issue was not, in other words, that it was impossible for territory to be indelibly stamped with certain obligations in favour of other States, but rather that the term 'servitude' was 'not the most satisfactory for defining the character of a real right in international law'.[561] There were, in the view of most, at least *some* territorial obligations that would come to inhere in territory (and hence survive a succession of States), albeit the case that it was 'impossible to say with precision which rights and obligations would be inherited automatically and which would not be'.[562] A typical list from the time would have included obligations

---

[554] Keith, above, n 285, p 22; G Crusen, 'Les Servitudes Internationales', 22 Hague Recueil (1928) 31. cf however UK's position in relation to Finland: there would be succession only as regards treaties which were 'in the nature of servitudes'. Yrbk ILC, 1970, II, p 32, doc A/CN4/224 and Add 1, para 3.

[555] McNair, above, n 552, p 122.

[556] PCIJ, (1923) Series A, no 1, pp 24–5 (in which the Court declared that it was 'not called upon to take a definitive attitude with regard to the question…whether in the domain of international law, there really exists servitudes analogous to the servitudes of private law.') Contra, Dissenting Judgment of Schücking who argued that '[t]he right to free passage through the Kiel Canal…undoubtedly assumes the form of a *servitus juris publici voluntaria*'. ibid, p 43.

[557] PCIJ, Order of 19 Aug 1929, Series A, no 22.

[558] LNOJ, Special Supp no 3 (1920) 16. The ICJ did not address the issue in the *Rights of Passage* case by reason of the fact that Portugal explicitly excluded that argument. But see, dissenting opinion of Judge Moreno Quintana.

[559] LNOJ, Special Supp no 3 (1920) 16. But see, *Aix-la-Chapelle, RR Co v Thewis and the Royal Dutch Government, Intervener*, 8 AJIL (1914) 907–13 in which mining rights under a Prusso-Netherlands Boundary Treaty of 1816 were regarded as 'a sort of international servitude'. Esgain points out, however, that since no third party was involved in this case, resort to the concept of a servitude was unnecessary. See also, *Tacna-Arica* 23 AJIL (1929) Supp 183.

[560] Váli, above, n 483, pp 56–63. He suggests that '[t]here is hardly any other concept or doctrine of international law which has suffered such contemptuous criticism and blunt rejection, and at the same time enjoyed such unsubstantiated approval and wanton praise', (p 42).

[561] O'Connell, II, above, n 72, p 19.

[562] FCO submission to ILA, UN doc A/CN4/224 and Add 1, Yrbk ILC, 1970, II, p 36, para 17.

concerning navigation,[563] irrigation,[564] fishing,[565] rights of way,[566] demilitarization,[567] non-fortification,[568] and neutrality.[569] In some, furthermore, capitulation agreements[570] and agreements establishing rights in relation to foreign military bases[571] might also have been mentioned.

In his survey of practice (much of which was taken from O'Connell) Waldock was to note a number of historic instances of practice confirming the permanence of rights and obligations associated with territory. These included British rights of navigation on the Mississippi under the Treaty of Paris 1763 which remained in force on the transfer of Louisiana to Spain;[572] Iraq's succession to Turkish rights over the Shatt-el-Arab waterway under the Treaty of Erzerum of 1847 between Turkey and Persia;[573] France's succession to provisions relating to the neutralization of Chablais and Faucigny under Article 92 of the Final Act of the Congress of Vienna of 1815;[574] and Egypt's succession to obligations under the Convention of Constantinople of 1888 in respect of the Suez Canal.[575] The latter two instances concerned regimes establizhed as part of some 'international settlement', the significance of which had been emphasized in the *Free Zones* and *Aaland Island* cases as well as by Judge McNair in his dissenting opinion in the *Status of South West Africa* case of 1950.[576]

---

[563] eg Nile Waters Agreement 1929, UN Doc A/5409, Yrbk ILC, 1974, II, paras 100–107; Berlin Act of 1885 (establishing régimes of free navigation on the Congo and Niger rivers); Suez Canal Convention of 1888.

[564] eg art 358 of the Treaty of Versailles which gave France the right to draw water from the Rhine (and imposed obligations upon Germany not to construct canals on the German side of the river).

[565] eg fishery rights in Newfoundland Waters established under Treaty of Ghent 1818 between Britain and the US.

[566] eg Articles 89 and 98 Treaty of Versailles, 1919; art 311 Treaty of St Germain; art 294 Treaty of Trianon. Waldock also suggested that this might extend also to air transport agreements, Yrbk ILC, 1972, I, p 249, para 85. On a dispute between Nigeria and France concerning the landing of aircraft on Nigerian soil see Elias, Yrbk ILC, 1972, I, p 261, para 88.

[567] eg Treaty of Paris 1856 concerning the Aaland Islands.

[568] eg duty not to fortify the Alsatian town of Hüningen under the Treaty of Paris 1815 survived the cession of Alsace to Germany in 1871 and its subsequent cession to France in 1919. See Oppenheim, (2nd edn 1912) I, p 207.

[569] Westlake suggested that France was obliged to recognize the neutrality of Chablais and Faucigny established under article XVII of the Congress of Vienna 1815 when they were ceded to it by Sardinia in 1860. J Westlake, *International Law* (1904, 2nd edn) I, p 61.

[570] eg O'Connell, II, above, n 72, p 292–9.

[571] eg, continuation of British-US base agreement in Newfoundland as confirmed by special agreement in 1952, cited in Váli, above, n 483, p 236 (see more generally ibid pp 208–52). For criticism see A Esgain, 'Military Servitudes and the New Nations' in W O'Brien, *The New Nations in International Law and Diplomacy* (1965) 78. On the American Bases in Morocco see Udokang, above, n 162, pp 353–7.

[572] O'Connell, II, above, n 72, pp 234–5.

[573] ibid 247–8.

[574] ibid 239–43.

[575] ibid 271–2.

[576] Advisory Opinion, ICJ Rep 1950, 153.

At the same time, however, Waldock was also to note several instances of practice that struck a dissonant chord. In case of the lease by Belgium of port sites in Dar-es-Salaam and Kigoma under agreement with Britain in 1921 and 1951 (the 'Belbases Agreements'),[577] the Tanganyikan government had declared that a lease in perpetuity of this nature was incompatible with the sovereignty of Tanganyika.[578] Tanganyika also declined to consider herself bound by the Nile Waters Agreement of 1929 between Britain and Egypt and was joined, in this respect, by Sudan.[579] Israel had repudiated, in line with its general stance in relation to all questions of succession, any responsibility under the Anglo-French agreements of 1923 and 1926 in respect of use of the waters of the River Jordan, and the various newly independent riparian States had abrogated the terms of the Berlin Act of 1885 and the Convention of St Germain-en-Laye of 1919 as regards the regimes of free navigation established for the Congo and Niger rivers.[580]

Waldock's pursuit of some conclusion, however, was to lead him to undermine systematically the force of all of these apparent 'exceptions'. The Tanganyikan opposition to both the Belbases and Nile Waters agreements were premised, in his view, on the incapacity of the British government as Mandatory authority to bind the territory for the future.[581] Israel's opposition to the Anglo-French agreements was simply a reflection of its unwillingness to consider itself a successor State at all,[582] and the position adopted by the riparian States in relation to the Berlin Act was constructed on the basis of the doctrine *rebus sic stantibus* rather than non-succession.[583] Lest he be accused of relying too heavily upon several fine points of judgment, however, Waldock was to come to the conclusion that the exception to the clean-slate principle:

seems to be limited to cases where one State by treaty grants, in respect of its territory or a particular part, rights of user or enjoyment [sic], or rights to restrict its own user or enjoyment, which are intended for an indefinite or for a specified period to attach to the territory or particular parts of the territory of another State rather than to the other State as such, or, alternatively, to be for the benefit of a group of States or of States generally. There must, in short, be something in the nature of a territorial settlement.[584]

[577] Udokang, above, n 162, pp 357–67; Makonnen, above, n 194, pp 305–8.

[578] Statement of the Prime Minister of Tanganyika, 11 ICLQ (1962) 1210, p 1212 ('We would not object to the enjoyment by foreign States of special facilities in our territory if such facilities had been granted in a manner fully compatible with our sovereign rights and our new status on complete independence. But such was not the case with the facilities which were granted to Belgium under the 1921 and 1951 Agreements. A lease in perpetuity of land in the territory of Tanganyika is not something which is compatible with the sovereignty of Tanganyika.').

[579] Rousseau, 64 RGDIP (1960) 88; O'Connell, II, above, n 72, pp 244–7; Udokang, above, n 162, pp 363–7; Makonnen, above, n 194, pp 303–5.

[580] T Elias, 'The Berlin Treaty and the River Niger Commission', 57 AJIL (1963); O'Connell, II, above, n 72, pp 307–10; Udokang, above, n 162, pp 367–76; Makonnen, above, n 194, pp 300–3; T Maluwa, 'Succession to Treaties and International Fluvial Law in Africa: The Niger Regime', 33 Neth ILR (1986) 334.

[581] Waldock, Fifth Report, above, n 60, p 56, paras 33–4.

[582] ibid p 57, para 38.

[583] ibid p 58, para 42.

[584] ibid p 59, para 45.

As with boundary treaties, Waldock subtly pushed the Commission to consider the question in terms of whether it was the treaty régime which continued in case of succession, or rather the customary rights and obligations that might have emerged consequential to implementation of the treaty (along the lines by which the ICJ approached the Portuguese claims in the *Right of Passage* case).[585] Predictably enough, the Commission was divided on the issue – some taking the view that such a régime could not survive without the treaty;[586] others, that there could be no survival of the treaty but only of the rights and obligations created by its execution.[587] In this case, the Commission adopted a text largely along the lines of the latter, providing that a succession of States should not affect obligations or rights established by treaty relating to the use of territory whether that be for the benefit of one particular territory, a group of States or all States.

Whilst there was almost unanimous endorsement within the Commission for the idea of the survival of territorial régimes in case of succession, it was also clear that this had been achieved by way of leaving unspecified the kinds of régime in question. References to agreements such as the Nile Waters Agreement of 1929, the Suez Canal Convention of 1888, the Lateran Treaties or the Belbases Agreements, provided some sense of the parameters of the idea, but in some respects it was the agreements that were not mentioned or discussed at any great length that stood out. The survival of military base agreements was obviously one,[588] but so also was the historic category of capitulations.

Capitulation agreements had assumed a central role in European relations with the North-African and Asian world over the previous three centuries and were typically characterized by the establishment, in favour of Western powers, of extraterritorial rights and consular jurisdiction within those territories.[589] By the early 20th century, however, many such régimes had been terminated or renegotiated and it may have seemed to Waldock, that there was little to be gained from addressing the issue.[590] But it was evident to others, nevertheless, that practice in relation to such agreements was significant. O'Connell, for example, was to maintain in both his 1956 and 1967 monographs on State succession that the historic survival of capitulation régimes in case of change in sovereignty was such as to exemplify the possible extension of the category of real rights 'to other types of privileges accorded by treaty'.[591] In this re-formulation, the doctrine of real rights

---

[585] ibid.

[586] eg Sette Câmara, Yrbk ILC, 1972, I, p 260, para 79.

[587] eg Ago, Yrbk ILC, 1972, I, p 264, para 18.

[588] Cuba, Yrbk ILC, (1974) II, p 74, para 417.

[589] For an historical review see C Alexandrowicz, *An Introduction to the History of the Law of Nations in the East Indies* (1967).

[590] Udokang, above, n 162, p 340 (asserting that capitulations 'have not been universally accepted as constituting an indispensable category of dispositive treaties which devolve automatically upon successor States'.).

[591] O'Connell, II, above, n 72, p 299.

would thus become 'a potential instrument for compelling a State to acknowledge the contractual relations of its predecessor when justice demands it'.[592]

On O'Connell's side was the fairly consistent practice, on the part of the US
and Britain in the early 20th century, in insisting that changes in the status of
dependent territories would not affect extraterritorial rights under capitulation
agreements if they were to become independent. Thus, although the Ottoman
capitulations had been suspended in case of Iraq and Palestine during the
period of British administration under the Mandate system, the general assumption was that on termination of the Mandate, those rights would require explicit
renunciation. Part IV of the Partition Plan for Palestine, for example, provided
that

States whose nationals have in the past enjoyed in Palestine the privileges and immunities
of foreigners, including the benefits of consular jurisdiction and protection as formerly
enjoyed by capitulation or usage in the Ottoman Empire, are invited to renounce any
such right pertaining to them to the re-establishment of such privileges and immunities
in the proposed Arab and Jewish States and the City of Jerusalem.[593]

It was assumed, in other words, that if a territory were to fall under the control of
a 'civilized' power,[594] pre-existent extraterritorial privileges would be suspended
(or even terminated), but if independence were subsequently to be gained, such
privileges would revive automatically albeit the case that they were thence open
to renunciation or re-negotiation.[595]

The significance of this residual doctrine concerning the survival of capitulation agreements was not, as O'Connell suggested, found in the fact that it seemed
to 'extend' the notion of real rights, but rather that it made clear the relationship
between a rhetoric of 'real rights' on the one hand, and an implicit bifurcation
between the 'civilized' and 'non-civilized' worlds on the other. Admittedly it was
rarely cast in such terms, but it was clear that the very framework of extrater-
ritoriality was embedded in deeply entrenched perceptions as to the inadequa-
cies of culturally specific modes of local administration or justice for which the
terms 'civilized' and 'uncivilized' were a not an infrequent shorthand. The key
was, however, that the survival of such capitulation régimes depended as much as
anything upon who it was who would be doing the inheriting, and who might
stand in the same sense on the side of 'justice'. This was not something reducible
to the abstract idea of sovereignty or indeed to a rule of inheritance governed
solely by the terms of the agreement, and does much to explain what might otherwise have seemed a fairly inconsistent array of practice.

---

[592] ibid.
[593] eg pt IV Partition Plan for Palestine Mandate (1947), UN doc 19/516, 25th Nov 1947, p 23.
[594] cf Japanese termination of extraterritorial privileges in case of Korea in 1910.
[595] This was the explicit position of Britain in relation to the suspension of capitulations on its
temporary administration of Cyprus in 1878. See O'Connell, above, n 72, pp 298–9.

The point to be drawn from this is that the historic association of the idea of territorial régimes, on the one hand, with systemic notions of dominance and subordination on the other[596] was one that coloured almost every instance of practice. For the most part the régimes in question had been put in place either as part of what might be referred to now as an imperial development project (Suez and Belbases) or as an expression of the superintendent authority of the Great Powers (Aaland Islands and Kiel Canal). Their survival was thus dependent either upon those agreements being read as favourable to the territory itself, or, and more commonly, as being in the interests of the 'international community'. This diffusion of particular State interests into the interests of the international community, of course, could always be seen to be a useful ideological subterfuge.

The general matter was to arise in a somewhat veiled way in Vallat's First, and final Report in which he sought to respond to remarks made by both Czechoslovakia and the GDR, both of which asserted that the draft article should not be used to justify the existence of territorial régimes based on 'unequal treaties'. They had suggested the inclusion of a clause limiting the application of the provision to territorial régimes that served the interests of international cooperation and were in accordance with the purposes and principles of the UN Charter.[597] Vallat's response, here, was to argue that a distinction had to be maintained between 'the validity of the treaty creating a territorial régime and the nature of the régime itself'.[598] As regards the nature of any such agreement, the matter would be regulated by Article 103 of the Charter so that in case of any conflict, the latter would prevail (even if it meant that the treaty would become 'inoperable'). As regards its validity, by contrast, it would be a matter determined by the normal rules of international law relating to treaties (as expressed, for example, in the 1969 Vienna Convention).[599] Vallat's response, no doubt, was well formulated, but it did raise obvious questions as to what kinds of regimes could properly be regarded as 'territorial' for such purposes, and as to whether the problem of unequal treaties had indeed been adequately addressed within the Vienna Convention of 1969. On both scores there were issues to address. In relation to the scope of the provision, the Netherlands government had already suggested that the reasons justifying the continuation of territorial arrangements could also apply to treaties protecting minority rights, rights of nationality or treaties protecting the rights and freedoms of the population in general.[600] Vallat's answer, here, was that this went 'well beyond the type of territorial régime to which' the article related:[601] but, of course, that only begged the question as

---

[596] Which had ultimately been fatal as regards the ILC's earlier work on objective régimes. eg de Luna, Yrbk ILC, 1964, I, pp 99–100; Jimenez de Arehcaga, ibid 100–1.

[597] Vallat, First Report, above, n 263, p 86, para 452.

[598] ibid, para 453.

[599] ibid.

[600] ibid, para 458.

[601] ibid, 87, para 459.

to what that 'type' was. As regards the issue of the validity of 'unequal treaties' it was by no means clear that the Vienna Convention did, in fact, prohibit the 'imposition' of treaties, or allow for the denunciation of such agreements already *in situ*.[602]

10. Final Moves: The Vienna Conference

By the end of its session in 1974 the Commission was able to submit to the General Assembly a set of final draft Articles with the exclusion of two matters which had only lately come before it: one concerning multilateral treaties of a universal character, and one relating to the settlement of disputes.[603] The draft consisted of 39 articles divided into five parts. Part I comprised of general provisions dealing with the scope of the provisions (Articles 1, 3, and 6), definitions (Article 2), its temporal applicability (Article 7) and other rules of a general character such as those governing succession to constituent instruments of international organizations (Article 4), devolution agreements (Article 8), unilateral declarations (Article 9), treaties providing for succession (Article 10), boundary treaties (Article 11) and 'other territorial régimes' (Article 12). Part II consisted of a single Article (14) dealing with succession in respect of part of a territory (ie cession). Part III covered provisions relating to newly independent States (Articles 15–29) in which the general principle of the 'right of option' was elaborated in detail – with provisions *inter alia* concerning treaties not yet in force, reservations, the effect of notification, and provisional application. Part IV contained provisions relating to the Uniting (Articles 30–32) and Separation (Articles 33–36) of States, and Part V 'miscellaneous' provisions relating to 'cases of State responsibility and outbreak of hostilities' (Article 38) and cases of 'military occupation' (Article 39).

In submitting the draft articles to the General Assembly the ILC offered to return at the following session to complete the final articles, but that offer was declined by the General Assembly which was keen to expedite the completion of the drafting process by way of convening an international conference for purposes of concluding a Convention on the subject. This was duly organized and the United Nations Conference on Succession of States in Respect of Treaties was convened in Vienna from 4 April to 6 May 1977 and, having not completed its work, again from 31 July to 31 August 1978. At the end of the second meeting, the draft Convention was opened for signature and ratification.... Thirteen States immediately put their name to the text. For the most part, the Convention followed the terms of the 1974 ILC draft, and final modifications were few in number. Indeed, in several respects it was the late additions made to the draft at the Conference that have subsequently been the cause for greatest concern.

---

[602] M. Craven, 'What Happened to Unequal Treaties?: The Continuities of Informal Empire' 74 Nordic JIL (2005) 335.

[603] On these see, Yrbk ILC, 1974, II, pp 172–3, paras 75–81.

As has been noted,[604] there were four main issues which gave rise to the most extended discussion at the Conference: 1) the temporal application of the Convention; 2) the recognition given to boundary and territorial regimes and their relationship to the principle of permanent sovereignty over natural resources; 3) the question of secession (separation of parts of a State); and 4) the provisions relating to dispute settlement. Of these, the first and last will be dealt with in relatively short order. As regards the question of its temporal application, the position adopted by the ILC in its 1974 draft (Article 7) had been that the articles would 'apply only in respect of a succession of States which has occurred after entry into force of these articles except as otherwise agreed'. This was a provision that had been proposed at the instigation of Ushakov[605] whose overt concern had been to prevent the Convention from being relied upon for purposes of validating the continuance of historic agreements marked by conditions of inequality. But the principle of non-retroactivity raised the obvious problem that the only way in which the Conventional provisions (as opposed to rules or principles in customary international law) could come to be applicable to a new State, would be by means of that State 'agreeing otherwise'.[606] In such a case, the Convention itself would seem to have limited value. Despite this, the Conference found no obvious way of sidestepping the problem: deleting the provision would not have avoided the general principle of non-retroactivity that was already enshrined in Article 28 of the Vienna Convention on the Law of Treaties; providing for retroactive application would have risked the re-opening of historic grievances.[607] The final text adopted at the Conference thus merely fleshed out the substance of Ushakov's proposal in a series of paragraphs, the substance of which provided that a successor State might make a declaration accepting the application of the Convention in relation to its own succession (effective in relation to other States choosing to accept that declaration).

In relation to the question of dispute settlement, although it was an issue that had long been flagged as one with which the ILC should deal, it was ultimately left to one side for lack of time. It was at the Conference, therefore, that the matter was fully discussed for the first time. Two proposals had been put forward – one by the United States[608] providing for compulsory arbitration (but allowing States to 'opt out'); the other by the Netherlands[609] providing for submission

---

[604] I Sinclair, 'Some Reflections on the Vienna Convention on Succession of States in Respect of Treaties', in *Essays in Honour of Erik Castren* (1978) 149, p 163.

[605] Yrbk ILC, 1974, I, p 80.

[606] The phrase 'otherwise agreed' obviously has two different connotations: one being that a successor State might agree 'otherwise' to apply the Convention notwithstanding the lack of any formal obligation to do so; the other being that it may 'otherwise' agree with other parties to vary the rules in the Convention even if they are formally applicable.

[607] UN Conference on Succession of States in Respect of Treaties: Official Records, vol I, pp 64–88.

[608] A/CONF80/C1/L38/Rev1.

[609] A/CONF80/C1/L56.

to arbitration or to the ICJ. After some discussion in which a range of different views were fielded – some of which recommended diplomatic negotiation, some conciliation, and some of which supported the proposal for compulsory arbitration – a working group produced a draft text that was finally adopted by the Conference and came to form Articles 41–45 of the Convention. These provide for a process of consultation and negotiation and following that, conciliation along the lines of the procedure annexed to the Vienna Convention on the Law of Treaties (1969) with the possibility of consensual resort to judicial settlement or arbitration. To this day, those procedures have not been invoked.

These two points aside, it is clear that the most significant aspects of the work of the Conference related to its consideration of boundary and territorial régimes and secession. Although there was considerable discussion of the provision relating to boundary régimes (with strong opposition from both Afghanistan and Somalia both of which had outstanding disputes with their neighbours), this provision obtained overwhelming support. As in the ILC itself, however, it was the provision relating to territorial régimes that was more problematic, with particular concerns being raised as regards the extent to which this might justify the continuation of foreign military base agreements and agreements for the exploitation of natural resources. As noted above, neither of these issues had been discussed at any great length within the Commission – a point which Vallat took as indicative of the fact that the ILC had not intended for either category to be regarded as constituting a territorial régime. Whilst there was little overt support for the continuance of military base agreements (to the extent that this did *not* extend to provisions relating to demilitarization)[610] there was less clarity as regards the implications of the principle of permanent sovereignty over natural resources. Some States, such as the UK and the USA, maintained that since many such agreements would seem to involve relations between what had become two newly independent States, any reference to the principle of permanent sovereignty over natural resources was largely irrelevant.[611] Underlying the dispute in this regard, as Sinclair put it, was 'the long-standing controversy concerning the relationship between the principle of permanent sovereignty over natural resources and international law itself'.[612]

The point to which Sinclair alluded was illustrated by a Statement of the UK in relation to a proposal for the inclusion of a savings clause stipulating that nothing in the Convention should 'affect the principles of international law affirming the permanent sovereignty of every people and every State over its natural wealth

---

[610] It was finally agreed that a third paragraph be added to art 12 excluding treaty obligations relating to 'the establishment of foreign military bases' from the scope of territorial régimes. See art 12(3) Vienna Convention (1978). For the declarations relating to demilitarization see UN Doc A/CONF80/C1/SR54.

[611] *Official Records*, I, pp 136, 137.

[612] Sinclair, above, n 604, p 171.

and resources'.[613] The UK delegation, affirming its adhesion to the principle of permanent sovereignty as spelt out in GA Resolution 1803(XVII), made clear nevertheless that 'its application was governed by the principles of international law which, in the final analysis, ought to be able to resolve any possible conflict between the principle of permanent sovereignty and other concepts, such as that of acquired rights'.[614] What the UK was alluding to in its reference to acquired rights, was the conflict that had surrounded recognition of the principle of permanent sovereignty as regards the level of compensation payable as a consequence of the 'expropriation' or 'nationalization' of foreign-owned undertakings or their property.[615] To some in the West, the assault upon the principle of adequate (or even 'appropriate') compensation of foreign owners in case of expropriation – as seemed to be evidenced in the rather equivocal obligation articulated in the Charter of Economic Rights and Duties of States – was tantamount to a rejection of international law. But what obviously went unmentioned, here, was that the very survival of rights and obligations under concession agreements in case of succession was itself a point over which there were clear differences of opinion. In order for a 'foreign' investor to claim compensation for loss of rights under an agreement concluded with the former colonial authorities, it had to be assumed that the agreement itself would have survived the transition to independence: compensation was dependent upon a prior claim to ownership. Despite the fact that there were only few instances in which such agreements were repudiated at the time of independence, and for all the 'traditional' insistence upon the intangibility of acquired rights, the debates within the ILC in the 1960s made very clear that this was not an assumption that could lightly be relied upon. In the event, however, the provision relating to permanent sovereignty was adopted by the Conference and was to become Article 3 of the 1978 Convention.

The final, and particularly controversial, issue raised at the Conference concerned Part IV of the ILC draft dealing with rules applicable in relation to the uniting and separating of States. As has been seen, the Commission found itself in an increasingly difficult position in attempting to differentiate between cases involving the emergence of a 'newly independent State' (for which a right of option was available), and 'other' cases of separation (for which a rule of continuity was applicable). In order to ameliorate the effects of this sharp distinction, the Commission had included in its final draft an exception to the principle of *ipso iure* continuity in case of the separation of a State (Article 33(3)) which read: 'Notwithstanding paragraph 1, if a part of the territory of a State separates from it and becomes a State in circumstances which are essentially of the same character as those existing in the case of the formation of a newly independent State, the

---

[613] Art 12 bis.
[614] A/CONF80/C1/SR55.
[615] See generally, Jennings and Watts, above, n 125, pp 911–27.

successor State shall be regarded for purposes of the present articles in all respects as a newly independent State'.

When the matter came under discussion at the Conference, two States (France and Switzerland) had put forward amendments seeking to eliminate the distinction that had been erected by the Commission between the two categories of secession. These were opposed on one side by those who were worried about the implications of conflating these categories in terms of encouraging secessionist groups, and on the other side by those who believed that it might undermine or downgrade the significance of the decolonization process itself. The implication of both positions, of course, was to cabin the principle of 'self-determination' in the draft to the context of decolonization. In the end, with the rejection of the Franco-Swiss amendments, so also was Article 33(3) deleted from the Convention leaving in its wake a very stark differentiation between colonial and non-colonial secession.

11. Reception and Reflection

Just as only a handful of States proceeded to sign the Vienna Convention of 1978, the reception it was given amongst the academic community was also largely mixed. The adoption of the Convention encouraged the production of a spate of articles and books on the topic many of which rehearsed lines of thought that had been debated at length within the International Law Commission.[616] Many authors spoke about the Convention as a kind of inevitable compromise: some saw it as seeking to 'balance' irreconcilable interests by resort to flexible

---

[616] eg E Bello, 'Reflections on Succession of States in the Light of the Vienna Convention on Succession of States in Respect of Treaties 1978', 23 GYIL (1978) 296; I Sinclair, 'Some Reflections on the Vienna Convention on Succession of States in Respect of Treaties', in *Essays in Honour of Erik Castren* (1978) 149; M Maloney, 'State Succession in Respect of Treaties: The Vienna Convention of 1978', 19 VaJIL (1978–79) 885; K Yasseen, 'La Convention de Vienne sur la Succession d'Etats en matière de traités', 24 AFDI (1978) 59; H Treviranus, 'Die Konvention der Vereinten Nationen über Staatensukzession bei Verträgen' 39 ZöV (1979) 259; R Szafarz, 'Vienna Convention on Succession of States in Respect of Treaties: A General Analysis', 10 PYrbkIL (1979–80) 77; D O'Connell, 'Reflections on the State Succession Convention' 39 ZöV (1979) 725; T Elias, 'The Contribution of Asia and Africa to the Contemporary International Law' 16 Africa Quarterly (1976) 1; R Lavalle, 'Dispute Settlement under the Vienna Convention on Succession of States in Respect of Treaties', 73 AJIL (1979) 407; Z Mériboute, *La Codification de la succession d'états aux traités* (1984); P Menon, *The Succession of States in Respect to Treaties, State Property, Archives and Debts* (1991). For reflections on the ILC draft art see G Caggiano, 'The ILC Draft on the Succession of States in Respect of Treaties: A Critical Appraisal', 1 Italian YBIL (1975) 69; J Stewart, 'Draft Articles on the Succession of States in Respect of Treaties: The Pragmatic Development of International Law', 16 HarvILJ (1975) 638. Some of the authors, such as Yasseen and Elias, had been directly involved in the process and their views were very much those of insiders. Others, such as Sinclair and Treviranus, had not been directly involved in the ILC's work, but had nevertheless been involved as members of State delegations at the 1974 Conference. Yet others, such as O'Connell, were figures whose work had been relied upon to a great extent during the drafting of the Convention, but whose general approach had been largely marginalized.

provisions,[617] others saw it in terms of a 'package deal', accommodating through abstract principles the conflicting interests of old and new States.[618] Others still saw the resort to 'selective precedents and flimsy doctrine' as an attempt to camouflage, or overcome, underlying political and ideological dissent.[619] The sense, for the most part, was that the project of codification would naturally assume a compromised character (particularly given the sharply 'divided' views of different States on the question of succession) and that this was simply an inevitable consequence of the process of codification.

By no means every aspect of the Convention was subject to criticism. A good number, for example, praised the ILC's commitment to the continuity of boundary and territorial treaties[620] even if the conclusion of Article 14 (a savings clause specifying that nothing in the Convention should be taken as 'prejudicing in any respect any question relating to the validity of a treaty') was such as to introduce an unworkable level of uncertainty into the issue.[621] Others praised the adoption of a rule of continuity in the formation and dissolution of unions of States, suggesting that this was a mark of 'innovation and courage'.[622] Few, however, stood out in support of the principles enunciated in respect of new States, and, commentators were largely unanimous in the view that the Convention seemed to be 'too much concerned with past problems bound up with the process of decolonization, and too little concerned with present or future problems'.[623]

The most intemperate of commentators by some degree was O'Connell, and it was his critique of the methodology and structure of the Convention that was both most acutely observed and challenging. O'Connell's central complaint was that the Conference had given 'scant indication' of any awareness of the fact that State succession to treaties was 'a matter of great intellectual, and hence of doctrinal, subtlety'.[624] It had, in his view, forced the topic 'within the constraints of inflexible dogmas that are at once over-simple and insufficiently comprehensive'.[625] The example he took to illustrate this point was the separation of Bangladesh from Pakistan. If, on the one hand, that separation was taken to be

---

[617] Maloney, above, n 616, p 911.
[618] Bello, above, n 616, pp 302, 304, 312.
[619] Stewart, above, n 616, p 647.
[620] Stewart, above, n 616, p 642; Treviranus, above, n 616, p 278; Bello, above, n 616, p 307. In the 1985 Maritime Delimitation case (Guinea/Guinea Bissau) 77 ILR 657, the arbitral tribunal held that 'the relevant provisions of this latter Convention [as it deals with boundary regimes] which is not yet in force, and which in fact neither Guinea nor Guinea Bissau has adhered to, are nonetheless held to reflect customary rules of international law'.
[621] Bello, above, n 616, p 307; Stewart, above, n 616, p 642. Maloney was critical of the Convention's apparent equivocation over the fate of boundary and territorial treaties which he saw to be a retreat from the 'bedrock principle of customary international law'. Maloney, above, n 616, p 905. See also P Pazartzis, 'State Succession to Multilateral Treaties: Recent Developments', 3 ARIEL (1998) 397, p 398.
[622] Maloney, above, n 616, p 913.
[623] Sinclair, above, n 616, p 181.
[624] O'Connell, above, n 616, p 727.
[625] ibid.

a case of secession (the emergence to independence from a condition of dependency) then Waldock's version of the clean slate would be applicable (Articles 16 and 17). If, on the other hand, it was to be characterized as the 'dissolution of a federation', the presumption would be that treaties would automatically continue (Article 34).[626] O'Connell was to point out, however, that neither solution would have been politically attractive. On the one hand

if Bangladesh chose to argue its case on the basis of secession that would have compromised its claims to a share of Pakistan's assets, including gold in the World Bank, and would have affected court actions which were launched in various countries to recover private property which had been subjected to Pakistan decrees during the liberation war.[627]

If, on the other hand,

Bangladesh chose to argue its case on the basis of the dissolution of the Federation of East and West Pakistan, it feared to be held liable to Pakistan's treaties. For, as a provincial government it had not even a list of these, let alone the texts.... Until several hundred treaties were identified, collected and examined it was not even possible to ascertain what the issues were for a policy decision, and... [in the event] it took three years to do so, by which time the whole matter had become past history.[628]

Although O'Connell ultimately took the view that the separation of Bangladesh had involved the dissolution of a federation, his concern was that the issues were ultimately compromised by the government's vacillation on this issue which facilitated decisions being made 'for it from outside'.[629] The point, however, was not that Bangladesh was to be blamed for its ambivalence, but that the inflexible framework of the Convention had forced it into such a position. It was surely nonsense, O'Connell maintained, to force a State like Bangladesh to adopt a position in which it 'inherits all or none of the treaties that previously applied to it'.[630] Common sense would surely suggest the best solution to be something in between, and the determination of that would be 'a matter of juristic function, not of legislative intervention'.[631]

The root cause of the problem, as O'Connell and others were to maintain, was the ILC's adoption of the clean-slate rule in case of newly independent States. In that context, the ILC had set aside 'reason' in favour of an approach formed within the ideological milieu of decolonization[632] 'around which' as O'Connell was to put it 'myth and emotion [had] accumulated like mists in the marsh'.[633]

---

[626] For a critique of a similar nature see P Kooijmans, 'State Succession and the 1929 Warsaw Convention: a Case Study', in T Masson-Zwaan and P Mendes de Leon (eds), *Air and Space Law: De Lege Ferenda* (1992) 113, pp 122–5.
[627] O'Connell, above, n 616, p 728.
[628] ibid.
[629] ibid.
[630] ibid.
[631] ibid 729.
[632] Stewart, above, n 616, p 641; Maloney, above, n 616, p 912.
[633] O'Connell, above, n 616, p 726.

This was evidenced, as far as O'Connell was concerned, in Waldock's slapdash methodology. The opinions of writers were referred to in an 'old-fashioned' form of 'head count' with no discrimination for specialist expertise and no appreciation that many such authors might have simply copied one another. Many instances of practice were lumped together despite their obvious dissimilarities, and little attention had been given to the very different circumstances that attended decolonization when compared with cases from the 19th century (the emergence of multilateral law-making treaties).[634] O'Connell also suggested that the proposed rule neither accorded with State practice during decolonization, nor was it consistent with the basic rule of consent in treaty law.[635] Ultimately, he reprised the position that he had favoured at least since 1962, to the effect that it would have been better to adopt a rule of continuity subject to the possibility of denunciation (either by way of treaty provision or by reliance upon the principle *pacta sunt servanda*).

What is most interesting about O'Connell's critique, however, is not his comments on methodology which only raise themselves a host of ensuing questions as regards how one should go about dividing the practice in a way that did not rely upon suppositions concerning the significance of 'personality' or a particular approach to decolonization. Nor is it his advocacy of treaty continuity – which in many respects did not entirely respond to the issues he raised in the case of Bangladesh. It is, rather, his observation that, in the latter case, the government was deeply ambivalent as to whether to pursue a general policy of continuity or discontinuity, and the relationship that appeared to exist between different issues – the preferred approach to treaties (wait and see) being at odds with the desire to inherit its share of the patrimony of the federation. This obviously raised questions as regards both the ILC's approach to treaty succession and O'Connell's own approach to continuity.

12. Conclusions

One of the very evident features of this story of codification is how, gradually, the topic became more complex and more involved, and yet, at the same time, more abstract and contemplative as it progressed. What, at the outset, had been a fairly concrete project concerned with supplementing existing rules of treaty law became, towards the final stages, a project mired in discussions as to whether cases such as that of Bangladesh would have more in common with decolonization than with the dissolution of a union of States, and whether all cases of unification were likely to take the form of that of the United Arab Republic. By the end, too much seemed to be asked at too great a level of generality, for views to harden in one direction or another. But at the same time, there seemed to be

---

[634] ibid 729–31.
[635] ibid 733.

an unwilled momentum, or gravitational pull, that took hold of the project once underway. Waldock's initial reluctance to look beyond the terms of the law of treaties and his similar equivocation over the significance of self-determination gave way in the later stages to a much more active contemplation as to what each might signify. What this spelled out, at the very least, was the obvious inability of those involved in codification, to deal with the problem of succession in a way that did not draw within it questions of identity and status, or conclusions about the relationship between international and municipal law.

What observations might, in general, be made about the project? There is no doubt that Waldock's approach to the process of drafting articles on succession in respect of treaties, as critics such as O'Connell were at pains to point out, was one marked by all the obvious methodological frailties associated with attempting to locate normative propositions in empirical observation. At moments, he was clearly highly selective in his choice of examples, at others, willing to identify practice as essentially inconsistent in order to make space for arguments of policy. At some points he was forensic in his attention to detail, at others, capable of wielding the broad brush. On some occasions, context was all important, on others largely irrelevant. But these, it must be said, were not problems peculiar to this particular project of codification. They were simply parts of a process of legal argumentation by which those such as Waldock (and, in his own work, O'Connell) sought to locate their normative intuitions in something other than personal taste or outlook. There was nearly always State practice to hand, but the key question was always about how to organize and interpret that practice and to determine what analogies might be used.

The central theme running through the whole process of codification, of course, was the place assumed by decolonization within it. It was evident to many from the outset that there was an inevitable tension between the idea of seeking to codify and develop rules of succession to govern future cases of political transformation, at the same time as concentrating upon the particular experience of decolonization whose course was almost run. There were those in the Commission – including Waldock and Ago – who clearly believed decolonization to be in no respect markedly different from other cases of separation or secession, and who thereby appeared to assume that the implications of self-determination were not confined to events in that particular era. But the effect of the Conference's decision to remove the qualifying clause within what became Article 34 (relating to cases 'analogous' to decolonization) was to concretize a sharp distinction between the colonial experience on the one hand (in which the principle of self-determination would be operative) and other cases of secession. Here one was to find in very concrete form an idea that was only otherwise hinted at in the practice of the UN, that self-determination was a principle whose content really varied quite starkly depending upon whether the relations in question assumed the aura of 'colonial' relations or not. That such an insight may now be thought mundane, is as much testament to the largely superficial equation of imperialism with 'formal' colonial rule, as it is with the idea that only some, but not all, might have a right to independent self-government.

There was obviously a considerable degree of commonality amongst members of the Commission and other commentators at the time that colonialism connoted a very specific experience discrete in both time and space. This idea itself was obviously problematic given the very different experiences of decolonization in different parts of the world, and given the time span over which it occurred. But even with this common starting point, there were obvious differences between the various scholars as regards the implications of decolonization. On the one side there were those, like O'Connell, Rosenne, and Keith who understood decolonization as a largely ordered process of governmental devolution characterized by high degrees of legal continuity at both the local and international level (indeed, on some accounts, these processes were closely intertwined). On the other side, there were the likes of Lester, Bedjaoui, and to a lesser extent Bartoš, who understood it as a revolutionary moment, the implications of which were to bring about a series of fundamental changes in the structure, process, and content of international law (the fulfilment, perhaps, of the ambitions elaborated in the UN Charter). For the first group, the problem posed by decolonization was essentially that of the potential incompatibility of the new circumstances with existing treaty commitments, and they thus saw the law of State succession as being oriented towards identifying the most convenient method of addressing that issue. This, as it turned out, was to maintain in principle the continuity of existing treaty obligations, but allowed for the possibility of termination, denunciation, or resort to the principle of fundamental change. Underlying this, of course, was a commitment to maintaining the integrity of international legal relations, which they saw to be ultimately challenged by advocates of the 'clean slate'.

For the second group, by contrast, the object of the law of State succession was not, strictly speaking, to 'resolve' the administrative or managerial problems associated with the devolution of authority, nor indeed to uphold the integrity of 'international law' in the abstract, but to realize the promise of political and economic self-determination and advance thereby the sundry objectives of what, in some circles, was referred to as the new 'law of decolonization'. Whatever the merits of maintaining existing treaty relations in place, this was a matter to be decided by newly independent States in their initial engagement with other international actors. For this second group, in other words, the issue was not the nature of the problem, but the question as to who might be entitled to resolve it.

Lying behind both of these accounts were particular constructions as to the relationship between colonial rule and the pre-independence identity of non-self-governing territories. As a way of pushing forward the project of decolonization, the General Assembly had insisted upon the separate legal identity of non-self-governing territories. This, of course, ran in line with both with the ICJ's approach to protected States, and with the general approach to trusteeship. But recognition of the pre-independence identity of those territories 'destined' for independence was clearly capable of being construed in quite different ways in terms of its implications for the law of succession. On the one hand, and most obviously for some, recognition of the separate identity of non-self governing territories signified a fundamental alteration in the terms of the legal relationship between colonizer and colonized. Colonial territories could no longer be represented as integral parts of the metropolitan State (as many Portuguese colonies appeared to remain for example) and colonial rule was rendered thereby alien, and perhaps occasionally 'illegal' in character. From this vantage point, two conclusions appeared to flow. First, it seemed to signify that treaties and other commitments concluded on behalf of those colonies could not survive independence merely by reason that power had been exercised in relation to the territory prior to that moment by the administering authorities. In the second place it also appeared to underpin the idea that the identity of metropolitan territories would remain largely unaffected by the process of independence – the transformation not going so far as to put in question the continuance of their rights and obligations as a consequence of the loss of empire.

On the other hand, the recognition of a pre-independence identity on the part of non-self-governing territories also suggested, to the contrary, that the movement towards independence was indeed gradual rather than sudden; evolutionary rather than revolutionary. If the territories in question already possessed a pre-formed legal identity, it was neither possible to argue that they were entirely 'new' at birth, nor that the administering authorities in the intervening time had no competence to transact on their behalf. In formalizing the relationship between colonizer and colonized, albeit in terms of alien occupant and subaltern populace, the General Assembly had appeared to regularise a relationship of authority and responsibility which could thereafter be taken as framing the terms under which independence was ultimately to be gained. The colonized territory might be said, thus, to have been called (interpellated) into the order of international law from which it was never destined to escape.

Here, of course, was the essence of the dilemma. Those pushing through what they took to be the logic of emancipation were unable to ignore the fact that the ascription of identity to those destined for independence was to disallow speaking about decolonization as something that had simply happened. Decolonization could not be understood merely as 'fact' to which scholars and practitioners attached certain consequences, nor indeed as a process of *de novo* self-determination, but as a regulated process by which the complex set of background legal relations were re-adjusted and re-ordered. This is clear in relation to the arguments concerning the executed effect of boundary and territorial regimes, it is also clear in respect of Waldock's formulation of the clean-slate principle. If a new State claimed a right of option in relation to pre-existing treaties, it did so under impress of a legal authority that simultaneously recognized its right of autonomous decision making, and the existence of a legally relevant and pre-existent bond between it and other treaty partners. No State, as some were to aver, could ever be regarded as entirely 'new' – they were always the progeny of a super-ordinating system of international law.

The idea, thus, that decolonization operated through pre-existent categories was, ultimately, thoroughly normalizing. What might have been cast as a revolutionary moment, a moment of expansion and change in international society, was immediately subverted by the idea that the sovereignty being obtained, was not a law-creative sovereignty, but a capacity already fully determined. When seen in that light, the arguments about the inheritance or otherwise of treaty obligations could not be fully described in terms of a commitment to, or disregard of, international law, any more than would arguments about the legitimacy of treaty denunciation or the invocation of the principle of a fundamental change in circumstances. All were, from one side at least, merely ways of qualifying what *pacta sunt servanda* might mean. In similar guise, when seen as a question of succession, the old opposition between self-determination and *uti possidetis* lost its decisive import by reason of the impossibility of self-determination meaning anything but independence within inherited borders – once the 'self' had been identified, any determination could operate only within the parameters of its own existence.

The normalizing effect of this approach to succession also meant that the arguments about inheritance were inevitably profoundly equivocal. It was always evident, for example, that with every argument in favour of the 'clean slate' went also an argument as to the importance of automatic inheritance to 'dispositive agreements', or the desirability otherwise of adhesion to multilateral agreements. Even with the emergence of an entirely 'new' subject, there were still legal relations applicable in respect of its territory that were there to be fulfilled. Succession merely indicated a change in the identity of the party responsible. So also, with every argument in favour of continuity, went arguments as to the possibility of denunciation or of open resort to the doctrine of fundamental change. That neither position seemed to be particularly attractive in unqualified form was, in many respects, related to an ambivalence as to the nature of what might, or might not, be inherited. As Bartoš had pointed out, States emerging from colonial rule, would not necessarily take it to be in their best interests to dispose of the entirety of their colonial heritage: certain treaties might have the character of colonial impositions, certain others may be useful or expedient. One could be fairly certain that they would not look upon a foreign bases agreement in the same light as they would an extradition agreement, or automatically accept the continuation of a capitulation regime in the same way as they might a treaty delimiting a border with a neighbouring State. In this regard, Waldock's version of the clean-slate rule was peculiarly attractive. As was made clear, it did not entail an inability to inherit treaties or represent an incapacity to be a successor State. It was, rather, a right to choose what would be inherited and what would not, and was largely premised upon the idea that new States should be encouraged to notify their succession as a matter of policy. It was, thus, by no means impossible that the outcome of his proposal would result in precisely the same treaties being subject to succession, as might otherwise have occurred under a rule of continuity. That it was to implicitly recognize both the significance and irrelevance of the relationship between the colonial territory and the former metropolitan power was only such as to affirm the moderated nature of his proposals.

This may all be such as to suggest that Bedjoui's concern as to the neo-colonial nature of the law of succession was, perhaps, overstated – or at least that such arguments did not translate quite so easily into conclusions concerning the survival or otherwise of treaty relations. Yet, at the same time, it was very much apparent that the terms of the debate were still very clear. The 6th Committee's opposition to the category of 'dispositive agreements', the Socialist States' arguments about the significance of 'social revolution', and Upper Volta's rejection of any succession to international agreements, all made clear the continuing suspicion with which arguments about continuity were held. By the same token, those favouring continuity were rarely short of arguments as to the implications of allowing new States to effectively set aside multilateral humanitarian agreements, or the chaos that might ensue from a disregard for the terms of territorial or boundary regimes. Even if neither side might have obviously triumphed in the articulation of rules relating to new States, the terms of the contestation were rarely far beneath the surface.

III

New Beginnings, New Ends

1. Introduction

The years immediately following the Vienna Conference on State Succession (1978) were a period of relative quiescence for those interested in the question of State succession. The process of decolonization had largely run its course, with Zimbabwe's independence coming in the same year as the Conference. The ILC, for its part, was in the final phase of its work on succession in respect of property, archives and debt with Bedjaoui's final 13th Report being presented to the Commission in 1981[1] leading to another Vienna Conference in 1983 and the final adoption of the Vienna Convention in the same year.[2] From here until the extraordinary events of 1989, only those watching the unfolding events in Namibia[3] might

---

[1] M Bedjaoui, 'First Report on Succession of States in Respect of Rights and Duties Resulting from Sources other than Treaties' UN Doc A/CN4/204 and Corr1, Yrbk ILC, 1968, II, 94; 'Second Report on Succession of States in Respect of Matters other than Treaties – Economic and Financial Acquired Rights and State Succession', UN Doc. A/CN4/216/Rev 1, Yrbk ILC, 1969, II, 70; 'Third Report on Succession of States in Respect of Matters other than Treaties', UN Doc A/CN4/226 Yrbk ILC, 1970, II, 131; 'Fourth Report on Succession of States in Respect of Matters other than Treaties', UN Doc A/CN4/247 and Add.1, Yrbk ILC, 1971, II, 157; 'Fifth Report on Succession of States in Respect of Matters other than Treaties', UN Doc A/CN4/259 Yrbk ILC, 1972, II, 61; 'Sixth Report on Succession of States in Respect of Matters other than Treaties', UN Doc A/CN4/267 Yrbk ILC, 1973, II, 9; 'Seventh Report on Succession of States in Respect of Matters other than Treaties', UN Doc A/CN4/282 Yrbk ILC, 1974, II, 93; 'Eighth Report on Succession of States in Respect of Matters other than Treaties', UN Doc A/CN4/292 Yrbk ILC, 1976, II, 57; 'Ninth Report on Succession of States in Respect of Matters other than Treaties', UN Doc A/CN4/301 and Add1, Yrbk ILC, 1977, II, 49; 'Tenth Report on Succession of States in Respect of Matters other than Treaties', UN Doc A/CN4/313, Yrbk ILC, 1978, II, 230; 'Eleventh Report on Succession of States in Respect of Matters other than Treaties', UN Doc A/CN4/322 and Corr1 and Add1 2, Yrbk ILC, 1979, II, 68; 'Twelfth Report on Succession of States in Respect of Matters other than Treaties', UN Doc A/CN4/333 Yrbk ILC, 1980, II, 1; 'Thirteenth Report on Succession of States in Respect of Matters other than Treaties', UN Doc A/CN4/345 and Add 1–3, Yrbk ILC, 1981, II, 4.

[2] On which see, B Stern, *La Succession d'États* (2000) pp 140–5; E Nathan; 'The Vienna Convention on Succession of States in Respect of State Property, Archives and Debts', *International Law in a Time of Perplexity, Essays in Honour of Shabtai Rosenne* (1989) 489; R Streinz, 'Succession of States in Assets and Liabilities – a New Regime? The Vienna Convention on Succession of States in Respect of State Property, Archives and Debts', GerYIL (1983) 198; P Williams, and J Harris, 'State Succession to Debts and Assets: The Modern Law and Policy', 42, HarvILJ (2001) 355.

[3] P Szasz, 'Succession to Treaties under the Namibian Constitution', 15 SAYrbk IL (1989/90) 65; UN Institute for Namibia, *Independent Namibia: Succession to Treaty Rights and Obligations*

have been concerned to engage with the issue. Even O'Connell was to lament, as early as 1979, that '[a]mong the diplomatic priorities of most governments, State succession is of a very low order'. Many States, he reported, had regarded the Vienna Conference as 'altogether unimportant and not worth expenditure of public funds'[4] – a view, no doubt, supported by the sluggish process of ratification following the adoption of the 1978 Convention.

All this changed with the dramatic events of the 1990s. Suddenly, with the dismemberment of the USSR and the SFRY, the partition of Czechoslovakia, and the unification of Germany (with the unification of the two Yemeni Republics,[5] the independence of Eritrea,[6] and the return of Hong Kong to China[7] as interesting sideshows) State succession, once again, came to the forefront. In the following decade a whole spate of new activity centred upon the issue. The ILA returned to the issue in 1994 producing a series of reports on succession in respect of treaties[8] and continued working on problems related to assets and debts.[9] The ILC, for its part, returned to deal with the question of nationality which it had left entirely to one side in the 1960s.[10] The Council of Europe began working through some of the questions arising within Europe with its Committee of Legal Advisers (CAHDI) initiating a Pilot Project on recognition and State succession[11] and the Venice Commission producing a Declaration on the question of nationality.[12] The Institut de Droit International drafted a set of 'guiding principles' in case of succession in respect of property and debts[13] and the International Court of

---

(1989); Y Makonnen, 'Namibia: Its International Status and the Issues of State Succession' 3 Lesotho LJ (1987) 183.

[4] D O'Connell, 'Reflections on the State Succession Convention', 39 ZaoRV (1979) 725, pp 726–7.

[5] Agreement on the Establishment of the Republic of Yemen, (1990) 30 ILM (1991) 820. See also, R Goy, 'La Réunification du Yémen', AFDI (1990) 249.

[6] R Goy, 'L'Indépendance de l'Erythrée', AFDI (1993) 337.

[7] R Mushkat, 'Hong Kong and Succession of Treaties' 46 ICLQ (1997) 181; P Yu, 'Succession by Estoppel: Hong Kong's Succession to the ICCPR', 27 PeppLR (1999–2000) 53; J Chan, 'State Succession to Human Rights Treaties: Hong Kong and the International Covenant on Civil and Political Rights', ICLQ (1996) 928; P Slinn, 'Aspects juridiques du retour de Hong Kong à la Chine', AFDI (1996) 273.

[8] ILA Committee on Aspects of the Law of State Succession, 'Rapport Final Sur La Succession en Matiere de Traites', 70 ILA Rep, New Delhi Conference (2002) 574.

[9] ILA Committee on Aspects of the Law of State Succession, 'Aspects of the Law of State Succession: Provisional Report', 71 ILA Rep, Berlin Conference (2004) 16.

[10] ILC, draft arts on the Nationality of Natural Persons in Relation to the Succession of States (1999), 54 GAOR, Supp no 10 (UN doc A/54/10).

[11] J Klabbers, M Koskenniemi, O Ribbelink and A Zimmermann, *State Practice Regarding State Succession and Issues of Recognition* (1999). The Committee also met on two occasions in 1992 the minutes of which were subject to analysis by Williams. See P Williams, 'The Treaty Obligations of the Successor States of the Former Soviet Union, Yugoslavia and Czechoslovakia: Do They Continue?', 23 DenvJILP (1994) 1, pp 16–19.

[12] Declaration on the Consequences of State Succession for the Nationality of Natural Persons, European Commission for Democracy through Law, 28th mtg, Venice 13–14 Sep 1996.

[13] Institut de Droit International, 'State Succession in Matters of Property and Debts', (Vancouver Session, 2001).

Justice became involved in the issue both in respect of the complex of interrelated disputes concerning the former Yugoslavia[14] and in relation to the *Gabčikovo-Nagymaros Project* case.[15]

To the extent that all those concerned understood themselves to be working within a tradition, the terms of which had been fairly extensively explored in the 1960s and 1970s, this was, in some respects, business as usual. Here was the opportunity to 'test' the utility of the two Vienna Conventions on State Succession:[16] to work out on the one hand which, if any, of their provisions could usefully be relied upon as a way of resolving the difficulties that were to emerge; and on the other, to evaluate the provisions of those agreements in light of the practice as it was subsequently to develop. Although neither Convention was then in force, they were frequently taken as the initial basis for discussion. The Arbitration Commission on Yugoslavia (aka Badinter Commission), for example, in being asked to respond to a series of questions put to it concerning succession to property, archives, and debts[17] took as its starting point the 'principles of international law embodied in the Vienna Conventions of 23rd August 1978 and 8th April 1983'.[18] Although the Badinter Commission subsequently downplayed the significance of the Conventions, the original intent was clear enough.[19] Similarly, the ILA's work on succession in the 1990s was initiated with a view to considering, amongst other things, 'the extent to which the United Nations Conventions on State Succession of 1978 and 1983 have contributed to the development of international law, having

---

[14] *Application of the Convention on the Prevention and Punishment of the Crime of Genocide, Preliminary Objections* Judgment ICJ Rep 1996, 595; *Case Concerning the Application of the Convention on the Prevention and Punishment of the Crime of Genocide*, Judgment, ICJ 26 Feb 2007; *Application for Revision of the Judgment of 11th July 1996 in the Case concerning Application of the Convention on the Prevention and Punishment of the Crime of Genocide (Bosnia and Herzegovina v Yugoslavia) Preliminary Objections (Yugoslavia v Bosnia and Herzegovina)*, Judgment, ICJ Rep 2003, 7; *Application of the Convention on the Prevention and Punishment of the Crime of Genocide* (Croatia v Serbia and Montenegro), 2 Jul 1999; *Legality of the Use of Force (Serbia and Montenegro v Belgium) Preliminary Objections,* Judgment ICJ Rep 2004, 279.

[15] *Gabčikovo-Nagymaros Project (Hungary/ Slovakia)*, Judgment, ICJ Rep 1997, 7.

[16] M Koskenniemi and P Eisemann, *State Succession: Codification Tested Against the Facts* (1997). For a largely positive view of the correspondence between the Conventions and practice in the 1990s see J Crawford, 'Remarks' 86 ASILProc (1992) 15, p 17.

[17] 32 ILM (1993) 1580. See generally A Pellet, 'Notes sur la Commission d'arbitrage de la Conférence européene pour la paix en Yougoslavie', AFDI (1991) 329; A Pellet, 'L'activité de la Commission d'arbitrage de la Conférence européene pour l'ancienne Yougoslavie' AFDI (1993) 268; M Craven, 'The European Community Arbitration Commission on Yugoslavia', 66 BYIL (1995) 333.

[18] Opinion no 9, 92 ILR 203. Significantly enough, the Republics had agreed that the two conventions should form the 'foundation for discussions between them on the succession of states at the Conference for Peace in Yugoslavia'. Opinion no 8, 31 ILM (1992) 1521, p 1524.

[19] By the time of its 13th Opinion, the Commission was to come to the conclusion that 'there are few well established principles of international law that apply to State succession' and that application of those principles 'is largely to be determined case by case, depending on the circumstances proper to each form of succession'. It concluded that the Conventions did, nevertheless, 'offer some guidance'. Opinion no 13, 32 ILM (1992) 1591, p 1592.

specific regard to State practice since the conclusion of those Conventions'.[20] In proceedings before the ICJ relating to the Gabčikovo-Nagymaros project, furthermore, Hungary and Slovakia spent a good deal of their time debating the applicability of Articles 12 and 34 of the 1978 Convention.[21]

In one sense, of course, this kind of retrospection was inevitable. Once it had been recognized that these kinds of political transformation constituted instances of succession, there was nowhere else to turn for legal insight. However problematic the Conventions might have been, they at least provided *some* answers to the questions that were being posed. Articles 11 and 12 dealing with territorial and boundary agreements, for example, were obviously less problematic points of departure.[22] On the other hand, however, and rather like in the case of decolonization, the turn to the disciplinary formality of the received law of State succession seemed to cut across what otherwise appeared to be a radical and disruptive change in the international order. As Koskenniemi was to describe the events of that time:

Rarely has territorial authority been reconceived and reallocated in as spectacular a fashion as in Europe since 1989. The collapse of the binary structure of the cold war undermined principles of identification on which political communities in Eastern and Central Europe had rested – with the result that old political structures disappeared, new ones were being proclaimed, and communities whose political identity had been held in abeyance during the long years of the cold war were reasserting themselves. 'Europe' was being reimagined in the East as well as in the West with a distinct message: 'real socialism' had failed, the future lies with liberal politics and the free market.[23]

To speak thus about the 'reimagination of Europe' in terms of the formulations given to the law of State succession during decolonization seemed altogether inappropriate. None of these States, after all, was emerging from a condition of colonial rule,[24] nor could the contingent assumptions made in respect of that process (the promotion of self-determination and liberation from 'imposed'

---

[20] Above, n 8, p 574.

[21] Above, n 15, paras 116–122.

[22] One can trace this in the ICJ's judgment in the Gabčikovo case in which it avoided the general discussion as to whether Art 34 of the Convention 'reflects the state of customary international law', preferring to focus attention instead upon 'the particular nature and character of the 1977 Treaty'. Ibid 71, para 123.

[23] M Koskenniemi, 'Report of the Director of Studies of the English-speaking Section of the Centre', in M Koskenniemi and P Eisemann, *State Succession: Codification Tested Against the Facts* (1997), 65, pp 65–6.

[24] For the argument that the dissolution of the USSR was 'a continuation of the process of decolonization' see R Mullerson, *International Law, Rights and Politics* (1994) pp 64–5. Also, A Beato, 'Newly Independent and Separating States' Succession to Treaties: Considerations on the Hybrid Dependency of the Republics of the Former Soviet Union', 9 Am UJILP (1994) 525. cf, G Bunn and J Rhinelander, 'The Arms Control Obligations of the Former Soviet Union', 33 VaJIL (1993) 323, pp 329–31.

agreements) be applied with similar ease.[25] The 'politics' of decolonization, as Koskenniemi was to put it, lay firmly in the past.[26]

That this conflicted sense of continuity and change was to become the decisive character of the 'new' engagement with the law of State succession is perhaps not so remarkable in itself. That, after all, had long been a possible consequence of the distinction between succession *de iure* and succession *de facto* (the latter signifying change, the former continuity). What was more significant was the character of the differentiation – what was it that seemed to continue, and what seemed to change? What seemed to be normal and what abnormal? Here, the change seemed to have two dimensions: one temporal, the other geographical. In a temporal sense, the change was that identified by Koskenniemi – between the 'new' and 'old' Europe, between socialism and democratic liberalism, between the pre- and post-cold war international orders for which the year 1989 seemed to represent a significant marking point. In a geographical sense (and as had already been highlighted by Schmitt)[27] the change was also that between revolution at the outer edges of empire on the one hand, and revolution in the European heartland on the other. This was not decolonization; it was political and economic 'transition'.[28]

The sense of continuity, by contrast, came first of all in the form of the continuity of international law. Lawyers were able to attribute decisive character to the changes taking place – here dismemberment, there unification – and to identify in the process a range of legal consequences that appeared to ensue therefrom. In some cases those consequences would appear axiomatic (Russia would retain its seat in the United Nations, Germany its membership in the European Union) in other cases they would leave open the possibility of negotiation and dispute (for example in respect of the property of the former Yugoslavia).[29] But for all the lack of clarity on certain points, it was rarely acceded that what was at issue was a 'gap' in the law or something incapable of regulation. There remained the clear sense that, for all their unpredictability, the events themselves were capable of being regulated within the terms of international law. Further to this, scholars were increasingly encouraged to identify rules of continuity – in

[25] See V Degan, 'La Succession d'États en Matière de Traités et les États Nouveaux (Issus de l' Ex Yugoslavie), 42 AFDI (1996) 206, p. 213.

[26] Koskenniemi (Rep), above, n 23, p 71.

[27] See above, pp 40–6.

[28] A literature burgeoned in the 1990s around the idea of both economic transition and transitional justice. Characteristically both of these literatures understood the economic and political changes in the 1990s as being largely distinguishable from the processes of decolonization that had preceded them. On economic transition see K Rittich, *Recharacterizing Restructuring: Law, Distribution, and Gender in Market Reform* (2002); on transitional justice see, R Teitel, *Transitional Justice* (2002).

[29] Agreement on Succession Issues, (2001) 41 ILM 3. C Stahn, 'The Agreement on Succession Issues of the Former Socialist Federal Republic of Yugoslavia', 96 AJIL (2002) 379; Williams and Harris, above, n 2, pp 383–400 (for background).

some cases extending across the spectrum of multilateral agreements,[30] in others confined to particular functional domains (humanitarian treaties or territorial regimes for example).[31] And here, as we shall see, one may identify the return of an agenda which had been set in the 1950s by the likes of O'Connell and Jenks, whose purpose had been on the one hand, to de-radicalize the process of decolonization and dissipate the destabilizing effects of national self-determination and, on the other, to underpin what they saw to be the 'interests' of the international community.

The significance of this re-instantiation in the 1990s of what was effectively a dissident agenda in the era of decolonization was quite evocative. To begin with, it marked out the 'new' international law of State succession as one which sought the erasure of the imprint of decolonization. The problem with the Vienna Convention of 1978 was that it really only *described* what had already happened, leaving entirely open the question whether it would have any significance thereafter. It represented, in other words, a necessary statement that decolonization had occurred – a way of *demonstrating* that international law had effectively shaken off its colonial heritage without necessitating any further deliberation on the issue. Those approaching the matter in the 1990s, therefore, could set aside any ambivalence as to the authoritarian or imperial thrust of the law of State succession, and embrace what had once obviously appeared to be a neo-imperial philosophy in the confidence that *those* conditions (the conditions of colonial domination) no longer pertained. This latter stage thus involved the strategic marginalization of the Vienna Convention as a way of eviscerating the lasting image of colonial rule that had remained as an ever-present shadow over its terms, and hence more generally over the doctrine of state succession. Only at this stage could international lawyers really say that the 'decolonization' of international law had been achieved.

Secondly, this decisively post-colonial orientation was to push to the background the old concerns (over sovereignty or consent) that had animated much of the discussion during the era of decolonization. Just as the privileging of self-determination during decolonization seemed to bring to the forefront concerns about authority, representation, or participation – reprising, as O'Connell put it, a redundant tradition of sovereignty – so the 'new' era could be shaped around the concerns of the international community, or the functional necessities of institutions and regimes. If sovereignty was relevant here, it was a new form of relativized sovereignty – one that was subordinated to cosmopolitan interests (human rights, or peace and security) and which was processed through mechanisms of institutional membership.

---

[30] eg, O Schachter, 'State Succession: The Once and Future Law', VaJIL (1993) 240.
[31] See eg, M Kamminga, 'State Succession in Respect of Human Rights Treaties', 7 EJIL (1996) 469.

2. Beyond Decolonization

In an article written at a fairly early stage in the unfolding events surrounding the dissolution of the Soviet Union and Yugoslavia, Oscar Schachter made a number of observations concerning what he saw to be the 'once and future law' of State succession.[32] The title of his article, which drew evocatively upon TH White's populist account of the Arthurian legend,[33] was to focus attention both upon the enduring nature of the 'human dramas' surrounding the break up of empires, the emergence of new identities, new voices, and new frontiers, and upon the distinctiveness of the contemporary context. Whilst he was to advert to the fact that even Aristotle had worried about the problem of State continuity,[34] it was his general view that the 'old formulas' that had shaped the legal discourse of State succession since the 19th century were no longer fit for current needs, and required remodelling in the light of, and in response to, 'political developments' in the contemporary era. In this regard, he was to reprise some of the same sentiments that had surrounded debates over succession during the time of decolonization.

Schachter drew attention to two particular ways in which he saw the 'future' of the law of State succession as markedly different from that of the past. The first concerned the evident relativity of the old distinction between State succession and governmental change. Noting with approval O'Connell's critique of this distinction,[35] Schachter went on to suggest that, ultimately, 'formal categories...are not as important as considering the practical consequences of political change in particular context [sic]'.[36] His contemporaries, he suggested with approval, tended to be much more pragmatic than their predecessors – concerned as they were with outcomes rather than formal structures, the implications of substantive commitments rather than with abstract deductions from status.[37] They were thus liable to think much more flexibly about the resort to doctrines such as *rebus sic stantibus*, and much less prone to dealing with problems in all or nothing terms. Secondly, and in contrast to the position widely advocated prior to the 1990s,[38] Schachter saw in the practice surrounding the dismemberment of the Soviet Union and the SFRY the emergence of

---

[32] Schachter, above, n 30.

[33] T White, *The Once and Future King* (1958). Although, in some senses merely a re-interpretation of Mallory's classic *Le Mort d'Arthur*, it may also be read as a political commentary and/or utopian tract designed to explore the conditions necessary for humankind's renunciation of violence.

[34] Aristotle, *The Politics*, (S Everson ed, CUP 1988) Bk III, ch 3.

[35] Above, pp 75–7.

[36] Above, n 30, p 254–5.

[37] ibid 255.

[38] Restatement (Third) of the Foreign Relations Law of the United States (1987), s 210(3), Reporters' note 4. ('When part of a State becomes a new State, the new State does not succeed to the international agreements to which the predecessor State was party, unless, expressly or by implication, it accepts such agreements and the other party or parties thereto agree or acquiesce.').

'a general presumption of continuity' in case of newly emergent States. Given his attention to context and outcomes, however, he was to suggest that this was a qualified presumption: it would not apply to membership in the United Nations or other general international organizations, nor would it allow the continuation of rights where that would be contrary to the object of the treaty (he cites here the Nuclear Non-Proliferation Treaty).[39] But it would have particular purchase in case of multilateral treaties of a 'universal' character or other 'law-making treaties'.[40] He summarizes his position in the following way:

> In this predictably pluralist world of kaleidoscopic change, stability in expectations will matter; it becomes more important than would be the case in a more settled period. The responses to the fragmentation of the Eastern European regimes revealed the concerns over the disruption of treaty relations. At the same time, the diversity and the particularities call for avoiding rigidities and for taking account of the context in specific cases. Contextual solutions may be facilitated by relying on treaty rules, such as *rebus sic stantibus* or on equitable principles applicable to state debts or liabilities.[41]

In his brief article, Schachter highlighted several issues that were to become characteristic standpoints in the ensuing decade – the key to which being his insistence that one should be 'pragmatic' about succession. For Schachter, and others who were also to align themselves with this idea,[42] this did not appear to be a position thoroughly worked out through the philosophy of Pierce, Dewey, or even Rorty, but one that loosely signified several different things. Being 'pragmatic' about succession appeared to mean, to begin with, thinking about the issue of succession in terms of 'problem solving'. Problem solving in the context of succession would tend to mean asking certain questions about outcomes (for example: who may be responsible for the external debt of a State after its 'dissolution'? What rights might a successor State have as regards membership in international organizations?) with a view to developing or employing various techniques by which one might go about managing, or dealing with, the problem. It would thus involve focusing somewhat less upon the nature of events giving rise to the issue, or the character and form of the wider relations in which the 'problem' is located and would place correspondingly greater emphasis upon the particular nature of the legal relations in question, the context in which they

---

[39] Above, n 30, p 257.
[40] ibid. 259.
[41] ibid 259.
[42] For others who speak about the necessity of pragmatism see, D Papenfuss, 'The Fate of the International Treaties of the GDR within the Framework of German Unification', 92 AJIL (1998) 469, p 470; G Hafner and E Kornfeind, 'The Recent Austrian Practice of State Succession: Does the Clean Slate Rule Still Exist?', 1 ARIEL (1996) 1, pp 22–6; K Bühler, *State Succession and Membership in International Organizations: Legal Theories Versus Political Pragmatism* (2001).

are placed, and the possibilities for negotiated settlement (by resort, perhaps, to fluid notions of 'equity').[43]

A further obvious consequence of this pragmatic mindset, as Schachter made clear, was that it was set against reliance upon the kind of formal categories that had hitherto marked the discipline. Whilst his particular target, in that respect, was the distinction between state and governmental change that had been the subject of O'Connell's critique in the 1960s, his scepticism also extended, obviously enough, to the distinction between continuity and succession more generally. Should it really matter, he seemed to ask, whether Russia was the continuation of the former Soviet Union or alternatively an entirely 'new' State? Are not such category distinctions ultimately arbitrary? And would it not, therefore, be preferable to seek a solution to all such problems of political change in terms that paid attention to the particularities of context? To the extent to which this was working against a tradition that regarded the distinction between continuity and succession as 'fundamental', it was a radical enough suggestion, but at the same time it did underscore a general perception that such ideas were as much part of the problem as the solution.[44]

Like O'Connell, however, Schachter was to understand that this subversion of the categories of continuity and succession could only operate in a context in which there was a general expectation of treaty continuity. Here, Schachter was to suggest that a general teleology might be ascribed to the doctrine of succession: namely one that prioritized the 'stability of expectations'. If the rule of law was to prevail in international relations, it had to take cognisance of the needs and expectations of its participants, and in doing so, could not sanction lawless disrespect for existing engagements. A principle of continuity, even if subject to category exceptions (such as in case of constituent instruments of international organizations), was thus a necessary correlate of a broader concern to ensure that the 'peace dividend' could be effectively cashed in. Where Schachter apparently re-asserts his pragmatism, is in his insistence that this is merely a general consideration (perhaps a presumption) which is subject to specific contextual examination. On one side, attention will necessarily fall upon the character of the agreement (certain treaties, therefore, being either automatically inherited, or

---

[43] cf arts 40 and 41, Vienna Convention 1983. For similar emphasis upon equity see, W Czaplinski, 'Equity and Equitable Principles in the Law of State Succession' 12 Developments and International Operation (1996) no 23, p 29; S Oeter, 'State Succession and the Struggle over Equity', 38 GYIL (1995) 73.

[44] For an articulation of this idea see T-H Cheng, *State Succcession and Commercial Obligations* (2006) 4 ('In the context of international commercial arrangements, the distinction between State and government succession does not adequately meet the needs of the global political economy. In both state and governmental successions, States, creditors and other international parties may demand that obligors and other parties take responsibility for pre-existing commercial obligations, or they may demand that obligations be terminated. International law should not draw doctrinal distinctions between State and government succession in response to claims that commercial arrangements survive or are terminated by succession. It should instead adjust these commercial arrangements to promote global order and development.').

incapable of inheritance). On the other, it will focus upon the character of the change (for which the principle *rebus sic stantibus* will be available).

3. The Perils of Formalism: Continuity, Personality, and Identity

Schachter's scepticism as regards the excessive formalism of the categories of continuity and succession drew, as suggested, upon the criticism launched by O'Connell in the 1960s against those who he believed placed undue reliance upon the idea of 'personality' as the medium by which one might address the problems arising from political change.[45] 'Personality' in the form in which O'Connell understood it, seemed to represent an *abstract* or *consequential* judgment as to legal capacity, not something that was typically *formative* (in the sense of determining itself what rights and obligations a legal subject might actually possess). If personality connoted nothing more than an undifferentiated 'legal capacity' it could not usefully be employed as a means of determining what rights and obligations a State might have as a consequence of a change in sovereignty, nor as a way of usefully separating the doctrine of succession from other forms of argument about legal change.[46]

For many looking at the changing landscape of Eastern Europe in the early 1990s, and trying to work out in that context what rules or principles of succession might come into play (if at all), the Vienna Convention provided little obvious help. As the account above indicates, towards the end of its work on succession in respect of treaties, the Commission had become increasingly mired in what seemed to be a fairly tendentious discussion as to how to categorize the various instances of practice with which it was faced.[47] Should it draw a parallel between decolonization and non-colonial secession or keep these separate? How should it distinguish, if at all, between cases of the dissolution of unions of States, and cases of secession in which the predecessor State continues to exist? For all its indecision on these points, the Commission felt compelled (for want, perhaps, of any other mode of generic differentiation) to make a series of distinctions premised upon the idea of 'personality', and in face of the criticism of people such as O'Connell.

To begin with, it is apparent that in concentrating on the position of 'newly independent States' the Convention gave articulation to one obvious category distinction which no one really questioned: that between the 'continuing' metropolitan State and the secessionist enterprise seeking its independence. This, of course, was to codify within the convention a Manichean divide between the

---

[45] See above, pp 75–7.
[46] See above pp 78–80.
[47] See above, pp 169–73.

'self' and the 'other': the selfhood of the metropolitan power being contrasted with the otherness of the decolonized population whose political 'amputation' was to leave, largely untouched, the legal (or indeed the political, social or cultural) identity of the former. As pointed out above, the very demand for 'self-determination' that underpinned the process of decolonization was one that had relied upon the pre-existing 'separateness' of the 'territories' destined for independence, and this no doubt was reinforced on the other side by a similar belief in the social and political separateness of the metropolitan 'homeland'. No question arose, therefore, as to the discontinuity of rights and obligations on the part of the 'continuing' colonial power and this itself was to place the focus squarely upon the situation of the 'newly independent State'. It was to have certain obvious consequences as regards any claim on the part of the newly independent States to resources or wealth that might have been extracted prior to independence.

Such considerations, of course, did not sit quite so easily in case of the 'separation' of part or parts of a State. In that context, there could be no obvious recourse to self-determination as an argument about the survival of pre-existent rights or obligations, nor could the invisible baggage of colonial history be taken as an unspoken starting point for analytical engagement. As we have seen,[48] the text of Article 34 of the Convention was ultimately an amalgamation of three different articles: one dealing with the dissolution of a union of States (for which the key example was the break-up of the United Arab Republic); the second being the dissolution of unitary States (for which there was little obvious practice); and the third being the separation of part of a State in which the predecessor State was regarded as continuing (the cases of Pakistan and Bangladesh being possible examples). These were ultimately combined under a single rubric in which treaty continuity was largely presumed and thus the distinction between cases in which the predecessor State continued, and those in which it did not, was regarded as immaterial. What suddenly became very important, however, was whether in any particular instance one was faced with a case for which the most proximate analogy was decolonization or the separation of a union of States.

There were two further contexts, however, in which the distinction between continuity and succession also appeared to be important. On the one hand, there was the question of unification, in relation to which the point had been raised during the drafting of the ILC's articles as to whether the rule elaborated took adequate account of the possibility that some cases of unification might be achieved by way of the 'absorption' of one State by another.[49] The fairly cursory dismissal of this point only thinly disguised the evident controversies that had surrounded some of the historic cases of unification (including the formation of Italy and the absorption of Texas into the United States) and the rule articulated by the Commission (to the effect that each element of the union retained

---

[48] See above, pp 166–73.
[49] See above pp 166.

the 'trace' of its personality within the union) was largely based upon one single exemplary case – that of the United Arab Republic. This only raised the obvious question as to whether, in other cases, one might identify with equal ease the 'trace' of personality that seemed to underpin the rule of regional treaty continuity, and whether such a solution was in any respects viable in cases in which the component parts of the union were contiguous rather than separated, like Egypt and Syria, by nearly 1,000 miles.

Finally, there was the issue of protected states which, as we have seen, the Commission engaged in a lengthy discussion of what seemed to be the implications of the ICJ's decision concerning the survival of the 'sovereignty' (and hence treaty obligations) of those States that pre-existed the creation of a regime of protection.[50] This again, was to lead to a certain ambivalence as to precisely what consequences might ensue therefrom, and in the event was an issue set to one side as historically contingent. But the idea upon which this discussion was premised – that of the survival of traces of indigenous sovereignty during periods of alien occupation or rule – was not so very far away from the Commission's approach to unification and, in any case, was an idea which clearly had purchase in relation to the circumstances of belligerent occupation. In the latter context, the Commission took the view that since the 'military occupation of a territory does not constitute a succession of States'[51] it was a matter to be excluded from the scope of the Convention, even if it seemed to raise problems 'analogous to those of a succession of States'.[52] In so concluding, and despite its desire not to 'prejudge' the issue, the Commission was to effectively to put in place the idea that, subject of course to any agreements which may have been affected by armed conflict or a permanent change in circumstance, treaties concluded prior to occupation would continue once that occupation had been terminated, and those applied to the territory by the occupant would not be open to succession.

Each of these three 'problems' of continuity was to come to some obvious prominence during the 1990s. In the first place was the obvious discrepancy between the posture adopted by the international community in respect of the Soviet Union on the one hand, and of Serbia-Montenegro (the 'Federal Republic of Yugoslavia') on the other.[53] Whereas, as pointed out above, it was generally accepted that Russia should be entitled to regard itself (for most purposes at least) as the 'continuation' of the former Soviet Union, that 'right' was denied to Serbia-Montenegro. However far commentators sought to rationalize the practice (as, for example, in Mullerson's combination of objective and subjective factors)[54]

[50] *Case concerning rights of nationals of the United States of America in Morocco*, ICJ Rep 1952, 172, p 188.

[51] See Commentary to draft art 38. Yrbk ILC, 1974, II, 174, p 268, para 2.

[52] ibid.

[53] See above, pp 70–5.

[54] R Mullerson, 'New Developments in the Former USSR and Yugoslavia', 33 VaJIL (1992–3) 299, pp 303–4; see also M Scharf, 'Musical Chairs: The Dissolution of States and Membership in the United Nations', 28 Cornell ILJ (1995) 29, p 67 (who includes in his determinants,

it was evidently hard to do so in any way that did not bring to the forefront the politics of institutional membership. Just as it seemed that the acceptance of Russia's claim to continuity was closely entwined with an unwillingness to open out discussion as to permanent membership in the Security Council, or as a convenient fiction accepted for purposes of negotiating the withdrawal of Soviet forces from the Baltic States,[55] so also it was hard to ignore the possibility that the refusal to allow Serbia the right to participate as the continuation of Yugoslavia within the UN and other international organizations was premised upon the idea that it should not be entitled to any 'benefits' that might result from a violent process of dismemberment for which its leadership appeared to be directly responsible.[56] There was, therefore, something distinctly tenuous about arguments to the effect that this was a decision informed by the size of the rump State, the location of the capital or indeed their legal history.[57]

The second context in which the question of continuity was to arise related to the process of German 'unification'.[58] In 1989 Chancellor Kohl had announced a ten-point program for unification of East and West Germany, which had envisaged the creation of a federal union of the two States much along the lines, one may suppose, of the United Arab Republic. As matters were to progress, however, following the conclusion of a Treaty between the FRG and the former GDR Establishing a Monetary, Economic and Social Union (State Treaty) in July 1990 an entirely different strategy was to emerge for unification. The Unification Treaty of 31st August 1990 made very clear that what was to be meant by 'unification' was not so much the merger of two independent States on an equal footing, but the 'absorption' of the GDR into the territory of the FRG.[59] Article 1,

possession of the following: the majority of the territory including its 'historic hub'; a majority of its population; a majority of its resources; a majority of its armed forces; the seat of government); and E Williamson and J Osborn, 'A US Perspective on Treaty Succession and Related Issues in the Wake of the Breakup of the USSR and Yugoslavia', 33 VaJIL (1993) 261, p 268 (who speak about Russia being the 'dominant part of the former Soviet Union in all relevant respects – land area, population, resources and military strength'.).

[55] R Mullerson, 'The Continuity and Succession of States by Reference to the Former USSR and Yugoslavia', 42 ICLQ (1993) 473, p 478; Williamson and Osborn, ibid 267.

[56] eg Williamson and Osborn, ibid 270 (who speak of the United States as being uninclined 'to bless Serbia-Montenegro as the legitimate heir to the SFRY'.).

[57] Scharf, above, n 54, p 53.

[58] Papenfuss, above, n 42; C Schricke, 'L'unification allemande' AFDI (1990) 47; F von der Dunk, and P Kooijmans, 'The Unification of Germany and International Law', 12 MichJIL (1991) 510; J Frowein, 'The Reunification of Germany', 86 AJIL (1992) 152; K Heilbronner, 'Legal Aspects of the Unification of the Two German States' 2 EJIL (1991) 18; S Oeter, 'German Unification and State Succession', 51 ZaöRV (1991) 349.

[59] Frowein puts it as follows: 'On October 3, 1990, the German Democratic Republic, a member State of the United Nations, ceased to exist and its territory became part of the Federal Republic of Germany. The five States formed in the German Democratic Republic (GDR) according to the Statute of July 22, 1990, Brandenburg, Mecklenburg-Vorpommern, Sachsen, Sachsen-Anhalt, and Thüringen, became Länder of the Federal Republic of Germany. On the same date, the territory of East Berlin became part of the Land Berlin which had been a State in the Federal Republic of Germany since 1949, though with a special status'. J Frowein, 'Germany Reunited' Zäo RV (1991) 333. See generally, Stern, above, n 2, pp 202–11.

for example, specified that 'upon the accession of the German Democratic Republic to the Federal Republic of Germany... the Länder of Brandenburg, Mecklenburg-Western Pomerania, Saxony, Saxony-Anhalt, and Thuringia shall become Länder of the Federal Republic of Germany'. Article 7 similarly provided for the extension of the financial system of the FRG into the territory of the GDR and Article 8 for the extension of its federal law. Both for purposes of organizational membership (including, notably, membership in the EU[60] and NATO)[61] and participation in other international agreements the idea was consistently pursued by the FRG that it continued to exist albeit in enlarged form, whilst the GDR had effectively disappeared as an independent State and with it, the treaties to which it had formerly been party.[62] Articles 11 and 12 of the Treaty of Unification provided, for example, that the treaties of the FRG would continue and would be extended to the territory of the former GDR,[63] but that, in relation to the treaties of the latter, Germany would enter 'discussions' with other contracting parties before confirming their continuation, adjustment or termination.[64] In respect of bilateral treaties, this arrangement worked relatively

---

[60] See Declaration of Dublin, 28 Apr 1990 and Memorandum of the Commission of the EC, COM(90)400 endg Vol 1, 21 Aug 1990, 29, 31. The Commission of the EC declared to the GATT in 1990 that; 'the German Democratic Republic has been united with the Federal Republic of Germany on the basis of an accession to the latter. Thus the territory of the Federal Republic of Germany, a member State of the European Communities, has been extended and, as a consequence, the territory to which the treaties establishing respectively the European Community for Coal and Steel, the European Economic Community and the European Atomic Energy Community apply, has also been extended to include the territory of the former German Democratic Republic and of Berlin (East)'.

Gatt Doc L/6759, 31 Oct, 1990, para 1. See C Timmermans, 'German Unification and Community Law', CML Rev (1990) 437.

[61] In a communication to the Secretary-General on 3 Oct, 1990, the Federal Minister for Foreign Affairs declared that: 'Through the accession of the German Democratic Republic to the Federal Republic of Germany with effect from 3 October 1990, the two German States have united to form one sovereign State, which as a single Member of the United Nations remains bound by the provisions of the Charter in accordance with the solemn declaration of 12 June 1973. As from the date of unification, the Federal Republic of Germany will act in the United Nations under the designation 'Germany'. For discussion of the question of EU membership see J-P Jacqué, 'German Unification and the European Community', 2 EJIL (1991) 1.

[62] Y Gamarra, 'Current Questions of State Succession Relating to Multilateral Treaties', in Koskenniemi et al, above, n 16, p 387, pp 402–3; K Bühler, 'State Succession, Identity/ Continuity and Membership in the United Nations' in Koskenniemi et al, ibid p 187.

[63] This is taken to be an application of the 'moving treaty frontier's rule'. See ILA Final Report, above, n 8, p 583. Some treaties mentioned in Annex I are excluded from this territorial extension – namely the treaties regulating the relations between the FRG and the Three Allied powers (the Convention on the Relations between the Three Powers and the Federal Republic of Germany, 26 May 1952, as amended 23 Oct 1954, 331 UNTS 327) and the treaties regulating the stationing of foreign troops in the FRG.

[64] 29 ILM 1186. Oeter, above, n 58, p 360. This procedure was confirmed in a letter by the Foreign ministers of both German States to the Four Allied Powers on the occasion of signing the Final Settlement concerning Germany on 12 Sep 1990, in Moscow. Following this communication, and in light of arts 11 and 12 of the Treaty of Unification, the Secretary-General proceeded to record 'Germany' as being party to all treaties to which the pre-unification FRG had been party.

well. Consultations were held with over 135 States, which resulted in agreement that the majority[65] of the former GDR's treaties had indeed lapsed. A few were continued,[66] some on a 'temporary basis',[67] and others simply superseded by the conclusion of new agreements.[68]

Whilst this approach to unification stood in sharp contrast to that adopted by North and South Yemen on their unification in the same year,[69] it is hard

In case of treaties in which formalities had been concluded by the GDR, the Secretary-General merely entered a footnote under the heading 'Participant' indicating the type of formality effected by the former GDR. Art 12 neither confirmed a principle of termination, or continuity, but simply affirmed the intention to discuss such matters with other parties taking into account the protection of the confidence (*Vertrauensschutz*) and interests (*Interessenlage*) of the States concerned. The Commission of the European Communities thus took the view that since the extinction of all GDR treaties could not be presumed, their continuity should be subject to negotiation. COM (90) 400, pt II, I, 1.

[65] There seems to have been doubt as to the precise number of treaties to which the former GDR was party. See D Papenfuss, 'Die Behandlung der völkerrechtlichen Verträge der DDR im Zuge der Herstellung der Einheit Deutschlands', (1997) p 68. According to Lee, however, 2,214 treaties or agreements of the GDR had been declared as terminated as at 1998. K-G Lee, *The Law of State Succession in the Post-Decolonisation Period with Special Reference to Germany and the former Soviet Union*, Unpublished Thesis, University of Cambridge, (1998) p 95.

[66] eg the Regulation of Open (Unresolved) Property Questions with Austria, Finland, Denmark, and Sweden, Papenfuss, above, n 65, pp 235–6.

[67] eg Treaty of 24 May 1960 between the GDR and the USSR concerning Cooperation in the Field of Social Security (GBI, 1960, 453).

[68] eg the Agreement Concerning the Demarcation of the Established and Existing Polish-German State Frontier, 6 July 1950, 319 UNTS 93 (between GDR and Poland recognizing the border between the States as being permanent).

[69] Art 1 of the Agreement of 22 Apr 1990 between the Yemen Arab Republic and the People's Democratic Republic of Yemen, declared that 'there shall be established between the State of the Yemen Arab Republic and the State of the People's Democratic Republic of Yemen...a full and complete union, based on a merger, in which the international personality of each of them shall be integrated in a single international person called the "Republic of Yemen"'. 30 ILM (1991) 820. See generally R Goy, 'La reunification du Yémen', AFDI (1990) 249. In a letter dated 19 May 1990, the Ministers of Foreign Affairs of the Yemen Arab Republic and the People's Democratic Republic of Yemen informed the Secretary-General of their intention to:

merge in a single sovereign State called the 'Republic of Yemen'...with Sana'a as its capital, as soon as it is proclaimed on Tuesday 22 May 1990. The Republic of Yemen will have single membership in the United Nations and be bound by the provisions of the Charter. All Treaties and agreements concluded between either the Yemen Arab Republic or the People's Democratic Republic of Yemen and other States and international organisations in accordance with international law which are in force on 22 May 1990 will remain in effect....

Accordingly, the Secretary-General adopted the practice of recording the Republic of Yemen as party to multilateral treaties to which he acts as depositary, from the date on which one of the two States first became a party to the treaty concerned. This 'first in time' rule ensures the maximum temporal application of the treaties concerned, but has the consequence that only those reservations or declarations recorded by the first party will survive. There is no evidence, as yet, as to whether other States parties are happy with this arrangement. A further important feature of this case is that although participation in treaties is neither linked to one or other of the former Yemeni Republics, the unified Yemen is not regarded as a successor State. This, in other words, is simply regarded as a case of treaty continuity and is viewed in the same manner as a case in which a State changes its name.

to think of this as anything other than a convenient managerial solution[70] to a problem whose most significant dimension was undoubtedly the question of EU membership. Certainly, the historical discord as to the status of the FRG and GDR after 1945 and their relationship to the Reich was not terribly illuminating,[71] nor was the 'solution' adverted to in Article 31(1) of the Vienna Convention (which would not recommend itself to a process of unification seeking the coordination of municipal law within a single constitutional and administrative framework).[72] There were, of course, legal 'costs': unification would obviously be incompatible with simultaneous membership in NATO and the Warsaw Pact, the EU, and the Council for Mutual Economic Assistance (CMEA).[73] It was also evident that 'negotiating' participation in multilateral treaties to which the GDR was formerly a party was not really a viable solution, and whilst the FRG promised to 'review' such treaties, it is apparent that a number fell by the wayside including the Convention on Privileges and Immunities of Specialized Agencies (1949),[74] the Convention on the Non-Applicability of Statutory Limitations to War Crimes and Crimes against Humanity (1968),[75] and the Apartheid Convention of 1973.[76] The same was the case in respect of a number of territorial agreements such as those relating to navigation, fisheries, and maritime frontiers.[77] But at the same time, there was very little sense that anyone regarded this 'solution' to be problematic.[78] In fact, the conclusion of the ILA was that given the evidence of this practice, the terms of article 31 of the Vienna Convention of 1978 were demonstrably

---

[70] It also conformed, generally speaking, to the approach adopted in the Third US Restatement on Foreign Relations Law 1987, which provides that 'when a State is absorbed by another State, the international agreements of the absorbed State are terminated and the international agreements of the absorbing State become applicable to the territory of the absorbed State'. s 210 (2), p 108.

[71] W Czaplinski, 'Quelques aspects juridiques de la réunification de l'Allemagne', AFDI (1990) 89; G Ress, 'Germany, Legal Status after World War II', EJIL (1987) 191.

[72] As Oeter notes, '[i]ntegration in these cases means assimilation of the legal order of the integrated territory to the legal order of the State supposed to be continued, and nothing could be worse in such cases than territorially limited continuation of the application of pre-existing treaties'. Oeter, above, n 58, p 355. The Dutch government, however, did argue that its consent was needed for the extension of the treaties of the FRG to the territory of the former GDR, invoking, in the process Art 31 of the Vienna Convention. See O Ribbelink, 'The Uniting of States in Respect of Treaties', NYIL (1995) 161.

[73] Rather than submit such treaties to a process of negotiation, however, the GDR denounced the agreements immediately prior to unification, invoking, in the process, the principle of *rebus sic stantibus* contained in article 62(1) of the Vienna Convention. Papenfuss, above, n 65, pp 85, 87–88.

[74] 33 UNTS 261.

[75] 754 UNTS 73.

[76] 1015 UNTS 243.

[77] ILA Rep, above, n 8, p 586.

[78] The one exception, here, was the Netherlands, which insisted that all bilateral treaties concluded with the FRG should be subject to renegotiation given their proposed extension to the territory of the former GDR. Whilst in the case of most treaties, the parties agreed to the extension without modification, two were deemed to apply only in amended form: the Treaty concerning the Regulation of Financial Matters and Benefit Payments to Dutch Victims of National-Socialist Persecution, of 8 Apr 1960, and the Supplementary Agreement of 14 May 1962.

'unsatisfactory' primarily because of the failure to distinguish between a case of 'incorporation' and one of 'unification'.[79] It was the Vienna Convention under scrutiny, not the terms under which unification was achieved in Germany.

The third context, in which the question of continuity obviously arose, was in respect of the three Baltic Republics' acquisition of independence in 1991.[80] In the beginning of 1990 the Supreme Councils of the three Baltic States (Latvia, Lithuania, and Estonia) resolved to re-establish their independence,[81] declaring in the process the illegality of the Soviet military occupation that had commenced in 1940. Pursuant to that idea, they re-established constitutional provisions that had applied prior to 1940, sought to continue treaty relations as if Soviet occupation had not occurred,[82] and took the position that they were (in principle at least) free of obligations which may have been assumed on their behalf by Soviet authorities. Even though the response of third States to Soviet occupation had been by no means unequivocal[83] (some refusing to recognize the legality of the occupation,[84] others accepting it de facto,[85] others still accepting occupation *de iure*)[86] there was a degree of acceptance of the three Republics' position. Thus, in

[79] ILA Rep, above, n 8, p 587.

[80] Mullerson, above, n 55; P van Elsuwege, 'State Continuity and its Consequences: The Case of the Baltic States', 16 Leiden JIL (2003) 377; R Yakemtchouk, 'Les républiques baltes en droit international. Echec d'une annexation opérée en violation du droit des gens', 37 AFDI (1991) 276; R Kherad, 'La Reconnaisance Internationale des Etats Baltes', 96 RGDIP (1992) 843; I Ziemele, *State Continuity and Nationality: The Baltic States and Russia* (2005).

[81] 'Act on the Re-establishment of the State of Lithuania' 11 Mar, 1990 (4 Lithuanian Foreign Policy Review (1999)); 'Declaration on the Renewal of Independence', Latvian Supreme Soviet, 4 May 1990, cited in Ziemele, above, n p 32; 'Resolution on the State Status of Estonia', Estonian Supreme Soviet, 30 Mar, 1990, cited in Ziemele, ibid 32.

[82] eg Latvia's notification of 14 Apr 1992 relating to the 1921 Convention Relating to the Non-Fortification and Neutralization of the Åland Islands, Multilateral Treaties Deposited with the Secretary-General, Status as at 31 Dec 1993, UN Doc ST/Leg/Sere/12, p 953, n 3.

[83] W Timmermans, 'The Baltic States, the Soviet Union and the Netherlands: A Historical Note', 32 Ned TIR (1985) 288; K Suter, 'The Australian Government's Policy of Recognition and Diplomatic Relations', 47 Aust Q (1975) 67, p 73; E Dunsdorfs, *The Baltic Dilemma. The Case of the* de iure *Recognition by Australia of the Incorporation of the Baltic States into the Soviet Union* (1975); W Hough, 'The Annexation of the Baltic States and its Effect on the Development of Law Prohibiting Forcible Seizure of Territory', 6 NYLSJICL (1985) 301; R Vitas, *The United States and Lithuania: The Stimson Doctrine of Nonrecognition* (1990); re Estonia see, *The Signe* (renamed *Florida*), AD 1941/42, Case no 19; *A/S Merilaid and Co v Chase National Bank of City of New York*, AD 1947, Case no 6; re Latvia see, *In re Graud's Estate*, AD 1943/45, Case no 10; *Latvian State Cargo and Passenger SS Line v Clark*, AD 1948, Case no 16; re Lithuania see, *The Denny*, AD, 1941/42, Case no 18; *A/C Tallinna Laevauhisus and Ors v Tallinna Shipping Co and Or* (1945) 79 Lloyd's LR; *Estonian State Cargo and Passenger SS Line v Laane and Baltser (The Elise)* AD 1948, Case no 50; H Briggs, 'Non-Recognition in the Courts: the Ships of the Baltic Republics', 37 AJIL (1943) 585; V Riismandel, 'The Continued Legal Existence of the Baltic States', 12 Baltic Rev (1957) 48; B Meissner, *Die Sowjetunion, die baltischen Staaten und das Völkerrecht* (1956) pp 291–312.

[84] eg Italy and the United States. See Ziemele, ibid 22–7.

[85] eg, position of Belgium, Norway, Switzerland, and UK. Ribbelink in Klabbers et al, above, n 11, pp 48–9. See generally, K Marek, *Identity and Continuity of States in Public International Law* (1954), pp 383–91.

[86] eg Finland, Sweden. See Ribbelink ibid 50. The Netherlands and Spain made no explicit mention of the Baltic Republics in their recognition practice with respect to the Soviet Union.

an Extraordinary Ministerial Meeting of 27th August 1991, the EC adopted a Declaration welcoming 'the restoration of sovereignty and independence of the Baltic States which they had lost in 1940' and confirmed their decision to (re)-establish diplomatic relations.[87]

There were various obvious consequences of the Baltic States' assertions in this respect. One was a refusal to accept any 'succession' to rights and obligations created in respect of the Baltic Republics during Soviet occupation. This was such as to lead, for example, to a denial of liability for loans assumed by the Soviet authorities,[88] and an unwillingness to continue treaties concluded on their behalf by the Soviet Union.[89] Another consequence of the 'Baltic thesis' was that it appeared to substantiate a claim for the return of property seized, or disposed of, by the Soviet Union during its occupation,[90] for the return of gold reserves in foreign bank accounts,[91] and for the revitalization (or 're-affirmation') of treaty relations as existed prior to 1940.[92] That, in some cases, bilateral treaties concluded between third States and the Soviet Union continued to be applied with respect to one or more of the Baltic States after the 'restoration' of sovereignty,[93] or were taken as a basis for the subsequent delimitation of boundaries or maritime zones[94] is perhaps not that significant other than as a recognition of the inevitably compromised character of their claim to continuity.[95] The most problematic issue arising as a consequence of the Baltic Republics' claims in respect of the restoration of their sovereignty,[96] however, concerned the question of citizenship.[97] Both Estonia and Latvia had determined to 're-establish' the citizenship laws that had been applicable prior to Soviet occupation in 1940, allowing those (principally of Russian origin) who had settled in those territories

[87] 7/8 Bull ec (1991) 1423. See, more generally, Ziemele, above, n 80, pp 63–93.
[88] *Skopbank v Republic of Estonia*, 21 Jan 1998 cited in Klabbers and Koskenniemi, above, n 11, p 128.
[89] Several States such as Belgium and Finland acquiesced in this. See generally, T Kerikmae and H Vallikivi, 'State Continuity in the Light of Estonian Treaties Concluded before World War II', 5 Juridica International (2000) 35; M Koskenniemi and M Lehto, 'La Succession d'Etats dans l'ex-URSS, ence qui concerne particulièrement les relations a vec la Finlanda', 38 AFDI (1992) 182, p 216.
[90] eg, claims relating to Estonian embassy in Berlin, Latvian embassy in Geneva, Estonian gold in the Bank of Sweden. Klabbers and Koskenniemi, 'Succession in Respect of State Property, Archives and Debts, and Nationality', in Klabbers et al, above, n 11, pp 126–30.
[91] eg, exchange of notes between UK and Lithuania, and Estonia, 45 UKTS (1992); 48 UKTS (1992). See generally, Ziemele, above, n 80, pp 84–7.
[92] eg, M Lehto, 'Succession of States in the Former Soviet Union', 4 Finn YIL (1993) 194; Mullerson, above, n 24, p 147.
[93] eg, Finnish-Estonian exchange of notes 20 Mar 1992 providing for the provisional application of 13 treaties with the Soviet Union relating to maritime boundaries, fisheries, and customs and environmental cooperation, taxation, legal aid, and investment protection.
[94] A Zimmerman, 'State Succession in Respect of Treaties', in Klabbers et al, above, n 11, 80, p 96.
[95] Koskenniemi and Lehto, above, n 89, pp 216–17; Ziemele, above, n 80, pp 78–81.
[96] Earlier cases include the re-emergence of Poland after partition, and the resumption of independence of India. For the latter see Judge Quintana. *Right of Passage* case, ICJ Rep (1960) 95.
[97] Ziemele, above, n 80, pp 143–74.

during occupation a right to 'naturalization'. That this obviously resulted in the rendering as stateless significant numbers of people within those Republics led to initiatives within the UN, the OSCE and the Council of Europe to affirm the right of habitual residents to the nationality of the successor State.[98] To the extent, however, that the various Baltic Republics maintained the view that they were not, in fact, successor States at all, this was only to bring back to mind the subtle complexities of the arguments about the survival of legal rights and obligations in case of protected States.[99]

Whilst each of these cases seemed to bring to the forefront the critical character of claims to State continuity in terms of their implications as regards the applicability and effect of rules of succession, there seemed to be no easy way by which such decisions could be made. Only in the case of the Baltic Republics did there seem to be any reliable principle upon which to articulate the claim (*vis* the prohibition against the annexation of territory by use of force), and otherwise scholars were largely at a loss.[100] The claims of the protagonists in question obviously had to be taken into account, so also the reactions of other parties,[101] but there didn't seem to be much else upon which anyone could base their assertions.[102] Certainly it was clear that the criteria for statehood didn't really go very far in determining whether, for example, Germany was entitled to characterize its own unification as one achieved by way of the absorption of the GDR, or whether Serbia-Montenegro could properly claim to continue the 'personality' of the SFRY. The existence or otherwise of a government controlling a defined population within a particular geographical sphere was not what was in question.[103]

The real conundrum, however, was how to square this apparent concern with the question of continuity with the equally pervasive sense that it was, as Schachter suggested, an issue largely to be avoided. O'Connell's response, as outlined above,[104] had been to try to shift the focus of attention away from the problem of status to the relationship between the severity of political change on the one hand, and the nature of legal relations on the

---

[98] Ottowa Declaration of the OSCE Parliamentary Assembly (8 July 1995); European Convention on Nationality of 1997; the Venice Declaration on the Consequences of State Succession for the Nationality of Natural Persons adopted by the European Commission for Democracy through Law in September 1996. J Chan, 'The Right to a Nationality as a Human Right: The Current Trend towards Recognition', 12 HRLJ (1991) 1.

[99] See above, pp 147–51.

[100] J Crawford, *The Creation of States in International Law* (2nd edn, 2005) pp 630.

[101] eg Williamson and Osborne, above, n 54, p 265.

[102] eg P Eisemann, Rapport du directeur d'étndes de la section de la langue français du Centre', in M Koskenniemi and P Eisemann, State Succession: Codification Tested Against the Facts (1997) 3 at p 40; Bühler, above, n 62, p 316; V Degan, 'Création et disparation de l'état (à la lumière du démembrement de trois federations multiethnique en Europe', 279 Hague Recueil (1999) 94, p 301.

[103] M Craven, 'The Problem of State Succession and the Identity of States under International Law', 9 EJIL (1998) 142.

[104] See above, pp 75–8.

other.[105] This was not such as to preclude reference to the categories in question – he still distinguished between various classes of succession – but was to suggest that those categories were significant only so far as they were expressive of the *likely outcomes*. Thus, he was to assert that although one might presume that treaties 'in principle survive the change of sovereignty...the presumption may well vary according to whether the case is characterized as one of annexation, cession, federation, secession, or independence'.[106] As a consequence:

> [w]hen the contracting State totally disappears as an administrative entity, it is likely that a wide range of treaties would cease to be performable in the changed circumstances, and the presumption might be against treaty survival. But when the change of sovereignty modifies the circumstances of performance only slightly, if at all, the presumption will be reversed.[107]

Here, the categories of succession to which his contemporaries normally alluded came to assume significance, not as *a priori* conditions for the application of particular rules, but rather as *descriptive categories* through which one might effectively predict whether, and to what extent, specific legal relations were likely to survive.

The question posed by O'Connell's thesis, in this respect, was how far could it be taken as a way of avoiding the issue of identity when dealing with problems of succession?[108] What it suggested, at the very least, was that the problem of status (continuity/ identity) was a *relative* one, dependent upon the particular character of legal relations.[109] This idea, in fact, became increasingly popular throughout the 1990s as people reflected upon the obvious difficulties of determining the issue of continuity. Tichy, Degan, and others, drew upon a stream of problem-solving scepticism as regards the utility of notions of continuity or identity that had been kept alive by scholars such as Brownlie. In the third edition of his book,

---

[105] There is an obvious relation, here, between the critique of international legal reasoning that places the notion of 'personality' at the forefront, and the Realist critique of reification of legal categories. eg F Cohen, 'Transcendental Nonsense and the Functional Approach', reprinted in L Cohen (ed), *The Legal Conscience: Selected Papers of Felix S Cohen* (1960) pp 33–76.

[106] D O'Connell, *State Succession in Municipal and International Law* (1967) II, pp 2–3.

[107] ibid.

[108] It is evident, to begin with, that his solution can only work if one takes as one's initial hypothesis, a general presumption as to the continuity of legal relations. O'Connell, himself, only appears to have taken this position in respect of treaties – his approach to contractual or other relations largely worked on the assumption that there was no continuity of legal relations (and partly explained by the fact that he viewed international law as having remarkably little relevance to such issues). J Crawford, 'The Contribution of Professor DP O'Connell to the Discipline of International Law', 51 BYIL (1980) 2, p 25.

[109] There are, of course, plenty of examples which may be drawn upon to support the view that claims to identity tend to be treated in different ways in different contexts. Thus, for example, in 1919 whilst the Soviet Union was for many purposes treated as continuing the sovereignty of the Tsarist State (in which its denial of responsibility for Russia's external debt was a matter that caused considerable tension), the US took the view that the Soviet Union did not 'assume the responsibilities of the previous Russian Government' as regards the 1865 Cape Spartel Convention. M Whiteman, *Digest of International Law*, (1963) IX, p 153.

Principles of Public International Law, published in 1979, Brownlie was to assert that:

The term 'continuity' of States is not employed with any precision, and may be used to preface a diversity of legal problems. Thus it may introduce the proposition that the legal rights and responsibility of States are not affected by changes in the head of State or the internal form of government. This proposition can, of course, be maintained without reference to a concept of 'continuity' or 'succession', and it is in any case too general, since political changes may result in a change of circumstances sufficient to affect particular types of treaty relations. More significantly, legal doctrine tends to distinguish between continuity (and identity) and state succession.... Unfortunately, the general categories of 'continuity', and 'State succession', and the assumption of a neat distinction between them, only make a difficult subject more confused by masking variations of circumstance and the complexities of the legal problems which arise in practice. 'Succession' and 'continuity' are levels of abstraction unfitted to dealing with specific issues. [Footnotes omitted.][110]

This relativity and lack of analytical precision led Brownlie to the inevitable conclusion that a functional approach was to be preferred: '[l]egal techniques may well entail relying on continuity in one context, but denying its existence in another'.[111] It might be plausible, in other words, to insist upon continuity in case of treaty participation but not in case of institutional membership. This view was to be echoed by Tichy in 1992 who suggested that acceptance of identity in one context 'does not necessarily prejudice the issue of "identity" in other areas'.[112] Identity, as he would have it, 'is not a simple fact that can be assessed objectively, but, rather, the grant of a special status by the other members of the international community'.[113] To similar effect, Bühler noted the varying approaches to succession adopted by different organizations, concluding in the process that 'even within one area of international law, such as the law of international organizations, a State could be considered new for the purposes of membership in the United Nations but – at the same time – identical in the framework of the WMO'.[114]

From one perspective, this emergent functionalism might have been such as to suggest that the idea of State identity needed to be re-imagined taking into account the 'multiplicity' of identities States may forge and develop in different legal contexts.[115] But of course, however much this might have seemed to reflect a thoroughly post-modern sensibility, it would only result in a loss of critical bite: how could a claim to continuity be maintained if there was nothing stable

---

[110] I Brownlie, *Principles of Public International Law* (3rd edn 1979) pp 84–5.
[111] ibid 85–6. See also, Degan, above, n 25, p 209 (referring to the Lighthouses arbitral decision of 1956).
[112] H Tichy, 'Two Recent Cases of State Succession – An Austrian Perspective', 44 AustJPIL (1992) 117 p 120.
[113] ibid.
[114] Bühler, above, n 62, p 314.
[115] Koskenniemi, above, n 23, p 124.

upon which it was based? Surely this would simply result in a kind of descriptive validation of whatever decisions were to be made on that score?

Two problems could be associated with this consequential 'relativization' of the notion of identity. The first was a point raised by Koskenniemi who suggested that such an approach may ultimately involve disregarding the perceptions of the protagonists themselves as concerns what they believe to be at stake. It ignored, in his view, 'current perceptions of the entity as a real life essence, and fails to take seriously national feelings of self-determination claims. In its rigorously anti-metaphysical stance, it fails to grasp the "internal view" of the participants in a political process. This in turn disturbs the interpretive context in which particular rights or obligations may seem either vital or outdated, worthy of continuation or liable to termination'.[116] Claims to identity or continuity, were thus still relevant and could be seen as determining outcomes 'through the back door' so to speak. The important point to note, however, was that it was impossible to fix those notions in advance,[117] or to determine for newly emergent political communities, the appropriate basis for their own political consciousness. However febrile, or fragile, those stories of nation building might be, they couldn't simply be ignored.

The second problem associated with the idea was that seeking to relativize identity in this way was, in some senses, fundamentally contradictory. In terms of their effect, one may understand claims to continuity as being aggregated claims relating to entitlements and responsibilities, whose distributional consequences range widely across different kinds of legal relations. The Russian claim to continuity, as most were aware, had relevance not merely for the question of its institutional membership in the United Nations, but also for purposes of arguments about treaty obligations (including most visibly, obligations relating to nuclear disarmament), deliberations on the distribution of the assets and debts of the former Soviet Union, and for questions of nationality. Arguably it was only at the point at which all such consequences were appreciated, that the Russian stance hardened and clarified (illustrated in the change in approach from Minsk to Alma Ata). Seeking to 'disaggregate' those claims – separate them out into individual, functionally specific, legal relationships – was really just to deny the possibility of making effective arguments at that level of abstraction. Saying, in other words, that a claim to continuity might 'work' in the context of institutional membership, but not in case of the partition of debt, was really just to admit that, as an argument, it was not a particularly strong one.

Yet, it is still possible to appreciate how arguments about continuity or identity may have become distinctly relative, even if not in the sense alluded to above. In the first place it is evident that each claim to continuity was of a different character. In case of Serbia and Russia, it was a question of their continuity respecting

---

[116] Koskenniemi, above, n 23, p 124.
[117] ibid 125.

the earlier incarnations of each (the SFRY and the USSR). In case of the unified Germany it was a question of its 'partial' continuity in respect of one of the two component parts of the 'union'. In case of the Baltic Republics it was a question of the continuity of their former identity that had been subsumed during the course of Soviet occupation (or, as some have put it, a case of identity without continuity). Whilst in all cases, therefore, the claim to continuity was opposed to the idea that the States concerned were 'successor States', the implications of that opposition were obviously quite different. In case of Serbia and Russia (and to some extent Germany), the concern was to exclude the possibility that as successor States they would lose certain rights and entitlements they would otherwise be able to rely upon as continuing States. In case of the Baltic Republics (and again, to some extent Germany), the claim to continuity was directed against any direct inheritance of rights and obligations in respect of the Soviet Union (or the GDR). The claims to continuity, in other words, operated in very different ways: in one direction towards maintaining in force existing legal relations (what might be called, for purpose of distinction, 'affirmative continuity'), in the other towards the disruption of those relationships ('discontinuous identity').

Of course, in each case, the meaning of such claims could only be determined by reference to the presumed content of the law of State succession. Making the claim, in other words, could only be really appreciated by reference to the alternative outcomes that one could presume to flow from either that claim being accepted or rejected. Here, one may appreciate what seemed to be an inextricable nexus in O'Connell's account between his dismissal of the category of 'personality' and the simultaneous advancement of a presumption of legal continuity. The greater the extent to which the law of State succession guarantees the continuity of legal relationships, he suggested, the less relevant or acute the question of State identity or continuity may become. In many cases it really wouldn't matter too much which side of the fence one was sitting on: all that would change would be the legal techniques available for disputing the continuity of a residual category of legal relationships whose continuance would be problematic (on the one side by reference to their personal characteristics perhaps, on the other, by reference to doctrines of changed circumstances). In such a context, claims to State continuity would thus only have legal relevance in relation to those rights or obligations incapable of being succeeded to.

The fact then, that the question of state continuity remained problematic at a time at which scholars and legal advisors were uniformly advocating a resurrection of O'Connell's presumption of continuity of rights and obligations was to signal two things. On the one side, it was to suggest that in cases of affirmative continuity, the real issue related to the (dis)continuance of those legal relations identifiable as specifically 'personal' – and for the most part, this seemed to concern institutional membership above all else.[118] That international organizations

---

[118] Art 4 1978 Convention provides that:
'The present Convention applies to the effects of a succession of States in respect of, (a) any treaty which is the constituent instrument of an international organization without prejudice to the rules

appear, then, to have assumed a central position, through rules precluding succession to membership,[119] in the determination of claims to identity is, perhaps, indicative not only as to how far any State's claim to a specific legal identity has become thoroughly functional,[120] but also of how responsibility for making such critical choices has apparently become diffused within systems of institutional voting. That such institutions may, by way of negotiating conditions for membership, also exercise considerable control over the distribution of significant resources (in the form, for example, of special drawing rights in the IMF or IBRD) is such as to highlight the disciplinary power that is now located at that particular decisional point.

On the other side, it was also to suggest that, in case of what I have called 'discontinuous identity', arguments about continuity have become a surrogate for substantive arguments about succession. Clearly, for all the obvious parallels between the assertions of the Baltic States and the 'sovereignty in abeyance' arguments raised and discussed in the context of Protected States,[121] had they argued their case in terms of article 17 of the Vienna Convention (in the name of 'self-determination') it would have been much harder for them to maintain their position. Not only would it have put in crisis the general affirmation of a presumption of legal continuity, but it would also have admitted the existence of a 'legal nexus', as Waldock put it, between the agencies of Soviet rule and the

concerning acquisition of membership and without prejudice to any other relevant rules of the organization'. Although this provision appears to admit the possibility of succession to constituent instruments, the ILC made clear in its commentary that, '[P]ractice appears now to have established the principle that a new State is not entitled automatically to become a party to the constituent treaty and a member of the organization as a successor State, simply by reason of the fact that at the date of the succession its territory was subject to the treaty and within the ambit of the organization'.
ILC draft arts, above, n 51, p 180, paras 10 and 13.
See generally, O Schachter, 'The Development of International Law Through the Legal Opinions of the United Nations Secretariat', 25 BYIL (1948) 91; O'Connell, above, n 106, p 183; L Green, 'The Dissolution of States and Membership of the United Nations', in Holland and G Schwarzenberger, *Law, Justice and Equity* (1967) 152, p 167; M Scharf, 'Musical Chairs: The Dissolution of States and Membership in the United Nations', 28 Cornell ILJ (1995) 29; P Williams, 'State Succession and the International Financial Institutions: Political Criteria v Protection of Outstanding Financial Obligations', 43 ICLQ (1994) 776; D Lloyd, 'Succession, Secession, and State Membership in the United Nations', 26 NYUJILP (1993–4) 763; Bühler, above, n 62.

[119] The rationale for non-succession is variously associated with the personal character of the obligations (K Zemanek, 'State Succession after Decolonization', 116 Hague Recueil (1965) 253; E Vallat, 'Some Aspects of the Law of State Succession', 41 Grotius Soc (1955) 123, p 134), the conditional character of membership (H Waldock, First Report on Succession of States and Governments in Respect of Treaties, A/CN4/202, Yrbk ILC (1968) II, 87, p 92), or the nature of the rights and obligations associated with membership (Williamson and Osborn, above, n 54, p 267; O'Connell, above, n 106, p 183).
[120] To this effect see Bühler, above, n 62, p 324 (suggesting that the overriding consideration determining whether succession will be admissible is not the character or weakness of association, or the requirement of formal admission, but rather 'a question of the functions and purposes of the organization concerned'. Those organizations with a 'functional' approach to membership such as WIPO will allow succession, those with a 'political' approach to membership will not).
[121] See above, pp 149–50.

newly independent Baltic governments. There could be no questioning, in that context, of the continuation of territorial regimes or of boundary agreements, nor any possibility of 'reactivating' membership in international organizations. Their claims to discontinuous identity, in other words, were far more radical than was even deemed possible for States emerging from decolonization. The key difference, here, seemed to be that the claims were not merely those associated with a right of independence or autonomy on the part of the Baltic states, but were, in effect, a vindication of international law itself.[122] However much their independence might have seemed to be a product of a revitalized politics of nationalism, what seemed to be significant was not that consciousness itself, but rather the affront to the principle of the non-use of force that was demonstrated in their continued occupation after 1945.

4. Treaty Continuity and Automatic Succession

For Schachter, and those participating in the symposium in 1992,[123] the problem of succession was situated against a background of 'unpredictable' and 'anarchistic' change.[124] The alternative to a rule of treaty continuity, in other words, was a chaotic and unstable world that would fundamentally undermine efforts to 'foster respect for the rule of law'.[125] In O'Connell's case, of course, this was not the sociology of political change that he experienced. His thesis had been built upon what he saw to be a relatively ordered process of governmental devolution in case of decolonization (captured, in many cases, by the incremental process of regional devolution prior to independence) and which he recognized as providing the theoretical foundations of a principle of continuity. O'Connell's notion of treaty continuity was thus posited on a sociological underbed of stable political change, whereas that of Schachter, and other contributors to the symposium, was upon the opposite. The interesting issue, however, is not whether O'Connell was right in his appreciation of the social and political nature of decolonization,

---

[122] The claim to discontinuous identity on the part of Germany after 1990 was obviously more problematic insofar as there was no obvious legal rationale other than what might have been seen to be the most convenient way of managing unification. At a time at which scholars were proclaiming the existence of a rule of automatic succession to multilateral agreements, and particularly those of a humanitarian guise, accepting that 11 labour conventions to which the former GDR was party were no longer in force for Germany was something of a reversal. It is clear, in any case, that Germany was forced, on several occasions to modify what seemed to be its clearly stated position – for example by way of agreeing to contribute (albeit on an ex gratia basis) in respect of the outstanding contributions of the GDR to international organizations, or by agreeing to settle with the United States outstanding property claims arising from expropriation and related activities of the GDR.

[123] Williamson and Osborn, above, n 54; D Vagts, 'State Succession: The Codifiers' View', 33 VaJIL (1992–3) 275.

[124] Schachter, above, n 30, p 259.

[125] ibid 264.

nor whether Schachter *et al* were right in their appreciation as to the nature of the post-Soviet 'transition', but rather the character of their engagement with international law.

For O'Connell, the problem of State succession was largely to be worked out in a marriage of sociology and philosophy. Law was a social phenomenon, ingrained in society, the needs of which would countermand any desire for it to be set aside. The very practical, sociological need for legal continuity at the local level (continuity in rights of possession and ownership) necessarily had implications for continuity of rights and obligations at the international level.[126] Since it would be expedient, for example, to continue air transport arrangements after independence, so also there would be undoubted pressure to admit the continuance of treaty relations upon which those arrangements were originally predicated. Whatever national, political passions might come into play in the context of independence, the practical reality was that most law and legal arrangements (whether of a purely domestic or more broadly international nature) would, and should, be continued. The exceptions, or those cases in which legal continuity was in practice denied, would have thus represented for O'Connell, the triumph of passion over reason.

Schachter's approach to the law of succession appears not to have been grounded upon this kind of local sociology. Certainly, he seems to have been in agreement with O'Connell as regards the desirability of legal continuity, but his concern was very much more for 'stability of expectations' in its general abstract sense. In this respect, he seems to have taken as the mainstay of his argument, the 'values' outlined by Vagts in his contribution to the same symposium.[127] In examining the 'characteristics of the international legal system' that appeared to support the development of a set of rules about the succession of States to treaties, Vagts highlighted the 'opportunity costs' that States incurred in arriving at and committing themselves to treaty obligations, and the corresponding reliance placed in that regard upon other States honouring those agreements. He was to declare that:

There are always costs to an unscheduled and unpredictable termination of commitments solemnly made, and the sum total of satisfied reliances plays a role in the general trust and confidence of states in the international legal system. Even occasional declarations that a treaty is merely a 'scrap of paper' can serve to undermine seriously the confidence of States in the reliability of the established treaty network and the key international law principles upon which that network is founded.[128]

For Vagts, the demand for continuity thus ensued from what was effectively a policy prescription whose advancement was necessary to regularize an otherwise anarchic environment. What was at risk, ultimately, was not the substance of any

---

[126] O'Connell, above, n 106, p 3–5.
[127] Vagts, above, n 123.
[128] ibid 281.

values or commitments that may have been codified in various agreements, nor indeed the welfare of those who may have been the 'subject' of succession, but the reliability of the international legal order as a means of protecting the various and multiple interests of its participants. As Crawford was to express this general sentiment, 'the international community cannot allow the negation of the extensive body of legal relations built up over time. It cannot allow communities simply to opt out of obligations and responsibilities, even by so fundamental and difficult a process as dissolution of or secession from a State'.[129] Whereas, thus, O'Connell saw the *law* of State succession as the outward expression of a domestic politics of reason, Schachter and his associates seemed to see the *policy* of State succession as an international prescription through which the international legal order itself might be defended.

One sees, in this, a double move in the justification for continuity offered by O'Connell on the one hand and Schachter and Vagts on the other. First of all, there is a move from law to policy – a move which crucially facilitates the elaboration of key norms or values without the necessity of locating those values in tradition, practice, or history, and which liberates the policy-maker from the formal constraints of arguments about sovereignty or consent. The policy maker can thus stand in a position of privilege, occupying the role of legislator for international common sense, unburdened by the past, and unencumbered by the problem of the analogy. Secondly, there is a move from a domestic sociology of order to an international sociology of instability. Here, and most critically, the argument becomes almost entirely solipsistic: a rule of continuity is necessary in order to protect the international rule of law.

The Vienna Convention itself, of course, appeared to work on an entirely different assumption. For all the evident continuity identified by O'Connell in the way in which colonial territories achieved their independence, it was taken to be the case (and indeed seemed to be an inexorable consequence of the application of the principle of self-determination) that colonial independence should be understood as a far more radical and disruptive event, in terms of its consequences, than other cases of the separation of territories from a state. The right of option in Article 17 of the 1978 Convention stood in contrast to Article 34 of the same Convention – which prescribed a rule of continuity (making no distinction, furthermore, between bilateral or multilateral treaties).[130] This, of course,

---

[129] J Crawford, *ASIL Proceedings* (1992), 15, p 21. See further Hafner and Kornfeind, above, n 42, p 27 ('The treaty relations among States belonging to such a community have reached a density which rules out any clear cut negative concept in state succession. Social life which possesses transboundary elements and is based on such circumstances undoubtedly relies on continuity. And these dense treaty relations do not only govern intergovernmental relations but also apply to individuals and create a legal standard applicable to private persons. A breakdown of this set in the case of a change of statehood would severely damage the stability of international society so that continuity would seem the only viable option.').

[130] It is notable that such a distinction was recognized in respect of newly independent States (art 24, Vienna Convention 1978).

was not a view that recommended itself to everyone – indeed the US,[131] the Netherlands,[132] and Austria[133] appeared to take the view, at least prior to 1990s that the clean slate applied in relation to *all* new States. But as far as the ILC was concerned, the key was the question of 'dependency' – a term which it employed in its definition of a 'newly independent State'. For the most part, colonial territories could be taken to be 'dependent' in this sense, but it was also apparent to members of the Commission that it need not be so confined.[134] As has been seen, that a provision to this effect (Article 33(3) of the ILCs draft)[135] was eventually deleted at the Vienna Conference did not, in the end, really detract from the ILC's obvious concern that the concept of 'dependency' was ultimately rather fluid given the different ways in which the former colonial powers had administered their overseas territories (Britain through the mediation of regional governments, Portugal largely directly), and the varying degrees to which there could be said to have been 'local consent' to the treaty-making of the metropolitan power. This, of course, was to put in question the conditions of local democracy and the extent to which the States emerging in Eastern Europe and Central Asia from the former Soviet Union and the SFRY had actively participated in foreign affairs. That the process of collapse of both States went hand in hand with the establishment of electoral democracy, and that the emergence to independence was frequently preceded by proclamations of national self-determination, was only to emphasize the Commission's original point.

The point that seems to emerge, however, is that whilst the ILC saw a clear correlation between the radical character of the change, and the necessity of allowing a freedom of choice on the part of the States emerging from that process, in a paradoxical reversal of this position, Schachter and others appear to have come to the opposite conclusion. The greater the degree of instability, rupture, and change, the greater the need for legal continuity.[136] When severed from the

[131] Restatement (Third) of the Foreign Relations Law of the United States (1987), s 210(3).

[132] A Bos, 'Statenpvolging in het bijzonder met betrekking tot verdragen', 111 Mededelingen van de Nederalandse Vereniging voor Internationaal Recht (1995) 55.

[133] Tichy, above, n 111, pp 123–4.

[134] The examples it had to hand were those of the separation of Pakistan from India, and the subsequent separation of Bangladesh from Pakistan, and Czechoslovakia and Poland, see Ago, Yrbk ILC, 1974, I, p 133.

[135] Commentary to arts 33 and 34, Yrbk ILC, 1974, II, para 27 Art 33(3) read in part 'if a part of the territory of a State separates from it and becomes a State in circumstances which are essentially of the same character as those existing in the case of the formation of a newly independent State, the successor State shall be regarded for the purposes of the present articles in all respects as a newly independent State'.

[136] Indeed there was a strand of thought that emphasized the *more* radical character of the events in the 1990s as compared to the order character of decolonization. Rosenne, for example, remarked, as regards the breakup of the former federal socialist States of Eastern Europe, 'There has been a combination of changes of the structure of the state, changes of government, and the dissolution of federal States leading to the creation of new States … something to be distinguished from the unification and separation of existing States which has been a feature of the decolonisation process, and which is addressed in the 1978 Convention'.

moorings of sociological continuity (*qua* Huber), or the continuity of the domestic legal order (*qua* O'Connell) all that is left is an abstract commitment to the bare value of international law or cosmopolitan virtue.

Whatever its basis, a remarkable feature of the analysis of succession in relation to treaties came to be the almost universal advocacy of a 'presumption of treaty continuity' along lines similar to that put forward by O'Connell back in the 1960s. Politically at least, this was forseen in the recognition policies of Western governments. The Guidelines on Recognition of New States in Eastern Europe and the Soviet Union adopted by the European Community on 16 December 1991, for example, required as a precondition for recognition the 'acceptance of all relevant commitments with regard to disarmament and nuclear non-proliferation as well as to security and regional stability'.[137] This was also echoed across the other side of the Atlantic:

We will welcome into the community of democratic nations those new political entities who believe in democratic values and follow democratic practices; who safeguard human rights, including equal treatment of minorities; who respect borders and commit to changes only through peaceful and consensual means; and who will adhere to international obligations and to the norms and practices of the Helsinki Final Act and the Charter of Paris.[138]

As far as commentators were concerned, this advocacy has not always been unqualified, nor necessarily formulated in absolute terms, but the general theme remains.[139] In its Final Report on succession to treaties, for example, the ILA Committee came to the following conclusion from its survey of recent State practice,

la règle générale est donc la négociation des traités au cas par cas, sur le fondement du principe de continuité, modulé par ses exceptions. L'importance de la mise en évidence du principe de continuité comme norme de référence ne doit pas être masquée par l'existence de ces négociations: c'est en effet la règle à laquelle il faut faire référence, pour dire le droit, en cas de désaccord des parties sur le devenir d'un traité de l'Etat prédécesseur.[140]

Similar conclusions, albeit in some cases more hesitant as regards the existence of a 'customary rule' in this respect, are to be found in the work of others such as

---

S Rosenne, 'Automatic Treaty Succession', in J Klabbers and R Lefeber (eds), *Essays on the Law of Treaties* (1998) 97, p 102.

[137] 92 ILR pp 173–4.

[138] J Baker 'America and the Collapse of the Soviet Empire: What has to be Done', 2 Dept State Dispatch (1991) 50.

[139] eg (in addition to those cited above): Williams, above, n 11; L Love, 'International Agreement Obligations After the Soviet Union's Break-up: Current United States Practice and Its Consistency with International Law', 13 VandJTL (1993) 373; S Oeter, 'State Succession and the Struggle Over Equity: Some Observations on the Laws of State Succession with Respect to State Property and Debts in Case of Separation and Dissolution of States', 38 GerYIL (1995) 73, p 74.

[140] Above, n 8, p 610.

Zimmerman,[141] Stern,[142] and Bothe and Schmidt.[143] Even those more sceptical, have tended to identify a much broader range of treaties to which succession may be said to be automatic than those admitted by the ILC in the 1960s,[144] and one major point of discussion in this respect has been the position of human rights, or humanitarian, agreements.[145] Zemanek was thus to conclude his analysis of contemporary practice with this observation,

> the so-called "clean-slate" rule, which proclaimed that a new State entered the international system without any international rights and/or obligations of its predecessor devolving upon it, and which was fashionable in certain circles during the decolonization period, has apparently lost its attraction.[146]

Contemporary practice, in other words, had decisively moved away from the faddish insistence upon the necessity of consent.

However expressed, the conclusions of all such authors have been largely predicated upon a particular methodology – which has been one of examining contemporary practice against the standards set out in the Vienna Convention. By far the most consistent, in that respect, was the practice accompanying the dissolution of Czechoslovakia.[147] Although Czechoslovakia had been party to 800 multilateral, and 2,000 bilateral treaties,[148] both the Czech Republic and Slovakia committed themselves to continue all existing treaty obligations in conformity with Article 34 of the 1978 Vienna Convention.[149] The principle was enunciated in their respective Constitutional provisions[150] and was subsequently confirmed in letters addressed to the UN Secretary-General.[151] In each case, the

---

[141] A Zimmerman, 'State Succession in Respect of Treaties', in Klabbers et al above, n 11, 80, p 116 (practice seems to indicate 'a certain tendency' towards the application of the model of automatic succession, but it would be 'too ambitious' to say that this had turned into a firm rule of customary international law).

[142] Stern, above, n 2, p 295 (there exists a 'rule of obligatory succession', but not one of 'automatic succession').

[143] M Bothe and C Schmidt, 'Sucessions d'États', 96 RGDIP (1992) 812, pp 839–40 (the general rule has been the continuation of existing legal engagements. This has not occurred 'automatically' but as a consequence of an obligation to cooperate in order to maintain in place, or adapt, existing legal relations).

[144] eg, Mullerson, above, n 24.

[145] Discussed by Stern, above, n 2, pp 295–310, pp 154–7.

[146] K Zemanek, 'The Legal Foundations of the International System. General Course on Public International Law', 266 Hague Recueil (1997) pp. 84–5.

[147] Cheng, above, n 44, pp 237–66; Gamarra, above, n 62, pp 406–11; Malenovsky, 'Problèmes juridicques liés à la partition de la Tchécoslovaquie', AFDI (1993) 305.

[148] ILA Rep, above, n 8, p 587.

[149] The Vienna Convention had been ratified by Slovakia on 27 Mar 1995 in which it made clear that it would apply the terms of the Convention to its own succession (as provided in Arts 3 and 7(2)). ibid 588.

[150] Art 153 Constitution of the Republic of Slovakia; Art 4 and 5 of the Czech Constitutional Law of 15 Dec 1992. ibid 588.

[151] As far as the Czech Republic was concerned, for example, it issued a letter dated 16th February, 1993 notifying the UN Secretary-General that, 'In conformity with the valid principles of international law and to the extent defined by it, the Czech Republic, as a successor State to

Czech and Slovak Republics provided lists of multilateral treaties to which they considered themselves bound.[152] Similar notes were sent to other organizations[153] and third States acting as depositary to multilateral treaties,[154] and there appears to have been little objection to such an assertion (with the exception of the continuation of Czechoslovakia's association agreement with the EC).[155] Succession by both States to the European Convention on Human Rights, for example, was finessed by a decision of the Council of Europe that admitted them to membership in June 1993 (which, under Article 66 of the Convention was a condition for becoming party to the Convention) but simultaneously declared them to have succeeded retroactively to the Convention with effect from 1st January 1993.[156] It was only really in respect of bilateral treaties that matters were a little more complex, requiring consultation with treaty partners with a view to agreeing (often by exchange of notes) as to which treaties would continue and which would not.[157]

In the case of the USSR, a similar public position was adopted as regards treaty continuity in the Alma Ata accords of 21 December 1991[158] in which it was proclaimed that, the States participating in the Commonwealth of Independent States (CIS) (which incidentally excluded not only the three Baltic States but also Georgia) agree 'in accordance with their constitutional procedures the discharge of the international obligations deriving from treaties and agreements concluded by the former Union of Soviet Socialist Republics'.[159] In the case of Russia, the continuity of existing treaty obligations appeared to be axiomatic, as indeed it seemed to be for Belarus and Ukraine in respect of the multilateral agreements to which they were already party. In respect of the other republics, however, practice has been somewhat less consistent. For example, whilst

the Czech and Slovak Federal Republic, considers itself bound as of 1 January 1993, ie the date of the dissolution of the Czech and Slovak Federal Republic, by multilateral international treaties to which the Czech and Slovak Federal Republic was a party on that date, including reservations and declarations to their provisions made earlier by the Czech and Slovak Federal Republic...'. A similar letter was issued by Slovakia on 19 May 1993.

[152] Not all treaties ratified by Czechoslovakia found their way onto the list eg the International Opium Convention.

[153] eg in case of both Republics this included the Director General of UNESCO (10 and 26 Mar 1993); Director General of IAEA (4 Jan and 8 Feb 1993); and the Director General of the ILO (Mar 1993).

[154] In the case of the Czech Republic, notes were sent, for example, to Hungary, Canada, Poland, Russia, the US, and the UK. ILA Rep, above, n 8, pp 589–90.

[155] ibid 592.

[156] Council of Europe Doc H/INF(94)1, p 1. See further, J Flauss, 'Convention européenne des droits de l'homme et succession d'Etats aux traités: une curiosité, la décision du Comité des Ministres du Conseil de l'Europe en date du 30 Juin 1993 concernant la République tchèque et la Slovaquie', 6 RUDH (1994) 1; Kamminga, above, n 31, p. 475.

[157] Some agreements were evidently 'localized' and therefore could only be continued by one party. eg, agreements with Hungary concerning frontier arrangements or customs cooperation. ILA Rep, above, n 8, p 592.

[158] 31 ILM (1992) 142.

[159] ibid 149.

Kazakhstan, Kyrgyzstan, Tajikistan, and Turkmenistan all succeeded to the Geneva Conventions and Protocols,[160] Armenia, Azerbaijan, Georgia, Moldova, and Uzbekistan all deposited fresh instruments of accession.[161] There is little evidence to suggest that this kind of inconsistency had geographical or other functional overtones. For example, whilst Kazakhstan registered its 'succession' to the Geneva Conventions, it registered its accession to other treaties to which the USSR was formerly a party.[162] There are also a number of multilateral treaties as regards which the successor States have failed to indicate their position one way or another.[163]

Similarly mixed practice may be appreciated in respect of successor States to the former SFRY.[164] In a general sense, all the successor States endorsed the principle of treaty continuity. Slovenia, for example, issued a notification of succession to the Secretary-General of the United Nations in respect of multilateral treaties to which the former SFRY had been a party effective as from 25th June 1991 ('the date on which Slovenia assumed responsibility for its international relations'). Similar statements were also issued by Bosnia-Herzegovina,[165] Croatia,[166] and Macedonia.[167] Subsequent practice, however, has been somewhat more uneven. For example, Slovenia rejected its succession to the 1980 Convention on Civil Aspects of International Child Abduction on the basis of children on the basis that, whilst it was ratified by the SFRY, the treaty was never applied to the territory Report of Slovenia.[168] Similarly, whilst it notified its succession to the International Covenant on Civil and Political Rights (1966) it acceded to the Torture Convention of 1984.

For all of their commitment to treaty continuity commentators were, in light of what they saw of State practice, somewhat unclear as to how precisely to characterize it. Certainly it was true that an absolute commitment to the clean-slate

---

[160] ICRC Annual Report (1994) 266.

[161] Stern's view is that Moldova, Uzbekistan, and Turkmenistan all adopted a posture of the clean slate in relation to treaties. B Stern, 'Rapport préliminaire sur la succession d'états en matière des traités, ILA Helsinki Conference 1996; pp 20–1; Koskenniemi, above, n 89, p 102. Further see T Schweisfurth, 'Das Recht der Staatensukzession: Die Staatenpraxis der Nachgolge in Völkerrechtliche Verträge, Saatsvermögen, Saatsschulden und Archive in den Teilungsfällen Sowjetunion, Tschechoslowakei und Jugoslawien' in U Fastenrath et al (eds), *Das Recht der Staatensukzession* (1995) 49.

[162] See in respect of International Covenant on Economic, Social and Cultural Rights (1966), Multilateral Treaties, IV, 4, 6, p 125.

[163] In case of the Anti-Doping Convention (1989) ETS no 135, for example, none of the republics has notified its succession to the Convention despite the fact that the USSR became party in February 1991. Ukraine, however, signed that Convention on 2 Jul 1998.

[164] Degan, above, n 25, p 206; Gamarra, above, n 62, pp 419–24; M Bojanic, 'Éléments d'Appréciation de la Practique Étatique en Matière de Succession aux Traités de la République Socialiste Féderative de Yugoslavie', RBDI (2000) 489.

[165] Gamarra, ibid 421.

[166] Degan above, n 25, p 223; Bojanic, above, n 164, p 491.

[167] Art 2, Declaration of Sovereignty and Independence of the Republic of Macedonia, 17 Sep 1991, cited in Gamarra, above, n 62, p 423; Bojanic, above, n 164, p 492.

[168] ILA Rep, above, n 8, p 596.

principle, by which 'new States' would have no entitlement, let alone obligation, to become parties to multilateral agreements, didn't seem to be reflected in practice (perhaps explaining Austria's change of mind on this score).[169] But neither did it seem that they simply succeeded *ipso iure* to existing treaties, independently of any act on their behalf (whether by way of notification of succession, or accession). Situating the practice in terms of Article 34 of the Vienna Convention was thus difficult precisely because of the apparent absence of any requirement of notification, even if it seemed obvious that such notification was the only way by which they might substantiate the presumption of continuity.[170] A suitable equivocation was therefore desirable – and one that took account of the possibility that the new States might opt to accede to such treaties rather than succeed – for which Stern's suggested 'obligatory' rather than 'automatic' succession provided a useful template. Yet it was also evident that an entirely different construction might have been placed on such practice – namely that it largely accorded with the terms of Articles 16 and 17 of the Vienna Convention – which envisaged the possibility of new States signalling their acceptance of international agreements by way of notifications of succession, or alternatively opting for accession. Oddly enough, the parallels were only rarely noted, and in large part for two reasons. On the one hand, was the reluctance to accept that Articles 16 and 17 were, in any respect, relevant to what had happened in Central and Eastern Europe; on the other, was a corresponding belief in the overriding desirability of treaty continuity.

The possibility that there might have emerged a general rule of continuity was debated at some length in the *Gabčíkovo* case. There, as has been observed above, Hungary had adopted a two-track strategy of arguing on the one hand, that it had legitimately terminated the 1977 agreement between Czechoslovakia and Hungary for the construction of Gabčíkovo-Nagymaros project, whilst also maintaining on the other, that Slovakia had not succeeded to that agreement following the 'Velvet divorce' (or, more precisely, that the treaty had 'terminated' following the disappearance of one of the parties).[171] In respect of this second contention, Hungary pointed out first of all, that it had explicitly refused to confirm Slovakia's succession to the 1977 Agreement.[172] Hungary argued, furthermore, that '[i]n respect of bilateral treaties (other than boundary treaties) there is no rule of international law which provides for automatic succession if part of a State separates, or if a predecessor State dissolves and several successor States emerge in its place'.[173] Succession to bilateral treaties was explicitly dependent

---

[169] G Hafner and E Kornfeind, above, n 42, p 24.
[170] Art 38 Vienna Convention, which speaks about the necessity of notification only in cases of arts 31, 32, and 36. See M Koskenniemi and M Lehto, above, n 89, p 200 (suggesting that there is no indication from practice that States regarded themselves automatically bound by multilateral treaties in virtue of art 34 of the Vienna Convention).
[171] See above, p 55.
[172] *Note Verbale* from the Hungarian Embassy to the Slovak Ministry of Foreign Affairs, 23 Dec 1992, reproduced in Memorial of Republic of Hungary, Annexes, vol 4, annex 110.
[173] Memorial of Republic of Hungary, vol 1, p 323, para 10.112.

upon agreement between the parties. Hungary relied, in that respect, upon section 210(3) of the US Third Restatement[174] which broadly confirmed the impossibility of succession to treaties, and Opinion No 12 of the Badinter Commission in which it had been held that 'the fundamental rule is that States must achieve an equitable result by negotiation and agreement'.[175]

Of course, in maintaining this position, Hungary necessarily had to deal with the question of Article 34 of the Vienna Convention which, contrary to its own position, articulated a rule of continuity in such cases without obviously distinguishing between bilateral and multilateral agreements. Hungary began by noting that the Convention had not been ratified by either Czechoslovakia or Hungary and that, given its 'legislative character' could not be regarded as 'a statement of existing general international law'.[176] This was particularly the case as regards Article 34 which, as academic opinion seemed to confirm (Jennings and Watts,[177] Brownlie,[178] and Mullerson),[179] the 'end product did not reflect any consensus as to the state of general international law, and was rather more influenced by concerns at possible secession of parts of independent States'.[180] Hungary was to add, furthermore, that even if a 'higher level of succession' could be observed as regards multilateral treaties,[181] practice since 1989 clearly indicated that succession to bilateral agreements was a matter negotiated between the successor States and other parties on a case by case basis.[182]

On this score, Hungary's argument seemed well supported in practice. In the case of the Republics of the former USSR, the general position as regards bilateral treaties was spelt out in the joint Memorandum of Understanding of 6 July 1992, by which the Member States of the CIS agreed that the fate of some bilateral treaties which concerned two or more of the Republics would be determined by them in negotiations with the respective third parties, and that other bilateral treaties (in particular border treaties) would remain in force for those Member States of the CIS who have a common border with a third State.[183] Although there seems to have been a general willingness to continue bilateral treaties where

---

[174] Above, n 38.
[175] Opinion no 12, 16th July 1993, 32 ILM (1993) 1586, p 1590, para 1. (The memorial itself erroneously refers to Opinion no 11.)
[176] Memorial of Republic of Hungary, above, n 173, p 324, para 10.116.
[177] R Jennings and A Watts, *Oppenheim's International Law* (9th edn 1992) I, p 236.
[178] I Brownlie, *Principles of Public International Law* (4th edn 1990) pp 668–70.
[179] Mullerson, above, n 55, p 488.
[180] Memorial of Republic of Hungary, above, n 173, p 325, para 10.117.
[181] It cited, in that regard, the EC conditions for recognition of the Republics of the former Yugoslavia and the Soviet Union in which it was expressly required that the new States demonstrate their commitment to be bound by existing boundaries, and by general principles relating to human rights and the rule of law. European Political Cooperation, Extraordinary Ministerial Meeting, Brussels, 16 Dec 1991, 'Declaration of the "Guidelines on the Recognition of New States in Eastern Europe and in the Soviet Union". See further R Rich, 'Recognition of States: The Collapse of Yugoslavia and the Soviet Union', 4 EJIL (1993) 36.
[182] Memorial of Republic of Hungary, above, n 173, p 325, para 10.117.
[183] 26 Revue Belge de Droit International (1993) 627–8.

possible, and although other treaty partners such as the US,[184] UK,[185] Germany, and Finland[186] sought to obtain a commitment to continuity, large numbers of those treaties were regarded as having ceased to have effect. Thus, for example, only 24 out of the 88 treaties in force between the United States and the USSR survived Ukrainian independence,[187] and only 5 out of 48 treaties concluded between the USSR and Finland.[188]

A similar story was evident in case of the former Czechoslovakia. The general presumption of continuity proclaimed by the two Republics extended to both multilateral and bilateral treaties.[189] In the case of bilateral treaty relations, however, each Republic held consultations with partner States leading to the confirmation and, in certain cases, the termination of agreements that were formerly in force in relation to Czechoslovakia. Thus, for example, in case of treaties concluded between the People's Republic of China and Czechoslovakia, 17 were confirmed as remaining in force and 6 'terminated' as regards the Czech Republic[190] and 20 remained in force as regards Slovakia[191] following exchanges of letters. In the case of Hungary, Slovakia had initially addressed a Note Verbale to the Hungarian embassy on 18 December 1992 indicating that 'in accordance with, and to the extent determined by, existing norms of international law' it considered itself bound by all bilateral and multilateral treaties to which Czechoslovakia was

---

[184] The US, in response to the declarations of independence of each of the former USSR Republics, sought to make it a condition for the establishment of diplomatic relations that they commit themselves to fulfil pre-existent treaty obligations. In a subsequent exchange of notes with each of the Republics, the governments took 'as a point of departure' the principle elaborated in art 34 of the Vienna Convention, and agreed to 'continue' those bilateral treaties that had not expired or were not obsolete. In each case, these treaties were spelt out in the Annex to the exchange of notes.

[185] See, BYIL (1992) 652–5, (1997) 535–6. Also, A Aust, *Modern Treaty Law and Practice* (2000), pp 313–14.

[186] This seemed to be the position adopted by Germany and Finland, Klabbers *et al.,* above, n 11, p 100, n 237.

[187] Ukraine and Belarus – two founding members of the United Nations – had already entered into a range of treaty obligations prior to the dissolution of the USSR (a power that was invested under the terms of art 80 of the 1977 Constitution of the USSR) and there has been no suggestion that those treaty obligations would not be continued.

[188] Lee, above, n 65, pp 128–9.

[189] Czech Republic concluded that in its practice, the provisions of art 34(1) (but not necessarily art 34(2)) 'received strong endorsement'. It was also able to claim that the continuity rule was applied in relation to all categories of treaties irrespective of whether they could be regarded as 'political' or 'dispositive', ibid 470. The significance of this claim, however, has to be viewed in light of the fact that many salient 'political' treaties had been formally terminated long before the date of dissolution. and it resolved to apply its terms not only to reservations and objections, but also to acts of signature, above, p 466. In the case of signature, the provisions of Art 37(1) of the Vienna Convention provided 'useful inspiration' for the practice in case of bilateral treaties in discussion with the Republic of Korea. *Lauder v Czech Republic*, UNCITRAL Arb (2001); *CME Czech Republic BV v Czech Republic*, UNCITRAL Arb (2001).

[190] 'State Succession in Respect of Treaties: Czech Republic (National Report)', in Klabbers *et al*, above, n 11, 400, p 440.

[191] 'State Succession in Respect of Treaties: Slovak Republic (National Report, January 1997)', in Klabbers *et al*, above, n 11, 478, p 510.

formerly party.[192] In the subsequent exchange of treaty lists, Slovakia indicated that it was prepared to continue some, but certainly not all bilateral agreements, and that it was, in any case, 'ready to hold negotiations' on the question of its succession to bilateral treaties with Hungary.[193] Hungary concluded from this, that the practice of Slovakia itself was 'inconsistent with the concept of automatic succession to bilateral treaties contained in Article 34 of the 1978 Convention.[194] Even if there was a rule of succession, furthermore, it would be subject to an evaluation as to what was 'workable' in the new situation, and to that end, negotiations would be essential.[195]

As Slovakia pointed out in its counter-memorial, the general thrust of the Hungarian argument on this point was somewhat tendentious – on the one hand it maintained that Slovakia was the sole successor State in respect of rights and obligations relating to the Gabčikovo-Nagymaros project, but on the other, sought to deny the continuance of the agreement on which those rights and obligations were based.[196] Hungary had admitted in its memorial that there was 'no rule of succession to international responsibility'[197] and that a successor State is not liable for the wrongful conduct of its predecessor.[198] It had suggested, nevertheless, that Slovakia had 'inherited the *situation* created by the illegal diversion of the Danube' and by failing to rectify that situation, had effectively adopted the wrongful conduct of Czechoslovakia.[199] This, of course, was to bring to mind the distinction articulated by the ILC in the context of territorial and boundary régimes, between the treaty on the one hand, and the dispositive character of the rights and obligations created pursuant to the treaty on the other.[200] And this was only to play into Slovakia's hands when it came to argue that the 1977 agreement was, in essence, a territorial or boundary régime within the terms of articles 11 and 12 of the 1978 Vienna Convention.[201]

But in terms of Hungary's argument as to the status of Article 34 of the Vienna Convention, Slovakia was to take an entirely opposed view. For its part, Slovakia maintained that the Hungarian contentions were baseless and that, in fact, the rules in the Convention were indeed rules of 'general international law'.[202] It rehearsed the history of Article 34 both within the ILC and at the Vienna

---

[192] Memorial of Republic of Hungary, above, n 173, Annexes, vol 4, annex 109.
[193] *Note Verbale* from the Czechoslovak Ministry of Foreign Affairs to the Hungarian Ministry of Foreign Affairs, 18 Dec 1992, ibid, annex 110.
[194] ibid 327, para 10.119.
[195] ibid 327, para 10.120.
[196] Memorial of Slovak Republic, p 12, paras 11–12.
[197] It cited, in that regard, *Robert E Brown* case (1923) 2 ILR 66; *Hawaiian Claims* 20 AJIL (1925) 381; *Lighthouses Arbitration between France and Greece, Claim No. 12a* 23 ILR (1956) 106. See above, pp 47–8.
[198] Memorial of Republic of Hungary, above, n 173, p 331, para 11.06.
[199] ibid 332, para 11.07.
[200] See below, pp 247–9.
[201] Memorial of Slovak Republic, above, n 196, pp 31–36, 58–63.
[202] ibid 51, para 3.07.

Conference of 1977–78, and argued that ultimately there was 'a near consensus amongst delegations that in case of dissolution and, in particular, in the case where the constitutive parts which separated had to some extent participated in the formulation of international relations or had been given limited international personality, the continuity principle was based on sufficient State practice.'[203] That consensus apparently also included Hungary.[204] Further to this, Slovakia maintained that its willingness to negotiate in respect of bilateral agreements was not, in fact, indicative of the absence of a rule or presumption of *ipso iure* succession. Article 34, after all, envisaged a series of exceptions such as where the States agree otherwise, where the application of the treaty would be incompatible with the object and purpose of the treaty, and where the treaty related to territory other than that of the successor State.

From this point onwards, the two parties merely reiterated their initial positions: Hungary continued to insist that there was no possibility of succession to bilateral treaties, and that the rule in Article 34 was over-generalized, Slovakia continued to maintain that succession occurred *ipso iure* and that, in any case, the treaty created a territorial regime within the meaning of Article 12 of the Convention. Of course, one of the difficulties for the Court when faced with such arguments about Article 34 was that both positions were equally plausible. Practice did seem to confirm that any continuation of bilateral agreements tended to be preceded by prior consultation and negotiation and that, in some cases (for example in respect of the EC accession agreement with Czechoslovakia) renegotiation was insisted upon by third parties. The very fact of negotiation, in other words, confirmed the absence of any *ipso iure* succession. On the other hand, it was just as possible to argue that the process of consultation was one necessitated by the fact that even under the terms of Article 34, the rule of *ipso iure* continuity wouldn't apply if the parties were to agree otherwise, or if the application of the treaty would be incompatible with the object and purpose of the treaty or otherwise would radically change the conditions for its operation. The fact of consultation, in other words, seemed to ensue merely from the necessity of confirming whether continuity was feasible in the circumstances, or whether one or other party might wish to raise a plea of *rebus sic stantibus*.[205] As the ILA Committee was to conclude in its Final Report on Succession to Treaties,

L'importance de la mise en évidence du principe de continuité comme norme de référence ne doit pas être masquée par l'existence de ces négociations: c'est en effet la règle à laquelle il faut faire référance, pour dire le droit, en cas de desaccord des parties suré le devenir d'un traité de l'Etat prédécesseur.[206]

---

[203] ibid 53, para 3.12.
[204] See UN Conference on the Succession of States in Respect of Treaties, vol II, 40th mtg, para 54, 41st mtg, para 48.
[205] cf Koskenniemi, above, n 23, p 105.
[206] ILA, Final Report, above, n 8, p 610.

But even if evidence of continuity might have been 'masked' by the existence of negotiations, it didn't necessarily follow that that was the rule in case of disagreement.

As was so obviously the case during the drafting of the Vienna Convention, the key to these positions was not so much what practice itself seemed to tell the parties about the international law of State succession, but rather the initial standpoints from which that practice was to be construed. For Hungary, it was a case of proving the existence of a rule of continuity; for Slovakia a case of disproving a presumption that had already been put in place in the Conference of 1978. From one point of view, these two standpoints seemed to be divided by reference to the respective emphasis placed upon the question of consent. Hungary, it might be said, prioritized the importance of consent in case of succession, whereas Slovakia prioritized the importance of legal continuity. But this only went so far. For Slovakia also emphasized consent in the form of its participation in the conclusion of the 1977 agreement prior to the dismemberment of Czechoslovakia, and Hungary also emphasized the importance of continuity in its arguments about Slovakia having assumed the rights and obligations created by the treaty. In each case, it was always possible to look behind the formalities: in case of consent, behind the idea of signature and ratification to domestic arrangements for participation; in the case of the legal regime, behind the formal status of the treaty itself. Each party, furthermore, availed itself of both formal and informal arguments. As argumentative positions, whether in formal or informal mode, they simply circled round an unresolved (and perhaps even unresolvable) difference in viewpoint.

Perhaps unsurprisingly, when the ICJ came to deliver its judgment on the merits, it quickly came to the conclusion that it was unnecessary for it 'to enter into a discussion of whether or not Article 34 of the 1978 Convention did indeed reflect the state of customary international law'.[207] It focused rather upon the particular nature and character of the 1977 treaty, which it found to be constitutive of a territorial régime within the meaning of Article 12 of the Vienna Convention, and which would hence be 'unaffected' by the succession of States. [208]

5. Functional Differentiation

In his article, Schachter had placed considerable emphasis upon the importance of context in the application of principles of succession. By 'context', of course, he wasn't thinking of the need to develop ever more complex typologies of event, but rather the need to pay attention to the very specific character of the

---

[207] Judgment, above, n 15, p 71, para 123.
[208] The only member of the Court who was to take the matter any further was Judge Bedjaoui who, in his separate opinion sought to flesh out, in greater detail, why it was that the treaty should be regarded as 'territorial'. Separate Opinion of Judge Bedjaoui, ICJ Report (1997) 7, p 125, para 22.

legal relationships in question, and their connection to the wider world. Here, Schachter was to draw upon what was already a fairly long-standing tradition of qualifying any general principle or rule of succession by reference to the nature or character of the legal relationship in question – a tradition which could be appreciated not only in terms of the articulation of distinctive rules for treaties, property, debt, and so on, but also in terms of a functional differentiation between different categories of treaty. The Vienna Convention of 1978 of course made several such distinctions: territorial and boundary regimes were given special recognition in Articles 11 and 12, constituent instruments of international organizations were given special mention in Article 4, and elsewhere liberal mention was made of the object and purpose of treaties for purposes of qualifying the general principles.

In its Final Report of 2002 the ILA Committee, in examining the question of succession to treaties in light of contemporary practice, highlighted four categories that warranted special attention. Two of these – boundary treaties and territorial agreements – were the subject of special régimes within the Vienna Convention and which at least one member of the Committee had already declared to be reflective of customary international law.[209] The two other categories – disarmament treaties and human rights treaties – were matters which had been highlighted by Schachter in 1992 and, in respect of the latter, there had developed quite an extensive academic discussion. In the words of the Committee, the recent changes in Europe had 'modified the approach to continuity and succession' in respect of such categories of agreement.[210]

In the case of the first two categories, the ILA Committee was to conclude that practice really confirmed what already seemed obvious: that each would remain in force as regards the successor State, albeit the case that the Committee added certain cautions.[211] In case of frontier treaties, the evidence it produced ranged across cases in which States explicitly accepted the continuation of existing boundary agreements (such as evidenced in the exchange of notes between Austria and Slovenia in 1992 and Slovakia in 1993);[212] those in which new agreements were concluded accepting the validity of existing frontiers (such as between Ukraine and Slovakia in 1993, and Belarus and Lithuania in 1994); and those, such as the German-Polish treaty of 1990 on the Confirmation of their Common Border[213] in which the line of the frontier was agreed to be that provisionally stipulated in earlier treaties (the treaty of Goerlitz of 1950 between Poland and the GDR and

---

[209] Stern, above, n 2, pp 165–8.
[210] ILA Final Report, above, n 8, p 610 ('Les récents changements, territoriaux survenus en Europe ont modifié l'approche de la continuité et de la succession en ce qui concerne deux types d'accords internationaux: les traités sur les droits de l'homme et les traités sur le désarmement.').
[211] ibid 613.
[212] ibid 612. Mention was also given to the maintenance in force of the Treaty of Osimo of 1975 between Italy and Slovenia.
[213] 31 ILM (1992) 1293.

the treaty of Warsaw of 1970 between the FRG and Poland).[214] Only in isolated cases (Russia-Lithuania; Ukraine-Romania) did the Committee recognize the continuation of existing border agreements to be a matter of dispute. It might also, of course, have mentioned the disputes between Russia and the Baltic states, particularly as regards territory 'lost' following administrative reorganization of the Republics whilst under occupation.[215] But here, there may have been some doubt as to whether what was in question was indeed a principle of succession.

The focus of the Committee, in this respect, upon State practice in Eastern Europe seemed peculiarly limited. To begin with, there was obvious support for the principle to be found in the ICJ's judgment in the *Libya/Chad* case, but which gained not even a passing reference.[216] There, the Court had concluded that, although the Franco-Libyan Treaty of 1955 describing the boundary envisaged the necessity of consultation with a view to reviewing the boundary after 10 years, it had in fact given rise to a permanent frontier with a 'legal life of its own' that existed independently of the fate of the 1955 Treaty itself. 'Once agreed' the Court advised 'the boundary stands'.[217] Further to this, the Committee seemed unwilling to engage in a broader discussion of the question of *uti possidetis* which had been the focus of considerable attention in the 1990s, and which was arguably central to the Badinter Commission's work in respect of the former Yugoslavia.[218] On one view, of course, the principle of *uti possidetis* was distinct, insofar as it concerned either the intangibility of external boundaries originating from a non-treaty basis (ie, through processes of recognition and acquiescence)[219] or the internationalisation of internal administrative boundaries.[220] In a formal sense, of course, the Committee could retain the distinction between boundaries established by treaty, and those otherwise created (whether or not through the principle of *uti possidetis*), but in doing so it was to miss the obvious point about Article 11 of the Vienna Convention, namely that it did not

[214] M Carrasco, 'Régimes de frontières et autres régimes territoriaux face à la succession d'Etats', in M Koskenniemi *et al*, above, n 16, 493, pp 549–50; M Bothe, 'Les traités entre L'Allemagne et la Pologne du 14 novembre 1990 et du 16 juin 1990', RGDIP 1990 357; R Piotrowicz, 'The Polish-German Frontier in International Law: The Final Solution', 63 BYIL (1992) 367. The recognition of border treaties concluded by the GDR, of course, stands in contrast to the position otherwise adopted in respect of Germany's non-succession to the agreements of the GDR. See above, pp 219–23.

[215] Estonia insisted upon the re-establishment of the border as described by the Treaty of Tartu of 1920. See generally, Mullerson, above, n 55, pp 148–50.

[216] ICJ Report (1994) 6, p 37.

[217] ibid.

[218] M Shaw, 'Peoples Territitorialism and Boundaries', 8 EJIL (1997) 478 and 'The Heritage of States: The Principle of *Uti Possidetis Juris* Today', 67 BYIL (1996) 75; S Ratner, 'Drawing a Better Line: *Ubi Possidetis* and the Borders of New States', 90 AJIL (1996) 590; S Torres Bernárdez, 'The "Uti Possidetis Juris" Principle in Historical Perspective' in K Ginther et al (eds), *Festschrift für Karl Zemanek* (1994) 417; J-M Sorel and R Mehdi, 'L'*Uti Possidetis* entre la consecration juridique et la practique: essai de réactualisation', AFDI (1994) 11.

[219] This was effectively the gist of the ICJ's interpretation of *uti possidetis* in the *Burkina Faso/Mali* case, ICJ Report (1986) 554, p 566.

[220] *Burkina Faso/Mali* case ICJ Report (1986) 554, pp 565–6; *El Salvador/Honduras* case ICJ Report (1992) 351, p. 386; Badinter Commission, Opinion no 3, 92 ILR 168, p 171.

speak of succession to boundary treaties as such, but merely provided that the boundary so established should be unaffected by a succession of States. Drawing a line here was somewhat question-begging.

When it turned to 'territorial régimes', like the ILC before it,[221] the Committee was somewhat more cautious. It noted, to begin with, that many authors seemed to accept the principle of succession to territorial régimes, that it had been included in the 1978 Convention without much opposition and that, finally the ICJ had recognized the principle to be one having the status of customary international law in the *Gabčikovo-Nagymaros Project* case. Rather than entering into an examination of this particular case, however, the ILA concentrated instead on what appeared to be the exceptions, for which no principle of automatic succession could be admitted. The first instance it mentioned concerned the Finnish-Soviet treaty of 1940 concerning the demilitarization of the Aaland Islands which had confirmed the general provisions of the multilateral Convention of 1921[222] and had also accorded the USSR the right to have a consulate on the Islands.[223] In its view, the case exposed the problem of treating 'localized' treaties such as this as subject to automatic succession: in theory, at least, that would have resulted in all of the successor States enjoying a right to a share of the consulate at Marienhamm. Its conclusion, following Koskenniemi,[224] was that the general provisions on demilitarization were 'objective' and hence, binding upon all, but that the provision relating to the consulate was a separate 'political' element of the régime which remained a right enjoyed only by Russia.[225] In fact, during subsequent bilateral negotiations with the other successor States, the agreement was either denounced or said to have expired.[226]

The second example concerned practice relating to the succession of Russia, Moldova, the Czech Republic, and Croatia to the Convention of Belgrade of 1948 governing the navigation of the Danube.[227] In the case of Russia, although it claimed to be the continuation of the USSR, it was obviously no longer a riparian State – a point which led to obvious complications concerning its participation in the work of the Commission of the Danube. Moldova sought to accede to the Convention as a riparian State, as did the Czech Republic[228] despite the fact that it wasn't a riparian State and that it had already been agreed that Slovakia would be the continuing State of the Czech and Slovak Republic in respect of

---

[221] See above, pp 187–94.
[222] Which had, in turn, reinforced the provisions on demilitarization of the Paris Peace Treaty of 1856.
[223] Carrasco, above, n 214, pp 565–8.
[224] M Koskenniemi, *Recent Finnish Practice on State Succession in Respect of Treaties* (1996) p 14; with Lehto, above, n 89, p 218.
[225] ILA Committee, Final Report, above, n 8, p 614.
[226] ibid.
[227] Carrasco, above, n 214, pp 562–5; Bokor-Szegö H, *Les Problems de la Succession d'Etats et la Convention relative à la navigation sur le Danube* (cited in ILA Final Report, above, n 8).
[228] Bokor-Szegö, ibid, p 4.

New Beginnings, New Ends

membership in the Danube Commission.[229] Croatia submitted a notification of succession to the Convention and membership in the Commission although it seems that States parties invoked Article 4 of the Vienna Convention by way of insisting that this was a decision for the 'organization' itself rather than for the successor States concerned.[230] Needless to say, by way of additional Protocol of 1998 amending the 1948 Convention of Belgrade, Russia, Moldova, Germany, Croatia, and Slovakia were all affirmed as parties to the Convention to which Serbia-Montenegro remained the depositary.[231] The Czech Republic, it seems, only obtained observer status.

On the basis of these two cases, the Committee ultimately came to the conclusion that 'il ne resort pas à première vue de notre analyse une thèse de la succession automatique aux accords concernant les régimes territoriaux particuliers'.[232] In any such case, the principle would be limited by reference to which States are 'directly concerned' and in accordance with the object and purpose of the agreement.[233] This was not, it must be said, the most enlightening conclusion.

For all the apparent certainty as regards the status of Article 12 of the Vienna Convention, similar difficulties attending the characterization of régimes as strictly 'territorial' had also been apparent in the ICJ's deliberations in the *Gabčikovo-Nagymaros Project* case. There, it was clear that both parties appeared to proceed on the basis that Article 12 of the Vienna Convention was, indeed, declaratory of general international law. Neither party disputed this idea and, in fact, both dedicated most of their efforts to arguing as to whether the 1977 treaty was of such a character as to be regarded as a territorial agreement for such purposes. For Slovakia, this was evident not only by reason of the fact that the agreement contained boundary provisions, but insofar as it created rights *in rem* independently of the personality of the original signatories. For Hungary, by contrast, the agreement was little more than a joint-investment project whose character as a territorial agreement depended upon it having been fully executed (which was obviously not the case). In its judgment, the Court concluded that over and above its 'nature as a joint investment' the treaty 'also established the navigational régime for an important sector of an international waterway'. In doing so, 'it inescapably created a situation in which the interests of other users of the Danube were affected'.[234] This being the case, the treaty did appear to constitute, in the Court's view a territorial régime within the meaning of Article 12 of the 1978

---

[229] Letter of Minister of Foreign Affairs of 12 Dec 1992 to the Director General of the Danube Commission, cited in Carrasco, above, n 214, p 564.

[230] ILA, Final Report, above, n 8, p 615.

[231] Additional Protocol of 26 Mar 1998 to the Convention on the Navigation Régime on the Danube of 18 Aug 1948, Art 1.

[232] ILA, Final Report, above, n 8, p 616.

[233] Carrasco suggests, by contrast, that there is evidence supporting the customary status of art 12 so long as it is understood as one that pertains to the rights and obligations in the régime, rather than to the treaty which created it (above, n 214, p 577).

[234] Above, n 15, pp 71–2, para 123.

Convention (which it held, without any further examination to be reflective of customary international law), and that it thus 'became binding upon Slovakia on 1 January 1993'.[235]

For all the confidence with which the Court proceeded on this point, it was also clear to it that what it proposed was not strictly in line with Article 12 of the Convention. Article 12 spoke about obligations and rights relating to territory being unaffected by a succession of States – the point being that there would be no succession to the treaty itself, but that the parties would simply be bound to honour the 'facts on the ground' so to speak. Interestingly enough, however, this was precisely Hungary's contention – that Slovakia had taken over an unlawful territorial situation and adopted it as its own.[236] And it was perhaps in recognition of the fact that this would have led to a somewhat one-sided appreciation of the issue (Slovakia being bound by obligations in respect of the implementation of the agreement, but not entitled to insist upon Hungary's compliance with the same agreement) that encouraged the Court to insist that it was indeed the treaty that was succeeded to and not merely its executed terms. To take this position, however, did involve the Court putting a favourable revisionist gloss on the work of the ILC in that regard – suggesting that the ILC had been concerned, above all, with the question of treaties 'no longer in force'.[237] This was clearly not the case.[238]

In respect of these two categories of case, the ILA clearly did not move very far from mainstream opinion, nor indeed from the position that had been adopted during the drafting of the 1978 Convention. In both cases, the question of continuity was taken to be largely axiomatic, even if there remained certain questions both as to the scope of such categories and as to whether it was indeed the treaty or the regime created in its shadow that would continue. It was, however, in respect of the other two categories of treaty – disarmament treaties, on the one hand, and human rights treaties on the other – that the ILA Committee most clearly saw matters changing.

In respect of disarmament treaties,[239] the ILA Committee began by noting that Western powers had insisted, from a fairly early stage that the States emerging from the former Soviet Union maintain their existing commitments to disarmament and nuclear non-proliferation. Indeed this was included as one of the conditions within the Declaration of the European Communities of 16 December 1991 concerning guidelines for the recognition of new States in East Europe.[240]

---

[235] ibid 72, para 123.
[236] There were obvious parallels here, between Hungary's claim and the conclusion of the tribunal in the *Lighthouses Arbitration*, 23 ILR (1956) 79.
[237] ICJ Report (1997) 7, p 72, para 123.
[238] See above, pp 177–85.
[239] Mullerson, above, n 55, p 488–9; Bunn and Rhinelander, above, n 24; Love, above, n 139; F Pagani, 'Identité et succession d'Etats aux instruments conventionnels relatifs au désarmement et à la maîtrise des armements', in Koskenniemi et al (eds), above, n 16, p 437.
[240] Declaration on the Guidelines on the Recognition of New States in Eastern Europe and in the Soviet Union, 16 Dec 1991, 31 ILM (1992) 1486. This was something, incidentally, to which

The most immediate issue, in that respect, seemed to be that four States of the former Soviet Union retained nuclear weapons (Russia, Ukraine, Belarus, and Kazakhstan), which posed obvious questions as to the implications as regards commitments under the Treaty on the Non-Proliferation of Nuclear Weapons of 1968 (NPT) and the, as yet unratified, Strategic Arms Reduction Treaty of 1991 (START) between the US and the USSR.[241] Following a flurry of diplomatic activity, the solution identified came in the form of the Lisbon Protocol of 23 May 1992 which provided on the one hand for a mechanism by which each Republic could become party to the START (which eventually entered into force following Ukraine's ratification of the instrument in 1994),[242] and, on the other committed Belarus, Kazakhstan and Ukraine to 'adhere' to the NPT as 'non-nuclear weapon States' in the 'shortest possible time'. Although the Lisbon Protocol specifically spoke of all four States as successor States to the USSR, it was clear that Russia was to be treated as the continuation of the Soviet Union for purposes of participation in the NPT as a nuclear power. As the ILA Committee noted, however, although there was considerable international concern to ensure the 'continuity' of such commitments, the real problem was that as a technique for achieving that end, 'succession' did not appear to be an option. The NPT created a regime of differential obligations as regards nuclear and non-nuclear powers (a nuclear power being defined in Article IX(3) as 'one which has manufactured and exploded a nuclear weapon or other nuclear explosive device prior to 1 January 1967') the general thrust of which was to restrict the number of nuclear powers to five. It thus seemed to the Committee that any formal succession would be precluded by reason of the object and purpose of the Treaty (in line with Article 34(2)(b) of the Vienna Convention)[243] and that therefore, arrangements for adhesion had to be developed through negotiation. Far from seeing this as an exception to the general rule, however, the Committee concluded, nevertheless, that the arrangements put in place were the 'equivalent' of a declaration of succession.

the relevant member States of the CIS committed themselves shortly after in Alma Ata. Under art 5 of the Agreement on Joint Measures with Respect to Nuclear Weapons, the Republic of Belarus and Ukraine undertake to accede to the 1968 Treaty on the Non-Proliferation of Nuclear Weapons as non-nuclear States. 21 Dec 1991, 31 ILM (1992) 152.

[241] Treaty on the Reduction and Limitation of Strategic Offensive Arms, 31 July 1991. This is supplemented by START II, the Treaty on the Further Reduction and Limitation of Strategic Offensive Arms, 3 Jan 1993.

[242] This appeared to be broadly consistent with Art 37 of the Vienna Convention which governs succession signed, yet not ratified, by the predecessor State. Pagani, above, n 239, p 461. On the negotiations prior to ratification, L Wolosky, J Malis, and D Schwimmer, 'Start, Start II, and Ownership of Nuclear Weapons: The Case for a "Primary" Successor State', 34 HarvILJ (1993) 581.

[243] Art 34(2)(b) provides that the principle of automatic succession does not apply if 'it appears from the treaty... that the application of the treaty in respect of the successor State would be incompatible with the object and purpose of the treaty or would radically change the conditions for its operation'. ILA Committee, above, n 8, p 617; Pagani, above, n 239, p 450; Bunn and Rhinelander, above, n 24, p 335.

Two other agreements were also relevant in this context. One was the Anti-ballistic Missile Agreement of 1972[244] as regards which the US made clear its expectation of participation on the part of all States of the CIS, and which resulted in a resolution being adopted by ten members of the CIS at the Bishkek summit in October 1992 indicating that they would commit themselves to 'implementing' the terms of the ABM Treaty.[245] This was later followed by a Memorandum of Understanding signed in 1997,[246] Article 1 of which provided that, subject to ratification, Belarus, Kazakhstan, and Ukraine, would join Russia and the US as parties to the ABM agreement. The MOU, however, was never ratified by the US which, in any case, denounced the agreement in December 2001. The other agreement was the Treaty on Conventional Forces in Europe of 1990[247] which, like START had not entered into force by the time of the 'disintegration' of the USSR. Negotiations proceeded amongst the eight former Soviet Republics possessing territory west of the Urals (Armenia, Azerbaijan, Belarus, Georgia, Kazakhstan, Moldova, Russia, and Ukraine) with a view to allocating weapon entitlements among themselves (set out in the Tashkent Agreement of 15 May 1992) for purposes of implementation. These allocations and the rights and obligations of the new States Parties were recognized by all Treaty members at their extraordinary meeting in Oslo, on 5 June 1992.[248]

Whilst much of this practice was set out by the ILA Committee, it was not entirely clear as to what conclusions were to be drawn from it. Reading between the lines, its general conclusion appears to have been that this practice essentially represented something that approximated a principle of obligatory continuity (following Stern) which, on the one hand, demonstrated a belief that continuity of such obligations was a necessity, whilst accepting, on the other, that adjustments necessarily had to be made in respect, for example, of matters such as arms quotas. Of course, this was not the only construction that could be placed upon such practice; indeed it might have been equally plausible to suggest that, on this evidence, there could be no succession to disarmament treaties as a consequence of the very 'personal' or 'political' character of those agreements. But such a suggestion, no doubt, was unappealing to the ILC Committee for the reason that it might seem to have implied a lack of concern for the problem of disarmament. What is very clear, however, is that as in case of its discussion of territorial régimes the Committee's commitment to minimize disruption to existing international relations was not necessarily to be achieved through the mechanism of succession.

[244] cit.

[245] Bunn and Rhinelander, above, n 24, p 340.

[246] Memorandum of Understanding Relating to the Treaty between the United States of America and the Union of Soviet Socialist Republics on the Limitation of Anti-Ballistic Missile Systems on 26 May 1972, 26 Sep 1997.

[247] 30 ILM (1991) 1.

[248] Similarly, when the Czech and Slovak Republics became separate States Parties, on 1 Jan 1993, their accession to the CFE Treaty was approved on 5 Feb 1997 and details of the division of the obligations of former Czechoslovakia were formalized accordingly.

The final category identified by the ILA Committee was one which had become a fairly consistent subject of attention in the literature on succession during the 1990s. A number of commentators – including Kamminga,[249] Simma,[250] Shaw,[251] Mullerson,[252] and Stern[253]– observed what they saw to be an emergent principle of automatic continuity in case of treaties of a humanitarian nature. Once again, this was frequently to be expressed in guarded or hesitant form (sometimes as an evolving principle, sometimes as a obligation to ensure continuation rather than specifically succession), and once again, the initial tone appeared to be set by the EC's guidelines on the recognition of new States in which recognition was made explicitly conditional upon respect for the provisions of the UN Charter, the Helsinki Final Act, and the Charter of Paris 'especially with regard to the rule of law, democracy, and human rights'.[254]

Kamminga was the one who sought to develop this idea most fully. He began his analysis with a reference back to Jenks's argument for automatic continuity in case of 'law-making' treaties.[255] Whilst Jenks's argument was undoubtedly influential, it had also been decried by commentators such as O'Connell as essentially confusing the relationship between conventional and customary international law – the 'law-making treaty' as a category was not something that was possible to comprehend in formal terms.[256] What Kamminga took from Jenks' article, however, was the idea that certain international instruments may effectively 'vest' rights in individuals or organizations. This he developed more generally into the idea that rights under human rights treaties were unaffected by State succession on the basis of the doctrine of acquired rights as recognized by the PCIJ in the *German Settlers* case.[257] Whilst he noted that the PCIJ was concerned, in that case, with property rights, he went on to suggest that:

As a matter of fact, private rights may consist not only of property rights but also of claims against other individuals and claims against the State. In this day and age, the most important category of rights that may be invoked against the State consists of basic human rights and fundamental freedoms deriving from both customary and treaty

[249] Kamminga, above, n 31.
[250] B Simma, 'From Bilateralism to Community Interest in International Law', 250 Hague Recueil (1994) 217, p 357.
[251] M Shaw, 'State Succession Revisited', 5 FinnYIL (1994) 34, p 84 ('One is on the verge of widespread international acceptance of the principle that international human rights treaties continue to apply within the territory of a predecessor state irrespective of a succession.').
[252] Mullerson, above, n 24, pp 154–8 ('New States should be born not only into general international law but also into those international human rights treaties which were obligatory for their predecessors.').
[253] Stern, above, n 2, pp 295–310.
[254] Above, n , p 1497. C Warbrick, 'Recognition of States: Part 2', 42 ICLQ (1993) 433.
[255] W Jenks, 'State Succession in Respect of Law-Making Treaties', 29 BYIL (1952) 105.
[256] O'Connell, above, n 106, p 5.
[257] *Settlers of German Origin in the Territory Ceded by Germany to Poland,* 1923 PCIJ, Series B, no 6.

law (including, but certainly not limited to, the right to own property). The doctrine of acquired rights therefore applies *a fortiori* with respect to human rights.[258]

Kamminga then supported this argument with an analysis of practice. He noted that the policy of both the ILO and the ICRC[259] had been to insist, or at least encourage, succession to ILO conventions and the Geneva Conventions respectively, and noted also the stance adopted by the UN Human Rights bodies in which they had insisted upon succession.[260] This was then bolstered by a discussion of the practice of the Czech and Slovak Republics, the FRY, the States emerging from the former USSR, and Hong Kong.[261] He concluded, in consequence that 'State practice during the 1990s strongly supports the view that obligations from a human rights treaty are not affected by a succession of States'.[262] This furthermore, occurred *ipso iure*, so there was no obligation to confirm that succession nor was there need for any consent from other parties.[263]

Other authors were certainly more muted on this score and the ILA Committee itself came to the rather cautious conclusion that even if doctrine appeared to be generally favourable to continuity in respect of human rights treaties, State practice was far from homogenous. Whatever else, it could not yet be regarded as a principle of customary international law.[264] In respect of the practice of the States emerging from the USSR and the SFRY the ILA Committee drew attention, first of all, to the fact that in many cases in which such States had notified their succession to human rights agreements, the date indicated for succession was that of their notification of succession rather than that of the moment of independence. This was to suggest that those notifications constituted something approximating a form of accession.[265] Secondly, it also noted that in many cases, such States deliberately chose to become party to such instruments by way of accession rather than succession. Thus, in case of the Genocide Convention of 1948, Slovenia, Bosnia-Herzegovina, the Czech Republic, and Slovakia all notified the depositary of their succession, whilst Armenia, Moldova, Georgia, and Azerbaijan all chose to accede to the Convention. It was also pointed out, that the dispute over Serbia and Montenegro's claim to continuity had spilled into dispute within

---

[258] ibid 473.

[259] H Coursier, 'Accession des nouveaux Etats africains aux Conventions de Genève', AFDI (1961) 760; B Zimmermann, 'La succession d'Etats et les Conventions de Genève' in Swinarski (ed), *Studies and Essays in Honour of Jean Pictet* (1984) 113.

[260] Commission on Human Rights, Resn 1993/23, 5 Mar 1993; Resn 1994/6, 25 Feb 1994; Resn 1995/18, 24 Feb 1995. CERD, General Recommendation XII (42), UN doc E/CN4/1995/80, para 7. For a discussion of the positions of various states in respect of Serbia and Montenegro's status as party to the International Covenant on Civil and Political Rights (1966) see, *Application for Revision of the Judgment of 11 July 1996*, ICJ Rep 2003, 7, p 18, para 36.

[261] J Chan, 'State Succession to Human Rights Treaties: Hong Kong and the International Covenant on Civil and Political Rights', ICLQ (1996) 928.

[262] ibid 482.

[263] ibid.

[264] ILA Committee, Final Report, above, n 8, p 620.

[265] ibid 619.

the UN Commission on Human Rights concerning its entitlement to be listed as party to human rights agreements without having notified its succession to those agreements.[266] As it happens, some of the States objecting to Serbia and Montenegro's claims in this respect, later reversed their position in 2001 when Serbia and Montenegro purported to accede to the Genocide Convention with a reservation to Article IX.[267]

The most vehement of critics of the general thesis of automatic succession was Rasulov, who suggested that there was remarkably little evidence in practice for any such contention. Starting with the proposition that automatic succession in its purest sense requires no notification (and further to this, that an act of notification of succession constitutes a *de novo* expression of consent)[268] the only instance he identified was that of Bosnia-Herzegovina's submission of a report to the Human Rights Committee prior to any notification of succession.[269] But even when he broadened the terms of the idea of automatic succession he was to identify little de facto continuity in the form of notifications of succession. His analysis of human rights and humanitarian treaties, in fact, showed that only a handful of states (Croatia, Slovakia, Bosnia-Herzegovina, Croatia, Slovenia, and the former Yugoslav Republic of Macedonia) had consistently become party by way of notification of succession, whilst several others (Armenia, Azerbaijan, Moldova, Uzbekistan, and Georgia) appeared never to have indicated their succession to such treaties, always opting, by contrast, to become party by accession.[270] Only in case of the Czech and Slovak Republics' position in relation to the European Convention on Human Rights was he to admit that something approximating automatic succession to human rights treaties appeared to have taken place.[271]

One possible objection to Rasulov's critique might be to suggest that, for all the emphasis he places upon the apparently voluntary character of successor States' decisions to accede rather than succeed to human rights and humanitarian agreements, ultimately, continuity of such commitments was clearly ensured. Stern takes up this point, suggesting that rather than think about succession in terms of automaticity, one might consider it as an obligation, the fulfilment of which might be achieved in various different ways (for example through accession as well as succession). Of course, in order to move in that direction, Stern needed to rely upon something other than practice itself – and here, she appeared to draw upon some of the ideas mooted by Judge Weeramantry in his Separate Opinion in the 1996 Bosnia case[272] – that tied an obligation of continuity or

---

[266] eg Declaration of Croatia, UN doc E/CN4/1995/121, p 2. Stern, pp 299–302.

[267] Application for Revision of the Judgment of 11 Jul 1996, ICJ Rep 2003, 7, p 22, para 53.

[268] A Rasulov, 'Revisiting State Succession to Humanitarian Treaties: Is There a Case for Automaticity?', 14 EJIL (2003) 141, p 148.

[269] UN doc E/CN4/1995/80.

[270] Rasulov, above, n 268, pp 159–65.

[271] ibid.

[272] Weeramantry, Separate Opinion, ICJ Rep 1996, 640, pp 645–52.

succession to the specific character of human rights treaties.[273] In Stern's case, she was to suggest that, just as territorial treaties seem to constitute objective régimes for the benefit of the members of the international community, so also, human rights treaties created objective régimes in favour of the individuals whose rights were the subject of protection, and in virtue of which they could be said to create a series of obligations which a successor State was not at liberty to ignore.[274] Support for this contention came in the form of the ICJ's classic statement in the Reservations case as regards the functionally specific character of the Genocide Convention as one concerned with the 'common interest' rather than the upholding of reciprocal rights and obligations[275] (a description which has subsequently been generalized across a range of human rights and humanitarian treaties).[276]

Of course, whether or not one could properly equate the idea of an objective régime with the non-reciprocal character of human rights treaties, Stern's arguments in this regard paralleled those of Kamminga (and endorsed by Rasulov) in his attempt to make an association between human rights on the one hand, and the doctrine of acquired rights on the other. The common feature of such arguments is to try to avoid the problem of succession as one of seeking to identify the existence of *external* obligations that are to be assumed on the part of the successor State (demonstrated, for example, by State practice), by suggesting that the very rights or entitlements of the successor State (ie what it may claim in the name of sovereignty) is already *internally* limited. This idea, of course, has certain parallels not only with old patrimonial principles such as *res transit cum suo onere*, but also with contemporary arguments about the right of intervention in case of States abusing human rights.[277] Most problematic, however, is the apparent revitalization of the doctrine of acquired rights which, as seen above, was regarded by many in the 1960s as a neo-colonial subterfuge, the purpose of which would be to continue imperial forms of domination and exploitation through private rather

[273] The reasons for this he saw 'partly on the basis that all definitions are hazardous and partly because many of those multilateral treaties are not limited in their object and purpose but are "multi-purpose"; and partly because many multilateral treaties, alongside their normative provisions as such, also contain procedural provisions applicable as between their parties – for example, in the case of the Genocide Convention... the provision conferring jurisdiction on the International Court'. Rosenne, above, n 135, p 103.

[274] Stern, above, n 2, pp 309–10.

[275] *Reservations to the Convention on the Prevention and Punishment of the Crime of Genocide, Advisory Opinion*, ICJ Rep, 1951, p 23, 'In such a Convention the contracting States do not have any interests of their own; they merely have, one and all, a common interest, namely, the accomplishment of those high purposes which are the *raison d'être* of the convention. Consequently in a convention of this type one cannot speak of individual advantages or disadvantages to States, or of the maintenance of a perfect contractual balance between rights and duties'.

[276] M Craven, 'Legal Differentiation and the Concept of the Human Rights Treaty in International Law' 11 EJIL (2000) 489.

[277] eg W Reisman, 'Sovereignty and Human Rights in Contemporary International Law', 84 AJIL (1990) 866.

than public relations.[278] That it re-appeared in such startling form in the 1990s, and came to be associated with the question of succession to human rights treaties, is only to draw attention to two perhaps contradictory ideas. On the one hand is the evident possibility of a continuing link between the 19th-century imperial project, and that associated with 'humanitarianism' in the 21st century, in which an emphasis on the continuity of individual rights only highlights the perceived frailty or authoritarianism of the newly emergent governments. On the other hand, however, it also seems to draw attention to the definitively 'post-colonial' orientation of the contemporary scene, which enables the existence of such parallels to remain entirely undisclosed (or if disclosed, irrelevant).

6. Conclusions

For most of those working on succession after 1989, the problem was how to square what they knew about the subject (for which the 1978 Convention was always a convenient starting point) with what appeared to be happening around them. For some, this was evidently a problem-solving exercise (for example, what might be the best posture to adopt in relation to participation in the NPT?), for others it was a question of principle (the consequences of unlawful annexation of the Baltic Republics), for others still it was simply a matter of mapping out what was taking shape by reference to the existing tenets of State succession as they saw them. With certain rare exceptions, it was the dissimilarity between past and contemporary practice that seemed most marked. There was no need to deal with the amorphous status of entities such as protectorates or mandated territories, no (or at least very little) anxiety as to the imperial orientation of Soviet rule, no sense that international law in a broader sense needed to be reshaped in light of what had happened. Even where there might have been certain obvious parallels with what had happened during decolonization, there appears to have been an intuitive resistance to recognizing their existence.

One salient example concerns the question of self-determination. As has been seen, this was a central principle around which much of the ILC's work in relation to decolonisation was structured. Yet, in the 1990s, although self-determination was vigorously debated in certain contexts (for example, in relation to the putative emergence of a right of secession,[279] or as a modification to principles of recognition)[280] it was rarely, if at all, seen to be relevant in relation to the discussion of succession.[281] A curious example of the discursive separation of the two ideas is found in the proceedings of the American Society of International Law in 1992 in

---

[278] See above, pp 82–90.

[279] eg A Cassese, *Self-Determination of Peoples: A Legal Appraisal* (1998).

[280] eg Crawford, *The Creation of States in International Law* (2nd edn 2006).

[281] An clear example of this is to be found in Mullerson, above, n 24, pp 58–91, 137–59 (in which he deals with self-determination and succession in entirely separate chapters).

which a panel of experts was asked to address contemporaneous issues of succession.[282] Half the panel seemed to understand the brief and spoke about the law of State succession;[283] the other half addressed, by contrast, the question of self-determination and secession.[284] For all the obvious lack of organization, the most striking feature of the panel discussion was that there was no apparent correspondence, or semblance of dialogue, between the two groups: they were simply addressing entirely separate issues. This, of course, was quite evocative in terms of what the various commentators seemed to see as happening around them in the 1990s. Whereas at the time of decolonization, self-determination appeared to be an idea associated with resistance to colonial domination, the consequences of which meant not merely self-government, but also a right to reshape (parts of) the legal environment in which that independence was to be achieved. In the 1990s, by contrast, self-determination seemed to mean *only* the right to self-government: the networks of legal relations pre-existing independence were not to be discarded or set aside, but were rather to be treasured as a final bulwark against an ever present threat of anarchy or lawlessness. The 'clean slate', so far as it had ever existed in the imagination of international lawyers, was a doctrine of a bygone era, to be overcome by progressive law-making.

In some senses this changing orientation to the question of succession was determined by an overtly pragmatic, policy driven, sensibility that cared little for historic precedent and which was decisively concerned, by contrast with the problems of the contemporary scene. It made little sense, in seeking to secure a stable international environment in the aftermath of the collapse of what many referred to as a bi-polar international order, to look for insights or solutions from the entirely different historical process of decolonisation. It also appeared anachronistic to have resort to the kinds of discussions of neo-imperialism that characterized debate in the 1960s and 1970s. The point was not that the Empire of the Soviet Union differed in so may respects from the imperial projects of colonization, but that there was no sense that international law itself was complicit in the process of subjugation – indeed, there was always the example of the Baltic States whose independence seemed to represent the triumph of an anti-imperial legality. It is not surprising, therefore, that O'Connell's approach to the question of succession found fertile ground: it could be adopted and redeployed without any sense of irony or scepticism.

But at the same time, this was a time of anxiety as to how precisely these intuitions could be shaped within the existing discourse of international law. To begin with, the simultaneous advocacy of an emergent presumption of treaty continuity, together with the identification of an expanded category of treaties to which succession would be automatic, was perhaps indicative of a 'belt and

---

[282] 86 AmSocIL Proc, 1 Apr (1992) 1.
[283] Rhinelander, 'Remarks' ibid 6; Williamson, 'Remarks', ibid 10; Crawford, 'Remarks', ibid 15.
[284] Albright, 'Remarks' ibid 1; Hamilton, 'Remarks', ibid 4.

braces' approach to succession: if not like this, then like that. But it was also indicative of a continuing insecurity as to how the evidence for one or other might be marshalled: what could one read into the fact that so many successor States chose to accede rather than succeed to international agreements? What, furthermore, could be made of the very fact of notification itself (did this imply that in absence of notification, no succession would take place)? What conclusions could be drawn from the practice of depositaries in that respect? Ultimately, it was evident that all such practice was open to quite contrasting conclusions which, of course, was to infuse all speculation as to the existence or otherwise of rules of continuity or even non-continuity with a polemical character. What appeared to matter, more than anything else, were the questions of policy: it was surely desirable, above all else, to insist upon the continuity of human rights agreements or more generally, multilateral treaties as a whole, than to suggest there might exist appropriate reasons for favouring their discontinuity.

Yet, at the same time, it was evident that a reprisal of O'Connell's position seemed, in some respects, too radical to be fully embraced. Just as much as he decried the falsity, or self-serving character of the differentiation between State and governmental succession, or that between the categories of succession and continuity, so also it seemed they could not be so easily dismissed. Too much still seemed to ride upon the distinction – whether in terms of failing to give appropriate recognition to the strength of nationalist fervour that underpinned claims to independence in Riga or Zagreb, or in terms of the need to address particular distributional issues such as the Belgrade government's access to gold reserves in bank accounts in London or Zurich.[285] Unless the law of succession was reformed in advance of such events, it was hard for anyone to take the stance that logic or analysis seemed to require. But of course, such arguments about continuity of personality, were really just arguments about change. Denial of Serbia's claim to identity with the former SFRY was in reality an argument about the significance of what had occurred in the territory of the latter during the early 1990s and an insistence upon its moral and political responsibility for the conflict; acquiescence in the Baltic Republics' claims to continuity was really an argument as to the momentous changes that had occurred in the USSR and the unsustainability of any claim to continue existing legal relations as if nothing had happened. So for those who were busy advocating the necessity of legal continuity in the turbulent changes that had enveloped Europe, there was also a sense that O'Connell's prescription really demanded too much. Change was also required, but it came in the form not of a law of succession as such, but in an apparently prior deliberation as to status the determination of which was to take place within the halls of international institutions.

---

[285] eg *In re AY Bank* [2006] EWHC 830 (Ch); *Republic of Croatia v Girocredit Bank AG der Sparkassen* (1997) 36 ILM 1520.

Conclusions

In his classic work, *Ancient Law*, Sir Henry Maine suggested that the hallmark of 'modern' society was found in the idea that whereas 'old law fixed a man's social position irreversibly at his birth, modern law allows him to create it for himself by convention'.[1] The imperative law of the sovereign which characteristically assigned power and authority in terms of birth and privilege had given way, in the name of emancipation, to an enlargement of the province of contract. This was such that:

> legislation has nearly confessed its inability to keep pace with the activity of man in discovery, in invention, and in the manipulation of accumulated wealth; and the law even of the least advanced communities tends more and more to become a mere surface stratum, having under it an ever-changing assemblage of contractual rules with which it rarely interferes except to compel compliance with a few fundamental principles, or unless it be called in to punish the violation of good faith.[2]

Whatever might be said of Maine's thesis in light of the vast expansion of State regulatory power and authority in the 20th century, his insights had particular resonance in the continuing debate over slave-holding in the late 19th century to which he consistently referred, and may also have been significant in the development of the post-industrial free market economy. In an entirely different sense, however, it may also be seen to have significance as regards the similar process of emancipation occurring in the middle of the 20th century in the form of decolonization, and for more recent debates concerning the putative 'fragmentation' of international law in the early 21st century.[3]

A large part of Maine's discourse on the development of contract law was concerned with tracing the sequential changes in the conception of the contract in Roman law. He was to observe that the idea of the contract was to begin to have an independent life of its own after its initial disassociation from the institution of the conveyance (the *mancipatio*). This 'emancipation' of the contract (its literal sense being 'out' or 'away' from the transfer of property) signalled, as far as Maine was concerned, something considerably more than an incidental change in the structure or conception of the contract, and was indicative also of a profound

---

[1] H Maine, *Ancient Law* (1861) (1920) 319.

[2] ibid 320.

[3] M Koskenniemi, *Fragmentation of International Law: Difficulties Arising from the Diversification and Expansion of International Law* UN Doc A/CN4/L682 (2006) reprinted (2007).

change occurring in the nature of social and commercial relations which had hitherto been dominated by a variety of hierarchical relations of authority (in the notions of _dominium, imperium, manus_ and _mancipatio_). The formal emancipation of the contract, in other words, connoted a more general social emancipation, and a move away from a hierarchical social order constructed in terms of ownership and inherited authority to one more profoundly egalitarian, premised upon the equal capacity of members of that society to promise and contract as autonomous, free-willing individuals. Ultimately, for Maine, the real meaning of emancipation seemed to be bound up with this idea of contractual autonomy.[4]

There are several features of Maine's account that appear to have significance in the context of the present project. To begin with, it is clear that as with Maine's account of emancipation, decolonization seemed to represent not only a move out of, or away from, a condition of ownership (the transformation of the colony from a piece of land to independent agent), but a broader transformation of international society from one premised upon hierarchy or status, to one that envisaged the independent contractual authority of the newly independent States as free agents in an undifferentiated world of sovereign equals. A necessary part of this change was to occur through the process of _self_-determination (which, in truth, was never really one of self determination, but merely _of_ determination) by which the colonized periphery was ascribed a transitional, aspirant, status as a way of pushing through the promise of 'national liberation'. A necessary consequence also, was the ability thereafter of the newly independent States to form their own contracts and promises, to develop their own position in the world independently of the conditions prescribed for them in virtue of their dependency. Viewed in terms of Maine's account, in other words, the new prerogatives of sovereignty, equality, and independence that were understood to be the outcome of decolonization were to find their parallels in the simultaneous development of the idea of the treaty as a 'contractual bargain': the capacity to promise, and be bound by promises, was the hallmark of freedom.[5]

Yet, for all the apparent simplicity of this story of emancipation it is evident that the story of decolonization was somewhat more complex. It may certainly be said that, by the inter-war years, international lawyers had increasingly sought to liberate the idea of the treaty as a 'contractual bargain'[6] from the evident role that such agreements had formerly played in the maintenance of a certain balance of

---

[4] Maine, above, n 1, pp 349, 373.

[5] cf W Jenks, 'State Succession in Respect of Law-Making Treaties', 29 BYIL (1952) 105, p 108 ('The obligations of multipartite legislative instruments are not, however, badges of continuing servitude; they are a necessary part of full cooperation in the international community and participation in them must therefore be regarded as _one of the hallmarks of emancipation_'. [emphasis added]).

[6] H Lauterpacht, _Private Law Sources and Analogies of International Law_ (London: Longmans, 1927) pp 155–67; A McNair, 'So-Called State Servitudes', 6 _British Yearbook of International Law_ (1925) 111, p 122 ('Most treaties or conventions between States are jurisprudentially contracts, and the private law of contract has proved an important source of rules for their formation, interpretation and dissolution'.).

power.[7] This encouraged, in fact, the development of a series of subtle doctrinal initiatives – the reformulation of the idea of revision into the doctrine of changed circumstances, and the formalization of the idea of consent to avoid the problem of 'lawful coercion'.[8] It may also have been the case that this insistence on consent and autonomy might have been indirectly related to what was happening in the colonies. But what occurred at the same time, however, was a simultaneous recognition of the highly variegated nature of the treaty. In an article written in 1930, McNair lamented international lawyers' reliance upon a singular set of universal rules when dealing with 'the only and sadly overworked instrument with which international society is equipped for the purpose of carrying out its multifarious transactions', vis 'the treaty'.[9] For McNair, various distinctions had to be recognized – between the 'conveyance' or the 'charter of incorporation' and the 'contract', between the 'contract' and the 'law-making treaty', and between treaties creating 'constitutional international law' and those creating or declaring 'ordinary international law'. Such distinctions, for McNair, all had a significance that went far beyond their mere form, and affected questions such as their interpretation, their continued applicability during war, their effects on third parties, and the possibilities arising for unilateral termination. He concluded by arguing that 'we' (international lawyers) needed to 'free ourselves from the traditional notion that the instrument known as the treaty is governed by a single set of rules, however inadequate, and set ourselves to study the greatly differing legal character of the several kinds of treaties and to frame rules appropriate to the character of each kind'.[10] What one finds, in other words, is that at precisely the same moment at which decolonization seemed to indicate a disciplinary move from 'status to contract' (read as a shift from 'subordination' to 'autonomy'), there was a simultaneous move to disaggregate the contract to allow the reassertion of a link between the contract and the conveyance. This was to take place, most

---

[7] Carty notes that 'both Britain and her opponents saw individual treaties in nineteenth century Europe as part of a framework of treaties which were to reflect as well as to maintain a material distribution of power' (A Carty, *The Decay of International Law* (1986) p 67). Bederman similarly notes that peace treaties 'were respected in an almost metaphorical way: they embodied the Concert of Europe'. D Bederman, 'The 1871 London Declaration, *Rebus Sic Stantibus* and a Primitivist View of the Law of Nations', 82 AJIL (1988) 1, p 7 . The 'realist' strain in 19th-century thought in this respect survived, in certain quarters, well into the 20th century. eg J Stone, 'De Victoribus Victis: The International Law Commission and Imposed Treaties of Peace', 8 VaJIL (1967–68) 356, pp 357, 358 ('While finding it morally outrageous that...a treaty should be legally binding even if imposed at the end of a war by a victorious "aggressor" on the victim of "aggression" [the writer has] seen no way of rescuing mankind *by legal precept* from this particular kind of outrage.... [There is no way] *whereby international law can summon sufficient power to defeat every victor at the moment of his victory*').

[8] M Craven, 'What Happened to Unequal Treaties? The Continuities of Informal Empire', 74 Nordic JIL (2005) 335.

[9] A McNair, "The Functions and Differing Legal Character of Treaties", 11 BYIL (1930) 100, p 101. See also, Réglade, 'De la Nature juridique des Traités internationaux et du sens de la distinction des traités-lois et des traits-contrats', 41 RDPSP (1924) 505.

[10] ibid 118.

overtly, in the form of Jenks's thesis relating to 'law-making treaties',[11] but it was also evident in the subsequent identification of a broad category of dispositive agreements whose terms would remain 'unaffected' by a succession of States. The story, in other words, was not one of pure emancipation, but of controlled, regulated, and disciplined independence, in which the question of status continued to be controlled through the medium of the treaty.

By the middle of the 1950s, many scholars were largely disenchanted with what they took to be the 'received tradition' of State succession which appeared either to confirm or deny the possibility of the inheritance of rights and obligations. Both positions were too absolute, too imbued with a speculative metaphysics, and far too concerned with questions of identity and personality at the expense of the needs or demands of 'international law' or the 'international community'. The emergent scholarship did not seek entirely to supplant or displace the idea of sovereignty as an idea that might influence the outcome of decisions concerning succession, but rather sought to set against the idea of 'sovereign autonomy', a range of ideas that stressed in its place, the perceived needs of individuals and societies in the world community and the changing environment of multilateral law making. The eyes were thus turned away from the structuring capacity of 'sovereignty' or 'personality' as an idea determining the outcome of decisions about succession (which might, or might not, endorse claims to autonomy or freedom from compulsory inheritance) to a demand for continuity based upon 'naturalized' arguments about the needs of the international community, the very pre-existence of which, made succession effectively non-negotiable.

Nevertheless, that it was still possible to speak about sovereign autonomy *and* the ordering capacity of international law, meant that the old opposition between advocates of the 'clean slate' and advocates of 'continuity' continued in revised form throughout the era of decolonization. However, it was at this moment that the politics of succession, so long buried beneath a formal and abstract rhetoric of statehood, sovereignty, and personality, came to life. Here, for the first time, it was possible to recognize what seemed to be at stake. On the one side was a neo-imperial rhetoric allied contiguously with the 'interests of the international community' and private entitlement. On the other side was an authoritarian rhetoric allied with what seemed to be an irredeemably formalist idea of 'statehood' and/ or sovereignty. In the crucible of the 'exception' was to be found a battle over the 'soul' of international law – a battle in which the radicals were apt to assume the garbs of 'tradition', and the neo-imperialists, those of a 'modernizing' tendency attuned to the dignity and interests of the individual.

The project of codification during the 1960s and 1970s situated itself within this battleground, the results of which appeared, on the face of it at least, to fall decisively on the side of the anti-colonial movement. This was represented, most

---

[11] Above, n 5.

obviously, in the vindication of Waldock's modified version of the principle of the 'clean slate' in case of newly independent States (Articles 16 and 17 of the Vienna Convention) even if that was tempered by the almost inevitable qualifications concerning 'territorial' and 'boundary' agreements, and even if the question as to what might constitute a 'dependent territory' for such purposes was never entirely clear. It was also apparent in Waldock's cursory dismissal of the legal significance of the various techniques that had been employed to ensure the survival of agreements and other rights and obligations on independence (devolution agreements and unilateral declarations) despite the fact that they had largely shaped outcomes up to that point.

One obvious qualification, however, has to be made to any such assessment. As many contemporaneous commentators unceasingly pointed out, by the time at which Waldock was drafting the Convention, many of his final conclusions were effectively rhetorical. Far from it being the case that the practice of decolonization was structured around the principle of the clean slate (or his version thereof), it was all too apparent that in only a very small minority of cases had newly emergent States rejected in their entirety existing international obligations. His argument that this was a matter of consent rather than obligation was only to go so far as to cast a shadow over the possible future relevance of that practice (which he ultimately admitted was to be the case in only few instances). It did, nevertheless, appear to give sustenance to the idea that what had, *in fact*, taken place was a process of decolonization in the name of self-determination. This was evidently important as a way of maintaining a continued commitment to the project on the part of the most important of the ILC's constituencies (the various organs of the United Nations General Assembly), and perhaps also as a way of ensuring that there would be no scope for revisiting existing settlements. But it was also a means of being seen to eradicate from the project – and from international law more generally –any final traces of neo-colonial influence. Only by the formal enunciation of this idea could it consistently be maintained, as Bedjaoui would have it, that the UN Charter had ushered in an era definitively opposed to colonialism. That this was ultimately a largely presentational position, however, also gave succour to those who may have, for one reason or another, been distrustful of the implications of leaving such decision-making authority entirely to the 'newly independent States' themselves.

In effect, what Waldock achieved was to capture, within the framework of a single convention, two largely inconsistent ideas: the first being that anti-colonial self-determination was a process which had marked, in revolutionary manner, the end of international law's surrogate relationship with colonialism and which had also ushered in a new era in which the ideals laid down in the United Nations Charter (sovereign equality, self-determination, and equal rights) could be brought into fruition. Against this, however, was the idea that the revolution had also been managed in a way that effectively denied its incipient radicalism: far from being a threat to international law and order, it had been thoroughly normalized even before the moment at which the revolution was proclaimed. The latter promulgation, thus, assumed the character of a revisionist gloss whose true implications were already lost to history, but which nevertheless represented a necessary ideological move to secure the socialization of new States into an international order whose decisive character remained the same.

When faced with this history, international lawyers in the 1990s were already fully primed in terms of their intuitive response to the events arising. Certainly the events themselves were radical enough, certainly also they seemed to usher in a new era of international law, but there was no 'baggage' here so to speak. It was not the case that the discipline had to divest itself of responsibility for the creation of the 'Soviet empire' (as it was sometimes referred to), nor any of the excesses of soviet rule (the Baltic Republics being a significant exception). There was thus no reason to insist upon the radically disruptive nature of its demise, or to characterize that moment as one requiring the transformation of international law *per se*. If anything, it seemed to be a moment of optimism and hope, in which old aspirations for an international order governed by and through effective global institutions could be dusted off and revived.[12]

This was to have particular consequences for the way in which scholars approached the question of succession. First of all, and most obviously, it precluded the need to speak about succession in terms of a radical disruption of legal relations. All were agreed that the 'new events' were profoundly different from the past, and the sense of contestation that had underpinned discussions during decolonization was almost entirely absent. There was no Bedjaoui insisting upon the reformulation or restructuring of international law to bring it into line with a postcolonial consciousness, no Nyerere denouncing the validity of agreements entered into by colonizing powers. Only in case of the Baltic States were arguments about discontinuity prevalent, but it was clear that what was being advanced, here, was less the idea of a reformist agenda associated with a general reshaping of the international legal order along new lines, and rather more a vindication of a pre-existent international legal status that had been submerged by the violence of occupation. This idea, of course, came to be expressed *outside* the context of the law of State succession – this was not a case of 'succession' at all, we were told, merely a refusal to admit the consequences of an unlawful occupation. The kind of disruption of legal relations that this appeared to entail, however, was far more radical and disjunctive than anything scholars had advocated during decolonization,[13] and far less concordant with the prevailing normative advocacy of the time.

Secondly, O'Connell's arguments about the social necessity of continuity and the relative value of the arguments about sovereignty or status, could all thereby be revived without any sense that this was the continuation of some kind

---

[12] M Koskenniemi, 'Why History of International Law Today?, 4 *Rechtsgeschichte* (2004) 61, pp 64–5.
[13] Whereas, it might be said, decolonization seemed to represent a vindication of autonomy and independence through, or in the name of, international law; the Baltic Republics represented the vindication of international law through, or in the name of, their autonomy and independence.

of neo-imperial dogma. On the one side there was a universal distrust of the principle of the 'clean slate', and a persistent search for evidence of continuity. Automatic continuity of treaty relations, nevertheless, was not an inevitable option – there would always be 'problems' to be addressed (such as in case of the idea of non-proliferation in the NPT, or in the determination as to whether a state was still a 'riparian State') – and it was fully apparent that resort was had to bilateral negotiation as a way of dealing with such issues. But this was just to signal, if nothing else, the sterility of much of the subsequent discussion. Arguments for continuity thus merged into arguments about functional specialization: the importance being to identify different kinds of treaty relations, in relation to which different kinds of legal response would be demanded.

On the other side, the absence of any obvious sense of contestation was to confirm the relativity of arguments about 'personality' and its correlates ('identity' and 'continuity'). The decision, for example, as to whether the unification of East and West Germany might be understood in terms of the formation of an entirely 'new' State, the resurrection of the old Reich, or by way of the absorption of the former by the latter, was one that could be addressed largely in managerial terms: how best to square the profound social and political changes that were in the process of taking place, with an evident desire to maintain intact the existing array of legal relations within which both were enmeshed. The framework chosen – that of 'absorption' – thus seemed to represent more a *technique* or *method* of overcoming the difficulties of merger, than as expressive of the *social ontology* of unification (what it seemed to mean in social, cultural, or historic terms) and it dealt very neatly with the obvious difficulties that might otherwise have arisen as regards German membership in international organizations such as the European Union. This was not, as many were keen to point out, a case of 'annexation' with all the obvious implications that such a term might have brought with it; it was still 'unification', albeit one of a special kind. That this approach to unification had, as some pointed out, certain unmistakable consequences – particularly as regards the non-continuity of the treaties of the former GDR – was notably not a cause of much anxiety, even if commentators were otherwise fully committed to ensuring the 'stability of expectations'.

The one obvious exception concerned the case of Serbia and Montenegro. Here, unlike any of the other claims to identity or continuity advanced at the time (on the part of Germany, Russia, Yemen etc) the issue was subject to significant contestation. The issue, of course, had all kinds of historical connotations – relating, for example, to the nature of the Socialist Federal Republic of Yugoslavia as a federal union, or to the process by which Yugoslavia came into being in the early parts of the 20th century – but it also had, more obviously, connotations relating to on the one hand, Serbia's right to defend its territorial integrity as against the secessionist movements and, on the other, Serbian claims in respect of assets and institutional membership. For all the pervasive scepticism as to the utility of arguments about status or identity, here at least the issue was hard to avoid: apart from anything else, it seemed to condition the outcome of a number of cases pending before the International Court of Justice. What one might discern in the discussion on this issue, however, were two things. First was the way in which the point of contestation relating to the problem of territorial change had subtly moved away from an argument about the substance of the law of succession, back to an argument about status. However far the international community was committed to ensuring the continuity of existing legal relations, Serbia and Montenegro's claim to continuity was one that effectively denied the possibility of the utilization of the law of State succession as a disciplinary tool. Resistance to that stance on the part of its European and North American counterparts can be read, therefore, as an insistence that Serbia and Montenegro's relationships with the outside world needed to be renegotiated. Far from it being the case that legal continuity will invariably be treasured, on some occasions, it seems, such continuity might actively be denied.

The second feature of the case of Serbia and Montenegro to be remarked upon was that the contestation over its claim to continuity took place in the context of institutional membership: the overt reason for which being the widely held belief that there could be no possibility of automatic succession to constituent instruments of international organizations. On the one hand this is to signal the continuing importance of the category of 'personal' treaties for purposes of managing processes of political change. It was here rather than, for example, in relation to Serbia's participation in multilateral human rights agreements, that the real force of the dispute could be felt. On the other hand, however, it also highlights the key role that international organizations now seem to assume in the context not merely of attributing a decisive character to the nature of the crisis, but also in the subsequent distributional issues concerning the external 'patrimony' of the State. The meaning of becoming independent, in other words, seems to have largely coalesced around the ideas of institutional membership and entitlement to overseas assets.

So where, finally, might one place the experience of decolonization in the context of the developing law of State succession, as experienced through the lens of late 20th-century transition? How might this story retain some relevance? One way to tell the story is by reviving Schmitt's analysis of the early 20th century, and to conceive of the current projects of succession as concerned with the instantiation of a temporal and spatial bulwark – between decolonization in the periphery of Empire on the one hand, and transition in the European heartland on the other. This may be such as to emphasize, in some ways, a thoroughly modernist agenda: decolonization representing the move from pre-modern to modern forms of statehood and self-government, recalling in the process a mythic foundational moment of autochthonous law-making; transition, by contrast, representing a move between alternative forms of the modern nation-State (in relation to which international law had always assumed a position of neutrality). On such an account, the context in which rules of succession might be thought to operate would be primarily a spatial one, determined by reference to the old standards of civilization and/or economic development: continuity would be sought and demanded in those contexts in which common principles of economic order or civilization might prevail, but might otherwise be dispensable or resisted elsewhere. If this were the case, of course, one could not look at European transition as anything other than just a highly contingent mode of political change.

Another way of telling the story is by way of revitalizing a sense of tragedy or loss. What might be said here is that whilst during the period of decolonization, the real meaning and implications of the law of State succession were to be clear, the sharpness of that agenda has since dissipated to be replaced by a species of pragmatic functionalism in which it is impossible to determine in any particular case what is at stake: whether continuity or discontinuity is to be preferred, or who may be empowered to make such decisions. The general insistence upon the need for legal continuity seems to be undermined by a simultaneous insistence that continuity cannot always be taken for granted. On one side the resort to negotiation, the application of principles of equity and the advocacy of functionalism and régime specificity have undermined in their turn, the general commitment to continuity rather than change. On another side, the need to uphold the values of the international system itself has given rise to arguments for legal change in a much more profound way than was ever admitted in the context of decolonization. In a plural and divided universe of régimes and institutions, thus, the scope for a univocal law of succession has largely disappeared. With it, also, the opportunity to articulate within that same language, opposition to the knowledge formations that are produced therein.

Select Bibliography

STUDIES AND REPORTS

Bedjaoui, M., 'First Report on Succession of States in Respect of Rights and Duties Resulting from Sources other than Treaties', UN Doc A/CN4/204 and Corr1, Yrbk ILC, 1968, II, 94.

—— 'Second Report on Succession of States in Respect of Matters other than Treaties – Economic and Financial Acquired Rights and State Succession', UN Doc A/CN4/216/ Rev 1, Yrbk ILC, 1969, II, 70.

—— 'Third Report on Succession of States in Respect of Matters other than Treaties', UN Doc A/CN4/226 Yrbk ILC, 1970, II, 131.

—— 'Fourth Report on Succession of States in Respect of Matters other than Treaties', UN Doc A/CN4/247 and Add1, Yrbk ILC, 1971, II, 157.

—— 'Fifth Report on Succession of States in Respect of Matters other than Treaties', UN Doc A/CN4/259 Yrbk ILC, 1972, II, 61.

—— 'Sixth Report on Succession of States in Respect of Matters other than Treaties', UN Doc A/CN4/267 Yrbk ILC, 1973, II, 9.

—— 'Seventh Report on Succession of States in Respect of Matters other than Treaties', UN Doc A/CN4/282 Yrbk ILC, 1974, II, 93.

—— 'Eighth Report on Succession of States in Respect of Matters other than Treaties', UN Doc A/CN4/292 Yrbk ILC, 1976, II, 57.

—— 'Ninth Report on Succession of States in Respect of Matters other than Treaties', UN Doc A/CN4/301 and Add1, Yrbk ILC, 1977, II, 49.

—— 'Tenth Report on Succession of States in Respect of Matters other than Treaties', UN Doc A/CN4/313, Yrbk ILC, 1978, II, 230.

—— 'Eleventh Report on Succession of States in Respect of Matters other than Treaties', UN Doc A/CN4/322 and Corr1 and Add1 and 2, Yrbk ILC, 1979, II, 68.

—— 'Twelfth Report on Succession of States in Respect of Matters other than Treaties', UN Doc A/CN4/333 Yrbk ILC, 1980, II, 1.

—— 'Thirteenth Report on Succession of States in Respect of Matters other than Treaties', UN Doc A/CN4/345 and Add1–3, Yrbk ILC, 1981, II, 4.

Declaration on the Consequences of State Succession for the Nationality of Natural Persons, European Commission for Democracy through Law, 28th mtg, Venice 13th–14th September. 1996.

Fitzmaurice, G., 'Second Report on the Law of Treaties', UN Doc A/CN4/107, Yrbk ILC, (1957) II (ii), 16.

—— 'Fourth Report on the Law of Treaties', UN Doc A/CN4/120, Yrbk ILC, (1959) II (ii) 37.

—— 'Fifth Report on the Law of Treaties', UN Doc A/CN4/130, Yrbk ILC, (1960) II, ii, 72.

ILA Committee on the Succession of New States to the Treaties and Certain other Obligations of their Predecessors, 'Interim Report', 52 ILA Rep Conf 14th–20th Aug (1966) p 574.

ILA Committee on the Succession of New States to the Treaties and Certain other Obligations of their Predecessors, 'Interim Report and Draft Resolutions', 53 ILA Rep Conf 25th–31st Aug (1968) 596.

ILA Committee on the Succession of New States to the Treaties and Certain other Obligations of their Predecessors, 'Report', 54 ILA Rep Conf 23rd–29th Aug (1970) 101.

ILA Committee on the Succession of New States to the Treaties and Certain other Obligations of their Predecessors, 'State Succession and Governmental Contracts' 55 ILA Rep Conf 21st–26th Aug (1972) 654.

ILA Committee on Aspects of the Law of State Succession, 'Rapport Préliminaire sur la succession d'Etats en matière de traités', 68 ILA Rep Helsinki Conference (1996) 655.

ILA Committee on Aspects of the Law of State Succession, 'Rapport intérimaire sur la succession en matière de traités constitutifs d'organisations internationals et de traités adoptés au sein des organisations internationales', 69 ILA Rep Taipei Conference (1998) 615.

ILA Committee on Aspects of the Law of State Succession, 'Rapport Final Sur La Succession en Matiere de Traites', 70 ILA Rep New Delhi Conference (2002) 574.

ILA Committee on Aspects of the Law of State Succession, 'Aspects of the Law of State Succession: Provisional Report', 71 ILA Rep Berlin Conference (2004) 16.

ILC Draft articles on the Nationality of Natural Persons in Relation to the Succession of States (1999), 54 GAOR, Supp no 10 (UN Doc A/54/10). GA Resn 55/153, 12th Dec 2000, Annex.

ILC Draft Articles on the Law of Treaties, Yrbk ILC (1966) II.

ILC Draft Articles on State Succession in Respect of Treaties, Yrbk ILC (1974) II, i, 174.

Institut de Droit International, 'State Succession in Matters of Property and Debts', (Vancouver Session, 2001).

Mikulka, V., 'First Report on State Succession and its Impact on the Nationality of Natural and Legal Persons', A/CN4/467, Yrbk ILC 1995, II.

—— 'Second Report', A/CN4/474, Yrbk ILC, 1996, II.

—— 'Third Report', A/CN4/480, Yrbk ILC, 1997, II.

—— 'Fourth Report on Nationality in Relation to the Succession of States', A/CN4/489, Yrbk ILC, 1998, II.

UN Secretariat, 'Survey of International Law in Relation to the Work of Codification of the International Law Commission', UN Doc A/CN4/1, (5th November 1948), reissued under symbol UN Doc A/CN4/1/Rev 1, 10th February. 1949.

UN Secretariat, 'Digest of the Decisions of International Tribunals Relating to State Succession', UN Doc A/CN4/151 (1962).

UN Secretariat, 'Succession of States in Relation to General Multilateral Treaties of which the Secretary-General is the Depositary', UN Doc A/CN4/150 (1962).

UN Secretariat, 'The Succession of States in Relation to Membership in the United Nations', UN Doc A/CN4/149 and Add 1 (1962).

UN Secretariat, 'Succession of States in Respect of Bilateral Treaties', UN Doc A/CN4/229, Yrbk ILC, 1970, II, 102.

UN Secretariat, 'Succession of States in Respect of Bilateral Treaties – Second and Third Studies', UN Doc A/CN4/243 and Add 1, Yrbk ILC, 1971, II, 111.

Vallat, 'First Report on Succession of States in Respect of Treaties', UN Doc A/CN4/278, and Add 1–6, Yrbk ILC, 1974, II.

Waldock, H., First Report on the Law of Treaties, UN Doc A/CN4/144, Yrbk ILC, (1962) II (ii) 27.

—— 'Second Report on the Law of Treaties', UN Doc A/CN4/156, Yrbk ILC, (1963), II, 36.

—— 'Third Report on the Law of Treaties', UN Doc A/CN4/167, Yrbk ILC, (1964), II, 26.

—— 'Fourth Report on the Law of Treaties', UN Doc A/CN4/177, Yrbk ILC, (1965) II (ii) 3.

—— 'Fifth Report on the Law of Treaties', UN Doc A/CN4/183, Yrbk ILC, (1966) II (ii) 51.

—— 'First Report on Succession of States and Governments in Respect of Treaties', UN Doc A/CN4/202, Yrbk ILC (1968) II, 87.

—— 'Second Report on Succession in Respect of Treaties', UN Doc A/CN4/214 and Adds 1 & 2, Yrbk ILC (1969) II, 45.

—— 'Third Report on Succession in Respect of Treaties', UN Doc A/CN4/224, and Add1, Yrbk ILC (1970) II, 25.

—— 'Fourth Report on Succession in Respect of Treaties', UN Doc A/CN4/249, Yrbk ILC (1971) II, 143.

—— 'Fifth Report on Succession in Respect of Treaties', UN Doc A/CN4/256 and Add 1–4, Yrbk ILC (1972) II, 1.

BOOKS AND ARTICLES

Acquaviva, G., 'The Dissolution of Yugoslavia and the Fate of its Financial Obligations', 30 DenvJILP (2002) 93.

Agrawala, S., 'The Doctrine of Act of State and the Law of State Succession in India', 12 ICLQ (1963) 1399.

Alexandrowicz, C., *An Introduction to the History of the Law of Nations in the East Indies* (Oxford: Clarendon Press, 1967).

Anghie A., *Imperialism, Sovereignty and the Making of International Law* (Cambridge: Cambridge University Press, 2004).

Anzilotti, D., *Cours de Droit International* (trad Gidel G., Recheil Sirey, Paris 1929).

Aust A., *Modern Treaty Law and Practice* (Cambridge: Cambridge University Press, 2000).

Baty T., *Canons of International Law* (London: John Murray, 1930).

'The Obligations of Extinct States' 35 Yale LJ (1926) 434.

'Division of States: Its Effect on Obligations' 9 Grot Soc Trans (1924) 119.

Baxter, Q., 'The Duty of Obedience to the Belligerent Occupant', 27 BYIL (1950) 235.

Beato, A., 'Newly Independent and Separating States' Succession to Treaties: Considerations on the Hybrid Dependency of the Republics of the Former Soviet Union', 9 Am UJILP (1994) 525.

Beckett, W., 'Decisions of the Permanent Court of International Justice on Points of Law and Procedure of General Application', 11 BYIL (1930) 1.

Bederman, D., 'The 1871 London Declaration, *Rebus Sic Stantibus* and a Primitivist View of the Law of Nations', 82 AJIL (1988) 1.

Bedjaoui M., *Law and the Algerian Revolution* (Brussels: International Association of Democratic Lawyers, 1961).
—— 'Problèmes Récents de Succession d'Etats dans Les Etats Nouveaux', 130 Hague Recueil (1970) 463.
Bello, E., 'Reflections on Succession of States in the Light of the Vienna Convention on Succession of States in Respect of Treaties 1978', 23 German YIL (1978) 296.
Benvenisti E., *The International Law of Occupation* (Princeton: Princeton University Press, 1992).
Berman, N., 'In the Wake of Empire', 14 Am ULR (1998–99) 1523.
—— 'Sovereignty in Abeyance: Self-Determination and International Law', 7 Wisc ILJ (1988–89) 51.
Blum, Y., 'UN Membership of the "New" Yugoslavia: Continuity or Break?', 86 AJIL (1992) 830.
'Russia Takes over the Soviet Union's Seat at the United Nations', 3 EJIL (1992) 354.
Bluntschli J., *Das moderne Völkerrecht der civlisirten Staten als Rechtsbuch dargestellt* (Nördlingen: Beck, 1867).
—— *Le Droit International Codifié* (trans. Lardy M., 3rd ed, Paris: Librairie de Guillaumin, 1881).
Bojanic, M., 'Éléments d'Appréciation de la Practique Étatique en Matière de Succession aux Traités de la République Socialiste Féderative de Yugoslavie', 33 RBDI (2000) 489.
Bokor-Szegö H., 'Identity and Succession of States in Modern International Law', in Bokor-Szegö (ed.). *Questions of International Law: Hungarian Perspectives* (Dordrecht, Neth.: Martinus Nijhoff, 1986) 15.
—— *Les Problèmes de la Succession d'Etats et la Convention relative à la navigation sur le Danube.*
Bos, A., 'Statenpvolging in het bijzonder met betrekking tot verdragen', 111 Mededelingen van de Nederalandse Vereniging voor Internationaal Recht (1995) 55.
Bothe, M., 'Belligerent Occupation' 4 Encyclopedia PIL (1982) 65.
—— and Schmidt C., 'Sucessions d'États', 96 RGDIP (1992) 812.
Brierly J, *The Law of Nations*, (Waldock, 6th ed., Oxford: OUP, 1963).
Briggs, H., 'Non-Recognition in the Courts: the Ships of the Baltic Republics', 37 AJIL (1943) 585.
—— 'Unilateral Denunciation of Treaties: The Vienna Convention and the International Court of Justice', 68 AJIL (1974) 51.
Broms, B., 'The Agreement on the Foundations of Relations between the Republic of Finland and the Russian Federation', 3 Finn YIL (1992) 615.
Brownlie, I., *Principles of Public International Law* (Oxford: OUP, 3rd edn, 1979).
—— 'The Calling of the International Lawyer: Sir Humphrey Waldock and his Work', 54 BYIL (1984) 7.
—— *Principles of Public International Law* (Oxford: OUP, 5th edn, 1998).
Bühler, K., 'State Succession, Identity/Continuity and Membership in the United Nations' in Koskenniemi, M and Eisemann P., *State Succession: Codification Tested Against the Facts* (Dordrecht, Nijhoff, 1997), p 187.
—— *State Succession and Membership in International Organizations: Legal Theories Versus Political Pragmatism* (The Hague: Kluwer Law, 2001).

Bunn, G. and Rhinelander J., 'The Arms Control Obligations of the Former Soviet Union', 33 Va JIL (1993) 323.

Bynkershoek C. van, *Quaestiones Juris Publici*, (Oxford: Clarendon Press, 1737; London: Milford 1930).

Caflisch, L., 'The Law of State Succession: Theoretical Observations', 10 Ned TIR (1963) 337.

—— 'Unequal Treaties', 35 German YIL (1992) 52.

Caggiano, G., 'The ILC Draft on the Succession of States in Respect of Treaties: A Critical Appraisal', 1 Italian YIL (1975) 69.

Cain, P., and Hopkins, A., *British Imperialism: Innovation and Expansion, 1688–1914* (London: Longmans, 1993).

Cansacchi, G., 'Identité et continuité des sujets internationaux' 130 Hague Recueil (1970) 1.

Carty, A., *The Decay of International Law* (Manchester: Manchester University Press, 1986).

Cassese, A., *Self-Determination of Peoples: A Legal Appraisal* (Oxford: Oxford University Press, 1998).

Castrén, E., 'Aspects Récents de la Succession d'Etats', 78 Hague Recueil (1951) 385.

—— 'Obligations of States Arising from the Dismemberment of Another State, 13 ZaöRV (1951) 753.

—— 'On State Succession in Practice and Theory', 24 Nord TIR (1954) 67.

Cavaglieri A., 'La dottrina della successione di stato a stato e il suo valore giuridico' 13 Archivio Giuridico (3d ser 1910) 297.

—— 'Regles générales du droit de la paix' 26 Hague Recueil (1929) 311.

Chan, J., 'State Succession to Human Rights Treaties: Hong Kong and the International Covenant on Civil and Political Rights', 45 ICLQ (1996) 928.

Chen L., *State Succession Relating to Unequal Treaties* (Hamden, Conn.: Archon 1974).

Cheng T-H, *State Succcession and Commercial Obligations* (Ardsley Park: Transnational Publishers, Inc., 2006).

Cohen, F., 'Transcendental Nonsense and the Functional Approach', reprinted in Cohen, L. (ed) *The Legal Conscience: Selected Papers of Felix S Cohen* (1960).

Cohen, R., 'Legal Problems arising from the Dissolution of the Mali Federation', 36 BYIL (1960) 375.

Cotran, E., 'Some Legal Aspects of the Formation of the United Arab Republic and the United Arab States', 8 ICLQ (1959) 346.

Coursier, H., 'Accession des nouveaux Etats africains aux Conventions de Genève', 7 AFDI (1961) 760.

Craven, M., 'The European Community Arbitration Commission on Yugoslavia', 66 BYIL (1995) 333.

—— 'Legal Differentiation and the Concept of the Human Rights Treaty in International Law' 11 EJIL (2000) 489.

—— 'What Happened to Unequal Treaties? The Continuities of Informal Empire', 74 Nord JIL (2005) 335.

Crawford, J., 'The Contribution of Professor DP O'Connell to the Discipline of International Law', 51 BYIL (1980) 2.

—— 'Remarks', 86 ASIL Procs (1992).

Crawford, J., *The Creation of States in International Law* (Oxford: Clarendon Press, 1979. 2nd edn, 2005).

Crusen, G., 'Les Servitudes Internationales', 22 Hague Recueil (1928) 31.

Czaplinski, W., 'Quelques aspects juridiques de la réunification de l'Allemagne', 36 AFDI (1990) 89.

—— 'La continuité, l'identité et la succession d'Etats – Evaluation de cas récents', 26 RBDI (1993) 374.

—— 'Equity and Equitable Principles in the Law of State Succession' 12 Development and International Cooperation (1996) No 23.

Debbasch, O., *L'Occupation militaire -Pouvoirs reconnus aux forces armées hors de leur territoire national* (Paris: Librairie Générale de Droit et de Jurisprudence, 1962).

Decamps, P., 'La définition des droit acquis', 15 RGDIP (1908) 385.

Degan, V., 'La Succession d'États en Matière de Traités et les États Nouveaux (Issue de L'Ex-Yougoslavie)', 42 AFDI (1996) 206.

—— 'Création et disparation de l'état (à la lumière du démembrement de trois federations multiethnique en Europe' 279 Hague Recueil (1999) 94.

Detter, I., 'The Problem of Unequal Treaties', 15 ICLQ (1966) 1069.

Dickinson E., *The Equality of States in International Law* (Cambridge, Mass.: Harvard University Press 1920).

Donati D., *Stato e territorio* (Rome: 1924).

Donner R., *The Regulation of Nationality in International Law* 2nd ed., (Irvington–on–Hudson: Transnational Publishers, 1994).

Dunsdorfs E., *The Baltic Dilemma. The Case of the de iure Recognition by Australia of the Incorporation of the Baltic States into the Soviet Union* (New York: Robert Spellers & Sons, 1975).

Eisemann, P., 'Rapport du directeur d'études de la section de la langue français du Centre' in Koskenniemi, M., and Eisemann, P., *State Succession: Codification Tested Against the Facts* (The Hague, Martinus Nijhoff: 1997) 3.

Elias, T., 'The Contribution of Asia and Africa to the Contemporary International Law' 16 Africa Quarterly (1976) 1.

Elsuwege, P., 'State Continuity and its Consequences: The Case of the Baltic States', 16 Leiden JIL (2003) 377.

Esgain A., 'Military Servitudes and the New Nations', in O'Brien (ed.). *The New Nations in International Law and Diplomacy* (London: Stevens, 1965) 42.

Evans, L., 'The General Principles Governing the Termination of a Mandate', 26 AJIL (1932) 735.

Fauchille, P., *Traité de Droit International* Public (Rousseau and Co, Paris, 1922) I.

Feilchenfeld E., *Public Debts and State Succession* (New York: Macmillan, 1931).

Fiore P., *Traité do droit international public européen et américain: suivant les progrès de la science et de la pratique contemporaines* (Paris: Pedone-Lauriel, 1885).

Fischer, G., 'L'indépendance de la Guinée et les accords franco-guinéens', 4 AFDI (1958) 711.

Fitzmaurice, G., 'The Juridical Clauses of the Peace Treaties', 73 Hague Recueil (1949) 259.

Fitzmaurice, G., 'The Law and Procedure of the International Court of Justice: International Organizations and Tribunals' 29 BYIL (1952) 1.

Flauss, J., 'Convention européenne des droits de l'homme et succession d'Etats aux traités: une curiosité, la décision du Comité des Ministres du Conseil de l'Europe en date du 30 Juin 1993 concernant la République tchèque et la Slovaquie', 6 RUDH (1994) 1.

Foucault M. 'Neitzsche, Genealogy, and History' in Rabinov P. (ed.). *The Foucault Reader* (Harmondsworth: Penguin, 1986) 76.

Franck T., *The Power of Legitimacy Among Nations* (New York: Oxford University Press, 1990).

Fricker K., *Vom Staatsgebeit, Gebiet und Gebietshoheit* (Stuttgart: J.B. Metzler, 1867).

Frowein, J., 'Germany Reunited' 51 Zäo RV (1991) 333.

—— 'The Reunification of Germany', 86 AJIL (1992) 152.

Gabba, C., 'Successione di Stato a Stato', in *Questioni di diritto civile* (2nd edn, 1885).

Gallagher, J., and Robinson R., 'The Imperialism of Free Trade', 6 *Economic History Review* (1953) 1.

Gamarra, Y., 'Current Questions of State Succession Relating to Multilateral Treaties', in Koskenniemi, M. and Eisemann, P., *State Succession: Codification Tested Against the Facts* (The Hague, Martinus Nijhoff: 1997) 387.

Gareis C. *Institutionen des Völkerrechts: ein kurzgefasstes Lehrbuch des positiven Völkerrechts in seiner geschichtlichen Entwicklung und heutigen Gestaltung* (Giessen, 1888).

Gautron, J., 'Sur Quelques Aspects de la Succession d'Etats au Sénégal' 12 AFDI (1966) 836.

Gentili A., *De Jure Belli Libri Tres* (1612, trans. Rolfe, Oxford: Clarendon Press, 1964).

Gidel, G., *Des Effects de l'annexation sure les concessions* (1904) unpublished doctoral thesis.

Gierke, O. von, *Die Genossenschaftstheorie und die deutsche Rechtsprechung* (Berlin: Weidmann, 1887).

—— *Natural Law and the Theory of Society 1500–1800* (trans. Barker E., Cambridge: Cambridge University Press, 1934).

Gong G., *The Standard of Civilisation* (Oxford: Clarendon Press, 1984).

Goy, R., 'La Réunification du Yémen', 36 AFDI (1990) 249.

—— 'L'Indépendence de l'Erythrée', 39 AFDI (1993) 337.

Graber D., *The Development of the Law of Belligerent Occupation 1863–1914: A Historical Survey* (New York: Columbia University Press, 1949).

Green L. 'The Dissolution of States and Membership of the United Nations', in Code Holland R. and Schwarzenberger G., *Law, Justice and Equity* (London: Pitman, 1967).

Grotius H., *De Jure Belli ac Pacis*, (1646, ed. & trans. F. Kelsey; Oxford: Oxford University Press, 1925).

Gruber, A., *Le Droit International de la Succession d'Etats* (Brussels, Bruylant, 1986).

Grzybowski, *Soviet Public International Law. Doctrines and Diplomatic Practice* (Leyden: Sijthoff, 1970).

Guggenheim P., *Traité de Droit International Public avec mention de la pratique internationale et suisse* (Genève: Georg, 1953).

Guyomar, G., 'La Succession d'Etats et le respect de la volonté des populations', 67 RGDIP (1963) 93.

Hackworth G., *Digest of International Law* (Washington, D.C.: U.S. Government Print Office, 1940–44).

Hafner, G. and Kornfeind, E., 'The Recent Austrian Practice of State Succession: Does the Clean Slate Still Exist?', ARIEL 1996/1, 1.

Hall W., *A Treatise on International Law* 4th ed. (Oxford: Clarendon Press, 1895).

Heilbronner, K., 'Legal Aspects of the Unification of the Two German States' 2 EJIL (1991) 18.

Henrich W., *Theorie des Staatsgebietes, entwickelt aus der Lehre von den lokalen Kompetenzen der Staatsperson* (Wien, 1922).

Hershey, A., 'The Succession of States', 5 AJIL (1911) 285.

Heyland C., *Die Rechtsstellung de besetzten Rheinlande nach dem Versailler Friedensvertrag und dem Rheinlandabkommen, zugleich ein Beitrag zur Lehre von der Besetzung fremden Staatsgebietes* (Stuttgart: W. Kohlhammer, 1923).

Hobson J., *Imperialism: A Study* (London: A. Constable, 1905).

Hoeflich, M., 'Through a Glass Darkly: Reflections Upon the History of the International Law of Public Debt in Connection with State Succession', Uni Ill L Rev (1982) 39.

Holtzendorff F von *Handbuch des Völkerrechts: Auf Grundlage europäischer Staatspraxis* (Berlin: C. Habel 1885–1889).

Hough, W., 'The Annexation of the Baltic States and its Effect on the Development of Law Prohibiting Forcible Seizure of Territory', 6 NYLSJICL (1985) 301.

Huber M., *Die Staatensuccession: völkerrechtliche und staatsrechtliche Praxis im 19. Jahrhundert* (Leipzig, 1898).

Hurst, C., 'State Succession in Matters of Tort', 5 BYIL (1924) 163.

International Law Association, *The Effect of Independence on Treaties* (London: Stevens, 1965).

Jacqué, J-P., 'German Unification and the European Community', 2 EJIL (1991) 1.

Jayakumar, S., 'Singapore and State Succession: International Relations and Internal Law', 19 ICLQ (1970) 398.

Jellinek G, *Allgemein Staatslehre* (Berlin: Springer, rev. 1905).

Jenks W., 'State Succession in Respect of Law-Making Treaties', 29 BYIL (1952) 105.

—— *The Common Law of Mankind* (London: Stevens, 1958).

Jennings R., *The Acquisition of Territory in International Law* (Manchester University Press: Oceana Publications, 1963).

Jennings R, and Watts A. *Oppenheim's International Law* 9th ed. (Harlow: Longman, 1992). I & II.

—— 'General Course on Public International Law', 121 Hague Recueil (1967) 112.

Jolowicz, H., *Historical Introduction to the Study of Roman Law* (Cambridge: Cambridge University Press, rev.1954).

Kaekenbeeck, G., 'The Protection of Vested Rights in International Law', 17 BYIL (1936) 1.

Kaikobad, K., 'Some Observations on the Doctrine of Continuity and Finality of Boundaries', 54 BYIL (1984) 119.

Kamminga, M., 'State Succession in Respect of Human Rights Treaties', 7 EJIL (1996) 469.

Keith A., *The Theory of State Succession with Special Reference to English and Colonial Law* (London: Waterlow and Sons, Ltd., 1907).

Keith, K., 'Succession to Bilateral Treaties by Seceding States', 61 AJIL (1967) 521.

Kellner H., *Language and Historical Representation: Getting the Story Crooked* (Madison: University of Wisconsin Press, 1989).

Kelsen H., *Principles of International Law* (New York: Rinehart & Co., 1952).

Kelsen H., *The Pure Theory of Law* 2nd ed. (trans. Knight, Berkeley, Los Angeles: University of California Press, 1964).

Kerikmae T., and Vallikivi H., 'State Continuity in the Light of Estonian Treaties Concluded before World War II', 5 Juridica International (2000) 35.

Kherad, R., 'La Reconnaisance Internationale des Etats Baltes', 96 RGDIP (1992) 843.

Kiatibian S., *Conséquences juridique des trans.formations territoriales des états sur les traités* (Paris: A. Giard et E. Brière, 1892).

Klabbers J., Koskenniemi M., Ribbelink O. and Zimmermann A., *State Practice Regarding State Succession and Issues of Recognition* (The Hague: Kluwer, 1999).

Kloppneberg J., *Uncertain Victory. Social Democracy and Progressivism in European and American Thought 1870–1920* (Oxford: Oxford University Press, 1986).

Klüber J, *Droit des Gens Moderne de L'Europe* (Paris: Guillaumin et cie, 1861).

—— *Europäishes Völkerrecht* (Schotthausen: Hurter 1951).

Kohen, M., 'Le Problème des frontiers en cas de dissolution et de separation d'Etats: quelles alternatives?' 31 RBDI (1998) 129.

Kooijmans P., 'State Succession and the 1929 Warsaw Convention: a Case Study', in Masson-Zwaan T and Mendes de Leon P. (eds.). *Air and Space Law: De Lege Ferenda* (The Netherlands: Martinus Nijhoff, 1992). 113

Korovin, E., 'Soviet Treaties and International Law', 22 AJIL (1928) 763.

Koskenniemi, M., and Eisemann, P., *State Succession: Codification Tested Against the Facts* (Dordrecht, Nijhoff, 1997).

Koskenniemi, M., and Lehto, M., 'La succession d'Etats dans l'ex-URSS, en ce qui concerne particulièrement les relations avec la Finlande', 38 AFDI (1992) 182.

Koskenniemi M., 'The Wonderful Artificiality of States: Theoretical Perspectives on the Transformation of Sovereignty', 88 Proc ASIL (1994) 22.

—— 'Report of the Director of Studies of the English-speaking Section of the Centre', in Koskenniemi M and Eisemann, *State Succession: Codification Tested Against the Facts* (The Hague: Martinus Nijhoff, 1997). 65

—— *The Gentle Civiliser of Nations: The Rise and Fall of International Law 1870–1960* (Cambridge: Cambridg University Press, 2002).

—— 'Why History of International Law Today?, 4 *Rechtsgeschichte* (2004) 61.

—— *Fragmentation of International Law: Difficulties Arising from the Diversification and Expansion of International Law* UN Doc A/CN4/L682 (2006) reprinted (2007).

Kratochwil, F., 'The Limits of Contract', 5 EJIL (1994) 465.

Kunz, J., 'Identity of States under International Law', 49 AJIL (1955).

—— 'Une Nouvelle Théorie, de L'Etat Fédéral', 11 RDILC (1930) 835.

La Forest, G., 'Towards a Reformulation of the Law of State Succession', 60 ASIL Procs (1966) 103.

Laband P, *Das Staatsrecht des deutschen Reiches* 5th ed. (Freiburg i. B., 1911).

Lagarde E., *La Reconnaissance des Soviets*, (Paris, 1924).

Lauterpacht, E., 'The Contemporary Practice of the United Kingdom in the Field of International Law: Survey and Comment, VI' 7 ICLQ (1958) 515.

—— *Jerusalem and the Holy Places* (London: Anglo-Israel Association, 1968).

Lauterpacht, H., *Private Law Sources and Analogies of International Law* (London: Longmans, 1927).

—— *The Function o f Law* (Oxford: Clarendon Press, 1933).

—— *Recognition in International Law* (Cambridge: Cambridge University Press, 1947).

Lauterpacht, H. *The Development of International Law by the International Court* (London: Stevens, 1958).

—— 'The Grotian Tradition in International Law', in Falk R., Kratochwil F., and Mendlovitz S. (eds) *International Law: A Contemporary Perspective* (Boulder: Westview Press, 1985) 10.

Lavalle, R., 'Dispute Settlement under the Vienna Convention on Succession of States in Respect of Treaties', 73 AJIL (1979) 407.

Lee K-G., *The Law of State Succession in the Post-Decolonisation Period with Special Reference to Germany and the former Soviet Union*, Unpublished Thesis, University of Cambridge, (1998).

Lehto, M., 'Succession of States in the Former Soviet Union', 4 Finn YIL (1993) 194.

Lenin, V. 'Imperialism: The Highest Stage of Capitalism', in 1 *Collected Works of V.I. Lenin* (1917) 495.

Lester, A., 'Bizerta and the Unequal Treaty Theory', 11 ICLQ (1962) 847.

—— 'State Succession to Treaties in the Commonwealth' 14 ICLQ (1965) 476.

Lissitzyn, J., 'Territorial Entities other than Independent States in the Law of Treaties', 125 Hague Recueil (1970) 64.

Lissitzyn, O., 'Recent Soviet Literature on International Law', 11 American Slavic and East European Review (1952) 268.

Liszt F. von, *Das Völkerrecht. Systematisch dargestellt* 12th ed. (Berlin: Häring, 1898).

Lloyd, D., 'Succession, Secession, and State Membership in the United Nations', 26 NYUJILP (1993–4) 763.

Löning, O., 'Das Subjekt de Staatsgewalt im besetzten feindlichen Gebiet', 28 Zeitschrift IR (1920) 287.

Love, L., 'International Agreement Obligations After the Soviet Union's Break-up: Current United States Practice and Its Consistency with International Law', 13 Vand JTL (1993) 373.

MacDonagh, O., 'The Anti-Imperialism of Free Trade', 14 Economic History Review (1962) 489.

Maine H., *Ancient Law* (1861). (London: Dent, 1917).

Makarov, A., 'Les Changements territoriaux et leurs effets sur les droits des particuliers', Annuaire Institut de Droit International (1950) 208.

Makonnen Y., *International Law and the New States of Africa* (Addis Ababa: UNESCO, 1983).

—— 'State Succession in Africa', 200 Hague Recueil (1986) 97.

—— 'Namibia: Its International Status and the Issues of State Succession', 3 Lesotho LJ (1987) 183.

Malenovsky, J., 'Problèmes juridicques liés à la partition de la Tchécoslovaquie', 39 AFDI (1993) 305.

Malone, M., 'Succession of States in Respect of Treaties: The Vienna Convention of 1978', 19 VaJIL (1978–79) 885.

Maluwa, T., 'Succession to Treaties and International Fluvial Law in Africa: The Niger Regime', 33 Neth. ILR (1986) 334.

Mann, F., 'The Assignability of Treaty Rights' 30 BYIL (1953) 475.

Marcoff M., *Accession à l'indépendance et succession d'Etats aux traités internationaux* (Fribourg: Editions Universitaires, 1969).

Marek, K., *Critique of Political Economy* (1859) Preface.

—— *Identity and Continuity of States in Public International Law* (Genève: Librairie E. Droz, 1954).

Martens F. de, *Traité du Droit International* (Paris, 1883-7).

Martens G. de, *Précis du droit des gens moderne de l'Europe* 2nd ed. (Paris: Guillaumin et cie, 1864).

Mazzini, G., 'The Duties of Man', in Dahbour, O., and Ishay, M., (eds) *The Nationalism Reader* (1995) 87.

McNair, A., 'So-Called State Servitudes', 6 BYIL (1925) 111.

—— "The Functions and Differing Legal Character of Treaties", 11 BYIL (1930) 100.

—— *The Law of Treaties* 2nd ed. (Oxford: Oxford University Press, 2nd ed. 1938).

—— 'The Effects of Peace Treaties upon Private Rights', 7 Cam LJ (1939–41) 379.

—— 'Aspects of State Sovereignty', 29 BYIL (1949) 6.

—— 'The General Principles of Law Recognised by Civilized Nations' 33 BYIL (1957) 1.

Meissner B, *Die Sowjetunion, die baltischen Staaten und das Völkerrecht* (Köln: Verlag für Politik und Wirtschaft, 1956).

Menon P., *The Succession of States in Respect to Treaties, State Property, Archives and Debts* (New York: Edwin Mellen Press, 1991).

Mériboute Z., *La Codification de la succession d'états aux traités* (Paris: Presses Universitaires de France, 1984).

Mervyn Jones, J., 'State Succession in the Matter of Treaties', 24 BYIL (1947) 360.

Miéville, C., *Between Equal Rights: A Marxist Theory of International Law* (London: Pluto Press, 2005).

Moore J, *Digest of International Law* (Washington, D.C.: U.S. Government Print Office, 1906).

Moore, R., 'Imperialism and "Free Trade" Policy in India, 1853–4', 17 *Economic History Review* (1964) 135.

Morgenstern, F., 'Validity of Acts of the Belligerent Occupant', 28 BYIL (1951) 291.

Morgenthau H., *Die internationale Rechtspflege: ihr Wesen und ihre Grenzen* (Leipzig: R. Noske, 1929).

—— *Politics Among Nations: The Struggle for Power and Peace* (London: McGraw-Hill, 1993).

Mullerson, R., 'New Developments in the Former USSR and Yugoslavia', 33 Va JIL (1992–3) 299.

—— 'The Continuity and Succession of States by Reference to the Former USSR and Yugoslavia', 42 ICLQ (1993) 473.

—— *International Law, Rights and Politics: Developments in Eastern Europe and the* CIS (New York: Routledge, 1994).

Muralt R. de, *The Problem of State Succession with Regard to Treaties* (The Hague: W.P. Van Stockum, 1954).

Mushkat, R., 'Hong Kong and Succession of Treaties', 46 ICLQ (1997) 181;

Mutua, M., 'Why Redraw the Map of Africa: A Moral and Legal Inquiry', 16 Mich JIL (1994–05) 1113.

Myers P., *Succession between International Organizations* (New York: Kegan and Paul International, 1993).

Nahlik, S., 'The Grounds of Invalidity and Termination of Treaties', 65 AJIL (1971) 736.

Nathan, E., 'The Vienna Convention on Succession of States in Respect of State Property, Archives and Debts', *International Law in a Time of Perplexity, Essays in Honour of Shabtai Rosenne* (Leiden, Brill: 1989) 489.

Nozari F., *Unequal Treaties In International Law* (Stockholm: Stockholm University, 1971).

O'Connell, D., 'State Succession in the British Commonwealth since the Second World War' 26 BYIL (1949) 454.

—— 'Economic Concessions in the Law of State Succession', 27 BYIL (1950) 93.

—— 'Secured and Unsecured Debts in the Law of State Succession', 27 BYIL (1951) 204.

—— 'A Re-consideration of the Doctrine of International Servitude', Canadian Bar Review (1952) 807.

—— ''Change of Sovereignty and the Doctrine of Act of State', 26 Aust LJ (1952–3) 201.

—— *The Law of State Succession* (Cambridge: Cambridge University Press, 1956).

—— 'Independence and Succession to Treaties', 38 BYIL (1962) 84.

—— 'State Succession and Entry into a Composite Relationship', 39 BYIL (1963) 54.

—— 'State Succession and Problems of Treaty Interpretation' 58 AJIL (1964) 41.

—— 'Independence and Problems of State Succession', in W. O'Brien, (ed.), *The New Nations in International Law and Diplomacy* (London: Stevens, 1965). 7

—— *International Law* (London: Stevens, 1965). I & II

—— *State Succession in Municipal and International Law* (Cambridge: Cambridge University Press, 1967). I and II.

—— 'Recent Problems of State Succession in Relation to New States', 130 Hague Recueil (1970) 95.

—— 'State Succession and the Theory of the State', Grot Soc Trans (1972) 23.

—— 'Reflections on the State Succession Convention', 39 Zaö RV (1979) 725.

Oakshott M., *On Human Conduct* (Oxford: Clarendon Press, 1973).

Oeter, S., 'German Unification and State Succession', 51 Zaö RV (1991) 349.

—— 'State Succession and the Struggle Over Equity: Some Observations on the Laws of State Succession with Respect to State Property and Debts in Case of Separation and Dissolution of States', 38 German YIL (1995) 73.

Onuma, Y., 'Nationality and Territorial Change: In Search of the State of the Law', 8 Yale JWPO (1981) 1.

Oppenheim L. *International Law*: A Treatise (London: Longmans, Green & Co., 1905). I

—— 'The Legal Relations between an Occupying Power and the Inhabitants', 33 LQR (1917) 364.

—— *International Law: A Treatise* 7th ed. (London: Longmans, Lauterpacht, 1952).

—— *International Law: A Treatise* 8th ed. (London, Longmans, Lauterpacht, 1955).

Pagani, F., 'Identité et succession d'Etats aux instruments conventionnels relatifs au désarmement et à la maîtrise des armements', in Koskenniemi, M., and Eisemann, P. (eds). *State Succession: Codification Tested Against the Facts* (The Hague, Martinus Nijhoff: 1997), 437.

Papenfuß D., *Die Behandlung der völkerrechtlichen Verträge der DDR im Zuge der Herstellung der Einheit Deutschlands* (Heidelberg, 1997).

—— 'The Fate of the International Treaties of the GDR within the Framework of German Unification', 92 AJIL (1998) 469.

Pashukanis, E., 'International Law' in Beirne, P., and Sharlet, R., *Pashukanis: Selected Writings on Marxism and Law* (London: Academic Press, 1980).

Pazartzis, P., 'State Succession to Multilateral Treaties: Recent Developments', 3 ARIEL (1998) 397.

Pellet, A., 'Notes sur la Commission d'arbitrage de la Conférence européene pour la paix en Yougoslavie', 37 AFDI (1991) 329.

—— 'The Destruction of Troy will not Take Place', in Playfair E., *International Law and the Administration of Occupied Territories* (Oxford: Oxford University Press, 1992). 175

—— 'L'activité de la Commission d'arbitrage de la Conférence européene pour l'ancienne Yougoslavie', 39 AFDI (1993) 268.

Pereira, A., *La Succession d'Etats en Matière de Traités* (Paris, Pedone, 1969).

Phillimore R., *Commentaries on International Law* (London: Butterworths ed. 1871). I-III

Platt, D., 'The Imperialism of Free Trade: Some Reservations', 21 *Economic History Review* (1968) 296.

Porter B., *Absent-Minded Imperialists: Empire, Society and Culture in Britain* (Oxford: Oxford University Press, 2004).

Pradier-Fodéré, P., *Traité de Droit International Public Européen et Américain* (Paris: Pedone-Lauriel, 1885) I & II.

Pufendorf S., *De jure naturae et gentium libri octo* (1698 trans. Oldfather and Oldfather, Oxford: Clarendon Press, 1934).

Quadri, R., 'La successione dello stato nel diritto internzationale privato', RDI (1958) 51

—— 'Cours Général de Droit International Public', 113 Hague Receuil (1964) III, 237.

—— *Diritto Internazionale Pubblico* 5th ed. (Naples: Liguori, 1968).

Radnitzky, E., 'Die rechtliche Natur des Staatsgebiets', 20 AOR (1905) 313.

Rasulov, A., 'Revisiting State Succession to Humanitarian Treaties: Is There a Case for Automaticity?', 14 EJIL (2003) 141.

Ratner, S., 'Drawing a Better Line: *Ubi Possidetis* and the Borders of New States', 90 AJIL (1996) 590.

Raz J., *The Concept of a Legal System* 2nd ed. (Oxford: Oxford University Press, 1980).

Réglade, M., 'De la Nature juridique des Traités internationaux et du sens de la distinction des traités-lois et des traits-contrats', 41 RDPSP (1924) 505.

Reid H., *International Servitudes in Law and Practice* (Chicago: University of Chicago Press, 1932).

Reisman, W., 'Sovereignty and Human Rights in Contemporary International Law', 84 AJIL (1990) 866.

Ress, G., 'Germany, Legal Status after World War II', 10 Encyclopedia PIL (1987) 191.

Ribbelink, O., 'The Uniting of States in Respect of Treaties', Neth JIL (1995) 139.

Rich, R., 'Recognition of States: The Collapse of Yugoslavia and the Soviet Union', 4 EJIL (1993) 36.

Riismandel, V., 'The Continued Legal Existence of the Baltic States', 12 Baltic Rev (1957) 48.

Rittich K., *Recharacterizing Restructuring: Law, Distribution, and Gender in Market Reform* (The Hague: Kluwer Law International, 2002).

Rivier A. *Principes du droit des gens* (Paris: Rousseau, 1896). I-II

Roberts A., 'Prolonged Military Occupation: The Israeli-Occupied Territories 1967–1988', in Playfair E., *International Law and the Administration of Occupied Territories* (Oxford: Oxford University Press, 1992). 25

Roberts-Wray K., *Commonwealth and Colonial Law* (London: Stevens, 1966).

Rosenne S., 'The Effect of Change of Sovereignty upon Municipal Law', 27 BYIL (1950) 267.

—— *Breach of Treaty* (Cambridge: Grotius Publications, 1985).

—— 'Automatic Treaty Succession', in Klabbers, J. and Lefeber, R. (eds.). *Essays on the Law of Treaties* (The Hague: Martinus Nijhoff, 1998). 97

Rousseau C., *Principes généraux du droit international* (Paris: Podone, 1944).

—— 'Syrie: Sécession de la Syrie et de la RUA', 66 RGDIP (1962) 413.

—— *Le Droit des conflits armés* (Paris: Pedone, 1983).

Rousseau J.J., *The Social Contract* (trans. Cranston M. London: Penguin, 1968).

Ruddy, F., *International Law in the Englightenment. The Background of Emmerich de Vattel's Le Droit des Gens* (New York: Oceana, 1975).

Sack, A., 'La Succession aux dettes publiques d'Etat', 23 Hague Recueil (1928) 145.

Said E., *Orientalism* (New York: Random House, 1978).

—— *Culture and Imperialism* (New York: Knopf, 1993).

Sayre, F., 'Change of Sovereignty and Concessions', 12 AJIL (1918) 705.

Scelle G., *Précis de Droit des Gens* (Paris: Sirey, 1932–4). I-II

—— 'Thèorie et Practique de la Fonction Exécutive en Droit International', 15 Hague Recueil (1936) I, 90.

Schachter, O., 'The Development of International Law Through the Legal Opinions of the United Nations Secretariat', 25 BYIL (1948) 91.

—— 'State Succession: The Once and Future Law', 33 Va JIL (1993) 240.

Scharf, M, 'Musical Chairs: The Dissolution of States and Membership in the United Nations', 28 Cornell ILJ (1995) 29.

Schmitt C., *The Nomos of the Earth in the International Law of the Jus Publicum Europaeum* (1950 Ulmen trans., New York: Telos Press, 2003).

Schönborn, W., *Handbuch des Völkerrechts* (1913) II, 32.

—— 'Staatensukzessione' in *Handbuch d hts* (Stuttgart: Kohlhammer, 1913). II

—— 'La nature juridique du territoire', 30 Hague Receuil (1929 II) 85.

Schricke, C., 'L'unification allemande' 36 AFDI (1990) 47.

Schwarzenberger G., *International Law* (London: Stevens & Sons Ltd., 1957).

—— *Law, Justice and Equity* (London, Pitman: 1967).

Schweisfurth T., 'Von Einheitsstaat (UdSSR) zum Staatenbund (GUS)' 52 Zaö RV (1992) 541.

—— 'Das Recht der Staatensukzession: Die Staatenpraxis der Nachgolge in Völkerrechtliche Verträge, Saatsvermögen, Saatsschulden und Archive in den Teilungsfällen Sowjetunion, Tschechoslowakei und Jugoslawien' in Fastenrath U. et al (eds.). *Das Recht der Staatensukzession* (Heidelberg: C.F. Müller, 1995). 49

Scott D., *Conscripts of Modernity: The Tragedy of Colonial Enlightenment* (Durham: Duke University Press, 2004).

Seaton, E. and Maliti, S., 'Treaties and Succession of States and Governments in Tanzania', *African Conference on International Law and African Problems* (1967).

Semmel B., *The Rise of Free Trade Imperialism: Classical Political Economy and the Empire of Free Trade and Imperialism 1750–1850* (Cambridge, Cambridge University Press: 1970).

Shaw, M., *Title to Territory in Africa: International Legal Issues* (Oxford: Oxford University Press, 1986).

——'State Succession Revisited', 5 Finn YIL (1994) 34.

——'The Heritage of States: The Principle of *Uti Possidetis Juris* Today', 67 BYIL (1996) 75.

——'Peoples Territorialism and Boundaries', 8 EJIL (1997) 478.

Simma, B., 'Reflections on Article 60 of the Vienna Convention on the Law of Treaties and its Background in General International Law', 20 Oest ZOR (1970) 18.

——'Termination and Suspension of Treaties: Two Recent Austrian Cases', 21 German YIL (1979) 74.

——'From Bilateralism to Community Interest in International Law', 250 Hague Recueil (1994) 217.

Simpson G., *Great Powers and Outlaw States: Unequal Sovereigns in the International Legal Order* (Cambridge: Cambridge University Press, 2004).

Sinclair I., 'Some Reflections on the Vienna Convention on Succession of States in Respect of Treaties', in Hakapää (ed.). *Essays in Honour of Erik Castrén* (Helsinki: ILA Finnish Branch, 1979). 149

Slinn, P., 'Aspects juridiques du retour de Hong Kong à la Chine', 42 AFDI (1996) 273.

Sorel, J-M., and Mehdi, R., 'L'*Uti Possidetis* entre la consecration juridique et la practique: essai de réactualisation', 40 AFDI (1994) 11.

Spivak, G. *A Critique of Postcolonial Reason: Toward a History of the Vanishing Present* (Cambridge, Mass: Harvard University Press, 1999).

Stahn, C., 'The Agreement on Succession Issues of the Former Socialist Federal Republic of Yugoslavia', 96 AJIL (2002) 379.

Stanic, A., 'Financial Aspects of State Succession: The Case of Yugoslavia', 12 EJIL (2001) 751.

Stern, B., 'Rapport préliminarie sur la succession d'états en matière des traités;, ILA Helsinki Conference 1996.

——*La Succession d'États* (The Hague: Martinus Nijhoff, 2000).

Stewart, J., 'Draft Articles on the Succession of States in Respect of Treaties: The Pragmatic Development of International Law', 16 Harv ILJ (1975) 638.

Stone, J., *Legal Controls of International Conflicts* (New York: Reinhart and Company, Inc., 1954).

——'De Victoribus Victis: The International Law Commission and Imposed Treaties of Peace', 8 Va JIL (1967–68) 356.

Streinz, R., 'Succession of States in Assets and Liabilities – a New Regime? The Vienna Convention on Succession of States in Respect of State Property, Archives and Debts', German YIL (1983) 198.

Suter, K., 'The Australian Government's Policy of Recognition and Diplomatic Relations', 47 Aust. Q (1975) 67.

Szafarz, R., 'Vienna Convention on Succession of States in Respect of Treaties: A General Analysis', 10 Pol YIL (1979–80) 77.

Szasz, P., 'Succession to Treaties under the Namibian Constitution', 15 SA Yrbk IL (1989/90) 65.

Tabata, I., 'The Independence of Singapore and her Succession to the Agreement between Japan and Malaysia for Air-Services', 12 Jap Ann IL (1968) 36.

Taracouzio, T., The Soviet Union and International Law (New York, Macmillan: 1935).

Teitel R., *Transitional Justice* (Oxford: Oxford University Press, 2002).

Tichy, H., 'Two Recent Cases of State Succession – An Austrian Perspective', 44 Aust JPIL (1992) 117.

Timmermans, C., 'German Unification and Community Law', CMLRev (1990) 437.

Timmermans, W., 'The Baltic States, the Soviet Union and the Netherlands: A Historical Note', 32 Ned. TIR (1985) 288.

Toma, P., 'Soviet Attitude Towards the Acquisition of Teritorial Sovereignty in the Antarctic', 50 AJIL (1956) 611.

Torres Bernárdez, 'The "Uti Possidetis Juris" Principle in Historical Perspective' in Ginther K., et al., (eds.) *Festschrift für Karl Zemanek* (Berlin: Duncker & Humboldt, 1994). 417

Treviranus, H., 'Die Konvention der Vereinten Nationen über Staatensukzession bei Verträgen', 39 ZaöRV (1979) 259.

Twiss T., *The Law of Nations* 2nd ed. (Oxford: Clarendon Press, 1884).

Udina, M., 'La Succession des États Qant aux Obligations International autre que les dettes Publiques', 44 Hague Recueil (1933) 665.

Udokang O., *Succession of New States to International Treaties* (New York: Oceana, 1972).

Vagts, D., 'State Succession: The Codifiers' View', 33 Va JIL (1992–3) 275.

Váli F. *Servitudes of International Law* (New York: Praeger, 1958).

Vallat, F., 'Some Aspects of the Law of State Succession', 41 *Grot Soc Trans* (1956) 123.

van Panhuys, H., 'Las succession de l'Indonesie aux accords internationaux conclus par les Pays-Bas avant l'independence de l'Indonesie', 2 Neth ILR (1955) 67.

Vattel E. de, *The Law of Nations* (1758 Chitty, J. trans., Philadelphia: Johnson Law Booksellers, 1863).

Verzijl J., *International Law in Historical Perspective* (Leiden: A. W. Sijthoff, 1974).

Vitas R., *The United States and Lithuania: The Stimson Doctrine of Nonrecognition* (New York: Praeger, 1990).

Vitucci, M., 'Has Pandora's Box been Closed? The Decisions on the Legality of Use of Force cases in Relation to the Status of the Federal Republic of Yugoslavia (Serbia and Montenegro) within the United Nations', 19 Leiden JIL (2006) 105.

Volkovitsch, M., 'Righting Wrongs: Towards a New Theory of State Succession to Responsibility for International Delicts', 92 Colum LR (1992) 2162.

von Bulmerincq, A., *Völkerrecht oder internationales Recht* (Freiburg: 1884) p. 195.

von der Dunk, F., and Kooijmans, P., 'The Unification of Germany and International Law', 12 Mich JIL (1991) 510.

Von Glahn G., *The Occupation of Enemy Territory: A Commentary on the Law and Practice of Belligerent Occupation* (Minneapolis: University of Minnesota Press, 1957). 31

Warbrick, C., 'Recognition of States: Part 2', 42 ICLQ (1993) 433.

Weber M., 'The Profession and Vocation of Politics', in *Weber: Political Writings* (Cambridge: Cambridge University Press, 1994). 309

Wharton, F., *A Digest of International Law of the United States, taken from Documents issued by Presidents and Secretaries of State and from Decisions of Federal Courts and Opinions of Attorneys-General* (1887) I–III.

Wheaton H., *Elements of International Law* 8th ed. (Dana R., 1866, reprinted Oxford 1936).

White H., *The Content of the Form: Narrative Discourse and Historical Representation* (Baltimore: Johns Hopkins University Press, 1987).

Whiteman, M., *Digest of International Law* (Washington, D.C.: U.S. Government Print Office, 1963).

Widdows, K., 'The Unilateral Denunciation of Treaties Containing no Denunciation Clauses', 35 BYIL (1982) 83.

Wilde, R., 'From Danzig to East Timor and Beyond: The Role of International Territorial Administration', 95 AJIL (2001) 583.

Wilkinson H., *The American Doctrine of State Succession* (Baltimore: Johns Hopkins University Press, 1934).

Williams, P., and Harris, J., 'State Succession to Debts and Assets: The Modern Law and Policy', 42, Harv ILJ (2001) 355.

Williams, P., 'State Succession and the International Financial Institutions: Political Criteria v Protection of Outstanding Financial Obligations', 43 ICLQ (1994) 776.

—— 'The Treaty Obligations of the Successor States of the Former Soviet Union, Yugoslavia and Czechoslovakia: Do They Continue?', 23 Denv JILP (1994) 1.

Williamson, E., and Osborn, J., 'A US Perspective on Treaty Succession and Related Issues in the Wake of the Breakup of the USSR and Yugoslavia', 33 Va JIL (1993) 261.

Wolff C., *Jus Gentium Methodo Scientifica Pertractatum* (1764 Drake., J. trans., Oxford: Oxford University Press, 1934).

Wolosky, L., Malis, J., and Schwimmer, D., 'Start, Start II, and Ownership of Nuclear Weapons: The Case for a "Primary" Successor State', 34 Harv ILJ (1993) 581.

Wright, Q., 'Conflicts between International Law and Treaties', 11 AJIL (1917) 573.

—— *Mandates under the League of Nations* (Chicago: University of Chicago Press, 1930).

—— 'The Status of Germany and the Peace Proclamation', 46 AJIL (1952) 299.

Yakemtchouk, R., 'Les républiques baltes en droit international. Echec d'une annexation opérée en violation du droit des gens', 37 AFDI (1991) 276.

Yasseen, 'La Convention de Vienne sur la Succession d'Etats en matière de traités', 24 AFDI (1978) 59.

Young Robert J.C., *Postcolonialism: An Historical Introduction* (Oxford: Blackwell, 2001).

—— *White Mythologies* 2nd ed. (London: Routledge, 2004).

Young, Richard, 'State of Syria: Old or New', 56 AJIL (1962) 482.

Yu, P., 'Succession by Estoppel: Hong Kong's Succession to the ICCPR', 27 Pepp LR (1999–2000) 53.

Zemanek, K., 'The Legal Foundations of the International System. General Course on Public International Law' 266 Hague Recueil (1997).

—— 'State Succession After Decolonization', 116 Hague Recueil (1965) III, 188.

Ziemele I., *State Continuity and Nationality: The Baltic States and Russia* (Leiden: Martinus Nijhoff, 2005).

Zimmerman, A., 'State Succession in Respect of Treaties', in Klabbers, J., Koskenniemi, M., Ribbelink, O., and Zimmermann, A., *State Practice Regarding State Succession and Issues of Recognition* (1999), 80.

—— *Staatennachfolge in völkerrechtliche Vertäge* (Heidelberg: Springer, 2000).

Zimmermann, B., 'La succession d'Etats et les Conventions de Gèneve' in Cwinarski, (ed) *Studies and Essays in Honour of Jean Pictet* (1984) 113.

Zorn A. *Grundzüge des Völkerrechts* 2nd ed. (Leipzig: J. J. Weber, 1903).

Zouche R., *Iuris et Iudicii Fecialis sive Iuris Inter Gentes et Quaestionumde Eodem Explicato* (1650 Brierly, J. trans., Washington, D.C.: Carnegie Institute, 1911).

Index